★　　　★　　　★　　　★　　　★　　　★

American Experiences in
MILITARY GOVERNMENT
in World War II

*With the exception of this title, the volumes in this series appeared under the editorship of Dr. Phillips Bradley.

↑ 805515

American Experiences in

MILITARY

GOVERNMENT

in World War II

CARL J. FRIEDRICH

and Associates

RINEHART & COMPANY, INC.
Publishers   *New York*

To
HENRY PARKMAN
in friendship

★   ★   ★   ★   ★   ★

Preface

MILITARY occupation and government have become a central concern of American foreign policy. They impinge upon our relations with virtually all the powers with whom we are in diplomatic contact. Like colonies, occupied territories complicate foreign policy, because the needs of the occupied country cannot be disregarded, except at great cost to the taxpayer of the occupying power; yet these needs may clash with the needs of adjoining nations. The problems raised by the Ruhr, its coal and steel production, and the role it might play in German and European reconstruction constitute only one of many such instances where the occupation officials, concerned primarily with the local situation, will differ sharply regarding policy from officials at home, especially those concerned with foreign policy in its over-all aspects.

At the same time military occupation and government is putting to a severe test the genuineness of our democratic faith. While intimately linked to the winning of the war, it is even more crucial in the winning of the peace. Who would question the urgency of democratizing Germany and Japan? Who would deny the paradox implied in trying to do it by force? Who would be ready to proclaim the success of denazification or demilitarization at this time? Or controvert the importance of these policies for the establishment of a lasting peace? How to carry forward these and similar policies, and not to become imperialist in the process, is the challenge confronting the United States as an occupying power today and for many years to come.

The issues which military government raises must therefore be faced and faced now. They confront the American people, and they confront all those who either inside or outside the military establishment are charged with carrying forward the American policies in this field. These issues must be the special concern of those who are called upon to prepare men for participation in occupation duties in Europe and Asia. Military government and civil affairs are becoming a part of the regular training of officers of the United States armed forces, as indeed they should be—and should have been. The importance of the field, hitherto almost completely neglected by American scholars, is attested by the appointment of a special panel on research in military government and overseas administration by the American Political Science Association of which the editor and coauthor of this volume has been asked to serve as chairman.

The confusions of policy which were responsible for many of our difficulties and failures should not blind us to the remarkable over-all accomplishments of the American military government. The basic common sense and humanity of most American military personnel, together with the American capacity for improvising ingeniously, overcame many a weakness in policy which might otherwise have proved disastrous. And these weaknesses were, after all, merely extensions of our prewar blundering. A study of the causes of many of our difficulties would have to delve into the period of hesitation, oscillation, and isolation between the two wars and explore the interrelation between our domestic and foreign policy, our peacetime military doctrine, and the methods pursued in personnel selection and training.

Military operations abroad were viewed with such aversion by the public that their study by the military was made difficult, if not impossible. It has been said that even in the late thirties the studies of the War Plans Division, War Department General Staff, were "essentially limited to an area bound by the bogs of New Jersey and the fogs of San Francisco." Naturally, any extended study of military government, involving as it does military operations overseas, was neglected. The shortcomings of military training generally are the consequence of the American refusal to face the likelihood of war and its aftermath.

A brief book such as this one cannot unfold the complete story of the unrealistic decisions made during the war in the field of military government, nor that of all the adaptations developed in the field to rectify the errors committed.[1] But it can serve as a record and as a basis for objective examination of the more serious kinds of errors committed, from planning to final execution. A recurring theme in many of the chapters is the need on the part of the key personnel of our armed forces for a political training as comprehensive as that required of the members of the foreign service.

The book is divided into four parts, followed by several appendices. In Part I, certain broad general aspects of military government experience are discussed, and an over-all picture of Axis occupation practices is given for purposes of contrast and comparison. The remaining parts are devoted to descriptive chapters of military government operations; Part II dealing with Italy, France, and Austria; Part III with Germany; and Part IV with the Pacific. Germany has received the fullest treatment, both because of the intrinsic importance of that occupation as a possible precedent, and because a greater amount of material is available. The Appendices includes a map and charts, the text of JCS 1067, the new directive revising it, dated July, 1947, and the text of General Joseph McNarney's statement of July 9, 1946, on the democratization of Germany.

The chapters in this volume were written by men who, though scholars in peacetime or civilian administrators, were participants in the activities they have recorded here. Most of them went overseas as members of the armed forces and became members of military government detachments, both at staff and field levels. As students of government and administration, the authors approach the performance of military government with more exacting standards than laymen in these fields. But their practical experience, too, should be borne in mind by the reader who might be surprised by the occasional sharply

[1]Since this book was planned and its writing completed, Hajo Holborn has published his valuable record of development at the policy level, entitled *American Military Government—Its Organization and Policies* (1947). However, this book makes no pretense at dealing with field experience. Harold Zink's *American Military Government in Germany* (1947), on the other hand, is a more detailed account of experience in a particular field, as seen by the author, himself a participant in military government at the central staff level.

critical note struck by these writers. Yet the editor feels that it would be a mistake for him to eliminate these personal observations, for it is only through such vigorous self-criticism that we can improve on experience.

The authors are avowed partisans of progressive democracy; they share a general outlook which derives from American intervention abroad a positive obligation to forward the forces of constitutional democracy with its social progress and civil liberties. Men with a different basic viewpoint would naturally arrive at a different evaluation of the events here depicted and assessed. For either a partisan of the Soviet Union, or a believer in a Tory philosophy of imperialism and the "white man's burden" will see failures and successes where the authors of this book might not.

Since it is inevitable that there will be changes in perspective as events progress, a final word ought to be said concerning the period covered. Most of the chapters were written in the spring and early summer of 1946. Chapters I and IX, written in August, 1946, are exceptions. The volume as a whole is concerned with developments from the early summer of 1943 to the summer of 1946.

The constant advice and encouragement of Colonel Herman Beukema of the United States Military Academy is responsible for much of the development of this volume. The editor has also been helped immeasurably by his associates at OMGUS, and especially by Mr. Henry Parkman, then Director, Civil Administration Division of OMGUS and his staff. He is also indebted to his research and editorial assistant, Mrs. Palmer Smith, Jr., and to Lt. Col. Robert H. Slover. Part IV could not have achieved its present quality without the aid of a junior colleague of the editor, Mr. Arthur Maass. The editor wishes to express his appreciation to the contributors to the volume who have borne patiently with his editorial vagaries. It is only fair to add that the book could not have been completed at this time if the editor's writing partner of many years had not come to his rescue after his return from Europe.

C.J.F.

Concord, Mass.
February, 1948

Contents

APPENDICES

Part I

Some General Problems of Military Government

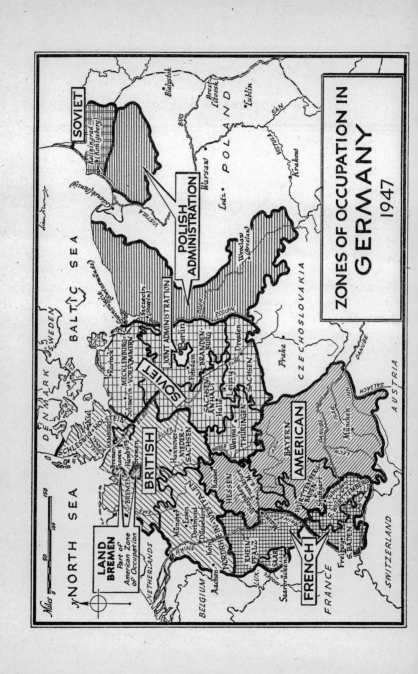

ZONES OF OCCUPATION IN GERMANY
1947

Chapter I

Military Government and Democratization: A Central Issue of American Foreign Policy

CARL J. FRIEDRICH

AMERICAN foreign policy has consistently maintained democratization of Germany and Japan as one of its major objectives in dealing with the defeated nations. In fact, democratization constitutes the major constructive aspect of American policy, the other major components being negative. Demilitarization, denazification, and deindustrialization were, of course, held to be essential conditions of democratization, but their purpose was obviously to eliminate obnoxious features of German and Japanese society, to wit: militarism, fascism, and the industrial war potential.

The four D's, as they are sometimes referred to, represent the effective compromise arrived at during the Teheran, Yalta, and Potsdam conferences of the Big Three. Nonetheless, democratization was perhaps more specifically an American objective. In any case, the changes envisaged by the Soviet Union under the same heading of democratization radically differ from the American concept. Specifically, the United States policy wanted to see established a system of free popular elections conducted by no less than two competing political parties which would be voluntary associations of citizens clearly distinguished from the government. The United States also wanted to establish the basic rights of the individual including freedom of speech, religion, assembly, and association, and other similar liberties. She also specifically desired the rule of law to be clearly recognized.[1]

American foreign policy finds its justification for its emphasis on democratization in its preoccupation with peace. Peace has been insisted upon as a basic interest of the United States time and time again in official documents.[2]

The Problem of Democratic Foreign Policy

Of all the different phases of public policy, foreign policy is the most elusive and the most difficult to define. The increasing interdependence of all the world has made it virtually impossible to draw a line between foreign and domestic policy as far as the substance of a government's objectives is concerned. The only reasonably pragmatic definition of foreign policy is one which relates to the dealings with foreign nations. We may, therefore, define foreign policy as that part of public policy which develops in connection with international negotiations carried on with one or more foreign nations. There has been a great deal of controversy within recent years concerning the broad issues of the foreign policy of the United States. Indeed, the very facts to be described under this heading are often the subject of argument and discussion.[3]

[1]See the "Statement of Policy" by General Joseph McNarney, July 9, 1946, describing the conditions which United States military government will consider a fulfillment of the process of "democratization." In a sense this statement merely elaborates the Berlin Protocol and hence could be claimed as general Allied policy. This "definition" is reaffirmed in the directive of July 15, 1947, to General Lucius D. Clay, U.S. Military Governor in Germany. This directive clearly puts democratization in the center of United States policy in Germany. (Cf. Sections 3, 5, 6, and 8.)

[2]The basic interest of the United States throughout the world is just and lasting peace. It is the recurring theme in speeches of the President and Secretary of State. Walter Lippmann in his United States Foreign Policy (1943), p. 50, has attacked this policy and maintained that American foreign policy should be directed toward survival.

[3]The issues of foreign policy, especially democratic foreign policy, have aroused increasing interest in recent years. The present writer analyzed its inherent weaknesses in a volume entitled Foreign Policy in the Making (1938). Other important contributions to the discussion are Cecil Carr, Twenty Years' Crisis (1938), the writings of Harold Nicolson, especially Peacemaking 1919 (1937), Sumner Welles, The Time for Decision (1944), Walter Lippmann, U.S. Foreign Policy, Shield of the Republic (1943). Charles A. Beard, American Foreign Policy in the Making (1946), Nicholas J. Spyk-

Too often it is assumed in speaking of "American foreign policy" that this term refers or should refer to a consistent whole. Actually, the exigencies in this field of policy, resulting from the actions of other governments, necessitate continuous adjustments. The criticism is frequently heard that the United States has no foreign policy. Such a view springs from unrealistic assumptions. It usually means that the writer or group expressing this view feels that the American government is not doing just what he thinks should be done in the field of international affairs. The unrealistic idea that the United States is free to do what she wants is nourished continuously by a group of columnists, each of whom speaks with considerable authority and advocates divergent courses of action for American foreign policy. In point of fact, the shifting exigencies of the situation allow the government of the United States control only to a limited degree. It is more in keeping with realities to speak of this field of governmental policy in the plural and to recognize that the United States has foreign *policies*. Some of these policies are, or at least seem to be, very stable. There is, however, a dangerous tendency to assume that the policy is stable because the formula remains the same. For example, the Monroe Doctrine is assumed by many to be such a stable element in American foreign policy, whereas actually it has undergone continuous evolution.[4]

Foreign policy makers in a democracy are particularly prone to seek an escape from the vagaries of popular control by rendering lip service to such verbal formulas. Postwar American policy in Europe is no exception to this general rule. Ever since the Potsdam Declaration was issued, American policy has been stated with reference to it.[5] Actually, however, American foreign policy has profoundly

man, *America's Strategy in World Politics* (1942), and the recent collective volume published by the Harris Foundation at Chicago (1947). These are only a few major items of the growing shelf of volumes showing the general concern with foreign policy. The general importance of foreign policy for the development of modern government forms the subject of Chapter IV of the author's systematic treatise, *Constitutional Government and Democracy* (1942).

[4] See Dexter Perkins, *The Monroe Doctrine, 1823–1826* (1927), *The Monroe Doctrine, 1826–1867* (1933), and his brief summary in *The Encyclopedia of the Social Sciences.*

[5] The Potsdam Declaration was released to the press on August 25, 1945. (*Department of State Bulletin*, Vol. XIII, 1945, pages 153–161.) This document is sometimes

changed as a result of the actions of other governments, especially those of France and the Soviet Union. The speech which former Secretary of State James F. Byrnes made at Stuttgart on September 6, 1946, shifted American policy decidedly toward Germany. This was immediately recognized at Paris and Moscow, yet the speech continually referred to the Potsdam Declaration and utilized its phrases.

Foreign policy in a democracy is, in other words, basically different from the traditional foreign policy of the past. The significance of this change is often overlooked. When such a democracy in turn has its most difficult dealings with a totalitarian dictatorship, a wholly novel situation is bound to present itself. Not since the period of the collapse of the medieval empire and the religious wars of the sixteenth and seventeenth centuries has the pattern of interstate relations changed as profoundly as it has within the last five years. A world dominated by two powers, one a full-fledged democracy and the other a totalitarian dictatorship, is bound to exhibit a different pattern of relations from the world as it existed in 1914 or even in 1930.

Democratization as a key feature of American foreign policy is very much involved in this change. There is hardly an issue on which the United States and the Soviet Union are farther apart than this one. To the concept of democratization which guides the United States, as outlined above, the Soviet Union opposes a concept derived from its own tradition and ideology. In fact, the Soviet Union proclaims this concept as the "true" democracy. To it the dictatorship of the proletariat and the absence of the capitalistic class are vital ingredients of this democracy.[6] It is obvious that the Soviet Union should have proceeded in its own way in carrying out the quadripartite policy of "democratization"; it was bound to do this in accordance with its own interpretation of the word "democracy." Democratization thus reveals the peculiar dangers of foreign policy by formula.

referred to as the Potsdam Agreement rather than Declaration. There seems to be no definite reason for using either expression in preference to the other. The Berlin Declaration, also known as the Berlin Protocol, was made on June 5, 1945. (See *Department of State Bulletin*, Vol. XII, pages 1051–1055.)

[6]For the Russians' insistence upon their democratic "ideology" compare the speeches by Molotov and Stalin on November 7, 1945, and February 10, 1946, respectively. See *The New York Times*, November 8, 1945, and February 11, 1946, for full texts.

Foreign policy of the traditional cabinet variety was believed to be subject to three established principles: first, it was assumed to be quite distinct from domestic policy and to take precedence over it; second, it was supposed to be as continuous and consistent as possible; and third, it was directed toward achieving a balance of power. Foreign policy in a democracy does not obey these principles. It is subject to the dynamics of democratic party politics. That means by definition that it is discontinuous. Furthermore, it is as inconsistent as public opinion. People who earnestly desire peace often vote for those who stand for policies which make for war. Similar contradictions develop in other fields as well. Thus a popular majority may at the same time decide to increase foreign trade and to raise tariffs. Examples of this type of contradiction in foreign policy could easily be multiplied. The American policy of democratization itself constitutes a striking example, for it was coupled at Potsdam and later with the policy of deindustrialization implied in the Morgenthau "plan," a policy which has created conditions in Germany now generally admitted to be very unfavorable to the development of democracy.[7]

If one were to state briefly some of the difficulties resulting from democratic control of foreign affairs, one would have to stress the consistent disturbing influence of special interest groups.[8] The people often force a bad policy and at other times prevent a good policy or develop a one-sided preoccupation with a particular phase of a given policy. Under such conditions governments are tempted to use popular opinion as a means of diplomatic pressure, thus producing a situation in which domestic concerns and party pressures take precedence over the problems of foreign policy. Democratic foreign policy tends to be party policy and representative bodies such as the Congress will continually be preoccupied with the requirements of the party policy even while they acknowledge the need of a bi-partisan policy.

If, as has been the case in recent years, parties establish contacts beyond national boundaries, the situation becomes even more unstable. While in one sense this represents a step toward One World,

[7]See Russell Hill, *Struggle for Germany* (1947), especially Chapters 4 and 5. The new directive cited above in footnote 1 presents an attempt to get away from this contradiction but it continues in American public opinion.

[8]See Charles A. Beard, *The National Interest* (1934), *passim*.

it yet has proved a very disrupting influence in foreign policy. This is, of course, particularly true of totalitarian parties such as the Communist and Fascist parties, but it holds true even in regard to other parties. Indeed, the very policy of democratization is in part conceived in such terms. Discarding the old doctrine of nonintervention, this policy proposes to support the "democratic" elements, which means an alliance with certain parties in the nation as contrasted with others. Thus in Germany today democratization policies oblige United States administrators to favor the democratic parties which agree with our concept of democracy while Soviet administrators, on their part, favor the Communist parties and their allies.[9]

Democracy, Self-Rule, and the Rule of Law

American authorities have persistently used the term "democracy," as well as its new derivative "democratization." The fact that they found themselves eventually obliged to clarify what they meant by "democracy" shows that there was disagreement among Americans no less than between the United States and foreign powers. Vast is the literature concerned with clarifying the meaning and concept of democracy.[10] Among the major lines of disagreement at least three can be clearly distinguished. The first view of democracy stresses its individualist aspect, and lays major stress upon the rights or liberties or freedoms of the individual. This view is strongly antisocialist, and its exponents incline toward the view that democracy and a socialized

[9]This range of problems is adumbrated in *Foreign Policy in the Making: The Search for a New Balance of Power* (1938), by Carl J. Friedrich, especially Chapters 2–5. For an earlier analysis of these problems see Joseph Barthélemy, *Democratie et Politique Etrangère* (1917), and D. C. Poole, *The Conduct of Foreign Relations under Modern Democratic Conditions* (1924).

[10]Besides the author's *Constitutional Government and Democracy* (1942) and *The New Belief in the Common Man* (1941) the following (arranged alphabetically) may be mentioned: Carl Becker, *Modern Democracy* (1941); Avery Craven, *Democracy in American Life* (1941); E. P. Herring, *The Politics of Democracy* (1940); H. D. Lasswell, *Democracy through Public Opinion* (1941); Charles E. Merriam, *What Is Democracy?* (1941); *idem, The New Democracy and the New Despotism* (1939); William F. Russell and Thomas H. Briggs, *The Meaning of Democracy* (1941). All these books contain further bibliographies to which may be added recent British works of importance: R. Bassett, *The Essentials of Parliamentary Democracy* (1935) and A. D. Lindsay, *The Modern Democratic State* (1943).

society are incompatible, that democracy presupposes a free, competitive economy based upon private enterprise. The second view of democracy maintains that while constitutional restraints upon governmental power are indeed important, regulation of the economy in the public interest is entirely in keeping with democratic ways, as long as such policies are clearly based upon the popular will. To put it another way, this view holds that the majority of the people are the final judges as to how far the government may go in restricting private enterprise. The third view insists upon this unrestricted power of the majority of the people to the virtual exclusion of constitutional restraints. It views all such restraints as encumbrances of the past which are reactionary and undemocratic, and considers such institutions as the judicial review of legislative acts as contrary to a fully developed democracy. It can readily be seen that exponents of these different viewpoints would often disagree rather sharply on what "democratization" in Germany (or Japan) would require on the part of Americans. These disagreements were further complicated by the fact that Americans sharply differed as to the prospects of any kind of democracy in Germany. For whatever view of democracy a man might take, he would be inclined to advocate different measures if he thought Germans were readily capable of organizing themselves democratically. On the whole, it can be said that the strongest genuinely democratic forces in Germany are those organized in the Social Democratic party and in the left wing of the Christian Democratic Union. These elements of the German population, formerly a minority, but now possessed of a majority in the British and American zones, happen to be very largely attached to the third view of democracy just outlined. American occupation personnel, particularly the higher echelons, including General Lucius D. Clay, on the other hand, more often believe in the first and second view. The evolution of American party politics from New Deal radicalism toward Republican conservatism has reinforced these attitudes. It is not too much to say that the present Congress in its majority strongly leans in this direction. In these circumstances, continuous misunderstandings were almost inevitable. When American authorities urged the establishment of constitutions, the German democrats viewed the step as premature. When the German constitutional assemblies desired to include socialistic programs in their constitutions, the American authorities questioned some of these programs as "undemocratic." When the Americans in turn insisted upon a federalistic pattern of states' rights, the Social Democratic party prevailed upon its representatives to vote uniformly and disregard local preferences. When the Germans hesitated to provide judicial review and to give the courts power to protect the constitution, the Americans exerted themselves to persuade the Germans to their view. These few instances may serve to illustrate the range of issues that are hidden behind "democratization," issues which divide Americans amongst themselves, as well as their allies and the Germans.

Fortunately, there is a common core which provides an area of agreement for all these differing views, except those which divide Americans from the Communists and the Soviet Union. This common core is often rather inaccurately referred to as the rule of law. For the expression "the rule of law" has a distinct and sharply defined meaning in the common law. According to Dean Roscoe Pound, it is the doctrine of the common law that the judiciary, in ordinary legal proceedings, may pronounce upon the legal validity of the acts of the king's ministers and servants and hence, in the United States, upon the validity of administrative, executive, and legislative action with reference to the constitution, and, in the case of administrative and executive action, the statutes governing such action. It has been called one of the three most distinctive institutions of Anglo-American law, along with trial by jury and the doctrine of judicial precedent. However, in the discussions on democratization in Germany, the expression "rule of law" has been employed in a broader meaning to designate the Continental doctrine of "government according to law" which the Germans traditionally refer to as *Rechtsstaat*. Since the idea of *Rechtsstaat* has a long and deeply rooted tradition in Germany, even under the Prussian monarchy,[11] and since it is an obvious requisite to the establishment of constitutional democracy, the likeli-

[11]The famous, albeit distorted, anecdote about Frederick the Great's readiness to submit to a court's verdict his quarrel with the miller of Potsdam illustrates this tradition. Cf. *Constitutional Government and Democracy,* p. 109, for the true story which in fact shows the Continental disregard for courts and judges.

hood of its re-establishment is greater than any immediate prospect of "democratization." It also is helpful to United States military government that much German criticism of the Hitler regime from both right and left was focused on the Nazis' destruction of the *Rechtsstaat*.[12]

The Paradox of Democratization by Force

Ever since the policy objective of democratization was first formulated, American criticism has been directed at it. Most of this criticism has taken the form of asserting that "you cannot impose democracy by force." Much of the best liberal and democratic tradition of the United States has been cited in support of the contention that democracy cannot develop as a healthy and lasting form of government unless the people to be democratized want it and are prepared to fight for it. This objection, whatever its intrinsic value, to be examined presently, does not apply to the establishment of the rule of law in the Continental sense. If the occupying powers are willing to impose upon themselves the self-restraint which governing according to law demands of them, they can initiate the *Rechtsstaat*. For no matter how severe their law, if they will subject themselves to the self-discipline of not doing what has not previously received the sanction of clearly enunciated law, the occupying powers will usher in a reign of law. The Americans and British have in the course of the last two years steadily progressed toward this objective.[13] At first numerous arbitrary acts were, of course, taken and justified as based upon military necessity.

[12]See for an earlier statement of what follows the author's article "Military Government as a Step toward Self-Rule" in *The Public Opinion Quarterly,* VII (1943). The indignation felt over the Nazis' utter disregard for the tradition of "government according to law" was effectively stated by Charles H. McIlwain in an article in *Foreign Affairs* (1937). The importance of the "rule of law" in the sense of *Rechtsstaat* was rightly brought out by Ernst Fraenkel, *The Dual State* (1941) where he showed the shadowy continuation of the *Rechtsstaat* tradition under the Nazis alongside the arbitrary party government.

[13]The importance of this issue was recognized in the revised directive to the Military Governor of July 15, 1947, Section IV, para. 11a. Even before this directive was issued, General Clay had instituted a broad program of indoctrination, not only for military government personnel, but also for officers and troops in the Constabulary and Military Police.

The military manuals do not include the establishment of self-rule or of democracy among the objective of military government. But they do include the establishment of law and order. They describe the purpose of this system of emergency government as essentially directed toward this end, once military needs are taken care of. It is, in essence, a security requirement.[14] To the extent that the establishment of government according to law prepares the ground for the setting up of constitutional government and democracy, military government is therefore bound to serve the purpose of democratization. Yet the primary task of military government, during the combat phase, is to assist the tactical troops in their military operations "by maintaining order, promoting security of the occupying forces, preventing interference with military operations, reducing active or passive sabotage, relieving combat troops of civil administration, and mobilizing local resources in aid of military objectives and carrying out governmental policies. . . ."[15] This primary task of military government in the early phases of occupation is often lost sight of by critics of military government who are concerned with democratization and similar postwar objectives. But while it is true that military necessity must come first, it nevertheless is likely that the conduct of military government has had and will continue to have a marked effect upon the re-establishment of orderly government according to law. Opinions will differ sharply among Americans as to the wisdom of military government and occupation troop practices in such matters as requisitioning of homes and other property, arrest and searches, censorship and control of the press and other means of communication.

Whatever one's view on such "undemocratic" procedures, there can be no doubt today that both British and American military authorities have steadily reduced their scope and importance. The Directive to the Military Governor and Commander-in-Chief of American Forces in the Euorpean Theatre issued on July 15, 1947, specifically

[14] See para. 9 of the revised *Field Manual* 27–5, issued in December, 1943, which appeared as *Joint Army-Navy Manual of Military Government and Civil Affairs* and was dated December 22, 1943. It superseded the preceding version of July, 1940, entitled *Military Government* and issued by the army alone.

[15] See *Field Manual* 27–5 (revised), Para. 4.

directed him as follows: "As a basic objective of the occupation is the re-establishment of the rule of law in Germany, you will require all agencies under your control to refrain from arbitrary and oppressive measures." Such decided efforts at self-restraint are clearly in line with the American policy of democratization. Yet they do not resolve the paradox of "imposing self-government by force." In any absolute sense those who insist that democracy cannot become firmly established, unless the Germans want it, are certainly right. Therefore the situation must appear hopeless to those Americans who have become convinced that most Germans were Nazis and that only "a handful" retained any belief in democracy. To people holding such views the entire occupation must seem absurd. General Lucius D. Clay has repeatedly stated it as his personal conviction that if such views are correct the only sound American policy is to evacuate Germany and leave her to such antidemocratic forces as might achieve supremacy—presumably the Soviet-led Communists who would establish the "true" democracy which they have already developed in the Soviet zone of Germany. But, as previously indicated, such counsels of despair are without foundation in historical fact. When the Hitler movement came into power in 1933, it did so by an alliance with undemocratic, conservative, and Nationalist elements[16] which nonetheless expected to maintain a government according to law. Hitler succeeded, however, in double-crossing these reactionaries in the name of "democracy" and in establishing his personal regime of ruthless totalitarian dictatorship without any mandate from the German people. For even the alliance between the Nazis and the reactionaries provided Hitler with only a bare majority of 51 per cent, and it will forever remain controversial whether a genuine election in the fall of 1934 would have led to his victory. However one may estimate the magnitude of Hitler's following at the time of the establishment of his personal tyranny after the Roehm *Putsch* and Hindenburg's death, it seems reasonable to assume that a large part of the followers of the Social Democratic, Christian Catholic, and Communist parties remained outside the Hitlerite fold. Without the Com-

[16]See for this issue Arnold Brecht, *Prelude to Silence—The End of the German Republic* (1944). The opening of the Nazi archives makes a new and more far-reaching study of the coming of the Nazis very urgent.

munists, who present a special problem when it comes to "democratization," these Social Democrats and Catholic and Christian elements presumably constituted about a quarter of the German population, even at the low ebb of democratic prospects. But whether 20 or 30 per cent, in any case they were a substantial minority, silenced by the terror of the regime with its concentration camps and secret police torture, but present and ready to come into action once their oppressors were removed. It is not necessary to engage in sentimental pro-German views to recognize the existence of this element. For it is this part of the German people which has provided the leadership as well as the mass support for whatever democratization and denazification has been accomplished in the British, American, and French zones of Germany. Once this situation is seen realistically, it becomes clear that American policy is not "imposing" democracy, but is imposing restraints upon those elements of the German population who would prevent democracy from becoming established. Force can be used, and has been used, for suppressing the Nazis. Force can be used, and has been used, for destroying the power of the big landowners and of the industrialists associated with them in supporting the Hitler movement, such as Thyssen.[17] Anyone who is even casually acquainted with the history of the first German Republic, and with the way in which successive reactionary maneuvers were initiated by this class in Germany, will realize that its destruction and elimination from German public life will assist those who desire to rebuild a constitutional democracy. In recognizing this patent fact, one need not jump to the conclusion that the future of democratization is insured thereby. Other, and equally threatening antidemocratic forces imperil the future of German democracy, as well as democracy elsewhere in Europe. The desperate economic plight engendered by the policies stemming from the vindictive ideas of Henry Morgenthau, Jr. and his circle threatens to engulf all of Western Europe in a catastrophe which would sweep the American policy of democratization into oblivion.

[17]See Fritz Thyssen, *I Paid Hitler* (1941), as well as the recent literature dealing with the conservative opposition, such as Bernd Gisevius, *To the Bitter End* (1947). Biased, but informative in its bitter hostility, is Frederick Martin's *The Junker Menace* (1945).

As was stated at the end of the last section, the practice of "govern-ment according to law" is capable of being developed by military government in its own operations. However, beyond that there exists the possibility of insisting that the groundwork be laid for such a system by the Germans. In short, military government could and did demand that the Germans draft, debate, and adopt constitutions. The means by which this was done are described in a later chapter (IX). It must suffice here to point out that the actual adoption of state con-stitutions in November, 1946, marked a most important practical measure in the direction of democratization. The step was criticized by America's allies as premature, but it has since been taken by all of them (though the constitutions in the Soviet zone are suspected of not being genuinely "democratic"). .

Since that time, the organization of the bizonal agencies and the control organ of the Bizone, the Economic Council, have prepared the ground for the eventual establishment of a German national con-stitution. A lively discussion over its problems has been going on for some time between the several political parties and in the press. Thus the way is being prepared for the eventual popular vote on a demo-cratic constitutional order.

Democratization and the Strengthening of Democracy

The policy of democratization in Germany is actually the spear-head of a policy of supporting constitutional and democratic forces throughout Western and Central Europe which has become an in-creasingly prominent ingredient of American foreign policy in Europe. The expression "imposing democracy" overstates the element of force in this policy; for it is not democracy which is being forced upon the people. Force is being employed for "containing" the anti-democratic forces throughout this area which the active support of the Soviet Union is seeking to strengthen. It should always be borne in mind that these antidemocratic forces are ready at any time to employ force and violence to cause further disorder, to disrupt pro-duction and distribution, and to strike at any and all weak spots in an admittedly shaky situation.

Perhaps some further insight may be gained by looking briefly at the difficulties and contradictions of American policy in Italy, where presumably the native forces of democracy were strong enough to permit military government to restrict itself to fostering these forces.[18] The operations of military government in this field have been severely criticized. It is, however, possible to show that the errors which military government committed were to a large extent a result of a faulty foreign policy. It is quite unfair to allow the poor results to obscure the remarkable achievements which American (and British) military government was able to accomplish, given the limitations created by the confusions in over-all policy. The good sense and ingrained ability of Americans to improvise practical solutions under great difficulties and their capacity for sustained enthusiasm helped to avert what might have been a catastrophe.[19] Great confusion resulted especially from the fact that overt policy and propaganda maintained that American foreign policy was primarily dedicated to the cause of promoting democracy in all liberated countries. Actually, this goal was subordinated to the task of splitting off as many of the satellites of Hitler Germany as possible. It is too early to decide whether the resulting conflicts in American policy could have been avoided. The "deal" made with Admiral Jean François Darlan which led to Casablanca showed how extremely difficult it was to strike a viable balance.[20] The battle cry of "Unconditional Surrender" first uttered at Casablanca was intended to still the doubts and fears of those who suspected the United States and Britain of being willing to compromise with the more moderate and opportunist elements in the Fascist camp.

Even at this early stage, the divergent views on Fascism and democracy which divided the Allies at home and abroad caused continuous difficulty. The fact that in the eyes of Communists anyone who is not

[18]See Chapter VI below.

[19]John Hersey's *A Bell for Adano* (1943) brilliantly portrayed the difficulties and perplexities of the average American military government officer. It is regrettable that the slightly sentimental tinge which crept into his original presentation was expanded into melodramatic proportions in the stage and screen versions of the story.

[20]See the valuable discussion in William L. Langer, *Our Vichy Gamble* (1947), pp. 321 ff.

a Communist is potentially a Fascist (had not even Trotsky been dubbed a Fascist wrecker?) exposed to serious misinterpretation any kind of American foreign policy designed to arrive at the surrender of conservative yet anti-fascist elements. Certain of the more radical American journalists bear their share of responsibility for the misunderstandings that arose. They pictured American military government officers as virtually engaged in unscrupulous plots to save Fascist necks, when in fact these officers were merely the victims of a contradictory and confused policy emanating from the highest quarters. If the governments of the United States and Great Britain chose to deal with Marshal Badoglio and the King of Italy, military government officers were, of course, prevented from ousting local officials whom they knew beyond all reasonable doubt to be Fascists, as long as such officials had the blessing of the Italian authorities accepted by American policy makers. It was, however, much easier to attack the luckless army captain than the President or the Secretary of State. This is not to say that either of the latter should have been attacked, except by those who take their cue from foreign powers as to what American policy should be. In any case, the desperate economic plight due to shortages of food and fuel which beset American military government in Italy would have hampered a policy of encouraging democracy.

At the same time, there exist deep-rooted "democratic aspirations" among the Italian people as well as traditions which could become effective elements in a vital and functioning democracy. But whether these will suffice to ensure democracy, no one can say at the present time. One cannot assess democratic prospects in terms of national character. What is really necessary for a democratic development are effective and broadly supported institutional devices which favorable material conditions enable to function to the satisfaction of a majority of the people. The mere provision of financial aid cannot solve the problems here involved. Without adequate controls to ensure that the financial aid is employed for the purpose of evolving workable institutions, such aid may actually weaken democracy. There is a tendency at present in all those countries, including Italy, who seek such aid from the United States, to protest against all such controls as "undemocratic," when as a matter of fact only aid combined with controls which foster democratization will be of lasting help.[21]

It is too often forgotten that the Fascists ruthlessly destroyed all social bonds and the numerous free associations and corporate enterprises in which human beings voluntarily band together for the pursuit of common aims, and by this destruction atomized the Italians and converted a once great people into an amorphous mass.[22] It has become the fashion to blame most of the agonies of Italy and the Italians since 1943 upon American ineptness and British imperialism and reactionary intrigues. But even if American and British policy had been superlatively skillful and inspired by saintly unselfishness, the inner disintegration of the Italian people would have blocked any rapid recovery. A failure to recover rapidly would in turn have stimulated a revival of Fascist symbols and activities. Furthermore, the tendency of the Communist party to call everybody a Fascist who is not a Communist has caused much confusion. While there are, no doubt, Fascist elements in the Chistian Democratic party, that party is surely not Fascist in its dominant outlook and policies.[23]

The search of military government for the personnel to take the place of the deposed Fascist cadres was frantic. Those who preferred purity of democratic purpose to technological competence and those whose preferences were the opposite were bitter in their mutual abuse. There is an active and underlying difficulty recurrent in this situation; a man might be a great scientist or engineer or administrator and yet be a Fascist or a Communist or a liberal of the old school, or simply an opportunist. It is equally possible to be any one of these

[21]See "Political Changes in France and Italy," by Mario Einaudi, *American Political Science Review*, XL (1947), 898 ff.

[22]The general significance of this destruction of the intermediary organizations between the state and the individual under a tyrannical government was stressed by Montesquieu. For our time, it was skillfully set forth as the destruction of democracy by Emil Lederer, *The State of the Masses* (1938). At one time a Marxist, Lederer clearly shows why the "classless society" is an amorphous society in which freedom cannot thrive, because no autonomous organizations, churches, unions, universities, etc., are permitted to exist.

[23]See "Christian Democracy in Italy," by Mario Einaudi, *The Review of Politics*, IX (1947), 16 ff.

and not amount to much as a technician. Much as we would like to
think that technical proficiency and moral worth go hand in hand,
all contemporary governments have had to admit the opposite to be
the truth. In the face of an utterly defeated and disorganized nation,
some Americans chose the pure of heart, others the skilled of mind.
By doing so they have helped to get things going, but they have not
succeeded in getting them going well.

It is always easier to see the flaws in an undertaking actually accomplished than to see errrors which might have been committed but
were in fact avoided. Three things might have happened in Italy as
part of a failure in military government: a deadlock in the Anglo-
American operation of military government; a serious breakdown in
American relations with the Soviet Union; and—perhaps most important—substantial setbacks for the advancing armies resulting from
a failure of the Italian civil administration under military government. None of these dangerous potentialities materialized, and much
of the credit for it should by right go to military government; the
broad foreign policy of the United States government certainly failed
to provide a clear basis for operations.

A World Revolutionary Situation: Fascism, Communism, and Capitalism

The preceding analysis would be incomplete if the underlying
world revolutionary situation were not given at least passing recognition. Democratization, whether of the American or of the Soviet
variety, is embedded in this revolutionary setting. Among the many
factors which differentiate the situation after the second World War
from that after the first, this rivalry between Soviet and Anglo-
American power is the most important. It polarizes the world ideo-
logically in the most dramatic fashion. It is customary to treat ideologies and the issues arising from them as more or less static. Actually,
ideologies are highly dynamic in their relation to each other and in
their effects upon public policies. One difficulty with a good deal of
democratic ideology and practice stems from a failure to recognize

what the revolution of 1917 and its aftermath have done to its underlying premise.[24]

Perhaps the most dangerous effect of this type of political color
blindness is an inclination to view the adherents of opposing ideologies as necessarily either stupid or criminal. In the field of foreign
policy here under consideration this prejudice leads to the assumption that all Communists (or most of them) are hirelings of Moscow
or the dupes of its wily agents. In point of fact, Communism is en-
demic all over Europe, and the Communists in Italy, France, Germany, and elsewhere can look back to a history of their movement
which antedates the establishment of the Soviet Union by many
decades. Fascism, in turn, is a pattern of reaction to Communism;
it arises from a democratic system at the point when that system's
prospects of continued successful operation have been placed into
jeopardy by Communist exploitation of its intrinsic weaknesses. If,
therefore, a policy of strengthening the democratic forces is to have
a chance of succeeding, it must be based upon a thorough grasp of
Communist and Fascist ideology. This sort of "intellectual penetration" of the adversary's lines of ideological resistance carries with it
a willingness to revise and develop democratic ideology to the point
where it actually meets the challenges of the opposing ideology. Thus
the Communist appeal to the landless tenant farmer of southern
Italy might have been anticipated and forestalled if a program of
effective land reform along democratic lines had been prepared as an
essential part of American policy. In point of fact, no such policy
was ever even adumbrated. Analogous tasks in Austria and Korea
were similarly left untouched as far as we know today. Criticism of
this kind is often countered by the remark that it is easy to be wise
by hindsight. Actually, these and other issues were repeatedly projected and urged by men whose knowledge of the countries was outstanding, while their continuous efforts on behalf of democracy and
against the totalitarian ideologies should have put their ideas beyond

[24]Harold Lasswell's study cited above, footnote 10, and the author's attempt at restat-
ing the concept of the common man in functional, nonrationalistic terms are essays
pointing in this direction. The work of Robert Lynd, especially his *Knowledge For
What?* (1940) and David Riesman's studies in the field of civil liberties also might be
mentioned.

suspicion.[25] Unfortunately, top policy makers in the United States showed themselves by their speeches and actions to be dominated by traditional and outworn conceptions of democracy, and a lack of comprehension of the views of its totalitarian detractors. The resulting policy is weak, since it does not command the support of youth, but only of a dwindling group of elderly Europeans. The large proportion of men over sixty among the supporters of American policy in Europe is a fair index of this weakness.

This difficulty will probably continue for some time. The fact that the Communists exploit the anticapitalist sentiment of the European masses does not justify us in pretending that the present conflict is merely one between tyranny and freedom. The shattered economies of many European nations, especially Italy and Germany, call for drastic plans. Any reconstruction whatsoever presupposes a vigorous facing of the problems of a directed economy, or so it seems to most Europeans. If this be socialism—and by nineteenth-century standards it certainly is—America, to be in the vanguard of democratization, will have to accept it as a part of the "democratic" future. Any insistence that the economic problems of reconstruction be handled by free enterprise will put America into a reactionary camp which is occupied mostly by men who have little use for democracy.

Summary and Conclusion

What does the preceding analysis of the American policy of democratization suggest? It has been shown that this policy has been very difficult to effectuate because of sharp disagreements regarding the meaning of democracy among the Allies and among Americans.

It is a policy which has been further handicapped by the fact that the other Allied policies have created a setting which is ill suited for the growth of democracy. Among these policies, deindustrialization and the division of the country into four (lately three) zones have

[25]For Italy, the most important study is that by Gaetano Salvemini and George LaPiana, *The Future of Italy* (1944). In spite of its anticlerical flavor, it pointed the way to a constructive prodemocratic policy. Mention should also be made of G. Borgese's *Common Cause* (1943).

been especially unfortunate because of the hunger and want they have entailed. Besides these, the policy adopted at Potsdam permitting the expulsion of from six to ten million people from one area into the overcrowded remainder of Germany has been calculated to impede democratization greatly by vastly enhancing the disunity of the electorate.

Since democratization spearheads the American policy of aiding the democratic forces of Europe, the responsibility of military government in this field has made their operations of crucial significance to American policy throughout Europe. Failure of democratization policies in Germany probably would entail the collapse of the entire United States policy in Europe of containing the antidemocratic forces. This conclusion is reinforced by the fact that further economic progress of virtually all the Western European countries who are seeking aid from the United States depends upon reconstruction of the German economy. American activity in this direction can, however, be justified only if there is a reasonable prospect of steady and orderly progress toward a democratic society in what remains of Germany. Thus it can be seen that the task of democratization is the vital one of military occupation in Germany. American military government authorities have been preoccupied with its requirements for some time. This is as it should be. General Lucius D. Clay is quite right in his frequently expressed thought that the success or failure of military government will be assessed in terms of this central task. Democratization is thus the heart of the military government enterprise.

Chapter II

The Development of American Military Government Policy during World War II

MERLE FAINSOD

Introduction

Public policy," observed an English judge more than a century ago, ". . . is a very unruly horse, and when you once get astride it, you never know where it will carry you." The development of official policy regarding military government during World War II serves as a vivid illustration of this maxim.

At the outbreak of World War II, it would have been difficult to find a systematic and coherent statement of official United States policy or doctrine with regard to military government. Of experience with military government there was no lack. In every major war since the War of 1812 the armed forces of the United States had found it necessary to establish controls over civilian populations in occupied territories. But this experience had been subjected to relatively little careful analysis. Policy was implicit in action rather than articulated in words. The written and unwritten rules of warfare, as defined by recognized authorities on international law and as established by the custom and usages of civilized nations; an occasional effort at synthesis such as Lieber's Code embodied in General Orders, No. 100 during the Civil War; the treaties to which the United States was a party, such as the Hague Conventions of 1899 and 1907—these defined the system of legal restraints that the United States accepted as obligatory in dealing with persons and property in occupied territory.

Underlying these rules was the now somewhat old-fashioned concept of "civilized" warfare, of military necessity tempered by the principles of humanity and chivalry. War was conceived as a battle between two armies, rather than as a total struggle in which the energies and destinies of whole populations were engaged. As Francis Lieber put it in 1863, "As civilization has advanced during the last centuries, so has likewise steadily advanced, especially in war on land, the distinction between the private individual belonging to a hostile country and the hostile country itself, with its men in arms. The principle has been more and more acknowledged that the unarmed citizen is to be spared in person, property, and honor as much as the exigencies of war will admit."[1]

In accordance with this traditional view of the responsibilities of the occupying power, military government operated within a framework of legal restraints. It abstained, as far as possible, from interference with established political, social, and economic institutions in occupied areas. It recognized an obligation to protect the enemy in his capacity as a private individual. These were the views that found acceptance in American policy expressions prior to the outbreak of World War II.

Field Manual 27-5

The first official statement of American policy on military government during World War II is to be found in the original edition of the War Department *Basic Field Manual on Military Government* (FM 27-5). It was released, significantly enough, on June 30, 1940, almost simultaneously with the completion of the Nazi blitzkrieg in the West and the capitulation of France. But the fertilizing ideas that nurtured it were not conceived in terms of the coming struggle with

[1] Article 22, Lieber's Code, General Order No. 100. U.S. War Department. The same outlook dominated the Annex to the Hague Convention of 1907. Thus:

Article 32. ". . . the occupant . . . shall take all the measures in his power to restore, and ensure, as far as possible, public order and safety, while respecting, unless absolutely prevented, the laws in force in the country."

Article 46. "Family honour and rights, the lives of persons, and private property, as well as religious convictions and practices, must be respected.

"Private property cannot be confiscated."

the totalitarian Nazi and Fascist dictatorships. They were largely the result of reflection on the American occupational experience in the Rhineland after the Armistice of 1918, and they expressed the liberal and humane spirit of Lieber's Code and the Hague Conventions.

The military government policies set forth in FM 27–5 for the guidance of the War Department were divided into two categories: basic and secondary. Five basic policies were outlined: (a) military necessity, (b) welfare of the governed, (c) flexibility, (d) economy of effort, (e) permanence. Military necessity was placed in the fore-front. "The first consideration at all times," stated the *Manual,* "is the prosecution of the war to a successful termination. So long as hostil-ities continue, the question must be asked, with reference to every intended act of the military government, whether it will forward that object or hinder its accomplishment."[2] Next in the list of basic ob-jectives comes the welfare of the governed. "Military government," the *Manual* continued, "should be just, humane, and as mild as prac-ticable, and the welfare of the people governed should always be the aim of every person engaged therein. As military government is executed by force, it is incumbent upon those who administer it to be strictly guided by the principles of justice, honor, and humanity—virtues adorning a soldier even more than other men for the very reason that he possesses the power of his arms against the unarmed. Not only religion and the honor of the Army of the United States require this course, but also policy. The object of the United States in waging any war is to obtain a favorable and enduring peace. A military occupation marked by harshness, injustice, or oppression leaves lasting resentment against the occupying power in the hearts of the people of the occupied territory and sows the seeds of future war by them against the occupying power when circumstances shall make that possible; whereas just, considerate, and mild treatment of the governed by the occupying power will convert enemies into friends."[3]

Concerning the other policies described as basic, relatively little needs to be said. The principle of *flexibility* means that a plan for

[2]*Basic Field Manual—Military Government* (FM 27–5), (1940), p. 3.
[3]*Ibid.*, pp. 3–4.

military government "must suit the people, the country, the time, and the strategical and tactical situation to which it is applied. It must be . . . capable of change without undue inconvenience."[4] *Economy of effort* implies minimum commitments consistent with "the proper functioning of military government." The principle of *permanence* requires that frequent changes in personnel or policy be avoided in order to insure "continuity of policy."

In addition to these so-called basic policies, a number of policies, somewhat misleadingly labeled "secondary," were also outlined. First came an explicit statement that the commanding general of the theater of operations should have full control of military government in his theater. Next, there was an instruction that separate personnel be provided for military government as long as hostilities continue, and that the personnel of combatant units be assigned to military government duties only when "the probability of a resumption of hostilities is extremely remote." Third, there followed an injunction on the retention of existing civil personnel in occupied areas. "The personnel of the military government should, so far as possible, deal with the inhabitants through the officers and employees of their own government."[5] Derived from this was a fourth principle, the avoidance of changes in existing laws, customs, and institutions.

The appearance of the original edition of FM 27–5 antedated Pearl Harbor by nearly a year and a half. In the intervening period interest in military government was quiescent. With the outbreak of hostilities, the whole atmosphere changed. Early in 1942 the War Department established the School of Military Government at the University of Virginia to train officers for occupational responsibilities, and by May, 1942, the training program was well under way.

Under the impact of war, and particularly a war in which the main foes were Nazi Germany and Japan, it was inevitable that the official doctrine of FM 27–5 should be subjected to critical re-examination. From the side of the military came the criticism that FM 27–5 neglected problems of military government in the combat phase, that it

[4]*Ibid.*, p. 4.
[5]*Ibid.*, p. 5.

assumed the kind of peaceful conditions that prevailed in the Rhineland during the American occupation after the Armistice of 1918. This line of criticism found striking expression in a lecture at the School of Military Government in Virginia. Referring to the original edition of FM 27-5, the lecturer stated: "[It] gives us the impression that the objective of promoting the welfare of the governed in occupied territory is almost as important as the objective of military necessity. In fact, you get the impression from the text that our principal objective in invading a foreign country is to bring light to the heathen. Now, I can assure you that that is not realistic. There is only one legitimate objective of military government, and that is to win the war. It is a method of fighting behind the lines, and it is done by holding the civil population in subjection. . . . Military government is not a missionary enterprise, and, while you do pay attention to the welfare of the governed, you do it because you are inherently decent and because paying attention to their welfare where you can will tend to avoid the more violent kinds of outbreaks against you; but it is utterly misleading to put the welfare of the governed on a par with military necessity. Everything you do in military government has to be tested in the light of whether it will aid or retard the campaign. . . ."[6] That this view was not without considerable influence

[6]Colonel Lewis K. Underhill, "Organization of Military Government" (mimeographed lecture at Charlottesville, 1943).

That Charlottesville was also a forum for the expression of views more consistent with the original philosophy of FM 27-5 may be illustrated by a quotation from Colonel Joseph P. Harris, also of that faculty. "Through all of these related programs for the training of administrators of occupied territories runs a fundamental philosophy —expressed or implied—that while the first and primary purpose of military government is to advance the cause of our arms and to promote the military objectives, there is also a secondary purpose and responsibility, under international law, to maintain law and order in the occupied area, to feed the starving, to protect the population against pestilence and disease, and, as far as military operations will permit, to aid the area to bind up its wounds, re-establish essential services, and start the healing processes of economic rehabilitation. Our purpose is not to loot or to despoil, but to lay the groundwork for the eventual restoration of the political and economic life of the area under conditions which will provide the basis of a lasting peace. Military and humanitarian considerations are not necessarily opposed to each other, though they may be so at times; and at those times military necessity must be the prime consideration."— "Selection and Training of Civil Affairs Officers," *Public Opinion Quarterly*, VII (Winter, 1943), 700.

will be demonstrated when the revised edition of FM 27–5 is subjected to analysis.

Another line of critical attack derived from a fundamental scepticism as to the capacity of the military to cope with problems of military government. Critics of this persuasion were convinced that the political and economic decisions that FM 27–5 vested in the military ought properly to be made by responsible civilian officials.[7] According to these critics, many of the functions entrusted by FM 27–5 to the military were essentially civilian in nature and would be most efficiently performed by civilians. This group argued that the responsibilities of the military for governing civilian populations should be delimited in scope almost from the beginning. Its slogan was civilian responsibility for civilian operations under military government. It was destined to have relatively little influence, at least while active hostilities raged.

The critical fire that raised the most fundamental long-term issues focused on the twin principles of retention of existing civil personnel in occupied areas and avoidance of changes in existing laws, customs, and institutions. Did these principles mean that it would be American policy to govern through Nazi or Fascist officials and to leave the entire structure of Fascist or Nazi administration undisturbed? Would the representatives of American military government undertake to enforce Nazi policy as embodied in Nazi legislation? The principle of economy of effort, with its reliance on supervision of a going administrative machinery, could be adduced to dictate an affirmative answer; military necessity, or at least military expediency, might serve to furnish reinforcement. Critics who put these queries argued a basic failure in FM 27–5 to visualize the impending war with the Fascist states and the political consequences that it entailed.

The Sicilian Directives

These questions, which supplied theoretical exercises in classrooms at Charlottesville and elsewhere, were soon to become issues that

[7]For an expression of this view, see Hiram Motherwell, "Military Occupation and Then What?" *Harper's Magazine* (Oct., 1943), pp. 439–446.

could not be evaded under the pressure of occupational imperatives. The amphibious assault on Sicily was launched on July 10, 1943. In thirty-nine days the Sicilian campaign had ended. For the first time, American military governors faced the test of applying their policies on Axis territory in Europe. (See Chapter VI.) The military government of Sicily was a joint British-American operation, but it is worth noting that one of the sources from which the plan for military government in Sicily was ostensibly derived was FM 27-5.

The experiences of military government in Italy are analyzed in detail elsewhere in this volume. What is of primary interest here are the directives that guided it, and their significance for the evolution of official American military government policy.

Two somewhat contradictory facets of the Sicilian directives warrant special discussion: (1) the problem of attitude toward Fascism and Fascists, and (2) the concept of nonpolitical administration. The Fascist problem proved troublesome from the outset. "The Fascist Party," read General Administrative Instruction No. 2,[8] "will be immediately dissolved. Fascist doctrines and propaganda in any form are to be prohibited. . . . The Fascist militia and all Fascist Youth organizations will be abolished. . . . The entire Fascist party leadership . . . should be removed from any posts of authority in the civil administration." But General Administrative Instruction No. 1 added some qualifications: "The Fascist Party machine will be broken up from the earliest possible moment and in every way in which it is open for us to do so, but the machine cannot be broken up or Fascist influence eliminated in a day. Since also nearly all Italian administrative officials are, at any rate nominally, members of the Party, it will not be possible to remove or intern all members of the Party. This would merely cause a breakdown, not only of the whole of the Italian administrative machine, but also of all technical services, such as transportation, etc. . . ." The application of this policy, which sought to reconcile the need for a stable administrative machinery with the elimination of the Fascists who were entrenched in it, was to prove difficult. It was subject to much misconstruction and much misunder-

[8]The proclamations and instructions used in Sicily have been collected in *Army Service Forces Manual* M-353-2 Supplement (1943).

standing. But it was not without significance that official military government policy was now committed, at least in theory, to the destruction of Fascism and all its works. Against the background of this development the doctrine of the old FM 27–5—that "the existing laws, customs and institutions of the occupied countries have been created by its people and are presumably best suited to them"—now made strange reading.

The Sicilian directives unveiled yet another important policy development in military government—the concept of nonpolitical administration. This concept was not to prove ultimately viable, and some of its difficulties were revealed at its birth. In General Administrative Instruction No. 1, military government officers were told: "Your job is to administer and not to frame policy or talk politics. You are not to discuss political matters with local Italians. You are not to discuss religious matters." And in General Administrative Instruction No. 2 the same point was reinforced: "Neither local personalities nor organized political groups, however sound in sentiment, shall have any part in determining your policies or course of action. It is essential to avoid any commitments to or negotiations with any local political elements, either in local or in general problems. Your job is to administer military government and to avoid any political discussion or commitment." Clearly the planners of military government had no desire to become embroiled in local political controversies. But their instructions to military government officers also read: "You should make it clear to the local population whenever opportunity presents itself that military occupation is intended a) to deliver the people from the Fascist regime which led them into the war and, b) to restore Italy as a free nation." It is impossible not to sympathize with the plight of the military government officers who were required to "avoid completely any political discussion," while delivering the above message. Sympathy heightens with the further revelation that they were to instruct Italians that "no political activity whatsoever will be countenanced" and to warn released anti-Fascist political prisoners that "political activity on their part . . . will not be tolerated." This negativistic concept of military government functioning in a political vacuum virtually reduced to absurdity the notion of a nonpolitical administration dedicated to the restoration of Italy as a free nation. It proved to be both unworkable and unwise. It subsequently had to be abandoned, but, as will be noted later, not before finding its way into the revised edition of FM 27–5 as an official expression of American military government policy.

The Revised Edition of FM 27–5[9]

The revised edition of FM 27–5 appeared on December 22, 1943, two years after Pearl Harbor. In the interim, American and Allied military government was beginning to make the transition from theory to practice. North Africa, Sicily, and southern Italy had been transformed into laboratories in which policy could be tested. The fundamental conceptions that endeavored to give shape to this experience were the same conceptions that were currently being incorporated in the revision of FM 27–5. They deserve careful analysis as indications of the transformations that American military government doctrines were undergoing at a point approximately midway in World War II.

Perhaps the most striking characteristic of the revised FM 27–5 is the triumph of the military point of view. Military government is visualized primarily in terms of the requirements of the combat phase, perhaps a natural and inevitable response to the urgencies of the moment. Relatively little thought or attention is devoted to problems of military government after hostilities cease.[10] As section 9a of the *Manual* has it, "The first consideration at all times is the prosecution of the military operation to a successful conclusion. Military necessity is the primary underlying principle for the conduct of military government. . . . The theatre commander must always have full responsibility for military government."[11]

Compared with the old FM 27–5, there is a marked hardening of attitude toward enemy populations in occupied areas. "Welfare of the

[9]The complete title is *United States Army and Navy Manual of Military Government and Civil Affairs* (FM 27–5 and OPNAV 50E–3), December 22, 1943.

[10]FM 27–5 was designed for the combat phase and not the post-combat. Further directives and policy statements were to be issued for the occupation phase.

[11]*Basic Field Manual—Military Government* (FM 27–5 and OPNAV 50E–3), p. 5.

governed" no longer is listed among the basic objectives of military government. References to the "virtues adorning a soldier" and pleas for "considerate and mild treatment of the governed," as a way of converting enemies into friends, cease to appear. "While the welfare of the inhabitants," notes the revised FM 27–5, "should be considered —for humane reasons and should be safeguarded as far as military requirements permit, the primary purposes of such treatment are to facilitate the military operations and to meet obligations imposed by law. . . . Such a policy, however, should not affect the imposition of such restrictive or punitive measures as may be necessary to accomplish the objectives of military government in any area, but especially in one in which the population is aggressively hostile and engages in active and passive sabotage."[12] "Fraternization," moreover, is strictly forbidden. "Civil Affairs officers and personnel, as representatives of the United States government, should keep their relations with local officials and inhabitants on a strictly official basis, avoiding unofficial social relationships."[13]

The provisions of the revised FM 27–5 with respect to the retention of local government departments and officials, as well as of existing laws, customs, and political subdivisions, mark a step forward in terms of the awareness shown of the problems created in imposing military government in areas formerly dominated by fascist regimes. The authors perceive that it will "usually . . . be necessary to remove high-ranking political officials from office." But the old principle of economy of effort, of lightening the burden of supervision for military government, operates in the revised FM 27–5 toward a cautious application of a removal policy. The formula evolved is as follows: "While membership in unfriendly partisan organizations or political parties may not by itself be cause for removal, such officials as have been active leaders of such organizations will ordinarily not be retained in office, nor will other officials who prove to be unreliable or unsatisfactory."[14] The formula on retention of existing laws and customs is even more general. "To avoid confusion and to promote simplicity of administration, it is advisable that local laws, customs, and institu-

[12]*Ibid.*, p. 7.
[13]*Ibid.*, p. 10.
[14]*Ibid.*, p. 9.

tions of government be retained, except where they conflict with the aims of military government or are inimical to its best interests."[15] But the problems created by the existence of fascist legislation and institutions are skirted rather than faced. Certain tentative instructions are given to restore the older legal norms that fascism destroys. Thus, "laws which discriminate on the basis of race, color, creed, or political opinions should be annulled as the situation permits."[16] The policy is stated that "to the extent that military interests are not prejudiced, freedom of speech and press should be maintained or instituted."[17] But unfortunately the very vagueness and generality of the revised FM 27–5 opened the way to extremely diverse interpretations. To some who put administrative efficiency or convenience in the forefront, it appeared to invite efforts to buttress a crumbling fascist administrative structure. To others it seemed to offer an opportunity to restore the older legal norms that fascism had sought to destroy. A prime difficulty was that the dominating preoccupation of the new FM 27–5 with military government during the combat phase led to an almost complete disregard of the post-hostilities problem of administering the receivership left by the bankruptcy of fascism. The emphasis on nonpolitical administration was a natural outgrowth of this disregard.

The concept of nonpolitical administration that guided the policy makers of the Sicilian occupation found full expression in the revised edition of FM 27–5. Thus, with regard to the selection of local officials, a warning is given that "appointments from a political faction or clique, *regardless of their friendly sentiment,* should be avoided, except in unusual circumstances."[18] Paragraphs that appear in the Sicilian instructions receive almost precisely the same formulation in the new FM 27–5. There is the same injunction that political activity on the part of released political prisoners will not be tolerated. And finally there is the same dubious formula already noted: "Neither local political personalities nor organized political groups, however sound in sentiment, should have any part in determining the policies

[15] *Ibid.,* p. 8.
[16] *Ibid.,* p. 12.
[17] *Ibid.,* p. 13.
[18] *Ibid.,* p. 10.

of the military government."[19] Precisely how this instruction was to be reconciled with the commitment of the military government to institute or maintain freedom of speech and press was not made clear.

A final contrast between the new and the old FM 27-5 deserves to be noted. The new FM 27-5 for the first time enters the area of economic policy. It sketches out basic economic policy as follows: "First, to revive economic life and stimulate production in order to reduce to a minimum the needs of the area for United States and allied assistance and to develop the area as a source of supply for further operations, and second, to use available goods and services as efficiently as possible for the satisfaction of military and civilian needs."[20] There follows a list of more specific steps that are to be taken, first, to guarantee supplies for the army, and second, to assure that "the population receive at least a minimum of necessary goods and services." What is significant about these statements, aside from their generality, is that they are dominated by the same fundamental military thinking that permeates all of the revised FM 27-5. The primary task is to win the war, not to take care of enemy civilians in occupied areas. If the minimum needs of enemy populations are supplied, this is to be done not primarily for altruistic or humanitarian reasons, but to protect the health of the occupying forces and to make certain that the pressing needs of the armed forces of the United States are met.

The revised edition of FM 27-5, like its predecessor, is important as a statement of general principles of military government as they were interpreted by the armed forces at the time of publication. But it should be stressed that the doctrine there elaborated was in no sense mandatory. The *Manual* clearly states that it is intended to serve "as a general guide" and it is explicitly recognized that departures may be required where "special circumstances dictate otherwise."

Among these "special circumstances" that were destined to become of increasing significance as the war moved to a victorious conclusion were the top-level political decisions made by the President and members of his Cabinet as well as the commitments entered into by the

[19] *Ibid.*, p. 10.
[20] *Ibid.*, p. 11.

chief executive with representatives of other nations. These decisions were to become particularly important in connection with the development of military government policy toward Germany.

Policy toward Germany—Early Aspects

Prior to American entrance into World War II, President Roosevelt and Prime Minister Churchill, in affixing their signatures to the Atlantic Charter (August 14, 1941), stated, among other things:

First, their countries seek no aggrandizement, territorial or otherwise; second, they desire to see no territorial changes that do not accord with the freely expressed wishes of the peoples concerned; third, they respect the right of all peoples to choose the form of government under which they will live; and they wish to see sovereign rights and self-government restored to those who have been forcibly deprived of them.[21]

These principles, which were potentially of great significance for military government planning, were later also subscribed to by the Soviet Union, China, and some forty-three other members of the United Nations.

As the war increased in bitterness and casualties mounted, the liberal humanitarianism of the Atlantic Charter came to be stressed less and less. The same hardening of attitude toward the enemy revealed in the contrast between the revised and the old FM 27–5 manifested itself at the level of high policy. At Casablanca in January, 1943, President Roosevelt and Prime Minister Churchill stated the intransigent formula of unconditional surrender, and at Moscow in October, 1943, their representatives joined with representatives of the Soviet Union and China in a similar declaration.

At the Moscow Conference the question of the treatment of Germany was discussed but, except for a declaration that those responsible for atrocities would be punished, and that Austria would be detached from the Reich and given independent status, no agreement was reached. Instead, the problem was referred to the European Ad-

[21]See *The Axis in Defeat* for the complete text of the Atlantic Charter, as well as for many other documents, important in the development of American military government policy.

visory Commission, composed of representatives of the United States, Great Britain, the Soviet Union, and, later, France. This body encountered major difficulties both in eliciting views from the participants and in reconciling such views as it succeeded in eliciting.

With the invasion of the Continent impending, the necessity for agreement on a German policy became more urgent. But invasion strategy and preparations tended to crowd German occupation problems out of high-level agenda, and the problem of obtaining agreement on an American policy toward Germany was rendered difficult by the hard versus soft peace debate that rose to a crescendo in the United States in 1944. While the top planning groups in the United States procrastinated, the SHAEF military government planners could not wait, and were compelled to elaborate their plans without decisive high-level political guidance. A draft of these plans came to the attention of Secretary of the Treasury Morgenthau. As he has recently related the story,

During a visit to the European theatre at that time [June of 1944], I had an opportunity to look into the plans for occupation of Germany which were then being prepared at SHAEF. This planning was being carried on by English and American officers in the staff divisions concerned with military government. It seemed to me that these military plans placed too great a share of the responsibility for rehabilitating Germany on the occupying forces rather than on the German people themselves, and that not enough emphasis was being placed on the task of destroying Nazi influence and eliminating Germany's industrial potential for war. In any event, it was clear that these were important issues of national policy which ought not to be decided at a technical military level.

On returning to Washington, [Morgenthau continues] I reported these impressions and views to President Roosevelt. I found that he, himself, had already given a great deal of thought to these issues and that his own convictions and views were in close accord with the opinions which I had expressed. Following my report to him, the President directed that the question of policy toward defeated Germany be considered by Mr. Hull, Mr. Stimson, and myself. In the ensuing month, the three of us explored and discussed this problem at considerable length. Failing to reach full agreement, each one submitted his own views to the President who made the final decision. That decision was essentially in accord with the President's earlier conclusions and it did not differ significantly from my own views of the subject.[22]

The Quebec Conference

The Quebec Conference in September, 1944, furnished the setting for the next act in the development of a German policy. Secretary Morgenthau, who was invited to participate in the conference by President Roosevelt, submitted a memorandum that called, among other things, for a partitioning of Germany, the deindustrialization of the Ruhr, reparations in kind, political decentralization, and the division of large estates.[23] That this document was not without effect is evidenced by a memorandum signed by both Roosevelt and Churchill at Quebec (September 15, 1944), dealing with the future disposition of the Ruhr and the Saar.[24] In this document they expressed agreement that "the industries . . . in the Ruhr and the Saar would . . . be put out of action and closed down, . . . that the two districts should be put under some body under the world organization which would supervise the dismantling of these industries," and that "this programme for eliminating the war-making industries in the Ruhr and in the Saar is looking forward to converting Germany into a country primarily agricultural and pastoral in its character." It was in connection with the approval of this memorandum that an agreement was reached between Roosevelt and Churchill that northwestern Germany, including the Ruhr, should be occupied by British forces.

It is no secret that the decisions reached at Quebec to convert Germany into a primarily agricultural country did not find ready acceptance in many quarters of the State Department, the War Department, and other federal agencies with an interest in the problem. The struggle to write the Joint Chiefs of Staff directive on German

[22]See Henry Morgenthau, Jr., "Postwar Treatment of Germany," *The Annals of the American Academy of Political and Social Science* (July, 1946), pp. 125–126. Compare Chapter X below for a divergent view.

[23]For the text of this memorandum see the preface of Morgenthau, *Germany Is Our Problem* (1945); cf. also Chapter X, pages 220–225.

[24]For complete text see *Annals, loc. cit.,* p. 126.

military government policy, which later became known as JCS 1067, reflected profound differences of opinion. In the end, as will be noted later, JCS 1067 represented an appreciably modified version of the original Morgenthau proposals.

The final version of JCS 1067 is dated April 26, 1945.[25] On September 11, 1944, the First Army had entered Germany. Pending the appearance of JCS 1067, military government officers in Germany operated on the basis of SHAEF directives, which were in turn based on policies contained in directives issued by the Combined Chiefs of Staff for application in the period prior to the defeat or surrender of Germany.

These policies formed a bridge between the revised FM 27–5 and JCS 1067. They reflect the influence of the Morgenthau proposals, and they represent a further stiffening of attitude toward the enemy as compared with the revised FM 27–5. The following basic principles were laid down to guide the occupation:

(i) No steps looking toward economic rehabilitation of Germany are to be undertaken except as may be immediately necessary in support of military operations.

(ii) No relief supplies are to be imported or distributed for the German population or for displaced enemy or ex-enemy nationals beyond the minimum necessary to prevent disease and such disorder as might endanger or impede military operations.

(iii) Under no circumstances shall active Nazis or ardent sympathizers be retained in office for the purpose of administrative convenience or expediency.

(iv) Although the Nazi party and all subsidiary organizations will be dissolved, administrative machinery of certain dissolved organizations may be used when necessary to provide essential functions, such as relief, health and sanitation, with non-Nazi personnel and facilities.

(v) Germany will always be treated as a defeated country and not as a liberated country.

This stern set of principles was an endeavor to set the tone for the occupation. A nonfraternization ban was imposed, but it soon proved unenforceable. Nor was the so-called "hard policy" outlined above

[25]For complete text see the Appendix, pages 381–402.

calculated to mobilize the support of such anti-Nazis as remained in Germany. An indiscriminate policy of denying food, forbidding economic reconstruction, and outlawing any form of social contact had the effect, whatever the intent, of driving home to the Germans that, in the eyes of the Americans, Nazi and non-Nazi alike were equally abhorrent and reprehensible. Such a policy, if persisted in, was calculated to drive antifascists to despair; it left them without hope and without any possibility for positive collaboration.

During the winter of 1944–1945, while the first efforts to apply this policy were being made in Germany, an Allied program for the occupation of the Reich was still lacking. The European Advisory Commission had failed to produce agreement; with the Nazis on the eve of collapse, decisions could no longer be postponed. At Yalta in February, 1945, the Big Three—Roosevelt, Stalin, and Churchill—made an effort to break the impasse.

The Yalta communiqué (February 11, 1945) announced a number of important decisions, immediately relevant to the problem of the occupation of Germany.[26] In the first place, in fixing the new Russian-Polish border approximately along the Curzon Line, it was agreed that Poland should be "compensated by substantial accessions of territory in the north and west." While a final determination of the Polish western boundary was postponed until a future peace conference, it was made clear that a very considerable part of eastern Germany would fall immediately into the area of Polish administration.

In the second place, it was decided that Germany would be partitioned into separate zones of occupation for military government purposes. The Big Three agreed to invite France to take over a zone of occupation, the limits of which were to be fixed by the four powers through their representatives on the European Advisory Commission. "Coordinated administration and control" of Germany was to be provided through a central control commission composed of the supreme commanders of the four occupying powers with headquarters at Berlin.

[26]For complete text see *The Department of State Bulletin* (February 18, 1945), pp. 213–216.

In the third place, the Yalta Agreement set forth certain general principles of denazification, demilitarization, and disarmament to guide occupation policy. The conference report declared:

It is our inflexible purpose to destroy German militarism and Nazism and to ensure that Germany will never again be able to disturb the peace of the world. We are determined to disarm and disband all German armed forces; break up for all time the German General Staff that has repeatedly contrived the resurgence of German militarism; remove or destroy all German military equipment; eliminate or control all German industry that could be used for military production; bring all war criminals to just and swift punishment and exact reparations in kind for the destruction wrought by the Germans; wipe out the Nazi Party, Nazi laws, organization and institutions, remove all Nazi and militarist influences from public office and from the cultural and economic life of the German people; and take in harmony such other measures in Germany as may be necessary to the future peace and safety of the world. It is not our purpose to destroy the people of Germany, but only when Nazism and militarism have been extirpated will there be hope for a decent life for Germans, and a place for them in the community of nations.

On its face the Yalta communiqué expressed the unity of Big Three policy. But the surface unity concealed deep and disturbing differences in fundamental outlook. The decision to compensate Poland with a slice of eastern Germany was made under Soviet pressure and involved Roosevelt and Churchill in an embarrassing repudiation of the principles to which they had subscribed in the Atlantic Charter. The decision to partition Germany into separate zones of occupation was an expression of disunity rather than unity, and it was to have serious consequences. The statement of principles to be followed in the occupation found common ground on what was to be destroyed, but it was essentially negative in its impact. Lack of agreement on positive policies to be followed after surrender reflected the divergent political and social orders of the Soviet Union and its Western allies. The reparations issue in effect was postponed, again perhaps a reflection of the fact that no real agreement was then possible.

Under the zonal system of occupation projected at Yalta, it was desirable that military government policy in all zones be synchronized if confusion was to be avoided. As the Allied armies pressed deeper into Germany, the need became urgent. No agreement, however, could be reached on a joint directive, and as a result each of the four powers destined to share in the occupation elaborated its own plan.

The Joint Chiefs of Staff Directive 1067

JCS 1067, which was issued to General Eisenhower in April, 1945, was designed to guide him in his role as military governor of that portion of Germany occupied by United States forces. While he was directed to urge the Control Council to adopt these policies in all parts of Germany, pending such adoption or agreement on some other plan, each member of the Control Council continued free to follow national instructions, which presumably were required to remain within the framework of the Yalta Declaration.

JCS 1067, as finally issued, may be described as a modified version of the Morgenthau plan. Like the Yalta Declaration, its emphasis was on what is to be destroyed and eradicated, rather than on what is to be built and rebuilt. In outlining the basic objectives of the occupation, JCS 1067 stated:

It should be brought home to the Germans that . . . the Germans cannot escape responsibility for what they have brought upon themselves.

Germany will not be occupied for the purpose of liberation but as a defeated enemy nation. . . . In the conduct of your occupation and administration you should be just but firm and aloof. You will strongly discourage fraternization with the German officials and population.

The principal Allied objective is to prevent Germany from ever again becoming a threat to the peace of the world. . . .

Decentralization of the German political, administrative, and economic structure and the encouragement of trends toward local autonomy were declared to be among the basic objectives of the occupation. But interzonal trading and the establishment of centralized administration or control of essential national public services such as railroads, communications and power, finance and foreign affairs, and production and distribution of essential commodities were to be permitted. A stern and far-reaching policy of denazification was ordered:

"All members of the Nazi party who have been more than nominal participants in its activities, all active supporters of Nazism or militarism and all other persons hostile to Allied purposes will be removed and excluded from public office and from positions of importance in quasi-public and private enterprises. . . ." Unauthorized political activity of any kind was forbidden. Military government was cautioned to avoid becoming committed to any political group. But occupational responsibilities were not conceived entirely in negative terms. One of the objectives proclaimed was "preparation for an eventual reconstruction of German political life on a democratic basis." The "self-organization of employees along democratic lines" and "free collective bargaining between employees and employers regarding wage, hour and working conditions" were to be permitted. The directive further stated that "a coordinated system of control over German education and an affirmative program of reorientation will be established designed completely to eliminate Nazi and militaristic doctrines and to encourage the development of democratic ideas."

The primary economic objectives were proclaimed as the industrial disarmament and demilitarization of Germany and the decentralization of the structure and administration of the German economy. To secure industrial disarmament, the production and development of all arms, ammunition, and implements and facilities of war were to be prohibited, and German industries that could be utilized for war production as well as excess capacity in certain other specified industries were to be subjected to stringent regulation and made available for reparations. German external assets were to be seized and impounded. To ensure economic decentralization, cartels were to be dissolved, and German participation in international cartels was to be prohibited. Agricultural output, however, was to be encouraged to the maximum extent possible. Measures were also to be taken to repair and restore essential transportation services and public utilities, to meet the minimum needs of the population for shelter, to stimulate the production of coal, and to revive the production of light consumer goods. Inflation was to be controlled and equitable interzonal distribution of available goods and services assured. The objective of the civilian supply program was "to prevent starvation or widespread

disease or such civil unrest as would endanger the occupying forces."
Germans were to be "made responsible for providing for themselves,
out of their own work and resources." Every effort was to be made
"to assure that German resources are fully utilized and consumption
held to the minimum in order that imports may be strictly limited
and that surpluses may be made available for the occupying forces
and displaced persons and United Nations prisoners of war, and for
reparation." No action was to be sanctioned "that would tend to
support basic living standards in Germany on a higher level than
that existing in any one of the neighboring United Nations" and
"appropriate measures" were to be taken "to ensure that basic living
standards of the German people are not higher than those existing in
any one of the neighboring United Nations when such measures will
contribute to raising the standards of any such nation."

JCS 1067 has been subjected to severe criticism from many sides.
For those of the Morgenthau school it does not go far enough to
ensure the impotence of Germany. By others it has been denounced
as "chiefly concerned with tearing things down rather than building
things up," as the embodiment of a harsh policy of retribution that
nourishes the seeds of future wars. Persuasive cases can be made for
both points of view, granted the premises from which the critics start.
JCS 1067, in its final form, represents a compromise between very
divergent views. Like most such compromises, it contains its telltale
uncertainties and contradictions. It assumed that American military
government would inherit a going concern with considerable economic virility and strength instead of a disrupted and paralyzed economy. It counted on interzonal collaboration to ameliorate the handicaps of quadripartite occupation. Because both of these assumptions
were faulty, JCS 1067 stood in need of revision even before the ink
was dry on its signatures.

Efforts to synchronize interzonal military government policy in
the months after the issuance of JCS 1067 did not prove notably
effective. The organization of the quadripartite Allied Control Council in Berlin was announced on June 5, 1945, ostensibly to "insure
appropriate uniformity of action in the chief questions affecting Germany as a whole." But the statement on control machinery made clear

that members would act "on instructions from their governments," and that decisions in the Control Council would have to be unanimous in order to have binding effect.[27] Germany was divided for purposes of occupation into four zones—an eastern zone to the Soviet Union, a northwestern zone to the United Kingdom, a southwestern zone to the United States, and a western zone to France. Greater Berlin in turn was split into four zones and made subject to a quadripartite Governing Authority (Kommandatura) consisting of four commandants, each of whom was to serve in rotation as chief commandant. This authority was to operate under the general direction of the Control Council.

Given the rule of unanimity, it became clear that synchronization of interzonal military government policy depended on agreement on the fundamental objectives to be pursued. Experience in the various zones in the first months after surrender revealed serious differences in national policies. The Big Three Conference at Potsdam (July 17–25, 1945) represented another effort to reconcile these divergent views.

The Potsdam Directive

A superficial reading of the Potsdam Declaration gives the impression that considerable progress was achieved in reaching agreement on occupational policy.[28] Many of the principles laid down in JCS 1067 were incorporated almost verbatim in the Potsdam Report. Disarmament, demilitarization, denazification, decentralization, and preparation for the eventual reconstruction of German political life on a democratic basis were proclaimed as the major occupational objectives. In some respects, the Potsdam Agreement goes beyond JCS 1067 in laying the groundwork for political reconstruction. It permits and encourages the establishment of democratic political parties; it promises the restoration of local self-government and the introduction of representative and elective principles into regional, provincial, and state (Land) administration as rapidly as experience justifies; subject to considerations of military necessity, it promises that freedom of

[27]For text see, *The Axis in Defeat,* p. 68.

[28]For complete text of the Potsdam Declaration see *The Department of State Bulletin* (August 5, 1945), pp. 153–161.

speech, press, and religion shall be permitted; it proposes the reorganization of the judicial system "in accordance with the principles of democracy, of justice under law, and of equal rights for all citizens without distinction of race, nationality or religion."

Agreement was also reached in principle on a degree of interzonal unification. "So far as is practicable," the declaration promises, "there shall be uniformity of treatment of the German population throughout Germany." While no central German government is to be established "for the time being," the declaration goes on to state that "certain essential central German administrative departments, headed by state secretaries, shall be established, particularly in the fields of finance, transport, communications, foreign trade and industry" and that such departments "will act under the direction of the Control Council." The statement of economic principles contains a flat declaration that "Germany shall be treated as an economic unit" and that "to this end common policies shall be established in regard to: (a) mining and industrial production and allocations; (b) agriculture, forestry and fishing; (c) wages, prices and rationing; (d) import and export programs for Germany as a whole; (e) currency and banking, central taxation and customs; (f) reparation and removal of industrial war potential; (g) transportation and communications."

The broad economic objectives stated do not differ markedly from those proclaimed by JCS 1067. The destruction of Germany's war potential, the elimination of excessive concentration of economic power in the form of cartels or other monopolistic arrangements, primary emphasis on the development of agricultural and peaceful domestic industries—all these familiar themes reappear in the Potsdam statement. Where JCS 1067 called for a basic living standard not higher than that existing in any one of the neighboring United Nations, the standard proclaimed at Potsdam was an average not to exceed the average of all European countries excluding the United Kingdom and the Soviet Union.

The Potsdam Declaration breaks new ground in its treatment of the reparation problem. The principle is laid down that "payment of reparations should leave enough resources to enable the German people to subsist without external assistance." In working out an export-import balance, it is further recognized that proceeds of exports from current production and stocks shall be available in the first place for payment of approved imports.

No attempt is made to fix a monetary value on property to be removed from Germany in the way of reparations. Instead, a determination is to be made of the amount and character of the industrial capital equipment deemed unnecessary for the German peacetime economy and therefore available for reparations. This determination is to be made by the Control Council, under policies fixed by the Allied Commission on Reparations (with French participation), and is to be subject to the final approval of the zone commander from which the equipment is to be removed. Reparations claims of the Soviet Union and Poland are to be met in the first instance from property located in the Soviet zone and from German assets in Bulgaria, Finland, Hungary, Rumania, and eastern Austria. Reparation claims of other countries are to be met from the western zone and appropriate external assets. The Soviet Union, however, is also to be entitled to 10 per cent of the capital equipment in the western zones deemed to be unnecessary for the German peace economy. In addition, it is authorized to draw an additional 15 per cent in capital equipment from the western zones, provided it furnishes such zones with food, coal, and other raw materials equal in value. This last provision does not constitute reparations in the strict sense; it is intended to serve as a sanction to induce an exchange of goods between eastern and western Germany.

The Potsdam Agreement also incorporated important boundary readjustments that were foreshadowed at Yalta. The conference approved in principle the transfer to the Soviet Union of the city of Königsberg and an area adjacent to it. Similar approval was granted to a proposal that the Polish western boundary be advanced to a line within fifty miles of Berlin. Thus, in effect, the map of eastern Germany was redrawn at Potsdam. No action, however, was taken by the Big Three on Germany's western boundary despite pressure from the French that the Saar be incorporated in France, the Rhineland be transformed into an autonomous area, and the Ruhr be placed under an international regime.

The illusory character of the "unity" achieved at Potsdam was soon revealed by events. French fears of a strong Germany and deep-seated differences between Soviet and Anglo-American representatives on the reparation question and the conditions of political and economic unification combined to block all efforts to create organs of German central administration.

Recent Developments

Political and economic policies, meanwhile, have taken divergent paths in the respective zones. In the Russian zone, industries have been nationalized on an extensive scale; a broad program of agrarian reform has been instituted; resources have been reserved for Russian exploitation; and every effort has been made through the new Social Unity party and the trade unions to expand Communist influence. In the French zone, all energies have been concentrated on incorporating in the French economy the resources and trade of the occupied area. In the British zone, coal mines have been nationalized, and some efforts have been made to build up the Social Democratic party, but occupational authorities have been slow to turn over authority to German agencies. In the American zone, a drastic policy of denazification has been combined with an accelerated program of building agencies of self-government, but economic policy has been lacking in positiveness and direction.

The failure to implement the Potsdam Agreement to treat Germany as an economic unit has confronted the American policy makers of military government with a dilemma. Neither the American nor the British zone is self-sustaining. Both normally depend heavily on food imports from areas in eastern Germany now in the Russian zone and in the area of Polish administration. These sources of food supply have been cut off. If access to these sources is not restored and starvation in the British and American zones is to be avoided, the only alternatives open to American and British policy makers are either to support the German population in their zones indefinitely on relief, or to seek to maintain industrial production and exports in their zones at a level that will pay for necessary food imports. The first alternative involves a heavy drain on British and American resources and is likely to be tolerated only as an emergency expedient. The second involves at least a partial abandonment of the program of de-industrialization embodied in JCS 1067 and the Potsdam Agreement.

The Allied Control Council Agreement of May 28, 1946, on the level of the postwar German economy, did not provide an escape from these alternations. That agreement was posited on the assumption that Germany would be treated as an economic whole. In order to attain such unification, American military government policy took a more aggressive line. The program of plant removals from the British and American zones was suspended, in the hope of exerting pressure on the Soviet Union to join in establishing the central organs of economic administration that the Potsdam Agreement authorized. Steps were also taken to break down interzonal barriers and synchronize policies between the British and American zones on the stated assumption that this action would induce the Soviet Union, and possibly France, to join in an integrated economic policy for the whole of Germany. If this four-power unification does not follow, the result will almost inevitably be a partition of Germany, in fact if not in name, with the eastern zone incorporated into the Soviet economic orbit and the western zones integrated into the economic system of western Europe, Britain, and the United States. Implied in this outcome is an almost certain modification, if not abandonment, of the deindustrialization program in the American and British zones, since such modification would be essential if western Germany is to be maintained on a self-sustaining basis. It may be that the far-reaching implications of such a partition of Germany will lead the Big Four to redouble their efforts to find common ground. But at this writing the prospects of success do not appear too bright.

American Military Government Policy in the Far East

While the policy of American military government in Germany has become enmeshed in the complexities and frustrations of quadripartite administration, its development in the Far East has followed a less tortuous path. Korea, however, constitutes an exception. There the division into American and Soviet zones has reproduced in miniature the same difficulties of interzonal cooperation that have plagued American military government in Germany. The agreement reached at the foreign ministers' meeting in Moscow (December 27, 1945) that a provisional Korean democratic government be established and that measures be taken through a joint Soviet-American commission to coordinate policy between the zones and to work out an agreement for a four-power trusteeship of Korea has thus far not been translated into actuality.[29] Basically different conceptions of democracy and social policy have collided head on, and up to this point no viable formula of reconciliation has emerged. As a result, Korea, like Germany, threatens to become a cockpit in which both the Soviet Union and the United States seek to defend their positions and expand their influence.

Japan's case is unique in the experience of American military government. There the United States is the sole power in actual military occupation. No problems of zonal partition exist. The policy directives originally prepared for the Japanese occupation were an exclusively American undertaking. Although there is multipartite representation both in the Far Eastern Commission and the Allied Council for Japan,[30] which were established subsequent to the issuance of the original directive, neither of these agencies is in a position to offer effective challenge to the policies that the United States desires to follow. The function of the Allied Council is purely advisory. The Far Eastern Commission's mandate extends to the formulation of policy to guide the occupation, but the fact that the United States, as well as the United Kingdom, the Soviet Union, and China, possesses a veto power over its decisions, means that no directive is likely to come from the Far Eastern Commission to which the United States strenuously objects.

The official statement of the policy of American military government for Japan resembles JCS 1067 and the Potsdam Declaration in its broad essentials.[31] Its stress is on disarmament and demilitariza-

[29]For text see *The Department of State Bulletin* (December 30, 1945), p. 1030. For a more detailed treatment see Chapter XVI.

[30]For agreement establishing these agencies see *The Department of State Bulletin* (December 30, 1945), pp. 1028–1030.

[31]For text see *The Axis in Defeat*, pp. 107–114.

tion. The policy of denazification in the German instructions has its counterpart in the injunction that "active exponents of militarism and militant nationalism will be removed and excluded from public office and from positions of substantial private responsibility," and that "ultranationalistic or militaristic social, political, professional and commercial societies and institutions will be dissolved and prohibited." The policy of economic decentralization involving the dissolution of large industrial and banking combinations also echoes the German policies. There are similarities also in the positive political policies adumbrated for the future. The encouragement to form democratic political parties; the stress on the fundamental freedoms of religion, assembly, speech, and the press; the stimulus to be given to "organizations in labor, industry, and agriculture, organized on a democratic basis"—all these reflect a common fount of policy making.

The most striking contrasts between the German and the Japanese instructions involve attitudes toward the central government and the head of the state. The German instructions are built on the assumption of a gradual reconstruction of political life from the ground up, with only such centralization tolerated as is necessary to provide essential economic integration between zones. The Japanese instructions leave the machinery of the Japanese central government largely intact. The Supreme Commander, General Douglas MacArthur, is authorized to exercise authority through central governmental instrumentalities, including the Emperor, to the extent that this satisfactorily furthers other American objectives. "The policy," says the directive, "is to use the existing form of government in Japan, not to support it." A caution, however, is added. "Changes in the form of government initiated by the Japanese people or government in the direction of modifying its feudal and authoritarian tendencies are to be permitted and favored."

The concept of military government that has evolved in Japan thus differs radically from its German counterpart. The German plan contemplated a relatively elaborate military government with personnel stationed at every level of local government down to the lowest important unit, and armed with power to issue commands to such units. The Japanese plan involves a relatively large central staff issuing orders to the existing Japanese national government, which in turn is to be held responsible for the local execution of such orders. Such limited military government personnel as operates in the field is primarily charged with responsibility for checking the execution of national directives. It does not assume powers of direct governance.

The first period of the Japanese occupation has passed with unexpected smoothness. Where the Germans in the American zone hoped for the best, only to be disappointed, the Japanese feared the worst, and their worst fears have not been realized. But despite the many surface signs of democratic resurgence in Japan, it is still far too early to be certain that the positive objectives of the occupation have been or can be attained.

The paradox which American military government confronted at the termination of hostilities both in Germany and Japan, was that it sought to build the peace with policy weapons forged in the heat of war. Clarity there was on what was to be destroyed or eliminated. But much more difficult was the realization that political reconstruction carries with it other imperatives—encouragement to groups that have repudiated Nazism and militarism, and the creation of conditions that make it possible for such groups to provide constructive leadership in new directions. Unless such realization comes and is acted upon, military government policy in the post-hostilities phase faces frustration. There are many signs that the paradox is beginning to be recognized and resolved.

Chapter III

Military Government Organizational
Relationships [1]

GEORGE C. S. BENSON and MARK DEWOLFE HOWE

THE fusion of organizational patterns as divergent as those of the army and of civilian government is apt to lead to conflicts. How these conflicts were resolved will be discussed in this chapter, which also reviews briefly some of the problems of civilian control, program planning, internal organization, staff concepts, military government personnel, its relationship to tactical units, and indirect administration which resulted from the organization of military government within the entire military organization.

Civilian Control

Although cooperation between military government and other sections of the American army was satisfactory, most of the more idealistically inclined people in military government tended to be dissatisfied with what was accomplished and to blame "the Army" for much of the failure of military government. The sincerity and intelligence of those who raised the issue are such that they merit careful consideration.

It would have been organizationally possible to reduce the army's influence on military government. In the later phases of occupation it

[1] The chapter which follows is the result of the joint efforts of the two authors listed in the table of contents and of Lt. Col. Robert H. Slover, formerly with G-5, SHAEF, and Office of Military Government USFET, who edited the two separate contributions under the general supervision of the editor of the volume.

might well have been desirable, but it would have been damaging to military government and dangerous to the army to have made a separation at an early stage. Military government had much to contribute to military facilities. The pattern of fairly speedy turnover from tactical units to territorial military government units established in Italy produced considerable advantage for both sides.

The real difficulty with military government operations in the countries observed by the writers (Italy, Austria, and Germany) was not so much lack of civilian control, as it was inadequate presentation of the civilian government viewpoint on the higher levels of the military hierarchy. There were civilians (or civilians in uniform) located in G-5 staffs of theater headquarters, the War Department Civil Affairs Division, and elsewhere. But few of them had had major governmental experience, and their chief was almost always a regular army or old-time reserve officer. G-5 was often worsted in intra-army disputes, and was frequently unable to evolve effective civilian policy. Some of the results of the inadequacy of G-5 staff supervision are given in Chapter VI on military government in Italy. Policy directives, often inadequate, were sometimes contradictory; moreover, staff supervision was almost completely absent.

This difficulty arose in part from the inevitable shortage of experienced administrative personnel in wartime, but more largely from the failure of top policy makers in Washington to appreciate the importance of putting informed, aggressive men of broad governmental experience in positions where they could have full staff supervision of, and staff responsibility for, military government. Had this been done, it is believed that line control of theater and army commanders would have proved to be largely compatible with civilian governmental needs and viewpoints.

Planning for the Job

The practice of intensively planning an administrative program before putting it into operation is not new to American governmental administrators. Before they start to enforce a new law or a new regulation, many federal agencies hold a series of conferences, but few of them carry this examining process to the length to which it is carried in the army. In the army almost everything is viewed as an "operation." It is inevitable that operations, which involve complicated movements of men and material against partly determinable opposition, should be most carefully worked out. Military government was, quite naturally, viewed as another operation, and as such it was planned out to surprising detail. A large staff of officers, for example, planned for six months for the Fifth Army's military occupation of Rome— an occupation which lasted about two weeks, though many of the officers concerned stayed in Rome much longer. Some officers in the American element of the Allied Control Commission for Austria "planned" for a year and a quarter before they came to Austria. In Italy, needed officers were frequently called away from regions and provinces to plan for areas farther north three or four months before they could possibly be used in those areas.

Planning for the assault on Europe was also extensive. G-5 of SHAEF had a large planning staff, besides supervising the Country Units, set up in London to work out detailed plans for each of the countries to be entered.[2] These were combined British and American staffs. Further down the military hierarchy, First U.S. Army Group had its planning staff and before D day the First Army's G-5 staff was organized, and later Third Army's G-5 staff. Handbooks for each country, proclamations and directives, and civil affairs annexes to the over-all army plan of invasion kept the planners busy. For each combat operation on the Continent the G-5 staffs were called on to furnish a civil affairs section for the plan.

Some of this planning, of course, proved unsatisfactory. For military operations the army is able to work out a detailed type of planning in which different individuals work out different parts of such an operation for someone higher up the line to put together. Government, on the other hand, requires first a statement of general principles from someone higher in authority; and, second, an opportunity for the planner to submerge himself in all the social, political, eco-

[2]For a discussion of the early planning for Germany see Chapter X, "Conflicts over Planning at Staff Headquarters."

nomic, and even linguistic factors of the country to be occupied, which might affect his particular area of activity and to which he must adjust his program as it develops. The army expected an unattainable degree of precision in military government planning and wanted it written out in specific reports. This sometimes led to absurd results, as in the instance in which the staff of officers planning for Vienna was forbidden to study German in order that it might concentrate on finishing a paper plan for the initial occupation of Vienna —and at a time that Russian troops were already commencing that occupation and there was no chance of the plan's being used. It often resulted in officers' neglecting background data they badly needed for the sake of a plan which would probably have to be altered greatly.

Internal Administrative Organization

Since no one has been able to devise a truly satisfactory grouping of the many activities of a modern government, it was natural that military government should undergo many trials and tribulations in arranging its specialist activities. In the early phases several efforts were made to fit military government into the traditional army staff organization. The example best known to the writers, that of the 42nd Division in Austria, worked out badly. There is no particular correlation between the activities necessary to govern a group of fighting men and those necessary to run a country. Over half the activities of military government would fall under G-4 if anywhere. G-4's planning of supply activities, however, leaves little opportunity for G-4 personnel to become aware of the many regulatory problems which military government and economic and supply agencies must handle. Efforts to supervise the legal activities of military government by G-2 were equally maladroit. Similarly, the military special staff activities are, with few exceptions, widely different in thought and outlook from the most nearly similar military government activities.

There are, however, some areas of control in which it may be suitable to allocate responsibility to the orthodox staff sections. It is doubtful, for instance, whether a need has been proved for public health and sanitation experts among the military government personnel. The surgeon and the engineers may be expected to deal with civilian health and sanitation problems as incidental to the protection of troops. The provost marshal may, similarly, be charged with responsibility for the organization of civil police services, without thereby interfering with the execution of his usual duties. Advance planning should be able to determine with reasonable accuracy whether special military government officers are required in particular fields in prospective areas of operations. No suggestion is therefore intended that every branch of civil government must be the sole responsibility of military government personnel wherever military government is established. The danger, however, is not that too many responsibilities will be assigned to military government staffs, but that they will be given too little scope.

One of the questions which has been much debated is whether the administration of justice in proceedings against civilians in military tribunals should be the responsibility of the Judge Advocate Staff Section or of legal officers with the military government staff. Here again it seems that no positive and invariable rule should be established. There is justification for the argument that serious offenses against military personnel in forward and rear areas alike can best and most effectively be prosecuted before conventional military tribunals by the judge advocate. Such treatment of the cases will not only serve to remind the population that the occupation is military in character, but it assures an appropriate formality in the proceedings. On the other hand, there is a great deal to be said for allowing the run of the mill prosecutions to be handled by special military government personnel. The procedures of courts established for the trial of curfew, black market, and petty theft cases should be flexible, summary, and informal. Furthermore, military government courts and their procedures, instead of conforming to American standards, can be modeled upon the court structure and procedures familiar to the population of the occupied area. It is therefore felt that the commander should provide for the establishment of military government courts, outside the army's judicial system and manned by personnel trained especially for the task.

Staff Concepts

Of all administrative thought patterns, the one most thoroughly ingrained in military minds is that of staff, both special and general. Since the commanding officers of military government units were usually Regular Army officers, it was inevitable that much thinking in military government organization should follow these patterns. The military concept of special staff was more satisfactory for military government purposes than a program that would have scattered these activities throughout the general staff organization.

Specialist staff exists everywhere. The only distinguishing feature of army special staff organization is that there is a fairly well worked out area in which a special staff officer acts on orders from the special staff officer in the next higher administrative echelon and another area in which the special staff officer takes problems to his over-all line commander. This management provides the over-all line commander with a clearly defined opportunity to protest against a staff order which he or his specialist advisers consider unworkable. Civilian specialists in uniform quickly develop the idea, so that military government suffered little from the uncertainty as to authority which characterizes many Washington–regional or state capital–field office relationships. All was not necessarily happy between military government national and local headquarters, however, since the lack of field experience for most of the national headquarters staff in both Austria and Italy resulted in questionable decisions. But the difficulties did not arise because of lack of proper understanding of interoffice relationships. As already noted in the example of the 42nd Division, the standard general staff organization pattern bore no relation to military government problems. In addition, the presence of the division general staff placed another administrative level between military government specialists in the province and the central Allied Commission. Every such step increased the problem of communications and decreased the possibility of the commission's issuing enforceable regulations. Finally, the injection of general staff control made more difficult the cooperation of military government divisions which happened to fall under different general staff divisions but had much in common with one another. The food officer, for example, in his concern over black marketing has far more to do with the public safety officer than he does with the public works officer. Yet the latter came under G-4 with the food officer, while the former did not and was moved into another building.

The reader may reasonably ask why the general staff idea works out successfully in strictly military organizations but not in military government. The answer lies in some basic differences of organization and personnel:

1) While it is true that an army, like a government, has many different activities to coordinate, their number is normally not so great as in government and the over-all objective is clearer. Hence coordination through a general staff agency is more possible in army than in governmental work.

2) The army has worked out training programs specifically designed to give officers the broad background in all sort of military activity essential for good general staff work. Almost no governmental experts are as broadly trained in the whole of government. Certainly no military general staff man is so trained.

3) Because of unforeseen effects or resistance, almost any administrative or economic program is liable to modification while it is under way. To hold the road open for adaptation it is necessary that the channels of communication between national and field offices be as short as possible. Insertion of a general staff unit lengthens those channels—an effect less damaging in military programs, which must be followed through, than in government.

In spite of the preceding discussion as to the difficulties of using existing general staff organization, military government may have an appropriate place as a G-5 on several levels of the military structure. The grouping of all military government specialist services in one place in the headquarters staff of an army or similiar level proved to be a very reasonable method of organization. When limited to a smaller number of officers, it constituted an acceptable part of a corps or division headquarters. One may ask if such a grouping should be part of the general staff or special staff unit. It seems to the writers that this detail of location makes little difference. It will have to be operated as a largely independent unit in any case, and will undoubtedly have a direct channel to the commanding general, no matter where it is located.

The concept of an entirely separate staff section to be concerned with civil affairs and military government activities won out in the planning for Northwest Europe. Accordingly, each command through the divisional level was ordered during the planning stage to set up a new general staff division, called G-5. All of the activities dealing with civilian contacts and controls were then centered in this division, which was on an equal footing with the G-1, -2, -3, and -4 divisions. This arrangement made for necessary close coordination in staff work with all the G sections as well as with the special staff sections. Such an organization prevailed throughout the combat phases in France, Belgium, Holland, and Germany, and during the early period of the occupation in Germany.

The internal organization of the staffs and of the civil affairs–military government operating detachments was made to correspond as nearly as possible to the organization of the government of the country to be occupied. Such a scheme of organization tended to follow the most important criterion of governmental organization—purpose of the job to be accomplished—and at the same time gave a type of clientele organization which greatly facilitated the indirect control discussed in a later section. At times this pattern encountered real difficulties where it ran against the grain of military organization. Most European countries have a department of the interior which, among other activities, includes control of over-all local government machinery. If military government had followed this pattern closely, it would have had a department of the interior section in national headquarters which controlled the over-all provincial commanders in military government. This departure from military organization principles in which each over-all commander reports directly to the over-all commander at the next higher level was not possible during combat. For Italy and Austria the result was that the interior divisions in both control commissions had little real connection with regional or provincial military government teams. Public safety, which is a part of the Ministry of Interior in both Austria and Italy, had to be handled by a separate division in both national and local military government headquarters for such important reasons as its relation to military security and to the intelligence branches of the military organization.

The internal organization of military government at times followed the tradition of both American civil government and military staff organization. It proliferated and multiplied organizational subdivisions, as in Italy, where an effort was made to create separate industry and commerce subdivisions. Officers in the field could not find the dividing line between these agencies. Another example occurred in Austria, where the American element of the Allied Control Commission produced a "military" division with no clearly discernible function. If any lesson is to be drawn from such organization it is simply that military government needs effective organization analysis as much as any other civil or military activity.

Military Government Personnel

Organization along lines similar to the organization of the government of the occupied country called for the concentrated attention of specialist personnel. The need for such personnel had been recognized in the early training programs. If civilian supplies are not brought forward with dispatch, if indigenous agricultural and other public services are not promptly reinstituted, military operations are jeopardized. It is evident that the efficient and prompt initiation of these services must be based upon extensive preliminary training in the economic and administrative problems of the area to be occupied. Essential resources may be present in one country and entirely lacking in another; methods of administration suitable in a democracy may not be adaptable to the area controlled by military government. For the solution of all these problems, which arise as soon as a community is subjected to the authority of the military government, special knowledge and special training are essential. The commander's task will be greatly simplified if the organization of his staff is so arranged that a particular group of officers and men is on hand in the forward area prepared to take the necessary action on his behalf.

A large number of military government officers in both the American and British armies were commissioned directly for military government work. In a considerable proportion of cases they were commissioned at a fairly high rank, including majorities and lieutenant colonelcies. They were not always carefully selected. Accordingly, one might expect that these men would have had considerable difficulty in cooperating with a group of combat officers who had won their gold and silver leaves by different processes.

It was a surprise to observe that only a minimum amount of friction existed. Even the most unmilitary of the military government officers seemed to be able to secure cooperation from army units which were concerned with his work. Cooperation with other parts of the army likewise remained a minor problem. The explanation for this striking harmony is to be found in several factors. A substantial number of military government officers were reserve officers or OCS graduates, and tended to smooth out misunderstandings between the ex-civilians and officers of tactical units. Not only had most of the officers in tactical units recently been civilians too; the uniform and insignia common to both groups bridged gaps very rapidly.

Relationship of Military Government to Tactical Units

The basic problem of organizing military government with relation to tactical troops is one of timing. It should change as the interest in a given area changes from that of the commander of troops, who for reasons of military security must have complete authority over all operations in this area, to that of restoring the civilian economy and government. The former purpose requires an organization of military government corresponding to tactical troop formations. The latter requires an organization corresponding to the governmental areas of the country being occupied.

This problem of the interrelationship between the tactical organization of forces in the field and the territorial organization of government has always been a tough one.[3] It is obvious that during active

[3] This problem receives further treatment in Chapters VI, VIII, and XI below. See especially pp. 118 and 245.

operations no commander is going to allocate area responsibility to his subordinate commanders in accordance with the internal political boundaries of the area of operations. He will not instruct corps commander A that his operations are to be confined within the borders of Province X, and corps commander B that he is not to pursue the enemy beyond the boundaries of Province Y—at least he will not give this instruction merely in order that the control of the provincial governments of X and Y may be simplified. No such instruction having been issued, let it be assumed that A occupies the whole of Province X and a portion of Province Y, including the capital of Province Y, where the principal offices of the civil government of the province are established. The balance of Province Y is occupied by B. Immediately problems are presented. B, quite properly, believes that he is charged with the maintenance of law and order in the area occupied by forces under his command. He finds, however, that the officials who normally direct the government in Province Y work in the capital of the province, which is occupied by the forces commanded by A. There are several possible solutions: liaison between the forces; purely local control before any type of centralized government is set up; or the assumption of direct responsibility for all phases of military government by a commander on a higher level. The most satisfactory solution was found by shifting areas from division to corps to army to base section jurisdiction as the tide of fighting moved forward. In military parlance this process is known as "phases." It thereby became possible to work out a clear-cut delineation of the authority of various levels of administration in each phase of military operations. If an Italian town was in a division area, combat engineering functions were handled by troops attached to the division. When, however, the division lost control of that area, road maintenance activities were undertaken by corps or army engineers. Each unit knew what activities it should undertake in each area.

Much of this military theory of "phases of operation" had, of course, to be used in military government. At the same time it became clear that the most important work of restoring civilian government had to be done during the time of army occupation (especially in Italy) and that continuity of officers in charge of an area was highly desirable. Furthermore, it was also desirable to bring higher levels of civilian government into operation as soon as possible, even though their areas frequently did not coincide with those of higher military units.

The solution finally developed for this problem in Italy was both simple and effective. Teams of military government officers were formed for each territorial unit of civilian government and were moved into their areas as soon as possible, but under the sponsorship of the appropriate military government staff section of tactical units. Thus the civil affairs officer of a commune usually moved into that commune under the sponsorship of the division military government officer. Provincial teams moved into their provincial headquarters under the sponsorship of army military government sections. To keep the number of echelons at a minimum the British Eighth Army kept corps military government units in strictly liaison capacity. The American Fifth Army practice on corps military government organization varied.

As soon as an occupied area ceased to be under the control of the army commander, the provincial team ceased to report to the army unit and began to report to the Allied Control Commission through a regional supervisory headquarters. In a few cases the regional headquarters was even brought into operation under army orders. While its area did not coincide with Army Area, its specialist staff did serve as a very useful supplement to the specialist staff of army AMG, and the opportunity for more continuous experience within their region was of great value to the regional staff. Without this opportunity there was real danger that the regional specialist staff would have to begin operations knowing far less about its territory than did the provincial teams already there.

The European Theater followed a similar pattern but made the mistake of putting fairly large military government specialist staffs on each of three higher military echelons, Army Group, Army, and Corps, in addition to the detachments. Government is a very complicated business to funnel through so many echelons of command. Communications from the bottom level reached the top level very slowly, and a series of highly unrealistic orders followed.

The other difficulty encountered by the European Theater was its failure to act promptly in depriving tactical units of control over military government and replacing them with over-all territorial units. VE day should have been a signal to eliminate tactical military government units below the level of Army or Army Group and to give full supervisory authority to the highest available territorial unit. As soon as the *Wehrmacht* surrendered, the purpose of military security was replaced by the purpose of governing and controlling the life of Germany. Instead of recognizing this fact, the ETO continued tactical control for several months. The most serious blunders in this respect were committed in Austria, where a division was kept in charge of military government until January, 1946.

The disadvantages of the continued control of military government by tactical units in the ETO seemed to be the following:

1) The great handicap imposed on the development of provincial or even township governmental institutions. The 3d Division in Salzburg kept a township military government unit away from the capital of its township. Provinces were severed into three or four different units by corps G-5's.

2) A natural corollary of this breakdown of governmental institutions was the paralyzing effect on trade. Corps headquarters, following the customary army tactics of thinking only of its own charges and having no knowledge of normal civilian movements, imposed limitations on export of foodstuffs, and on any civilian travel. Even milk was kept away from dairies for weeks after VE day by blind tactical unit orders.

3) The fact that tactical unit headquarters had no normal place for contact with responsible civilian authorities kept it in a condition of ignorance regarding the effect and implications of any orders which it might issue.

The reader may wonder if close control of military government activities by tactical units does not ensure a closer cooperation between tactical units and civilian authority, as represented by military government. In fact, tactical unit control, by lower echelons, speedily broke up the whole purpose of military government. There was cooperation with military government, but it was cooperation in seizing local supplies or accomplishing other ends of the troops. G-5 units, however, seemed to keep their fundamental purpose clear through Army level. From Corps on down there was a recurrent tendency for tactical troop commanders to overlook the special tasks of military government officers.

Indirect Administration

Handbooks of military government administration usually stress the fact that military government should, wherever possible, operate through the native government of the occupied area.[4] Experience in both Austria and Italy indicated that this instruction was correct. Operations progressed more rapidly and smoothly, fewer major mistakes were made, and more genuine cooperation was secured when the military government officer did not try to do things himself or through the American organization. To take one outstanding example, the Allies did not succeed in stopping the wholesale looting of imported foodstuffs in Italy until they commenced the practice of turning the foodstuffs directly over to Italian agencies and making them financially responsible.

In the liberated countries of France, Belgium, the Netherlands, and Luxembourg, the policy was at all times to reconstitute the local government as rapidly as possible. Liaison officers attached to Allied forces were used to assist in making necessary appointments, clearing out collaborators, and, in general, organizing the new governments. Agreements had been drawn with several of the governments in exile in London, clearly delineating army and local governmental responsibilities.

The problem of Germany was, of course, different. Here the purpose was to wipe out completely the Nazi pattern and re-establish democratic methods and institutions. Although some functions were abolished, and Nazi-minded officials were removed, the same general pattern of local governmental structure was retained. At the top, the central governmental organization was completely destroyed and not

[4]For a discussion of this principle as shown in the original edition of FM 27–5 and the revised edition see Chapter II, "The Development of American Military Government Policy during World War II."

reconstituted in any form. The initial complete control of all government offices and activities in Germany gradually developed during the occupation phase into a policy of supervision and observation.[5]

Unfortunately this method of indirect control did not coincide with the administrative habits of many officers in military government. The Regular Army officers were least fitted for this type of operation since much of their professional life had been spent as company or regimental officers directly supervising administrative minutiae. Almost as bad were a number of military government officers who had been recruited from private business or smaller governmental jurisdictions where administrative operations were directly supervised. It took a great deal of experience with the disadvantages of direct control before these officers learned that the easiest and best way was to delegate matters to the responsible native officials.

A few examples will illustrate the results of this initial clash of administrative habits. In army organization it is quite properly considered essential that every supply officer should know the current position of his stocks. In a governmental jurisdiction, on the other hand, daily stock reports would require a proportion of time on the part of the operating officials which is unjustified by the value of the report received. The customary practice in military government was to require weekly or fortnightly reports from provincial authorities and to check those reports carefully. Periodically military government officers were subjected to criticism by their superiors, who felt that the system must be wrong if they could not get a report of food stocks today but must wait till Wednesday. It was a difficult task to explain that civilian government organizations, unlike military supply departments, are not generously staffed; that periodic reports, if properly used, are just as adequate a control as daily reports; and that preparation of a sudden, unexpected report "for the Americans" would throw a whole provincial department into confusion for two or three days.

This same clash of administrative practices continues as long as the military share in control. Three months after the United States had recognized an Austrian national government and eight months after

[5]For a more complete discussion of this subject see Chapter XII, "Denazification."

the Americans had set up a provincial government in Salzburg, American military courts were still trying Austrians for illegal parking, American police were directing traffic, American officers were directing snow removal, street cleaning, and a variety of miscellaneous tasks. The commanding generals, if queried, would undoubtedly have said that they were permitting the Austrians to operate everything in accordance with the doctrine of indirect control. But their passion for direct control, strengthened by years of army experience, kept leading them back to direct operation.

The best examples of indirect control came from two groups of men who were accustomed to that method of operation. One group was composed of the American agricultural officers, who did excellent jobs in both Austria and Italy in reviving and stimulating civilian agriculture departments. It took little perception to see that they were merely using techniques they had learned in American agricultural administration, where so much control is indirect. The other exception was a group of British officers who had learned something of the technique of indirect control by experience in British colonial practices. It was a striking fact that the areas they controlled "came back" faster economically than those the Americans controlled.

Although the mental habit of indirect control was most important to such a system, there were other requirements. As indicated in an earlier section, indirect control can be considerably handicapped by an internal organization in military government which does not correspond to that of the civilian government. It is, of course, also essential in the occupation phase that tactical units at lower levels be kept out of military government operations. Finally, it is necessary that a substantial degree of civilian cooperation be secured—a condition which was never hard to obtain.

Important in the policy of indirect control is the problem of the removal of undesirable individual officials.[6] For example, it may, with sound reasons, be decided in advance that a particular police agency, national or local, is to be continued in operation. It is virtually certain, however, that within that branch of the police system there

[6] For detailed data compare Chapter VI, pages 122–136, Chapter VIII, pages 177–180, and Chapter XII.

will be a large number of officers and men whose political convictions and past records are such that their removal from office is essential. Their retention would not only lead the population of the occupied territory to doubt that a complete transfer of authority to the military government had occurred, but it would lead to doubt among the allies of the occupant as to whether the common political objectives of the war were taken seriously by the military governor. It is in problems of this sort that the local commander is first called upon to make those wise political and military decisions upon which the success of his government will ultimately depend. The workings of Allied policy in the opening phases of the operations in Sicily in 1943 showed how important this matter may be. It was then the policy of the American and British occupying forces to permit the retention in office of Fascist officials when their retention seemed expedient from the military standpoint. Inevitably, this broad license led to the temporary continuance in office of many corrupt officials. Disregarding entirely the resulting criticism in the United States and Great Britain, which had unfortunate repercussions on all future efforts of the military government of occupied European countries, it can easily be demonstrated that the Italian anti-Fascists lost faith in the purposes of England and the United States. The loss of that faith not only made the problems of government more difficult than they would otherwise have been, but indirectly affected military operations.

Experience has shown that mere administrative convenience and expediency should never justify even the temporary retention of an official whose loyalty to the principles of a government with which the United States is at war is so undivided that he has gone beyond the duties of patriotism to the excesses of fanaticism. In only one highly exceptional circumstance should an official of this character be continued in office: when the necessities of tactical operations actually require his retention. In making a decision on this matter the commander should never permit considerations of governmental efficiency to affect his decision. It is naturally tempting for the commander who wishes the government to operate smoothly to consider that an experienced official, no matter what his past record may be, will be of advantage to him. He easily assumes that since all authority is in his own hands, no harm can result from acts of the disqualified official. In that, the commander is probably right, but he should never forget that his government will succeed only if it seems to the local population and to the Allies that the principles for which the war is being fought have not been compromised. If the people of the occupied territory doubt the good faith of the occupying forces with respect to their political objectives, a sullen suspicion, at the least— and acts of sabotage, at the worst—may be expected.

The relevance of these considerations to problems of organization may not be evident, but experience indicates that mistakes are frequent if the organization of military government is planned without regard for the political purposes being pursued. If action with respect to the removal of officials and the reorganization of government must be taken as soon as an area is occupied, it is essential that officers be available in the forward areas to take the necessary action, and to take it not merely casually and as incidental to the performance of their other military duties, but as their first and principal responsibility.

Conclusion

Some of the persistent problems of organization for civil affairs and military government operations have been treated in broad outline. It is, of course, impossible to find solutions to these problems in textbooks and tables of organization. The questions of military government are among the most subtle and complicated which a commander must solve, for they concern the political life of the people governed and the political objectives of the occupying power. It will be only through close study of past experiences, successful and unsuccessful, orthodox and innovating, that guidance for the future will be obtained. One lesson has been learned that never should be forgotten: military government will be successful and effective only if its subtleties are appreciated and only if personnel trained for its efficient and imaginative administration are made available to the commander. The military governor will be successful in the fulfillment of his mission only if he possesses political understanding of its purposes and an organization trained for their achievement.

Chapter IV

Political Intelligence and Its Relation to Military Government[1]

ROBERT G. NEUMANN

In every known form of civil or military government, the collection, analysis, and dissemination of information are among the most vital staff functions, without which the executive would be unable to carry out his task. Unless he knows the effects of his measures, unless he is aware of the social, economic, and political forces with which he has to deal, unless he retains an intimate knowledge of the working of his administrative machinery, effective government soon comes to a speedy and ignominious end. This is even more true of the military governor than of the ordinary civil administrator. The loyalty of subordinate officials and employees, which the civil executive can generally take for granted, is by no means a foregone conclusion for the military governor. The effect of military government laws and decrees is not immediately apparent as would be the case in a country with a free press and an articulate public opinion. The forces of political opposition in an occupied country do not ordinarily appear on the surface before they have taken on menacing proportions, and

[1]Military intelligence deals, and dealt during the war, primarily with the military intention and capabilities of the enemy or prospective enemy. Political intelligence, therefore, is not really a part of it. And military government is not ordinarily concerned with the strength and deployment of the enemy. For administrative purposes, the Office of Strategic Services and the Counter Intelligence Corps were, in their field operations, part of G-2. But in actual fact they constituted separate entities. Some G-2 officers had a wide and farsighted view of their functions and were deeply interested in political as well as military intelligence, often considering it one of their important tasks.

even indispensable collaborators among the loyal and constructively democratic forces may be inadvertently alienated by a military governor ignorant of interparty agreements and intraparty relations and jealousies.

To a reader unacquainted with the actual operation of military government this may seem like a statement of obvious facts, especially since much has been said and written about the importance of intelligence for military operations. Yet during the war military government teams were and are being sent into enemy or near-enemy territory without the benefit of any organization which would undertake to keep them informed on all the currents and undercurrents with which any government has to deal. It is true that various organizations and individuals have at one time or another attempted to bridge the gulf between the military government officer and his subject matter. The Office of Strategic Services, the Psychological Warfare Division, later the Information Control Division, and the Counter Intelligence Corps did much good work. Occasionally, some extraordinarily alert G-2 and G-5 officers and enlisted men devoted some of their time to the problem, and at times a better-than-average military government officer made a concentrated effort to break through the vacuum surrounding him.

But all these efforts lacked organization and consolidation. Instead of receiving one well-edited and integrated intelligence report, a military government officer may have received none, or five, or ten, some of them containing contradictory statements. No wonder that these reports were often pushed aside unread.

Military government officers are themselves required to write numerous reports. But most are of a purely technical nature, and those which touch political questions hardly penetrate the surface, as the average officer has little opportunity and aptitude to make a profound and well-informed analysis of the political situation.

Best coordinated of the various intelligence agencies is the Counter Intelligence Corps, but its personnel would have had to be increased to cover its assignment adequately. Moreover, counter intelligence duties, the ferreting out of clandestine enemies, are by no means the only problems facing military government.

Training for Political Intelligence

Would better and longer training of military government officers alleviate these difficulties? Undoubtedly to some extent, but a real remedy is not to be found there. In the United States, military government is still looked upon as an administrative rather than a political job. Consequently, prospective military government officers are usually selected for their administrative ability; and the assessment of a strange political situation in a foreign country may not be within reach of their talents and training. Moreover, language difficulties often preclude a free and easy exchange of views between military government officers and native politicians, and frequently make for an excessive influence of interpreters and their friends whose political antecedents are often questionable.

Furthermore, the official position and power of military government officers tend to turn into a formal affair of state any exchange of views with native officials or politicians, preventing the establishment of confidential contacts which might produce valuable inside information. And even if the military government officer were a paragon of inquisitive skill, he would remain unaware of trends and subterranean events in districts other than his own. Yet such knowledge would seem to be essential for a correct analysis of important political trends, as well as a warning of impending developments.

The ideal setup would have been an intelligence organization established prior to the invasion of the Continent of Europe. Working through G-2 and G-5 of Supreme Headquarters, and with field teams attached to the field armies, a comprehensive coverage could have been instituted from the first. Actually OSS and PWD teams did accompany the armies and prepared political reports. But these teams, though well trained, were far too small to provide anything like full coverage. Frequently as few as two or three men would cover an entire army area. Naturally, intelligence targets had to be picked almost at random and it was seldom possible to follow up on a previous target, which would have provided an important basis of comparison.

Ferreting Out Underground Activities

One of the principal tasks of an intelligence service is keeping a sharp lookout for traces of underground activities directed against the occupying powers as well as against those native elements which are sincerely collaborating. This part of the work is largely of a secret, often undercover, nature, and was originally done in Germany by the Counter Intelligence Corps and by branches of the Office of Strategic Services. These organizations came to Germany well prepared with dossiers of potential and real troublemakers, and they had a fairly good idea of the form which dangerous activities were likely to take. But in order to guarantee the absolute safety of German democratic administrators and leaders, and in order to stamp out every vestige of real and potential resistance, it would have been necessary to cover the country with a network of agents who would have had to follow up every lead, keep their eyes on every gathering and group, and have a sufficient number of undercover agents ready to participate in any native enterprise and thus determine its real character. Unfortunately, the available personnel did not have the man power to fulfil this task. Even when redeployment had not yet torn deep holes in the Counter Intelligence fabric, there was a general shortage of man power. However, it might have been possible to take care of this problem to some extent by a more skillful personnel policy.[2]

Under these circumstances, all hands were busy ferreting out important Nazis. Little attention could be paid to minor but potentially dangerous elements, and many, whose offices and ranks had placed them on the automatic-arrest list, found themselves released without any worse consequences than those disabilities which generally rest on Nazi party members. At the time that more and more German soldiers, and particularly officers, were returning, the cadres of the Counter Intelligence organization were being so steadily depleted through redeployment that there has now arisen a dangerous situa-

[2]Cf. page 179. On the whole, qualitative rather than quantitative factors are decisive in intelligence work. In short, denazification policy established by JCS 1067 and the directives issued under it forced upon the intelligence services a vast task for which they were not fully prepared. See Chapter XII.

tion in which subterranean movements cannot be watched effectively until they swell to considerable size. This cannot but encourage the already rebellious and discouraged returning soldier and ex-PW who find an emotional outlet in secret conclaves and "debating circles" full of ominous portents for the future, although not an immediate menace. These groups recruit their members from the same type of men who became stormtroopers and entered the various "Free Corps." Obviously it is easier to watch these groups and apply appropriate countermeasures to them in their incipient stages than when they have assumed menacing proportions.

The creation of a network of secret police agents, the infiltration of undercover agents, has at times been called a bad copy of the late Gestapo. The Western world, used to the security of its democratic tradition, looks with suspicion on any such enterprise. But military government is not democratic government. If normal democratic government were possible, a military regime would be superfluous. Although this fact unfortunately has not been explained adequately to the German people, it is nevertheless a plain truth. Transitional and educational as its character may be, military government is by force of necessity an undemocratic regime, and it must have the means to deal with those elements which might endanger its existence and effectiveness. The first step toward such measures is accurate information. In the absence of a reliable intelligence organization which can gather such information, underground movements, whispering propaganda, and a campaign of threats and terror against loyal German officials increase daily in scope. It is easy enough to arouse the disillusioned younger generation against "foreign oppressors" and "native traitors," especially when the danger of being caught is slight.

While the need for counter intelligence—the fight against the negative elements—is of utmost importance, the systematic collection and analysis of overt, positive intelligence, i.e., intelligence concerning potentially constructive elements, is even more important. Yet it is even more neglected. Experience has shown that an effective intelligence agency must operate on a high level and in some respects be independent of local or even regional military commanders.[3] It is

[3]For further comment see page 77.

not the business of intelligence agents to inspect and criticize the operations of military government, but it is nevertheless unavoidable that occasional reports on the political situation in a certain locality may reflect adversely upon the local commanding officer or members of his staff. If such an adverse report is justified by facts, it is all the more important that higher echelons should be cognizant of it in order that the situation may be repaired. After all, the purpose of military government is not to provide sinecures for its members but to achieve certain political and administrative results.

On the other hand, there has been a tendency among some members of reporting intelligence organizations to look upon all military government officers as incompetent and to assume the role of a visiting inspector general. Such hasty judgment frequently sprang from their lack of acquaintance with the actual problems facing military government officers. Perhaps more intelligence personnel should have been given the military government training program. An added period of practical experience in military government would also have been helpful.

There are many instances in which, because of inadequate information, the wrong type of German was picked for a responsible post. There were even a few cases in which prominent Nazis were elevated to high office, in one instance even to that of a provincial governor. Such cases are, of course, hard to excuse. The fact of the provincial governor's affiliation with the Nazis party must have been well known in the area in question, and only a great lack of efficient political intelligence could have allowed military government to remain so completely out of touch with the population. Although most of these mistakes were eventually corrected, they did not benefit the reputation of the occupation authorities or strengthen the position of other, bona fide appointees.

The important point here is that the needed information for forming a sound judgment was not secret or difficult to secure. It is this type of *available* political information which often turns out to be the most valuable for the man who is making decisions on policy. The difficulty is one of efficient correlation, selection, and analysis. The problems are essentially political in scope and require seasoned personnel, preferably civilian, and of mature judgment. In any case, it is the task of such officers, whether military or civilian, to keep a constant watch on political groups, their leaders, and membership, and it is rarely necessary to disguise their purpose. Certainly most Germans have been found to talk more than freely, and even the Communists usually do not present great difficulties if they are treated with a moderate amount of skill and urbanity. More often than not these political groups wish to bring their opinions and problems to the attention of the occupation authorities, and what is hidden by one group will almost certainly be revealed by another. Political leaders of all parties complained to interrogators time and again that they had little or no opportunity to acquaint the military government officers with their political problems. Often certain officers, in their efforts to remain objective, shunned all politicians. Sometimes, the intricacies of European political life seemed incomprehensible to men who had formerly been city engineers in Kansas or Missouri. Surprisingly often political leaders are reluctant to speak openly in the presence of military government interpreters whose discretion and political reliability they distrust, frequently with good reason. Nevertheless, politicians and politically conscious people in occupied areas welcome regular contacts with informed American officers. Naturally the person interrogated will usually try to make a case for his own ideology rather than give objective information. But this bias should not trouble a well-trained intelligence officer.

Apart from an intimate knowledge of the history, economy, and political structure of the occupied country, the intelligence officer must have a conversational knowledge of the language of the country. The presence of interpreters stifles unbending, and much can be learned over a glass of wine that would never be revealed at a conference table. Other equally important prerequisites are tact and a capacity for at least an appearance of sympathetic understanding. One would assume this gift to be indispensable for all military personnel, but their position of authority has afflicted too many officers and enlisted men with a master-race complex.[4]

[4]The abuses resulting from such an attitude are indicated in Chapter VIII, pages 187–188 and Chapter XII, pages 249–250.

Intelligence and Military Government

Two subjects have frequently been discussed by intelligence agents in Germany: their relationship with local military government; and their relationship with those of their colleagues who are engaged in the collection of secret information. With regard to the first question, there are those who insist on dealing only on the highest level, and others who would rather help the perplexed local commander. It is true that many valuable contributions to effective military government were lost by an unswerving insistence on high-level dealings and a complete disregard for the crying needs of the working level. But on the other hand, if an intelligence officer whose principal advantage is independence from departmental responsibilities allows himself to become enticed into direct participation in military government, his usefulness to his own work will soon come to an end. Such involvement is not always easy to resist, since the training of the intelligence officer, particularly his linguistic abilities, makes him a desirable target for an overworked commander who may try to "pull" his superior rank in order to get the newcomer to work for him. Besides, the intelligence officer may feel reluctant to refuse to make a contribution to an essential piece of work, particularly when he knows that he could probably do it better than some other, less well-prepared person. Nevertheless, it is necessary that the intelligence officer should concentrate on the specific intelligence function and participate in operations in an advisory capacity only.

The question concerning the nature of relations between overt and secret operators is not quite so easy to decide. It goes without saying that undercover agents must abstain from contacts which might give them away. But should the fruits of their labor be communicated to their openly working colleagues? Persons engaged in secret intelligence tend to regard all those outside their particular bailiwick as unfit to be trusted with any really secret material. There are, of course, occasions when the knowledge of certain secret facts may color and influence the approach of an overt intelligence officer and thus nullify the discovery of important material. Yet the contacts which this officer makes in the course of his work will often enable him to follow the trace of some political event originally discovered by a secret agent, and he may do so with greater accuracy and dependability than the undercover agent if the latter were left to unearth the entire story. The overt intelligence officer is, or should be, selected for his position because of his analytical ability and his understanding of political and economic affairs in the occupied country. Secret agents are primarily chosen for their great personal courage and their ability to dissimulate their true character. If analytical gifts are also present, so much the better, but they cannot be counted on in the great majority of agents. It is perhaps the greatest weakness of secret intelligence that an agent often overlooks important developments and concentrates on more spectacular trivia. It stands to reason, therefore, that the overt intelligence officer should cover all those fields which can possibly come within his reach—and this reach can be greatly enlarged by an intimate collaboration between the secret and the overt intelligence branches.

Of particular importance is the relationship between the field teams and the regional office which collects and integrates all intelligence from the entire country. The distance between field and regional offices should be as short as possible, with a frequent and regular air pouch available in either direction between them, since connections by field telephone are notoriously unreliable, frequently inaudible, and quite lacking in security. Because only coordinated intelligence is of material value, all distribution to the various commands must emanate from regional headquarters. Thus the military government officer for Munich should receive his intelligence report from Frankfort, Wiesbaden, or Berlin—wherever intelligence headquarters for Germany are located—although those reports which concern him will have primarily originated in Munich. This may seem like a roundabout, bureaucratic route, but to the political observer it must be obvious that one of the most important questions is whether a particular incident or movement represents a trend or merely constitutes an accidental, local occurrence. Trends cannot be studied locally.

Duplication in Reporting

A third question which has been much debated among intelligence personnel is whether individual pieces of information should be sent out as such, merely with a classification attesting to the probable reliability of the news and its source and perhaps an explanatory comment, or whether such information should be integrated with similar stories from other sources and presented in a manner which would give a fairly complete picture. Secret information is not always easy to integrate into a picture. It consists frequently of a few lines stating that in a certain cellar preparations are being made for the storing of arms, or that certain persons have held a secret meeting somewhere. Yet it is difficult for an intelligence officer to suppress such information and wait until a pattern is visible, for somewhere in the army some person may be working on a project or on a certain line of investigation to whom this small piece of information is of the utmost importance. As long as the present system—or rather, lack of system—prevails, in which various intelligence organizations cover the same ground, sometimes even competing with each other, it will be necessary to distribute these individual pieces of intelligence without any attempt to coordinate them. This fact alone would highlight the importance of a single, all-embracing intelligence organization which would know precisely what sort of information is needed, and by whom. The average officer, across whose desk streams a daily flow of seemingly unrelated items, finds them far too much to digest, and he may even fail to perceive those reports from which his work could gain real benefit. Thus all intelligence reports tend to become pieces of paper which clutter up the desk, and important information disappears under a mountain of unimportant papers. If individual tidbits of information must be sent out, a careful appraisal of the "client" should be made and he should receive only that which is germane to his work and his needs. The task is relatively easy in a single intelligence department, but almost impossible when rival organizations, by going into mass production, are trying to win first place in the race for recognition.

The problem for overt intelligence is somewhat simpler. This material, which has been gathered by a trained observer, will already be in an analytical form. It should not be too difficult to integrate such items into a series of reports which, taken together, should give a detailed, though readable report on the situation. The editing of these reports, which must be combined to show trends in different areas, is therefore an important function for which special training and ability are necessary. Suitable secret information should also be incorporated. These consolidated reports should be issued at regular intervals and, if they are to be weekly reports, on the same day each week in order to create a "reading habit" among their recipients. Frequently military government officers must be educated to the realization that they need better information; if they become used to receiving a certain report on a certain day each week, a "reading habit" will probably be created, particularly if the consolidated report appears on their desks in a colorful cover which distinguishes it from the usual drab army correspondence.

From time to time various intelligence organizations published so-called special studies which were usually less concerned with recent intelligence than with the historical, sociological, or economic background of certain events, institutions, or groups. Such reports, which often fill a real educational need, are not strictly intelligence, but the members of an intelligence organization are probably best suited to write them in the form of separate studies.

The Office of Strategic Services

During the war and for some time thereafter, one of our foremost intelligence agencies, the Office of Strategic Services, presented a somewhat anomalous picture. This organization developed out of an attempt to coordinate all information from whatever source derived, and therefore stayed clear of all definite ties to any of the services. In 1942 it came under the direction of the Joint Chiefs of Staff. Since OSS remained aloof from the individual branches of the service, it continued to maintain its own intelligence services. Thus the Military Intelligence Division of the Army and the Office of Naval Intelligence continued their activities without introducing much inter-service coordination. Agencies such as the Foreign Economic Administration also entered the picture. In due course, the Office of Strategic Services established branch offices abroad and engaged in field operations. But there soon developed a difference of opinion between the Washington office and the field staffs, particularly in the Research and Analysis Branch, which dealt primarily with questions of overt intelligence. The home office looked upon the field staffs as existing exclusively or at least mainly in order to feed it intelligence material and to carry out such projects as the home office might desire. It appeared to the Washington heads of the organization that their work, being of the highest level directly under the Joint Chiefs of Staff, was to be paramount. But the field staffs very soon became aware of the great need for special intelligence in the various theaters of operation and therefore sought closer ties with the staffs of the theater commanders. Since this difference of opinion was never quite decisively resolved, a large part of the personnel was retained in Washington, which left the European theater without the necessary staff for a thorough coverage of all intelligence activities.

Equally lacking in clarity was the relationship between the Office of Strategic Services, especially its Research and Analysis Branch, and the regular military commands. While all activities were technically under the authority of the theater commander, the Office of Strategic Services attempted to maintain its dual role as a branch office of its Washington headquarters and as a full-fledged theater agency. The result was to be foreseen: it failed to become fully integrated on either side of the Atlantic.

Even in civilian government, the appearance of independent agencies causes a good deal of confusion. In a territory governed by the military, the effect is worse. The army, with its strict table of organization and its time-honored concept of the functions thereunder, does not take kindly to ill-defined organisms which are neither fish nor fowl. Consequently the Office of Strategic Services frequently found itself out in the cold and actually looking for "customers." Customers it did find because of the excellence of its operative personnel, but it was piecework rather than a steady job, and its frequently sound intelligence reports, instead of being required reading for all concerned, had to be thrust upon indifferent and sometimes even unwilling recipients.

After the end of hostilities, the intelligence picture became more confused. The Office of Strategic Services had expected to become the principal intelligence agency of the American element in Allied Control Council for Germany. In fact, tentative agreements to that effect had been concluded. But as soon as the German armies had surrendered, Germany was deluged with intelligence teams and commissions of inquiry of every possible description as well as by army personnel—often high ranking—from Washington. In this general melee and struggle for information, organized intelligence work became impossible. Various groups worked at cross-purposes, information was not exchanged, Germans in important political or technical positions were interrogated innumerable times by various persons and most of the time were asked the same questions. Needless to say, even the best source of information will dry up under such treatment. Moreover, the busy military government officers who had to receive some intelligence team almost every day grew less responsive to them and their innumerable, and often conflicting, reports. Under those conditions the establishment of a single, integrated intelligence service was, of course, impossible. In addition, the trained field reporters dwindled away when their point score became high enough for redeployment, as has been mentioned before, and many civilians who had served as field reporters during the war (particularly with the Office of Strategic Services) resigned and went home.

Counter Intelligence Corps

It is probably true that the Counter Intelligence Corps and the Secret Intelligence Branch of the Office of Strategic Services did the best possible job with the personnel at their disposal. Nevertheless, criticism has been leveled against the Counter Intelligence Corps either for being too strict or for not catching and detaining all Nazis. Undoubtedly there is some substance in all the charges and countercharges which always flow so abundantly when the battle is done.

But counter intelligence work is largely made up of painstakingly detailed effort—and nobody who has seen the Counter Intelligence Corps in operation can escape the impression that it was almost always pitifully understaffed. Under those handicaps it probably did the best possible job.

The same statement cannot be made of overt political intelligence in the European theater. In that type of work, the great bulk of all pertinent facts is easily accessible to the trained observer. Moreover, in a country like Germany, where the masses of the population are still largely apathetic in political matters, most events of political significance originate in a fairly small circle of persons. As a result, a large staff is not required to canvass the occupied country in order to supply the military authorities with reliable and regular information on all political developments.

Conclusion

What lessons are to be learned from all this? It would seem that the most careful attention must be paid to the training of political intelligence officers. A thorough knowledge of the history, the political and social conditions, and the economy of the occupied country is essential. There is an unfortunate tendency in many branches of the armed services to get rid of substandard officers by transferring them to "Intelligence." Such misfits, of course, are only a minority among intelligence officers, but they do exist and, since they are incapable of operating on the working level, they frequently become administrators and thereby help to make the organization top-heavy, paralyzed by red tape, and unwieldy. An effective political intelligence organization need not be particularly large. Through a discriminating and strict personnel policy it can always be kept down to a relatively small but well-knit team.

A second lesson is that the intelligence organization must become a definite part of the table of organization of military government. Its functions must be well defined and, within their field, exclusive. If other agencies wish to conduct surveys of any kind they should perhaps be cleared through the intelligence agency. Only in that way is it possible to avoid much duplication and to protect sources of information from being wearied until they dry up. Too many agencies and groups were permitted to send separate teams to Germany and Austria to gather information readily available through intelligence channels.

Third, it is essential that the problem of military command and channels be carefully reconsidered. It would seem that at least some political intelligence officers on the several levels of military government should be responsible only to the highest level of military government command. These officers, though available for consultation, must not get involved in actual military government work, except for the purpose of gaining experience. It is highly desirable that intelligence officers be on good terms with the military government officers of the area in which they operate. In fact, inability to get along may seriously impair the value of an intelligence officer. But his considered appraisal of the political or economic situation and his report thereon to his superiors must be free from local censorship.

A fourth lesson derived from experience is the advisability of allowing an intelligence officer to operate in the same territory for a long time. It takes time to establish useful contacts and confidence among native personalities. "Doing" a town in a few days and then pushing on, never to see it again, is probably better than nothing—but not much better. Since political intelligence officers work quite openly for the most part, their prolonged residence does not harm their work unless it results in the creation of preferences and dislikes which impair the necessary objectivity. In such cases, rotation would be called for.

Finally, it is necessary for intelligence officers to remember at all times that they exercise a staff, not a command, function. Because of their special insight and knowledge, they may often be keenly aware of mistakes made by others, and the temptation to step in to "set things right" may be overwhelming at times. However, such forays into direct administration will almost certainly be resented, and if they become a frequent occurrence, they will raise such animosity as to impair the value of the intelligence organization. Staff work is self-effacing, anonymous work. Most important of all, it is service. A person who is emotionally unfitted to be content with rendering a vital service should not be used in the intelligence organization.

The occupation of Germany is a long-range task. It cannot succeed through intelligence work alone. But without effective political intelligence it is eventually doomed to failure.

Chapter V

Military Occupation Policy of the Axis Powers

FREDERICK M. WATKINS

The Objectives of Axis Occupation Policy

In spite of the radically different conditions prevailing in Europe and East Asia, the occupation methods adopted during the last war by the leading Axis powers were very much the same. This similarity was due to the fact that Germany and Japan were both guided by the same basic theory of military government. The traditional concept of occupation, as embodied in the Hague Convention and other sources of international law, assumed the existence of a world composed of fully sovereign states. Since war was concerned with the external relations rather than with the internal organization of these states, the function of military government was viewed in essentially conservative terms. Subject only to the requirements of military necessity, the duty of occupying authorities was to preserve the existing bases of social and political order, leaving the final allocation of sovereignty to be determined in the course of peace negotiations. The purpose of Axis warfare, on the other hand, was essentially revolutionary. Like the English and French revolutionists of the seventeenth and eighteenth centuries, the Axis powers were interested not in the conservation but in the destruction of established principles of political legitimacy. Their purpose was to create a new international order by placing themselves in a position to dominate the domestic and foreign policies of their weaker neighbors. According to this conception, the function of military government was not to preserve the existing foundations of sovereignty, but to lay the groundwork for a thorough reorganization of political and social relations. Although Italy, in its relatively restricted field of influence, was never able to accomplish much in this direction, the more successful Axis nations had ample opportunity to reveal the revolutionary nature of their objectives. This places the German and Japanese occupations in a class by themselves, and accounts for the marked similarity of the methods used in all the various regions which fell within their respective spheres of interest.

Fundamentally, the Nazi conception of a New Order in Europe, and the Japanese conception of Greater East Asia were nothing more than an attempt to revive an old-fashioned form of racial imperialism by the use of modern means. The idea of exploiting conquered populations for the benefit of a conquering race is one of the oldest conceptions in the repertory of political thought. With the growth of modern nationalism, however, it has tended to become increasingly obsolete. By the end of the nineteenth century, the difficulty of coping with nationalist resistance in disputed areas like Alsace-Lorraine, and the manifest weakness of multinational states like Austria-Hungary, had forced most statesmen to agree that Europe itself could no longer be regarded as a profitable field for imperialist expansion. The progress of nationalism in twentieth-century Asia has led to a similar discrediting of colonial imperialism in that area as well. In the light of these experiences, most people have concluded that the principle of racial exploitation can no longer be regarded as a possible basis for international order. The German Nazis and the Japanese militarists were alike, however, in refusing to accept this conclusion. At a time that more experienced imperialist powers were gradually becoming reconciled to the abandonment of their pretensions, they employed every device of modern propaganda to inspire their fellow citizens with a newly fanatical faith in their right, as representatives of a superior race, to impose their will on racially inferior neighbors. In the course of their rise to power within their own countries, the Axis leaders had discovered that the social and political conditions of modern life offer many hitherto unexploited opportunities for the centralized control of mass populations. By applying similar methods to the government of subject peoples, they believed that an ambitious system of racial imperialism could once again be placed on firm foundations. Their experiments in military government were devoted to the furtherance of that end.

Police Methods

From the standpoint of the Axis powers, no aspect of modern life was more important than the developments which have recently taken place in the field of military and police technique. The terroristic use of military power has always been an essential means for the control of subject populations. Efficient and ruthless police forces have also played a large part in the establishment of all colonial systems. Recent technical advances have made it possible, however, to go much farther than ever before in the use of these time-worn means. A modern army with bombers and machine guns is in an incomparable position to work its will on unarmed civilian mobs. A modern police force, with its elaborate methods of detection and registration, is able to exercise remarkably close supervision over the activities of dangerous individuals. In establishing control over their own countrymen, the German Nazis and the Japanese militarists had already gained a great deal of experience in the application and development of new coercive techniques. The efficacy of such institutions as the concentration camp, originally devised for the purpose of overcoming domestic resistance, had left them with a high degree of respect for the potentialities of systematic intimidation. These were the resources on which they relied, in the first instance, in establishing their power over the populations of occupied areas.

In their use of military and police power, the purpose of the Axis leaders was not merely to provide support for the conduct of military operations, but also to undermine the authority of all social and political institutions which might offer ultimate resistance to the establishment of a new order. According to the classical theory of occupation, the duty of occupying authorities is to maintain the highest possible degree of public order. The policy of Axis occupation, on the other hand, was based on a full recognition of the advantages of calculated disorder. In their own rise to power, the German Nazis and Japanese militarists had found that the creation of an atmosphere of unbearable insecurity provided one of the most effective means of undermining the position of established institutions in their own countries. By using their police resources to destroy the Communists and other radically hostile groups, and by making the security of other groups entirely dependent on their will, they soon persuaded the people of Germany and Japan that the only way of preserving their lives and property was to abandon their old loyalties and to accept the rule of their new masters. A similar combination of actual and threatened violence formed the basis of their subsequent activities in occupied regions. In places like Denmark or Siam, where they had reason to hope that the mere threat of disorder would suffice to hold the support of the local population, their policy was to create as little disturbance as possible. In places like Poland or China, where a more uncompromising attitude was feared, correspondingly rigorous methods were adopted. By inaugurating a period of absolute violence and chaos, complete with rape and pillage, the attempt was made to create a condition of life so radically intolerable that people would ultimately be eager to accept any new order able to promise a reasonable degree of peace and security. Thus the power of granting or withholding public order was deliberately used as a device to break the old loyalties of conquered peoples, reducing them to a position of absolute dependence upon the will of the conqueror.

In this respect, however, there was one significant difference between the occupation practice of the German Nazis and of the Japanese militarists. Western armies have been so long trained to respect the rights of civilian populations that it would have been difficult and dangerous to use the German army as the principal agency for the terrorization of Nazi occupied areas in Western Europe. Thus the regular military forces were encouraged, with some notable exceptions, to maintain an attitude of strict "correctness," and the execution of terroristic policies was left in the hands of independent party organizations. The traditions of Asiatic warfare, on the other hand, have accustomed the armies and peoples of the Far East to a rather less scrupulous level of military behavior, and made it possible for the Japanese militarists to use regular army units for the accomplishment of their purposes. The rape of Nanking, which has become notorious as the classic modern instance of unrestrained military brutality, is sometimes explained as the consequence of an unpremeditated collapse of military discipline. In the light of comparable episodes at Hong Kong and elsewhere there can be little doubt, however, that the destruction of public order by military violence was a calculated element of Japanese occupation policy. More systematic methods of coercion, such as the maintenance of concentration camps, were also left in the hands of military organizations, the most notable of which was the famous Kempei or military police. In this way the Japanese army, unlike its German counterpart, was made to assume direct responsibility for the worst abuses of military government.

Political and Administrative Policy

The essentially revolutionary character of Axis occupation policy was most clearly revealed in its treatment of the conquered ruling classes. At the time of occupation each of the conquered regions had its own system of social and political organization, under the direction of national or colonial administrations. If its population was to be incorporated successfully within the framework of a new order, it was necessary that the existing system should either be destroyed or else be made subservient to the will of the conqueror. In view of the fact that no organization can act without effective leaders, the easiest way to accomplish this result was to exterminate or intimidate the various individuals on whom the conquered populations had been accustomed to rely for leadership. The German Nazis and the Japanese militarists in their own countries had already demonstrated the possibility of controlling large populations by killing off the more recalcitrant leaders of opposing organizations, and using the threat of force to inhibit the action of the rest. Their occupation policy was an attempt to extend the scope of this experiment. In areas where the existing leadership was wholly unacceptable, police measures were taken to eliminate the entire ruling class. The Japanese conquerors of regions formerly subject to Western colonialism accomplished this purpose by the simple expedient of arresting the bulk of the dominant

European population, and by subjecting these prisoners to indignities calculated to make them lose their last marks of prestige in the eyes of their onetime subjects. The German practice, as exemplified in Poland and in certain other Slavic areas, of arresting and killing a large part of the native intellectual elite was similarly designed to deprive the conquered society of its normal sources of leadership. In other areas, like China or France, the bulk of the previous ruling group, while permitted to remain in existence, was curbed by the constant threat of police supervision. By these methods it was hoped that the conquered populations, having been deprived of independent leadership, would be rendered incapable of resistance to the establishment of a permanent new order.

In their attempt to curb the independence of native elite groups the Axis powers could not afford to go so far, however, as to put them entirely out of action. Except in a few areas, such as western Poland and New Guinea, which were scheduled for mass resettlement by the "master race," the aim of the new order was to exploit rather than to destroy the resources of existing populations. The supervisory and managerial personnel needed to maintain a modern level of productivity in a continental empire was far too numerous to be recruited, except at the very highest levels, from the ranks of the ruling nations. As soon as possible after the inauguration of military government, the Axis authorities tried, therefore, to conserve their own limited man power by selecting reliable members of the native population to take over the performance of executive functions. Existing police organizations, once they had been purged of undesirable elements, were generally allowed to assume the main burden of police supervision. Native bureaucrats, under similar restrictions, were allowed to carry on the regular work of civil administration. Many conquered regions were also forced to contribute to the military power of the Axis by maintaining armies of their own. Because of the shortage of competent and reliable native personnel, the occupying authorities often found some difficulty in carrying out this policy. This was particularly true in the onetime colonial areas conquered by the Japanese, where the wholesale removal of the European ruling class, and the low educational level of the native population, made it hard to find the requisite human material for the creation of an effective local administration. The Japanese tried to meet this problem by inaugurating police institutes and other specialized training programs in the various occupied areas, and by sending selected native students to Japan for advanced study. For all their emphasis on the unique capacities of the master race, the German Nazis and the Japanese militarists were far too realistic to assume that their own peoples could supply all, or even the major part, of the talent needed for the management of continental empires. To supplement their own man power from native sources, without at the same time losing their capacity to control the imperial system, was the basic problem of their occupation policy.

In order to secure the requisite degree of local cooperation it was necessary that political as well as administrative responsibility be entrusted as far as possible to local leaders. Colonial powers have always recognized the fact that the easiest way of controlling an alien population is to leave the formal exercise of political authority in the hands of native rulers whom the people are in the habit of obeying, and who can at the same time be coerced or bribed into following the dictates of the paramount power. At a time when the peoples of Europe had long been accustomed to national self-determination, and when most of the peoples of East Asia were already in revolutionary opposition to the continuance of alien rule, the advantages of indirect government were particularly obvious in these parts of the world. From the beginning, therefore, Axis occupation policy in most areas was directed toward the establishment of puppet states. The ideal situation from their standpoint would have been to replace all military governments by formally independent regimes headed by native statesmen influential enough to hold the allegiance of their own fellow nationals, and subservient enough to give unquestioning obedience to the commands of the master race. These specifications were not easy to fulfill. In some regions, genuinely influential national figures were available for Axis purposes. This was especially apt to be the case in areas like Burma or Croatia, where well-organized national movements were already seeking liberation from an alien national or colonial regime. In return for a formal grant of freedom, the leaders of these movements were often willing to lend more or less wholehearted support to the Axis. In politically disunited countries, like France or China, it was possible to find men like Pétain or Wang Ching-wei who, without being able to speak for the country as a whole, were sufficiently influential to bring a considerable part of their fellow nationals within the Axis orbit. In politically sophisticated countries like Norway and Denmark, or in politically undeveloped regions like Malaya and Sumatra, it was often impossible, on the other hand, to find any native leader willing or able to swing any considerable number of people in the Axis direction. But even under the most unfavorable circumstances, the general Axis policy was to build up the available local leadership during the period of military occupancy in the hope that it would ultimately be strong enough to assume the full responsibilities of puppet rule.

Among peoples already accustomed or aspiring to the right of national self-determination, the problem of maintaining popular allegiance to foreign-dominated puppet regimes was obviously difficult. On the basis of experience in their own countries, however, the German Nazis and the Japanese militarists believed that the newly discovered techniques of totalitarian government would suffice to solve the problem. The Russian Communists had been the first to show that a small but determined minority, united by the hierarchical discipline of a totalitarian party, and vested with an effective monopoly of coercive and propagandist resources, could reduce the population of a modern state to a position of absolute dependence on the will of its rulers. This political technique, applied and developed in the course of their own rise to power, was used by the Axis leaders as the basis of occupation policy. Although local conditions made it impossible to apply identical measures everywhere, the general purpose of their military governments was to undermine the position of liberal institutions and to lay the foundations for an effective totalitarian regime. Local fascist parties, under the protection of the occupying authority, were encouraged to expand their coercive and propagandist activities at the expense of their rivals. Whenever the circumstances seemed to warrant, they were also allowed to take over the widest possible range of administrative and political responsibility.

In countries like China, where the Kuomintang had already familiarized people with one-party government, it was comparatively easy to transfer authority to a Japanese-sponsored totalitarian party. In countries like Norway and Holland, where the native fascists had never been more than an inconsiderable minority, it was necessary to proceed with greater caution. Even under the most unfavorable circumstances, however, the policy of military governments was to foster the growth of totalitarian regimes. By establishing their own totalitarian pattern as a universal norm, the new imperialists felt that the internal authority of their puppet regimes could ultimately be placed on firm foundations.

In basing their hopes upon the spread of totalitarian government, the Axis imperialists were faced, however, with an extremely difficult problem. Experience has shown that, under the conditions of modern industrialism, a considerable amount of popular enthusiasm is needed to ensure maximum productivity. Totalitarian imperialism, unlike the older forms of colonial imperialism, was accordingly based on the proposition that subject peoples should be deliberately aroused to political consciousness by mass indoctrination. Once a people has been inspired with a vivid sense of national self-consciousness there is always the danger, on the other hand, that the power of the organized masses will be used for the furtherance of purely national interests. The strength of fascist movements in Germany and Japan was largely due to the fact that they promised to place the peoples of their respective countries in a position of imperial predominance over their neighbors. In their attempts to gain popular support, totalitarian puppet regimes were forced to make a similar appeal to the national aspirations of their own peoples, aspirations which in the long run were bound to come into conflict with the plans of an alien master race. Can a totalitarian regime be made strong enough to control and mobilize the resources of a native population, without at the same time becoming too strong to be effectively controlled by an external imperial authority? This was the essential problem faced by the exponents of Axis imperialism.

The Russian Communists, as pioneers in the development of modern totalitarianism, were able to offer an effective answer to this problem. Before the Russian Revolution, most national imperialists in Europe, and many colonial imperialists in Asia, including the Japanese themselves, had tried to minimize or eliminate local differences by assimilating conquered peoples within the body of the imperial nation. The results of this policy, as applied in Alsace-Lorraine and elsewhere, were uniformly disappointing. Forewarned by such experiences, the Russian Communists decided that the best way to unite their extremely polyglot empire was not to suppress but to encourage the spread of linguistic and cultural differences. This policy relieved the central government of many unpleasant responsibilities, and served at the same time to divide the non-Russian population into fragments far too small and impotent to challenge the position of a compact Russian majority. The value of this solution to the problem of totalitarian imperialism was fully recognized by the Axis leaders. The Russian nationalities policy was accordingly adopted as the model for their own imperialist experiments. Except in a few areas scheduled for mass resettlement by the master race, their powers of military government were not used in an attempt to assimilate the local population. Their efforts, instead, were directed to the task of breaking up the conquered territories into the largest possible number of distinct national and regional units. In Europe submerged nationalities like the Croatians and the Slovakians were given separate statehood, and regional autonomists, even in so firmly united a nation as France, were granted every possible consideration. In the Far East, colonial peoples who had shown any signs of national self-consciousness were stimulated with the gift or promise of independence. By the establishment of separate regional administrations, and by the encouragement of regional dialects, an attempt was also made to undermine the unity of nations which, like China, were inconveniently large and powerful. Thus the divisive potentialities of modern nationalism were systematically used for the purpose of exalting the relative power and importance of the master race.

In their encouragement of local nationalism, the Axis imperialists were doing nothing more than applying a modernized version of the ancient policy of divide and rule. Before the rise of nationalism, colonial powers were generally able to maintain their position by diverting

the energies of subject peoples into the mutually self-destructive channels of religious or class antagonism. National jealousies, deliberately
fostered, provided the new empire builders with a similar opportunity. By granting varying degrees of political autonomy to their several client peoples, they were able to set them in competition with one
another for the favor of the master race. By awarding disputed territories to those claimants who showed the greatest willingness to
support the new order, they could play upon the hopes and fears of
rival nationalities. Thus the Rumanians and the Hungarians, with
their conflicting claims to Transylvania, could be made to vie with
one another in support of the Nazi war effort, while Burma and Siam,
in their common desire for territorial expansion at the expense of the
Shan states, were similarly tempted to bid for the favor of the Japanese. Since national rivalries were more extensively developed in
Europe than in East Asia, the German Nazis were able to go especially far in this direction. By setting up an elaborate hierarchy of
inferior and superior races, and by correlating it with an equally
elaborate schedule of differential wage rates, rationing levels, and
the like, they used their occupation powers for the deliberate purpose
of creating ill-feeling between the various subject peoples. In the Far
East, where common opposition to the forces of Western colonialism
had served in some measure to inhibit the growth of national rivalries,
opportunities for this sort of thing were comparatively restricted. The
occupation policies adopted in both areas made it abundantly clear,
however, that the German Nazis and the Japanese militarists were
equally prepared to use the tactics of divide and rule as an essential
element in the establishment and maintenance of the new order.

Economic Policy

The encouragement of local nationalism also provided an excellent
basis for the exercise of economic control over the newly conquered
empires. With the development of modern industrialism, economic
power has tended to become even more important than military or
political power as a basis for imperial unification. In the Soviet Union,
where over-all planning and direction in the economic realm has been

reserved as a function of the central government, it has been possible to grant linguistic and cultural self-determination to local groups without endangering the effective unity of state action. This is a reflection of the fact that small territories under modern conditions are no longer capable of commanding the material resources necessary for military or political self-sufficiency. Nations large and rich enough to support the full apparatus of modern technology are the only ones capable of genuine self-determination in the modern world. In their respective spheres of influence, Germany and Japan were much the strongest economic units. By using the resulting power to gain a strangle hold on the economies of neighboring nations, they were in a position to make substantial grants of political and administrative autonomy to carefully restricted areas without sacrificing the reality of imperial predominance. This was one of the primary objectives of Axis occupation policy.

The simplest and most direct means of accomplishing this end was to increase the existing margin of German and Japanese economic superiority by transferring productive capacity from peripheral regions to the homeland of the master race. In the early days of Western colonialism, the preponderance of the imperial power was ensured by forcing colonial areas to devote themselves to the production of raw materials, while manufacturing processes were concentrated in the home country. The progress of modern industrialism, with its constant multiplication and elaboration of the stages of production, has opened the way to ever new possibilities of refinement in the application of these old methods. By limiting subject peoples to the production of unfinished and semifinished goods insufficient in themselves for the maintenance of a wartime or peacetime economy, a highly industrialized imperial people can easily maintain a monopoly over the essential resources of modern technology. This fact has given a new lease of life to the hopes of modern imperialism.

That this was the essential aim of the Nazi and the Japanese empire builders is shown not only by the evidence of their theoretical writings, but also by the conduct of Axis military government. In the initial phases of occupation, many factories engaged in essential phases of production were dismantled and shipped to the home country. By the withholding of raw materials and other restrictive devices, many other establishments were deliberately immobilized in order that native workers, under the pressure of unemployment, might be induced or coerced to leave their own countries and join the labor force of the imperial power. Although the Nazi-dominated nations of Europe, being much more highly industrialized than the Japanese-dominated nations of East Asia, offered the most fertile field for the application of these policies, the Japanese militarists were no less interested than the German Nazis in applying these measures. The progress of the war did, to be sure, make it impossible for either of these groups to proceed as far in this direction as they would have liked to do. As the air and sea power of the Allies reached its climax, the deterioration of Axis communications and the need for anti-aircraft dispersion compelled them to slow down and even to reverse the process of industrial concentration. The rapid deterioration of the Japanese position made it particularly necessary for them, in the last years of the war, to build up the economic self-sufficiency of conquered areas which could no longer be supplied with Japanese goods. But if the Axis powers had succeeded in gaining military victory, they would undoubtedly have returned to the methods which marked the earlier stages of their occupation policy.

Deliberate changes in the location of industry were by no means the only resource available, however, for the establishment of economic control. Modern developments in the field of commerce and finance have led to the creation of many institutions admirably adapted to the purposes of economic imperialism. In an age when the essential medium of exchange consists of fiat currencies and bank credits, the control of central credit institutions provides an easy means of dictating the economic destinies of whole peoples. The development of cartels, holding companies, and other devices of large-scale integration has made it possible, through the domination of a few central control institutions, to direct the operations of a vast number of individual producing units. Government monopolies and trading restrictions provide an even more potent means of regimenting economic processes which in an earlier age, would have been governed by market considerations. To exploit and extend these various means of economic centralization was one of the important tasks of Axis military government.

In view of the fact that the territories under their control were economically the more highly developed, the German Nazis were naturally able to go farther than the Japanese militarists in the use of modern economic methods of control. Their advantage in this respect was less, however, than one might at first be tempted to believe. In so far as East Asia was still a land of primitive and relatively self-sufficient village communities, it could not easily be subjected to the control devices proper to an advanced capitalist economy. But if the economic life of the region was uncommonly backward in some respects, it was at the same time uncommonly advanced in others. In Europe and America the modern trend toward economic concentration has been inhibited by the continuing existence of small-scale organizations inherited from the earlier phases of capitalist development. In the Far East, capitalism from the beginning has tended to assume the form of large-scale corporate and governmental enterprise. Colonial economies long dominated by institutions like the Dutch East India Company, and integrated by the control mechanisms of an international business community, offer a particularly convenient field for imperial exploitation. So far as the most important sectors of economic life were concerned, therefore, the Japanese were hardly less well situated than the Germans, and the measures adopted by each of these groups were substantially the same.

Manipulation of the circulating medium is perhaps the simplest means of modern economic control. As recent victims of one of the worst inflation disasters of modern times, the Germans were particularly well acquainted with the revolutionary potentialities, social and economic, implicit in any really drastic experience of monetary disorganization. One of the first tasks of every Axis occupation was, therefore, to disrupt the bases of the local currency and to lay the foundations for a new monetary system which would be permanently subject to Axis dictation. Sometimes the first steps in this direction were actually taken prior to the occupation itself. Several days before the capitulation of Hong Kong, for example, the Japanese were able to bring the economic life of that colony to a virtual standstill by

announcing that the existing currency would be demonetized immediately after their arrival. Even in those cases where direct demone-
tization was not attempted, the policies adopted by Axis military governments were regularly designed to produce similarly disruptive
effects. Wherever the German and the Japanese armies advanced,
they were furnished with lavish issues of unbacked occupation currency which, freely used to finance the private and public expenditures of the occupation forces, subjected the conquered territories to
all the hazards of runaway inflation. By charging the local population
with grossly inflated occupation costs, and by calling upon them, as
a token of loyalty to the new order, to make extravagant contributions
to the Axis war effort, they also forced the local authorities to inflate
their own currencies. Unfavorable trade agreements, which called
for the export of goods and services in return for blocked credit accounts in Berlin or Tokyo, provided another effective means of weak-
ening the local currency situation. The ultimate purpose of these
various measures was to reduce the satellite economies to a state of
bankruptcy so complete that they would be forced to apply to Germany and Japan for the financial resources indispensable to ultimate
currency stabilization. Once this result had been accomplished, the
imperial nations would be in a position to exert virtually unlimited
power over the monetary policy of every state incorporated within the
structure of their respective new orders.

But for all their value as a means of over-all regulation, currency
controls in themselves were insufficient to ensure control over the
operations of particular industries. For this purpose it was necessary
to acquire dominance over the corporations, cartels, and other regulatory mechanisms which play a decisive part in the operation of every
advanced capitalist economy. Axis military governments accordingly
devoted a good deal of attention to the task of acquiring a leading
position in all the more important of these control institutions. The
simplest way of doing this was to expropriate the original owners of
all crucial corporations, by confiscation or by purchase, and to vest
the controlling ownership in the hands of Axis nationals. In East
Asia, where a large part of the existing industrial wealth, as the property of foreign enemies, was liable to military seizure, this procedure

was particularly easy to apply. In deference to local nationalist sentiment, however, the Axis powers generally found it advisable to leave
the ownership of local industry largely in the hands of reliable local
supporters, exercising their own control functions through channels
less direct and obvious. As the unfavorable currency situation made
foreign banks increasingly dependent on the financial resources of
Germany and Japan, local banking policy would, without any change
of management or ownership, be quietly dictated in favor of the particular industries and enterprises which the imperial masters wanted
to encourage. In certain cases, particularly in those Japanese-occupied
areas where the elimination of European-born personnel had left a
severe shortage of experienced managerial talent, it was possible to
insist upon the appointment of foreign managers for the direction of
native-owned factories. The industrial predominance of Germany
and Japan, newly backed by the threat of force, also made it easy for
the representatives of those countries to dictate regional cartel agreements in line with their own national policies and interests. The fact
that the divorce of ownership and control has long been recognized as
one of the more notable features of modern capitalistic development
made it comparatively easy for Axis military governments, without
committing themselves to a policy of thoroughgoing expropriation,
to subordinate locally owned industries to the requirements of their
own version of economic imperialism.

Under modern conditions, however, direct government regulation
has tended, particularly in wartime, to take the place of other forms
of economic control. This development provided the Axis powers
with precedents and institutions very useful to their purposes. During
the initial stages of occupation, military governments were able on
their own authority to assume a power of life or death over all forms
of productive enterprise. By rationing the available supplies of raw
material and man power, and by limiting various forms of activity
to holders of specially approved licenses, they were in a position to
integrate the economic life of all the various occupied regions within
the framework of a single master plan. When military governments
were replaced by ostensibly independent local regimes, direct responsibility for the manipulation of these control devices passed into

the hands of local authorities. The political and economic dependence of these puppet states was so complete, however, that this transfer of authority involved no real impairment of imperial power.

By monopolizing the processes of international trade, the Germans and the Japanese were also able to retain a considerable degree of direct government control over the economic life of ostensibly independent states. Most local economies of modern times depend on the maintenance of a substantial volume of imports and exports. This is especially true of the colonial regions of East Asia, which have long been geared to the requirements of world trade rather than to the requirements of local self-sufficiency. By retaining control over foreign trade facilities, the imperial authorities were in a position to turn the mutual interdependence of nations to their own advantage. Satellite states were forbidden to make direct trade agreements with one another, and forced to do everything through the mediation and under the supervision of Germany and Japan. Foreign exchange ratios between the various local currencies were settled in terms of their relationship to the imperial currencies, as determined by the central banking institutions of the imperial power. Import and export quotas were fixed in terms of the shipping space made available by the central authorities. In this way all the resources of modern economic regulation were used to provide the master race with an effective monopoly of economic planning functions.

These various economic controls were designed to serve not only the economic but also the political purposes of the Axis powers. The success of totalitarian control in the Soviet Union is based on the fact that political leadership in all the member nations is exercised by a native elite whose personal careers are made or broken by a centralized Communist party to whose discipline most of them are completely subjected. By making private property dependent on the will of the imperial power, Axis military governments were in a position to use the hopes and fears of native property owners as a basis for the creation of similarly disciplined local elites. People whose bank accounts and bond or mortgage investments could be wiped out by the collapse of an Axis-sponsored currency had a natural interest in staving off that disaster by supporting the Axis cause. Factory

owners and managers whose enterprises could be ruined by confiscation, or by the unfavorable application of rationing and other
control measures, were bound by elementary considerations of economic prudence to seek the favor of the occupying authorities. For
those who succeeded in gaining that favor, moreover, there was a
prospect of substantial reward. Although the lion's share of prosperity under the new order might go to Axis nationals, the share of
the jackal was by no means unattractive. Whenever the occupation
authorities or their puppet associates confiscated the property of enemy
nationals, domestic insurgents, Jews, and other repressed groups,
favored members of the local property-owning class could generally
count on receiving a substantial part of the spoils. People with the
right banking or party connections could also hope to expand their
own enterprises. Newly established government monopolies provided an especially profitable field for these activities. In occupied
China, for example, followers of the puppet leader Wang Ching-wei
were rewarded by membership in official trading associations, which,
being vested with an exclusive legal right to engage in the purchase
and distribution of rice and other vital commodities, were in a position to secure enormous returns for the favored few. By allowing
trusted natives to assume a leading economic role, the Axis authorities were able to shift responsibility for many unpopular measures
upon their shoulders, and at the same time to surround themselves
with a group of local adherents whose economic interests and personal safety were intimately bound up with the success of the new
order. These were the people who formed the nucleus of every puppet
regime.

Propaganda Policy for the Axis

Men do not live by bread alone. If a political regime is to maintain
an effective hold over the lives of men, it must appeal not only to
the personal fears and hopes of its supporters, but also to their broader
aspirations. The uncommon success of the Communist party in securing the loyalty of men drawn from various nationalities is due to the
fact that, in addition to promising distinguished careers to its abler

members and adherents, it has been able to inspire them with the vision of a better world to come, in which all men equally will be allowed to share in the blessings of a fully rationalized technological civilization. If the Axis powers were to achieve equal success in uniting their various local supporters, it was necessary that they also should be inspired with devotion to a common cause. From the ideological standpoint, this was the crucial problem of Axis occupation policy.

The easiest way of uniting men is to inspire them with hatred for a common enemy. The appeal of the Communists has always been based in large measure on their success in arousing workers and technicians to a mood of violent opposition toward the capitalist class. The propaganda policies of the Axis powers were directed to the comparable task of stimulating the latent fears and hatreds of those peoples who came within their respective spheres of influence. By encouraging colonial and semicolonial nations in the belief that Western imperialism was the source of all their woes, the Japanese tried to unite them in a common crusade against the Western world. By playing upon the anti-Semitic and anti-Bolshevik sentiments of the European middle classes, the German Nazis made equally strenuous attempts to join the peoples of Europe in a community of hate. In the course of their rise to power the Axis leaders had found that the policy of attacking convenient scapegoats was one of the most effective means of gaining political support among their fellow nationals. The propaganda policies adopted by their military governments, and continued by the ensuing puppet regimes, were an attempt to apply comparable methods in the field of international relations.

The negative emotion of hatred can never be fully satisfying, however, unless it is complemented by positive aspirations. In the case of Communist ideology, opposition to the capitalist class is justified on the grounds that capitalist property relations constitute a hopeless obstacle to the attainment of desirable technological results. A corresponding emphasis on the positive potentialities of the new order was ultimately needed to ensure the success of Axis propaganda. During the period of military occupation, therefore, the Axis authorities did everything in their power to impress their subject peoples with the vision of a better world to come. Like the Communists, they appealed to the modern desire for technological progress by emphasizing the possibilities of effective rationalization implicit in the establishment of supranational units of economic cooperation and control. The term "Co-prosperity Sphere," under which the Japanese militarists tried to popularize their new colonial system, is a characteristic example of this particular type of appeal.

Because of their racist ideology, however, the Axis leaders tended on the whole to lay even greater emphasis on motives of racial imperialism. The nations of Western Europe, after more than a century of successful colonial imperialism, were in the habit of regarding themselves as the representatives of a race uniquely qualified for the high task of ruling inferior peoples. As the heirs of an expansive Chinese civilization which had once held sway over many barbarous and semibarbarous races, the nations of East Asia were similarly disposed to think in imperial terms. By convincing Europeans that their waning predominance over other regions could be restored only under German leadership, and by persuading Asiatics that their unique civilizing mission could be resumed only under Japanese hegemony, the Axis propagandists hoped to unite their subject peoples in a fellowship of common imperialist enthusiasm. The prospect of sharing in the glory of future world mastery was offered in both cases as a positive inducement to cooperation.

Conclusion

The event has shown that the methods used by the Axis totalitarians were inadequate to the accomplishment of their purpose. To some extent this failure was no doubt due to the fact that military defeat came before they had had a chance fully to exploit the resources of their new technique of revolutionary imperialism. Their ultimate military weakness, however, was in itself a reflection of the inadequacy of their particular version of the totalitarian formula. Unlike the Communists, who grant equal status to all party members regardless of national origin, the German Nazis and the Japanese militarists were committed to the practice of uncompromising racism.

Although they might allow neighboring peoples to share in the privileges and responsibilities of imperial rule, there could never be any question of equal partnership with the master race. In an age of rising national self-assertion, the prospect of association on terms of permanent inferiority could never be wholly satisfactory even to the most highly favored members of other national groups. This made it difficult to awaken genuine enthusiasm, even in puppet circles, for any of the ostensibly independent national regimes set up by the Axis. Resistance movements, supported in many cases by a large part of the favored propertied classes, arose to constitute a serious drain on the military and economic efficiency of the new order. By committing themselves to a policy of racist exclusivism, the Axis leaders had subjected their version of totalitarian imperialism to a handicap from which it was never able to recover.

In spite of its ultimate failure, the Axis experiment has had a profound and, to all appearances, lasting effect upon the development of modern international relations. In order to undo the political and social consequences of the totalitarian concept of revolutionary occupation, the Allied victors have themselves been forced to abandon the conservative presuppositions which formerly governed this particular field of international law. The idea that military government should be limited by the requirements of military necessity has been replaced by the assumption that it should be used as an instrument for the complete reorientation of political and social life in occupied regions. To destroy the last vestiges of German and Japanese militarism, and to establish a new order concordant with the desires of the victorious nations, has become the publicly avowed objective of Allied occupation policy. The traditional concept of military occupation was based on the assumption of an essentially stable international order. Now that the revolutionary dynamism of the twentieth century has upset the political and social bases of nineteenth-century conservatism, revolutionary action has become an inescapable condition of survival in the field of international politics. In a period of revolutionary unrest, conservative principles of occupation provide no answer to the problems of military government. The victors of World War II, in their attempts to prevent the re-emergence of fascism, have already found it necessary in their respective areas of occupation to apply the whole totalitarian repertory of police coercion, official propaganda, economic controls, and puppet politics. As long as revolutionary conditions continue to exist, revolutionary rather than conservative standards are bound to prevail in the field of military government. Thus the Axis experiments in occupation policy are likely to exert a lasting influence upon the course of twentieth-century politics.

Part II

Descriptive Accounts and Evaluations of Experiences in Italy, France, and Austria

★　　★　　　★　　　★　　　★　　　★

Chapter VI

American Military Government in Italy

GEORGE C. S. BENSON and MAURICE NEUFELD

Nature of the Problem

THE Allied armies first waded through the clear invasion waters of the Mediterranean onto the mined beaches of the southern coast of Sicily on July 10, 1943. American military government officers, nearly a hundred of them, armed with twelve proclamations and general orders, landed with the 1st, 3rd, and 45th Divisions and Seventh Army Headquarters at Gela, Licata, and Scoglitti, while civil affairs detachments of the Eighth Army came ashore near Catania. On July 22, after a dash across the island, General Patton rode into unresisting Palermo accompanied by American military government officers. In Rome, on July 25, Mussolini was dethroned, without a struggle, by the Fascist Grand Council and the king, creatures of his own making.

Completely and quietly, without the shrill drama of great historic events, a synthetic political philosophy, an elaborate administrative system, an empire, and a new social order—the entire Fascist Revolution—dissolved. This actual end of classical Fascism was more ignominious and conclusive than even the collapse of the Nazi-propped Fascist Republic of the North and Mussolini's assassination less than two years later. But neither the British nor the Americans, nor the world at large, could believe that the end of Italian Fascism had come. From the ignorance of internal conditions before the event, from the resulting incredulity when the event occurred, and from the consequent lack of preparation for seizing the moment prepared by the forces of history, emerged the errors of Allied military strategy on the peninsula as well as the faulty planning, the vacillating policy, and the administrative and political shortcomings that covered the entire career of AMG in Italy like a slow and steady rain of ash.

The sway of Rome over the Italians and its dictates never represented a return to the ancient tradition of imperial centuries. It represented, indeed, an age-old return of memories: hatred and sabotage of central power and oppression by Roman Caesar, Church, and modern State. The *Risorgimento,* which unified Italy in 1859 and threw the Italian people headlong and unprepared into the European stream of democratic development, was so fearful of the dangers of local attachments and loyalties that the able leaders of that period made a political mistake of the gravest nature. To create the semblance of nationhood, they placed power in Rome. The union of Italy took and kept a form of tightly controlled monarchy derived from the small state of Piedmont, its laws, customs, institutions, Army, and royal house. Before the united kingdoms could learn to live together as a regional federation, to fuse into a common life the powerful social, political, and economic regional forces which produced the desire for union, tight central control was thrust hastily upon Italy. The *Risorgimento* even imported from Piedmont the French system of provinces and prefects into a country where loyalties have always been directed first to the family, then the village, town, or city, then the region, and finally the nation. The province has never held meaning for an Italian. Yet it was precisely here that Mussolini expended his administrative efforts. He imposed again a northern form of discipline by developing still more extremely the centralizing mistakes of the *Risorgimento* against the wishes and aspirations of Italy's freer, bolder, and more realistic intelligences.

Municipal liberty in Italy, despite operatic pretensions of freedom and ancient reference, had, since the Kingdom, been controlled by Rome through strong administrative restraints. Yet certain local powers had remained. They were vested in popularly elected mayors and municipal councils and in provincial councils and *giunta,* composed, in part, of representatives of the various municipalities. The *giunta* controlled the prefect. At these levels of elections, at least in southern Italy and Sicily, Mussolini had been opposed, and candidates hostile to him were elected to office. As early as 1923, Mussolini told the Senate that it was "monstrous to think that . . . minor public bodies may follow political ends in contrast with those of the Government of the State. . . ." Between 1925 and 1928 all elected local governmental agencies were abolished. The podestà replaced the mayor, and like the provincial prefect, was appointed by the Ministry of the Interior. The prefect was made more powerful locally and more dependent upon Rome and upon the party hierarchy. He assumed greater control over the budget process and the resolutions and acts of local authorities. Powerful rights of surveillance over municipal affairs in his province were added to his duties and he could, under the law of October 23, 1925, impose his views on laws and regulations. His wider powers of maintaining orderly processes and progress in the province gave him the weapon of fear and reprisal for unspecified acts and hostile attitudes and thought. He was even dignified with the title of "Excellency," an honor dear to the Italian heart. Certain committees were created to replace the democratically elected provincial and municipal bodies by cooperating with the podestà and prefect. Since they were appointed by the various associations of employers and employees, created by the corporative state and by Fascist party officials, they were designed to guarantee to the local authorities the loyalty of the economically and socially important classes. In 1928, the chief administrative official of the cities and provinces, the permanent, and consequently powerful, secretary general, was made a state official, who entered service only after severe competitive state examination.

Uniform policy could be imposed throughout the country with this system of administration, running in continuously controlled channels from the Duce to the mayor. In addition, Fascist officials were often dispatched from Rome to make mayors and prefects conscious of their duties to the state and to the party. Theoretically, the system could have meant efficiency, even though it thwarted local initiative and responsibility. Actually, since the national government was the Fascist party and the party was, in truth, a vast and corrupt political machine directed by ludicrous and maladjusted mediocrities of Mussolini's early days of rise to power, the local machinery, expressing party and not local will, became establishments for carrying out and paying for public works schemes which Fascism needed to stay in power.

With the invasion of Sicily, local and party officials and their top appointees fled the island. Subordinate officials, who had stayed on had neither the training, the ability, nor the will to take their place. They had obtained their unimportant jobs through party favor and had kept their posts through loyalty and fear. They were unprepared for supervising or directing the activities of which they were a part. Nor could they help to devise new administrative techniques for an emergency situation. Soon, moreover, it became clear that the organizations which controlled every aspect of Italian life—the collection of grain, oil, and other staples; the slaughtering of cattle; transportation; fuel; and commerce, industry, rationing, employment, and social security—had collapsed long before the Allies reached Africa. Farmers had sold wheat on the black market for years before the Allied invasion. Few honest citizens could live on the official ration, since many items had not been regularly distributed, though books contained stamps for meat, fats, sugar, and coffee. Even the protection of citizens against air attacks had been neglected.

In summary, the problem confronting military government in Italy was that of dealing with a people of high pretensions, including, in the past, democratic idealists, but who had suffered from two decades of an overcentralized, corrupt, and bombastic regime. As a result of this regime, Italian governmental services were incompetent, at times almost nonexistent. The population of Italy was not unfriendly to the Allies, but it was too badly organized to express its friendship in any concrete way.

Even the narrowest conception of purpose of military government—the securing of lines of communication of the army—requires some kind of government. What steps were the Allied armies going to take to see that some sort of government existed? The following sections will review the command and organizational arrangements, and the policy determinations with which Allied military government attempted to solve its problems in Italy.

Command and Organization of Military Government

As a result of the necessity of recognizing Italian territorial entities and Allied military organizations, the command structure of military government had to be complicated. After the first few months in which the officers operating in Sicily were definitely on their own, a regional unit was established for Sicily. After the signing of the armistice, an Allied Control Commission (later Allied Commission) was established to work with the Italian government. After this commission came into authority, the chain of command was from Allied Force Headquarters (Mediterranean Theater of Operations) to the Allied Control Commission, to Military Government Regional Headquarters (or, on an equal basis for staff control, Army Headquarters) to Provincial Military Government teams, to municipal AMG's. Each of these organizational levels from Allied Commission down will be discussed in turn, as to jurisdiction, staff, and competence.

Although the Allied Control Commission included a Russian member, the staff was entirely Anglo-American. The British headed a large majority of the "subcommissions," as its divisions were called, though, at first, a majority of officers were American. The British predominance in higher rank arose in part out of their policy of granting rank to their officers commensurate with the positions they held, regardless of their permanent rank. The American army did not follow this policy and its officers thus often found themselves outranked. The British preponderance in the higher ranks had a good deal of effect on the work of the commission.

The jurisdiction of the commission during most of its history included three main fields:

1) General control of governmental policy in all parts of Italy not held by the Germans. This control included approval of laws and decrees of the Italian government in the so-called "Kings Italy"— the area in which the Badoglio, Bonomi, and Parri governments ruled—and a staff supervision of military government policy in the area controlled by the Allied armies.

2) Complete control of military government policy and operations

in the regions—i.e., areas which had passed out of control of the armies but were not yet under "Kings Italy."

3) Assignment of all military government personnel in Allied-held Italy. Naturally the armies had some degree of autonomy in selection of their personnel. Personnel could not be withdrawn from army AMG's without consent of the army AMG commander.

Theoretically the commission reported directly to Allied Force Headquarters (AFHQ) for the Mediterranean Theater. AFHQ had a G-5 section of able officers who exercised an intermittent and in general surprisingly ineffective staff supervision over the commission. The commission also had consultations with, and sometimes received instructions directly from, the State Department, or the British Foreign Office, or the Combined Chiefs of Staff in Washington. The commission also could not ignore the presence of the smaller, primarily tactical Headquarters of Allied Armies in Italy (sometimes called Fifteenth Army Group). As will be pointed out later, a large part of the reconstruction of the Italian governmental machinery was done during the first or Army phase of occupation. Since the armies operated under AAI headquarters, the latter at times took an active interest in military government policies. For a number of months in 1944–1945 a fairly active military government section in AAIHQ undertook some liaison work between army AMG units and the Allied Commission. Most of this staff was withdrawn in early 1945.

Few higher headquarters are liked by field officers, and the Allied Commission was no exception. For a variety of reasons, the commission did not have the reputation of being a highly efficient headquarters. The better officers avoided assignment to the commission whenever possible. This situation was especially tragic because, as noted in the next section, policy directives from headquarters above the commission were not clear. The commission had to develop a great deal of policy on its own, and found itself handicapped by an inadequate staff.

The general pattern of field organization was one in which over-all officers (civil affairs officers), assigned to communes or groups of communes, worked under the supervision of a provincial headquarters. The latter included a few specialists in such fields as food and supply, public safety, public works, public health, and finance. The provincial team reported to a regional headquarters (or in certain cases to an army AMG unit, as discussed in a later paragraph), which included a larger number of specialists. There was a great deal of flexibility in personnel assignments. Immediately after occupation a large commune might have several officers working in it. If the armies were moving forward rapidly, the number would be sharply reduced in two months. Similarly, the size of provincial and regional headquarters varied greatly in accordance with the stage of military operations.

The quality of regional and provincial headquarters varied as much as the size of the staff. Usually the personalities of the regional commissioners were the determining factor. These officers were either lieutenant colonels or colonels—fairly evenly distributed between the two armies. The deputy regional commissioner was usually not of the same country as the commissioner. Only one regional commissioner had had any important political or administrative experience prior to joining military government. It is probably fair to say that in general the regions were not very effective intermediate units.

In many ways a more creditable job was done at the provincial level. This was the lowest level at which specialists appeared (except as a few public safety officers were assigned to larger communes during the first few days of occupation), and it was the only level at which specialists had daily contact with functioning Italian governmental groups. The province is the level at which the bulk of the work of Italian local government is performed, so that the provincial specialists had an excellent opportunity for constructive work.

Each of the armies had a military government organization, paralleling other staff activities. The commanding officer of the headquarters group was usually located at army advance headquarters, but most of the specialist staff was at main headquarters. Liaison officers were attached to each corps and division, and a few "spearhead" officers worked with these liaison officers, aiding in the initial occupation of newly captured communes.

Army AMG's were much more important than the small strip of land—usually about two provinces wide—which they controlled would indicate. Since they were operating in the area of greatest military concentration, they had to deal with the toughest problems of civil-military relationships—billeting, maintenance of order and military security, looting, and requisitioning. In addition, the fact that they selected the first Italian communal and provincial officials and issued the first military government decrees made them the pattern setters. Since army headquarters had more continuity than any regional headquarters military government officers had more opportunity than others to influence Allied Commission policy and to devise their own policies when Allied Commission had none.

Relationship of Territorial and Tactical Military Government

So much confusion arose over the organizational problem in both Italy and the European Theater that the pattern finally evolved in Italy should be noted. Two important and apparently conflicting goals had to be harmonized: the necessity of a commanding general having control of all operations in an active combat area; and the necessity of continuous development of territorial government. Each goal required different types of military government organization.

The pattern developed in Italy to resolve this dilemma was relatively simple. When areas were occupied, corps and division liaison AMG officers installed in the communes the officers who were slated for those towns as a part of the territorial AMG organization. As soon as the provincial capital was occupied, the provincial headquarters team was installed by AMG. Armies then immediately began to route communications to communal military government officers through the provincial headquarters. Corps and division officers were kept out of the chain of command as much as possible. The Eighth Army, which even functioned through a regional AMG organization at one time, developed this system more fully than the Fifth, but the basic plan of operating through territorial units was followed by both armies.

As noted above, provinces were turned over to regions under the Allied Commission as soon as they passed out of Army Area. Later the Allied Commission turned them over to "King's Italy," by which time all provincial military government staff had usually been ordered out.

The American and the British armies made sincere efforts to locate suitable personnel for military government. Both utilized officers already in the army and commissioned other men directly from civilian life. Both countries probably recruited as high-grade personnel as they could in the lower and intermediate officer ranks, considering that they had to use army personnel offices, which are designed for a different sort of recruitment, and that much of the best personnel was already tied up in other parts of the war effort. It is perhaps true that the State Department, or Foreign Office, or other civilian agency with special experience in foreign affairs could have selected personnel who would have understood better how to work with Italians. But remembering the limitations of army personnel work, a passable personnel job was done in the lower and intermediate ranks.

The great difficulty lay in the personnel selected for the higher brackets—from the grade of lieutenant colonel on. Military government needed men of major political and administrative experience to fill the vacuum resulting from the lack of clear policy directives and to prevent the type of inefficient administration to which it was by nature liable. Instead of insisting on such men, both armies often took the path of least resistance and used military government as an answer to that ever-present problem of what to do with surplus higher-ranking officers. Among these were many able American reserve or British territorial officers who had helped greatly in building up their units during the first part of the war but had to be replaced by younger, more physically fit officers as soon as enough of the latter were trained.

Allied Military Government Policies

Italy has been pictured thus far as a country without a government, and AMG as a willing but uncoordinated group of officers. With clear-cut policies, both of these difficulties could have been overcome. But AMG had no practical plans. As has been indicated in an earlier chapter, the initial orders for AMG in Italy were naïvely unworkable.

The incomplete, faulty, and poorly conceived doctrine of military government for Italy came from the past. The planners found in the Civil War and the occupation of the Rhineland during and after World War I the dead experience from which to formulate living policy. A basic military government concept was repeated in army classes, handbooks, manuals, and directives like dogma: the chief function of AMG would be the job of securing the army's rear lines of communication. Whether this principle of limits of responsibility had validity in modern warfare, whether it was possible to administer at all on such a narrow scale, or whether the narrowed scope was consistent with Allied promises and the democratic hopes of occupied countries were questions left, unfortunately, to the slow process of learning by making mistakes. The error was inevitable, since the planners of military government had had more experience in law offices than in public administration. Consequently, no imaginative projection of specific problems into the administrative machinery created on paper ever took place. Yet a chain of command, the subjection of AMG to army habits of thought and action, a personnel policy, and an entire administrative structure were built upon a mistaken, confused, and limited notion. Even when it became mandatory to change thought and action during the period that later came to be known as the second phase of operations, the shift could not easily be made, regardless of pious declarations or directives. The realization of inadequacy came so gradually and grudgingly that AMG personnel could not adjust, without further training, to wider concepts and responsibilities.

Actually, the chief concern of AMG could never remain for long a hemmed-in preoccupation with the army's rear lines of communication. Any provincial commissioner or a city civil affairs officer, confronted with daily problems of extreme moment to thousands of human beings, belied the theory at once. Even mediocre administrators tried to alleviate the sufferings of their communities. Moreover, at home—and this might have been foreseen—were too many Americans of Italian extraction to make the original and limited concept politically feasible in election years. Accordingly, before AMG was ended in Italy, an entire program of economic and social reconstruction had been undertaken. Detailed directives had been issued to provide for the restoration of economic life, for the elimination of Fascists and Fascist institutions, for the maintenance of public security, and for handling political parties and partisan movements. Some of these regulations went into great detail. Unfortunately, many of them came long after the problem had arisen. In the following sections a few of the more specific fields of action will be reviewed.

Although AMG entered Sicily with no clear-cut policies, with many mistaken notions, and in ignorance of many important fields of administration, one elementary principle, enjoined repeatedly, had been clear beyond doubt: the principle of indirect rule after the initial phase. All plans and operations, the number and quality of personnel, and the schedule of achievement had been predicated upon the notion that Italian agencies and personnel were to be used as quickly as possible to perform the task of governing. This principle, which had been developed because of the limitations of Allied skills and man power, was also sound in theory, since it put to work Italian knowledge and ability. The failure of the principle in practice was due to the fact that certain fields, because of lack of knowledge, were overstaffed while other vital areas of activity were understaffed. Public safety was thought, at the beginning, to be the chief problem in a fascist, and consequently, hostile country. There were many public safety officers, with good training, assigned to this job. Certain basic activities for developing a new democracy were neglected: education, labor, and epuration (elimination of Fascists). Other fundamental areas of government were also overlooked and understaffed: rationing, transport, and food control. These were fields, too, where Italians were inadequate and where fascist controls had broken down. In other older agencies like public health, welfare, finance, and public works, Italians were adequate. In these fields adequate Allied personnel also existed. However, the realization of faulty planning and of Fascist governmental bankruptcy in certain important fields came so late to higher headquarters that alternative methods of government became impossible. Indirect rule had to be more emphasized in some Italian agencies and less stressed in others. In desperation, without policy or knowledge, AMG fell into the error of leaving

Italian political life free and undirected, after twenty years of civic slavery, and imposing vast tasks upon all levels of those parts of Fascist administration which were powerless, through lack of ability and training, to act. At points where Italians needed skills, specific help, and close supervision from capable and numerous Allied specialists, they received vague directives and advice from officers unqualified to devise or advise. In those administrations where Italians were experienced and informed, they were often subjected daily to persistent and carping nagging because their methods, long tested on the Italian scene, were different from Allied ones.

Elimination of Fascists

The simple chronology of the epuration in Italy illustrates abundantly the inability of the Allies to buttress declarations of high principles with workable administrative techniques designed to give body and substance to lofty intentions. The goal was the clearest of all AMG objectives: the total elimination of Fascism from Italian life and the removal of Fascists from positions of economic influence and power and from all levels of government. The statement of this crucial doctrine was simple. Actual epuration, however, involved exact knowledge of the complex relationship of Fascism to economic life and to government, Italian psychology, the impact of Fascism upon public morality, the influence of politics on a drastic and uncompromising program, and the administrative effects of stringent action upon the feasibility of indirect rule. Intelligent appraisal of these considerations should have been made before the basic policy was announced to the world. Basic policy should have been molded to administrative, psychological, and political realities and given definite form before the Allies landed. Instead, epuration languished as the administrative responsibility of no single agency or individual at Allied Control Headquarters for more than a year after the occupation of Sicily; during this period no directive was ever issued establishing a complete and orderly procedure for epuration.

General Alexander, through Proclamation 7, issued in July, 1943, dissolved the Fascist party and organizations affiliated with the party and provided for the disposition of Fascist property through AMG channels. Former top governmental officials were automatically dismissed by AMG, and new officials were appointed after screening by individual officers in charge of special activities like education, finance, or welfare. Prefects, mayors, and local officials were screened by provincial and local civil affairs officers. No detailed or comprehensive written rules existed to guide AMG officers. Screening, in the hands of busy men during the early days of greatest activity and confusion, was necessarily slipshod and based on hearsay rather than facts, which were difficult to obtain. Months after D day, AMGHQ in Sicily finally set a single officer upon the preparation of a personnel questionnaire, to be filled out by all governmental officials and designed to detect the Fascist culpability of individuals. Not until December 2, 1943, was a memorandum issued in Sicily stating in detail how AMG and civilian administration employees were to be examined and calling for completed personnel questionnaires (*schede personali*). Although AMG landed with printed proclamations abolishing Fascism, it had no *schede* for detecting Fascists until this late date.

AMG officers entered Naples on October 1, 1943. On December 20, 1943, a very general order was sent from regional headquarters to Naples, Benevento, and Avellino provinces directing the dismissal from public office of persons falling into four high Fascist categories (*squadristi, marcia su Roma, sciarpa littorio,* and *gerarchi*) and other Fascists guilty of attacks against personal liberties. The order was short and generic, a simple statement, making no provisions for administration, methods of appeal, or the handling of doubtful cases. This AMG order was followed by the Royal Decree Law of December 28, 1943, 29/B, which specified the categories to be purged and prescribed the administrative machinery for handling cases at different civil service grades both at state and provincial levels. This decree was to apply to King's Italy, and recognized the complexities of the epuration program. The decree foreshadowed, too, Italian reaction to severity of application with which AMG unsuccessfully had to cope later. Although at the time it was thought that this attitude was limited to the government of Badoglio, this proved a naïve judgment.

On January 1, 1944, the Regional Commissioner of the Naples Area issued an order for prefects to communicate with all department heads. Weeks were spent in an attempt to write a satisfactory directive. Epuration by flight in all directions rather than by system was the rule. Those who lived in King's Italy were suspended or dismissed from jobs under one set of laws and decrees; those who lived under Allied rule lost their livelihood under other laws and decrees.

Five weeks later came a regional order elaborating a plan for the careful and orderly elimination of Fascists from public life. Issurance of local orders was requested in March from Allied Control Headquarters but was delayed until Allied Control Headquarters could draw up an order for all AMG territory.

Almost a year after D day a conference met to discuss alternative methods, but meanwhile the Italian government was growing impatient of AMG indecision. Italian political opinion demanded action, and by various royal decrees the epuration process was speeded.

On June 2, 1944, the Regional Commissioner of Region 3, in final desperation over delay at Allied Control Headquarters, issued Administrative Order 3, the first detailed and inclusive epuration decree published in AMG territory. Other epuration orders issued later were based on this model.

The various formulas for ridding Italy of Fascism—some with King's Italy, some with AMG, and some with army labels—operated simultaneously within a small radius of each other in the minor portion of the Italian peninsula liberated from dictatorship.

With the issuance of the Sforza law (Royal Decree 159), the first Italian law to deal comprehensively with all phases of Fascist activities, concrete anti-Fascist provisions were decreed. No AMG decrees were as inclusive. At long last, in Italian territory, total and consistent administration of all phases of epuration was possible. AMG decrees, known as the Poletti epuration laws, were directed toward the purging of administrative or governmental agencies. These decrees listed 33 Fascist categories and later others were added. That part of the Sforza law which paralleled the Poletti decrees was not as rigid as the Poletti laws, and proof of Fascist activity was more difficult to establish.

When the north was liberated in the spring of 1945, the problem of epuration was at last handled uniformly through General Order 35, which listed specific categories and provided for provincial commissions and the filing of *schede personali* by all governmental officials. This Allied Control order followed the Italian law and made possible the orderly shifting of the administration of epuration from AMG to Italian government supervision. By May 21, 1945, the epuration commission of Milan was at work.

Since the north was the last place of refuge for Fascists and harbored the last-ditch Republican Fascists as well, the problem of epuration was intensified. For about a month after the liberation of the north, the Patriots handled the worst Fascists, torturers, and collaborationists by quick and effective methods. As soon as order was re-established, a sufficient police force was available, and AMG had established its unquestioned authority, special courts of assize were set up to handle the worst cases for which death or long prison sentences were necessary.

In southern and central Italy, the problem of dealing with private commercial and industrial agencies had never been acute. In the north it became necessary to displace badly compromised industrial and commercial heads of firms with special temporary commissioners. Later, through General Order 46, drafted by the Regional commissioner of Lombardy and a representative of the Italian government and issued by Allied Control Headquarters, an orderly procedure for the epuration of private industry was established. In each firm, a commission of three was appointed by the provincial epuration commission created by General Order 35. Methods of appeal were explicitly described.

By spring, 1945, 120 auxiliary decrees had been added to Royal Decree 159. Of 4,600 cases investigated for possible punishment for Fascist crimes and acts of violence, 4,398 were sent to trial. The high court tried 22 cases and found 16 guilty. Of 4,400 cases involving recovery of wealth obtained corruptly, 1,300 were prepared for hearing and 554 orders were issued sequestering property. By April 1,

1945, in liberated Italy, some 300 hearing commissions had been appointed for the epuration of state and nonstate organizations. Of 485,741 state and nonstate employees on the books, 165,254 had been investigated, and 26,331 referred to hearing commissions. The commissions disposed of 11,102 cases; 2,330 were dismissed or retired, and 4,831 given lesser punishments. Of 98 prefects of liberated provinces investigated, 34 were sent to trial, 6 dismissed, and 16 punished. However, the people of the liberated provinces would not countenance the continuance of these prefects in their territory, and those found not guilty by the Italian government had to be transferred elsewhere.

After the proclamation of the Italian Republic in June, 1946, a general political amnesty was announced. Persons dismissed for former Fascist activity would not lose pension rights, and leniency would be shown to those not too flagrantly compromised. This action was consistent with the victory of the Christian Democrats and the widespread inclination of Italians in political life, as evidenced by Croce earlier, and later in the Sforza decrees, not to deal with former Fascists too harshly. With few exceptions, most of the men in Italian politics today had not been in exile during Fascism but had lived on and not too badly in Italy during Mussolini's regime. Understandably, most of them were compromised in varying degrees with Fascists and Fascism. Anti-Fascists, if not too actively hostile to the regime, usually had a powerfully placed Fascist to whom they could turn for help when needed. During the Partisan movement of the North, many Fascist officials, gambling both ways, aided the Patriots. Italians are realistic. When they sit in the cabinet, on epuration commissions, on special courts of assize, or on departmental committees, and are called upon to judge a former Fascist, they must consciously think: "There, but for the grace of God, go I." No one can keep alive in a fascist country for twenty years without compromise. From the beginning of the feeble Allied attempts to impose a stringent epuration program upon Italy, Italians resisted the effort. Better than the victors they knew what could be done and what could not.

Political Activity

Like the story of epuration, the story of political activity in Italy indicates that without clear, constructive policies and without enough able administrators, allied military government was unable to accomplish the democratic reconstruction it wished. At the same time this story does show that there were times when the allies helped the Italians redevelop their free political activities and in the long run did not suppress them.

Italian habits of logical political thinking, coupled with deep and violent feelings about intellectual matters, have led to the pluralism of Italian politics. This phenomenon does not represent political immaturity, excessive individualism, or lack of civic responsibility. It reflects the nature of the Italian intellectual enjoyment of fine distinctions, logical if heated discussion, loyalty to local rather than to national institutions, and a peculiar bent for compromising in deeds but not in thought.

Ironically enough, Allied officers—career military men, lawyers, engineers, physicians, finance experts, and other specialists, with that characteristic distaste for politics which these groups share in England and the United States—were placed in positions of authority to determine in many indirect ways the political activities and future of Italy. The very men who regarded politics at home as an unsavory activity, better left to those unsuccessful in the business world or professions, were expected to understand Italian political life, in which is to be found the best talent of the nation. As a result, none of the Allied agencies—the Army High Command, the Allied Commission, most regional headquarters, or the representatives of the State Department and the Foreign Office—ever came to comprehend or feel from within the purposes and exigencies of Italian political affairs, nor were they ever able to present realistic and unbiased information on political trends for the guidance of Washington and London.

The six-party system of Italy which existed during the Occupation (reading from left to right: Communist, Socialist, Action, Democracy of Labor, Christian Democrat, and Liberal) was constructed in Bari, in January, 1944. Because no national elections were possible with the greater part of Italy still under German control and the relative strengths of the parties consequently unknown, each party agreed to treat the other five as equal in authority. These six parties were the constituent elements of the various provincial and regional committees of liberation formed later throughout Italy. They were also the parties of the future national committee of liberation and of the national coalition government.

Actually, after years of political enslavement, the parties lacked mass support, especially during the early days of liberation. Each grew to be, quite naturally, an organizing committee for the principles it advocated, hoping that in time those who came to adhere to the tenets of the party would help to form a nation-wide organization of influence. For twenty months, the design for political living that started at Bari worked exceptionally well. Despite political crises in Rome, this coalition weathered changes in cabinets and ministers and provided Italy with a government until the national elections in the summer of 1946 could be held.

Some of the underlying difficulties in Italian politics under AMG are perhaps best illustrated in Sicily. Sicily, preponderantly agricultural, showed little interest in normal politics. The independent-Sicily movement under Finocchiaro Aprile antedated the occupation of the Allies and sprang from the hatred of Sicilians for Rome, which neither under the democratic kingdom nor under Mussolini had done more than promise to alleviate Sicily's poverty, illiteracy, and social retardation. As conditions on the island grew worse when the Allies withdrew and Sicily became part of King's Italy, mass support for independence strengthened. Financial support did not, however, come from the masses, who were unaware of the complexities of the movement. The large landowners feared Rome because they feared an eventual socialist government. The signs of the times were visible even in Sicily. The Communists, the Socialists, and the liberal wing of the Demo-Christians were, of course, opposed to independence on economic and social as well as on political grounds. They showed statistically that the central government, even in normal times, had made up the budget deficit, for Sicily, despite Aprile's assertions, had never been self-sufficient in foods or manufactured products. They

agreed that the national government would have to raise the standard
of living in Sicily by providing more roads, schools, scientific agriculture, and industrialization.

Because military government's regional commissioner in Sicily had
been an administrator and politician of considerable experience in
the United States, he understood the psychological and economic
motivations of the independence movement and sought to disarm
them through an administrative device of the greatest significance for
the future of Italy: the creation of Sicilian regional government. The
Italian prefect of Palermo, a Socialist protégé of the great Orlando
and a lawyer of extraordinary capacity and integrity who had never
joined the Fascist party, was made High Commissioner of Sicily. He
chose anti-Fascists of recognized ability to act as regional health, welfare, commerce, supply, public works, labor, and agricultural administrators. Prefects having over-all administrative problems to discuss, instead of having to go to Rome for decisions as they normally
did (and this was impossible physically, given the military situation),
could consult with the high commissioner, who had authority from
AMG to act. An Italian provincial health administrator could obtain
similar action from the head of the regional health office. Fundamental policy decisions could be discussed with the high commissioner who, in turn, looked to the Allied regional commissioner for
guidance. Not only was uniform policy established and the possibility
of rapid decisions ensured, but Sicilians came gradually to be aware
of Sicilian administrative autonomy and to be proud of it. The fact
that the provinces no longer had to wait many weeks for Rome's
decision removed the psychological block of depending upon and
resenting the central government. If independence was to be discouraged, local responsibility and pride had to be created.

When Sicily was returned to the central government early in 1944,
only the form of the high commissioner was retained. Old civil
servants, plodding their appointed way through set tasks, could not
have been expected to understand the subtleties of political administration. Soon the provincial health administrator found that he had
to deal with the Ministry of the Interior directly and that time was
wasted as before. The Sicilian regional health administrator found

himself thwarted. The top cabinet members in Rome, and Badoglio as well as Bonomi, were too engrossed in political maneuvers to understand the importance not only for Sicily, but also for other regions in Italy, of some degree of real regional autonomy and the administrative reforms implied. Unrest in Sicily mounted, open riots quelled by *carabinieri* increased, Aprile grew to the stature of a prophet, and finally the cabinet, in desperation, and as a sop, appropriated hundreds of millions of lire for public works and reconstruction in Sicily, forgetting the historic and psychological bases of the movement. Aprile was chosen by the Sicilians in June, 1946, as one of Sicily's representatives in the Constituent Assembly.

In Naples, the regional commissioner who succeeded the original head of civil affairs in February, 1944, began dealing immediately with the committee of liberation composed of the six parties. From the committee, under the chairmanship of a highly respected Neapolitan lawyer and Socialist who is married to an American, came lists of potential candidates for public offices. From the committee, too, came the first draft of the epuration laws which were finally approved by the Allied Commission and made into law by the Italian government. The policy of seeking the political advice of the committee, of asking its guidance in the selection of worthy and able anti-Fascists for public office, ensured Italian cooperation with the men whom the Allies selected and placed responsibility for administration upon the parties which had had a voice in the selection of the directing official. This pattern of consultation continued throughout Italy as other regions were liberated and was extended to the provinces and the communes wherever local committees of liberation could be found.

The parties in Naples also disclosed to discerning AMG officers what political compromise on a large scale could mean and how much the parties of the left, dependent upon leaders who had spent many years in exile, had still to learn in the conference room. Before reaching Naples, Badoglio's cabinet represented only his own personal choices. With the occupation of the Campania region, it became necessary to enlarge the government. But Prime Minister Churchill had remarked to the House of Commons on February 22, 1944, that a more representative government would come after the liberation of

Rome. In protest, the six parties planned a ten-minute work stoppage for March 4. Time lost was to be made up by fifteen minutes of work at the end of the day. A shivering ACHQ forbade the strike on the superficial grounds of its interfering with the war effort and compromised, it thought shrewdly, by allowing a tremendous mass meeting on March 12 in the Galleria. The Communists, Socialists, and some leaders of the liberal wing of the Demo-Christians had at first insisted that they would never become members of a government under the old king, who had betrayed the country and bartered with Mussolini to save his throne. They were loud in their declarations, especially the Communists and Socialists, that they could be true neither to their own consciences, principles, and followers, nor to the democracies of the world in accepting the discredited monarch. These statements were widely publicized. The private views of the Communist leaders were even more uncompromising. Then Soviet Russia recognized the Badoglio government on March 14. Next, Palmiro Togliatti, the present leader of the Communists in Italy, who had been in exile in Russia for many years, was flown back to Italy with the consent of the Allies on March 26. The party line shifted completely on April 1, leaving both the second-line Communist leaders, the Socialists, and the liberal Demo-Christians considerably embarrassed. The Socialists, still living in the shame of twenty years earlier, when their failure to cooperate with the Communists resulted in the ascendancy of Mussolini, like many other Italians confused the strength of the Italian Communists with the demonstrated strength of the Red Army. Instead of having the political sagacity to place the Communists in an untenable position—an incongruous government of the old king, Badoglio, and the Communists—where they would have been laughed out of office by Italy and the outside world, they chose on April 6 to accept the king with the proviso that he would step down in favor of his son when the Allies entered Rome. On April 12 the king announced his intention of complying with the proviso. A new cabinet still under Badoglio, including representatives of the six parties, met for the first time on April 27, 1944, and stated that they would all work for the war effort and postpone the institutional question until the end of the war.

This entire episode demonstrated that the parties to the left had considerably less political skill and wisdom than the more conservative parties, that the Communist party of Italy would respond to signals from Moscow, and that none of the parties had a clear knowledge of the actual sentiments of the people. The disgust of most Italians, even in the southern and most conservative part of Italy, with the House of Savoy was a fact that neither high-ranking Allied officers nor most Italian politicians in power would recognize. Not until the Demo-Christians in party convention rejected the monarchy by a three-to-one vote in May, 1946, was this truth finally conceded. The seemingly strong monarchist vote in southern Italy and Sicily represented the cumulative resentment of neglected regions against Rome more than any intense feeling of loyalty to the House of Savoy or to the Crown Prince, or even to the idea of monarchy.

To politically astute AMG officers, and to most Italians, the fall of Rome meant the fall of Badoglio. He had served Mussolini well. On the façade of his Roman house, presented to him by the grateful Duce, were emblazoned the words, for all Rome and the world to see, that he, Badoglio, at the head of his troops, had entered Addis Ababa. This record in stone was a quotation from his telegram to Mussolini signaling the arrival of Fascism in the imperialist world. But after the surrender of Rome Badoglio was retained. Badoglio was charming, educated, and shrewd. Thanks perhaps to his peasant background his love of tangible property was so strong that he could easily shift his allegiance to those who could protect or augment it. With specific instructions to retain Badoglio, Lieutenant General Noel Mason Mac-Farlane, the Chief Commissioner of the Allied Council, and the most able head that that confused Allied body ever had, proceeded to Rome with Badoglio on June 8, 1944. Badoglio had resigned his government and had actually hoped to form a new one including the Roman parties. General MacFarlane, who knew the realities of the political scene and recognized impossibilities, yielded to the inevitable, and a new government under Ivanoe Bonomi, a former prime minister of democratic days and chairman of the Rome committee of liberation, was accepted by the Allies. On June 22, General MacFarlane, who had carried on his heavy duties despite a serious illness, went back to England to undergo a difficult operation and a long convalescence. The liberation of Rome and the negotiations with Badoglio and the Allies freed Italians from any remaining illusions that Allied democracy was in any way connected with political liberalism or ideals.

During the six weeks between Mussolini's fall on July 25, 1943, and the surrender of Italy on September 8, 1943, every anti-Fascist in the country exposed himself. Throughout Italy, the people, under the new anti-Fascist leaders, were rallying. Then, in the period of Allied hesitation, the Germans swept down the peninsula. In some cities, all anti-Fascist leaders were destroyed. In Rome, a reign of SS and Gestapo terror began. The Italian film, *The Open City,* made a few months after Rome was freed, and later shown in the United States, is the simple, stirring record, almost documentary in its objectivity, of the life of a resisting city under the Nazis.

Now began for all of German-occupied Italy a trial by Allied bombing and fire and Nazi brutality and torture. In this period was born —for Italy north of Rome, and especially north of Bologna, where Fascism had been conceived and organized—the true liberation of Italy by the Italians themselves. The Patriot movement—in which exiles returned from foreign hiding, army officers, former Fascists, young intellectuals, bankers, and manufacturers fought and worked together—grew into one of the noblest resistance movements in Europe, a movement that freed every important city in north Italy once the Allied troops had taken Bologna. The entire population resisted. Max Ascoli describes this total revolution: "There were industrialists in the north who paid their workers to go on anti-Fascist strikes or commit acts of sabotage. The agents for the financing of the resistance were the two great commercial banks. In Rome, the most accomplished forger of identification papers and ration cards was a Monsignore. In the same city, two thousand British soldiers who had escaped from prison camps were hidden by the people for months."[1]

Before May, 1945, when the entire country was freed, the committee of liberation of north Italy, CLNAI, achieved, for a six-party coalition, remarkable unity. The president was Longhi (his underground name), a nonparty member, an independent. Alfredo Pizzoni (his

[1] Max Ascoli, "Politics in Italy," *Free World*, II, No. 1 (January, 1946), p. 19.

real name) is now president of the Credito Italiano, the largest commercial bank of north Italy. His great ability helped to finance the resistance. He and the future prime minister, Parri, known as Maurizio to the underground, had made several dangerous clandestine trips to Rome and Caserta to obtain money for the Patriots. Longhi received millions of lire from General Alexander, every penny of which was accounted for. In Rome, the man who was to be the regional commissioner of Lombardy had the opportunity to consult with Pizzoni, Parri, and Arpesani, a Liberal and later vice-premier under Parri, to discover the state of conditions in the north, and to make specific plans for administration once the Germans were driven out. Arpesani, on the other hand, learned the Allied administrative division of work, and CLNAI then reordered its affairs to conform with Allied health, commerce, industry, labor, finance, public works, and public welfare arrangements so that all activities could be coordinated.

But, characteristically, the unity of the resistance did not last long after freedom. Ostensibly because he belonged to no party, but actually because the Communists and Socialists wished to consolidate power, Pizzoni was ousted as head. Thus the familiar pattern developed: wrangling among the parties of the committee, war within each party over principles and personalities, and the inevitable campaigns for party membership.

Throughout the regions of Genoa, Milan, Venice, and Bologna, the people were saying that the Wind of the North (CLNAI) would wipe Rome clean, that a government of the people would at last be formed, that the sacrifices of the resistance would be reflected now, at long last, in the very heart of administration. But the Patriot politicians, brilliant at underground sabotage and united by necessity, did not count on the political sagacity of the southern politicians in Rome. Instead of insisting, when their prestige was at its height, that the government in Rome come to Milan to enter into negotiations for its widening, they chose to go to Rome. They went disunited and without precise plans for action and demands. Weeks dragged on, with Bonomi's nonrepresentative government still in power and the north in political turmoil. Italy's unsolved administrative, economic, and social problems deteriorated. Finally, Parri, representing the Action party, was named prime minister, with many of the old ministers continued in office, and with most of the parties and their heads supporting him as the least of evils. In the meantime, Socialist Nenni, Communist Togliatti, Demo-Christian de Gasperi, and the monarchist Liberals continued their public game of playing up the strength of their respective parties, as yet undetermined by the people, beyond the influence each would properly have once the elections were held.

In Rome, Parri worked too long, sleeping at his office, absorbed in administrative details, forgetting the fences which needed repair, speaking out with his St. Francis-like candor when he promised the Italians nothing but hard work and little bread, refusing to picture Italy as anything but a wrecked country completely dependent for life upon Allied good will. His aides, too few of them, were new to administration, ignorant of the skills demanded of them, dependent upon civil servants who were largely unsympathetic to the government's program and unsure of the direction that future governments might take. In those circumstances, ineptitude and procrastination combined to make effective administration impossible. The Allies, in turn, naïvely insisting upon complete political liberty for the Italians in combination with strict administrative control, were scornful of Italian inefficiency, forgetful of their own less justified administrative and economic failures, and blind to the fundamental proposition that politics and administration cannot be divorced. The Parri government, sabotaged by Italians and Allies alike, fell in the autumn of 1945 and was replaced by a government of Alcide de Gasperi, Parri's Demo-Christian foreign minister. The other ministers were largely carry-overs. Parri's Action party, a small, but intellectually influential one, split asunder.

The consultative assembly that met in Rome in the fall of 1945, though not chosen popularly, in the absence of elections, afforded Italian political leaders a chance to function under the rules of parliamentary procedure after twenty years of rustiness. As a gesture against British interference in Italian politics, Count Sforza, who had engaged in a public dispute with Churchill, was elected president. Although the assembly had no real powers, it could make suggestions to the government, which would have to give some thought to its proposals since it represented a wide segment of party and public opinion.

Gradually, Italians acquired a new political experience in local and regional party activity, in provincial and national administrative offices, in the cabinet, and in the consultative assembly. If the Allies made no real contribution to Italian political life, at least they did not stifle completely Italian efforts to learn by blundering, a process certainly familiar to democracy in the United States.

Economic Problems

AMG control was more obvious in Italian economic than political life. That the Allied Commission had regulations in most important fields of economic life the following summary will indicate.

Even before Allied troops landed in Sicily, propaganda to the Italians had announced that surrender would result in better feeding. Since the Germans had not concerned themselves about feeding Italy, this was an important promise that should have been kept. But unfortunately supply and propaganda agencies were not coordinated. Although Churchill and Roosevelt promised the Italians food, the army refused to schedule an initial shipload for Sicily. When supplies did arrive they were generally inadequate. Not until the breakthrough at Cassino did military government learn to plan movement of civilian supplies as part of military operations.

The sheer size of the job of civilian supply was undoubtedly underestimated by military government as well as by propagandists. The task was huge. In the spring of 1945 before the final campaign in north Italy, 24,000,000 people in the least productive part of Italy had to be fed. More than 2,500,000 tons of all sorts of supplies, worth $300,000,000, had been imported. This figure included 1,000,000 tons of wheat and flour.

Distribution of this great quantity of supplies was the first great problem and the first great object lesson of military government supply officers. As soon as the first foodstuffs had arrived at the port of Naples, military government ordered them shipped out to communes by American army trucks. Army truck drivers misunderstood orders, or deliberately disobeyed them, and sold to black marketeers—with the result that one third of the first shipments in the Naples area did not reach its destination. Military government was not a very successful wholesale grocer.

Recognizing the evil, if not the source of it, Allied Commission, in the winter of 1943–1944, took fairly vigorous steps. It set up AMG warehouses and staffed and even guarded them with AMG officers. Supply accounting staffs were established to follow up on the sale of supplies to Italian communes.

But the real answer was not in AMG warehouses. It was Italian control. After the breakthrough at Cassino and the occupation of the Rome area, the regional staffs at Rome developed new methods of turning foodstuffs and supplies over to Italian civilian authorities immediately. This method made the Italians responsible for losses, relieved AMG of detailed responsibilities of guarding and accounting, and provided an excellent opportunity for schooling Italian local officials in administration.

Second in importance to foodstuffs in Allied imports were petroleum supplies, essential for vital transportation needs. By April, 1945, 90,000,000 gallons of gasoline and oils had been imported for the Italians. Imports of "POL" (petroleum, oils, and lubricants) were turned over to the *Comitato Italiana Petrolio,* an organization made up out of the remnants of Italian privately owned oil companies by the Petroleum Section of AFHQ. CIP representatives worked closely with military government supply officers and were the primary instrument for carrying out the rationing of petroleum supplies ordered by AMG. They also assumed the financial responsibility for supplies issued to them from army petroleum distribution points.

The development of civilian agencies for receiving Allied imports did not mean that civilian supplies were not closely controlled by AMG orders. Allied Commission and subordinate AMG units issued regulations prescribing in detail rations for normal civilians, for heavy workers, for army workers, for guards, for hospitals, and so on. Special attention was even paid to the amount of food to be retained by farmers.

The desirability of entering into this close degree of control of smaller aspects of a conquered nation's economy is open to question. If military government officers are tied down by a mass of detail, smothering Italian agencies with petty regulations, and trying to supervise Italian habits that they cannot understand, the disadvantages are obvious. On the other hand, the necessity of importing these supplies gave the Allies a legitimate concern over whether the Italians used them carefully.

AMG at no time "spoiled" the Italians. There were never as many as 1,000 calories a day on the ration card, and often there were many less. This low level was only partially offset by the large Italian consumption of fruits and vegetables (which were not rationed) and the extensive black market. Other distributions were also minimal. Clothing was never allocated in quantities adequate for any substantial group of the population. Petroleum products were allocated on a basis which allowed doctors with large cars only fifteen gallons a month. The Allies tried to be generous with the Italians but their generosity was not overwhelming.

The AMG record on price control was far less distinguished than that on supply. This important feature of any wartime scarcity economy was especially essential in poverty-stricken Italy, where several years of war had left a complete dearth of raw or manufactured materials. The situation was sufficiently bad so that probably no Allied measures could have prevented a substantial amount of inflation. Yet a prompter and more effective price control policy and a more generous currency policy on the part of AMG would have greatly reduced the size of the present Italian inflation.

The administrative record of AMG on price control was shockingly ineffective. Although prices had been controlled fairly well by the Fascists, and the Italians were more or less accustomed to the idea of control, AMG started off with an early Victorian scorn for this interference with laissez faire. In Naples, no prices were posted and no discernible effort was made to control prices until the area had been occupied for about three months. There was a general provision in military government regulations that prices and wages were to be frozen as of the level at the time of occupation, but for months no effort was made to put administrative pressure behind it. The first price list that appeared in Naples was one on semiluxury articles imposed at the insistence of military authorities for the protection of troops. Stores were declared off limits or were closed for failure to comply with this regulation. The stores then went under cover on such materials.

In the winter of 1943–1944, the Allied Control Commission began to realize the dangers of the situation and, under prodding from AFHQ and Washington, appointed an anti-inflation committee. A subcommittee of the latter recommended stricter enforcement of prices and a price control committee. The latter recommendation was administratively naïve. Effective staff supervision of as difficult a problem as price control in as lax an organization as ACC could come only by appointing some vigorous, high-ranking officer for that job alone.

After the price control committee was appointed, its staff consisted of one or two low-ranking officers or administratively ineffective civilians from the United States. No effective staff supervision on price control was ever given to the regions or the army AMG's. In spite of a statement sent out about a price control office to be established in the Italian government, no very effective help was given to that office by ACC. As late as early 1945, it was very difficult, if not impossible, for an army or a regional AMG to find out what the legal price was on any particular item.

With such ineffective operation from the central point of policy making, it was improbable that the regional units in the AMG hierarchy would accomplish any more. Price control must, by its very nature, be a centralized operation. Without central support, most regional units did not even have a man designated as the price control officer.[2]

The army AMG's, who were in a key position to start Allied occupation of new territory with a policy of price control, had diametrically opposite policies. The Eighth Army made a genuine effort to

[2]Regions III and IV under Colonel Poletti were exceptions. Some of the regional commissioners believed that the Manchester economics they had learned at the university in the early 1900's were applicable to wartime Italy, and no staff officer in the commission knew enough or was forceful enough to set them straight.

secure enforcement of a schedule it had prepared, but the Fifth Army paid almost no attention to prices until it reached Florence. Since the Fifth Army initially occupied the populous western cities, its laissez-faire policy gave inflation a tremendous impetus.

This basic failure to place administrative controls on prices was doubly unfortunate since the rate of exchange set for the Italian lira (100 to the dollar) represented a sharp drop over its preceding value and led many Italians to think that inflation was intended. Shopkeepers often quadrupled their prices, on the ground that the lira was now at one fourth of its former value. Financial experts could easily justify the 100-lira exchange rate on the ground that it was a higher value than Italy could subsequently support. This argument was valid, as the subsequent further devaluation indicated. But the experts overlooked the tremendous effect of an occupation currency paid to a large occupation army in a country short of supplies. American private soldiers could draw and spend in Italy as much money as an Italian prefect received. The British and Canadian armies wisely withheld portions of the pay of their officers and men, but the American army made no such move. After a time, Italian restaurants were declared off limits, but there were many other ways in which American troops could inflate the Italian economy with their wads of occupation currency.

Italian police, in general miserably paid, in ragged uniforms, often without shoes, and treated contemptuously by American soldiers, would have found it difficult to enforce a sensible price control and currency program. They found it impossible to enforce AMG's policies.

When black markets are once allowed to start on a grand scale, they become almost uncontrollable. Laxity of control in the early days in Naples and southern Italy permitted the development of an underworld machinery almost rivaling that developed in the United States during prohibition days. Prices became so high and the *sub rosa* merchants so well organized that it was not possible to collect in legal channels as much as one half the prewar production of olive oil.

Wage control is, of course, essential to effective price control. Unfortunately, wages shared the unhappy history of prices during AMG operations in Italy. The initial theory of freezing wages was soon disregarded; in fact, American army units led in the raising of wages in the Naples area under the economically naïve theory that they were thus raising the standard of living of Italian workers. Elaborate wage scales were then published for the guidance of employing military units but were frequently disregarded. They seemed to be enforced somewhat more by British army units because of a British audit on military expenditures that included the maximum-wage scale. A curious psychological reasoning that affected the disregard for this scale by American units was the tendency to compare lira wages with standard wages in the United States, with no effort to evaluate the tremendous, obvious difference in over-all living standards.

As a result of rising prices and rising illegal wages, the legal maxima went through two large upward movements. The first was a 70 per cent increase on the lowest incomes and the second was about as large. It is probably fair, however, to say that wage increases never corresponded to price increases. Throughout the entire period of AMG control, the position of the working classes thus declined, though probably not as much as that of the middle classes, whose salaries are fixed.

Attention should be drawn to the immense effect of Allied military units in breaking down price and wage controls. Above-ceiling prices and wages were paid regularly by American units and often by British units. There were half-hearted efforts on the part of American and British staff units to secure some degree of compliance with price and wage orders, which had, of course, been regularly issued to troops. But the armies were basically uninterested in such economic problems, and staff enforcement was poor.

Agricultural experience in AMG illustrates the advantage of securing people of governmental experience to undertake to solve governmental problems. A number of officers, most of whom had had experience with agricultural administrative work in the United States or England, did a constructive job of eliminating Fascists from agricultural agencies, foreseeing the farmers' needs, and trying to secure necessary materials. Although there were competent agricultural technicians among the Italians, the services of this AMG group seemed to be generally appreciated. Perhaps the knowledge of indirect administrative control techniques learned in American agricultural administration helped these officers to understand the indirect control techniques needed in military government.

A few examples will illustrate the achievements of this group. In 1944 a harvest of 9,000,000 quintals (a quintal is approximately $3\frac{2}{3}$ bushels) of wheat had been collected in freed Italy. In 1945 collections south of the Rimini line were over 11,000,000 quintals. Grain collections were far from complete, but averaged far better than under the Fascists. Fisheries were re-established promptly enough to bring in 30,000 tons in the year 1945. With Allied help the Italians produced 13,500 tons of sugar in the same year.

Just as the mistakes listed in the preceding sections were a result of the weakness of AMG in economic personnel, the splendid record in restoring engineering facilities indicates the strength of Allied armies in technical matters. Both armies were, of course, anxious to restore essential facilities for purely military reasons of transportation, communication, and health. To a limited extent they competed with essential civilian services for scarce materials. But army engineers were generous in reconstructing some bridge, roadway, or power line of primarily civilian and but secondarily of military importance.

Taken in combination, the efforts of AMG and the armies to restore public facilities were one of the bright spots in the Allied record in Italy. All main-line roads were opened and kept open immediately after the Germans were driven out. Although the British had to take up their Bailey bridges on some side roads in order to use them again farther north, this removal was made only after clearing with AMG as to civilian use. Certain main arteries to the front had to be closed to civilian traffic in army areas but army AMG trucks were permitted to use these roads to carry supplies to civilian areas in critical need. As soon as military necessity permitted, the roads were opened to civilian traffic again. In spite of the Germans' thorough demolition program, railroads were miraculously restored by a clever use of secondary routes, and tonnage was made available for civilian lighting, flour milling, and other essential purposes.

A few more specific examples may be enlightening. In Sicily a year after the Allied arrival, all railroad bridges, important highways, and other public works were restored. Another remarkable achievement was the restoration of parts of the Terni and Tivoli power plants within a year. Since army engineers lose interest in areas they are vacating, AMG officers found part of their usefulness in arranging for continuity between army reconstruction projects and subsequent civilian projects. Frequently the same contractor and the same fiscal arrangements continued—an arrangement somewhat simplified by the fact that all reconstruction was charged to the Italian government.

The other main task of the AMG public works officers was, of course, to reorganize and epurate Italian public works agencies and to stimulate and help them to the task of reconstruction. A main task was to help them find essential materials and tools. The requisitioning of supplies by the *Wehrmacht* and later by Allied armies frequently left major shortages which could be solved only by issues from Allied armies or, even though it involved the same problem of material shortages, by starting industries to work.

At first, AMG paid relatively little attention to the revival of Italian industry, presumably because it was not related to "military necessity." When, however, the Allied Control Commission came into authority in early 1943, and it became apparent that AMG was in Italy for a long stay, the necessity of doing something about Italian industry became apparent. Existing stocks would not provide 45,000,000 Italians with such everyday necessities as matches, clothing, or kitchen utensils. There was not the faintest chance that Italy could pay for the imports of such items (or of foodstuffs) if she did not make something out of her industries. As a result, senior officers who began operations in Italy with an unsympathetic attitude toward the inhabitants slowly came around to the conclusion that the wheels of industry must be started.

This conclusion led only to more difficulties. Despite the substantial development of her hydroelectric power facilities, Italian industry was based on the use of imported coal. Aside from some poor lignite deposits and some low-grade Sardinian coal, Italy had no coal. But importation of coal was long delayed, and when it did arrive it was frequently adequate only for Allied troops and such vital civilian purposes as hospitals.

Other raw materials were in equally short supply. There was, for example, no cotton for the textile plants of northern Italy until very recently. Where materials could be found, they were frequently tied up for possible military use by the requisitioning process described in later paragraphs. Or it proved impossible to transport them to the few factories that had not been requisitioned by troop units for repair of equipment or other military purposes requiring tools and equipment.

Hence it was clear that cessation of military occupation was necessary before substantial progress could be expected. What advances were made were slow and painful. For example, it took Allied Commission eight months to send to Washington a requisition for raw materials for a vitally important civil-military plant. The new French government prepared a requisition for the same materials for a similar plant in two months. In 1945 a $100,000,000 credit was granted to Italy for American materials. Ostensibly, this was recompense for the pay of American soldiers in occupation lira. Actually, it was, of course, response to the sympathy for Italy in America.

Allied Control Commission was so occupied in preparing its own brand of militarized controls on the Italian economy that it did not have much time to concern itself with the removal of the remnants of the Fascist "corporate" system. Actually, there was not much to worry about. Most of the corporations had existed only on paper or in small ineffectual offices. The few which had operated went out of business very rapidly. In conjunction with the Italian government, decrees were prepared to separate the provincial chambers of commerce from the provincial economic control office, but nothing more was necessary.

One of the most difficult problems of military government is the allocation of scarce materials between the armies and the civilian population. The Allies entered Italy with full rights of requisition and a general theory that the rights of their armies and "military necessity" were superior to all other rights. In a few months, however, it became clear that in a poverty-stricken country like Italy, the economic condition of the civilian population was itself of military importance. Disease, starvation, lack of clothing, other wants in the civilian population have an effect on the troops of humanitarian countries like England and the United States which no amount of military regulations can neutralize.

The problem of rationed food supplies was answered with relative ease. Since the Allies were importing foodstuffs for civilians whom everyone knew were hungry, it was obvious and easy to forbid purchase of rationed foodstuffs by military personnel and to place civilian restaurants off limits to military personnel. Both these regulations were usually put into effect and were in general moderately well enforced.

Fresh vegetables and eggs presented a more difficult problem. The ration of the British Army was based on the assumption that there would be a certain sum of expenditures per man-day for fresh food and vegetables. Substantial purchases were made in Italy. Up to August, 1944, the Allied armies had eaten 150,000 tons of fresh foods and 110,000 sheep purchased in Italy.

Although the ration of the American army included canned vegetables, its more opulent messes did not readily abandon the idea of greenstuff, especially in a country like Italy, where vegetables are grown in abundance. Both armies seemed to have a mania for fresh eggs and paid black market prices for them.

Purchases of fresh foodstuffs by smaller messes were never brought under control. The larger purchases for the British army ration were controlled in Army Area largely because of the cooperative relationship of AMG in the Eighth Army structure. Both quantity and price of vegetables purchased by the army were first approved by AMG. No such control was, however, worked out for the rear areas. An Allied Forces Local Resources Section attempted to allocate fresh produce to Italian military units and to hospitals.

More difficult problems were raised over the allocation of scarce metals, building materials, electrical materials, timber, and other materials that were scarce and of immediate importance both to the armies and to the civilian economy. In an effort to balance these competing claims fairly, with full knowledge of demand and supply,

AFHQ Local Resources Section attempted to build up a system. Recognition was given to immediate operational necessity by permitting requisition by units in Army Area. If, however, materials in Army Area were not immediately requisitioned, they, along with materials in rear areas, should be reported to the Local Resources Section of AFHQ. At monthly meetings of a local resources board, such materials were allocated between competing army claims and civilian claims as presented by the Allied Control Commission.

Like all allocation systems, this was logical but difficult to administer. Neither AMG nor military services wished to take time to report materials for ultimate allocation by some distant body in AFHQ. Worth-while reports were received only when local resources officers were sent out from AFHQ and AAI. After the conclusion of hostilities much-needed goods were kept from civilian use for months, except as they filtered into the black market.

Requisitioning procedure was largely handled by the appropriate officers in each army and was important to military government only in three respects:

1) A certain amount of requisitioning had to be done for AMG's own needs. The regulations here were, quite properly, that AMG should requisition only through the authorized army officers.

2) AMG officers needed to know the procedure for payment of requisitions, since they were frequently questioned by Italians on the subject.

3) AMG, with its responsibilities for price control, was concerned as to the prices paid by the armies for requisitioned materials. In general, however, it was not consulted because it had not established price policies and did not possess specific price information. In default of AMG advice, American and British engineers worked out their own price scales on requisitioned building materials.

Results of Allied Military Government in Italy

In terms of the limited objective set by higher headquarters for the first military government officers to land in Sicily, AMG in Italy was an unqualified success. It did help to safeguard military lines of communication. The docility of the Italians, and their predisposition to the Allied cause after the armistice made this maintenance a relatively easy task.

But this first limited objective was an error, as a whole series of later, and belated, directives for the political and economic reconstruction of Italy demonstrated. A process of piecemeal thinking slowly brought the military government staff officers of Mediterranean Theater Headquarters—and of Washington—to a realization that most Americans thought of themselves as fighting a war for democracy in Italy, as well as elsewhere, and that Italian democracy could be restored only by a series of broadly constructive political and economic steps.

Even after the idea of reconstruction had replaced the idea of merely safeguarding military lines of communication, grave difficulties handicapped the higher levels of military government. The planners of AMG in Washington were not men who understood public administration in the United States; moreover, their information about Italy was spotty and unreliable. Hence they evolved in Washington administratively unrealistic plans. The relatively low quality of AMG personnel in higher headquarters in Italy, and the complicated organizational structure of those headquarters made it impossible to work out on-the-spot improvements in Washington's vague and unworkable policies. It is a credit to the sincere, though unqualified, personnel of military government, and to the cooperative attitude of the bewildered Italian officials that much reconstruction was accomplished in spite of the uncertainties of the top policy makers.

Chapter VII

Civil Affairs in France[1]

MERRITT Y. HUGHES

WHATEVER ground in fact there may be for the view that President Roosevelt hesitated to "accept the French Committee *de facto* authority for the civil administration in France," and did so only on condition that "complete authority should be reserved for General Eisenhower to do what he felt necessary to conduct military operations,"[2] there can be no doubt that civil affairs officers in France were governed by the order[3] of the Supreme Commander that "Civil Administration in all areas will be normally controlled by the French themselves."[4] The Third Army went into action with the understanding that "any semblance of military government in France was to be scrupulously avoided, and that the French would resume full civil activity as fast as conditions permitted."[5] In all echelons the spirit and letter of the Supreme Commander's order were felt as corresponding to the use of the official designation "Civil Affairs" rather than that of "Military Government," which was to obtain in Germany. From the first landing on the Norman coast, civil affairs officers were instructed to secure the cooperation of civilian police, transport, and communications authorities without infringing French

[1]The writer served as Field Historian with the Third Army, G-5; hence this chapter deals mainly with Civil Affairs as seen from Third Army Headquarters in the French and Luxembourg areas.

[2]Captain H. C. Butcher, *My Three Years with Eisenhower* (1946), p. 610.

[3]*After-Action Report, Third U.S. Army, 1 Aug. 1944–9, May 1945*, I, 63.

[4]*After-Action Report, Third U.S. Army*, II (G-5 Section), 2.

[5]*Ibid.*

rights or sensibilities, and to keep watch upon themselves to avoid all appearance of usurping the powers of military governors.

Public safety—which required the immediate appointment of reliably patriotic mayors to assist in civilian traffic control—was an urgent challenge to the diplomacy of civil affairs officers in the field. The mayors at first were usually appointed by Allied CAO's in consultation with De Gaulliste liaison officers and they promptly recruited large special police forces, mainly from boys of the *Resistance,* to reinforce the *Gardes Champêtres* and gendarmes in Normandy and Brittany. Recruits were screened by their own authorities and, if possible, by the Counter Intelligence Corps, then equipped with a firearm and a brassard. At first the bulk of recruiting was handled by the local resistance leaders acting with French police officials. Later it was handled by the gendarmery. All told, about eight thousand arm bands were distributed through controlled French channels from Third Army Headquarters, and about that number of auxiliary police was believed to have assisted in the handling of civilian traffic in the army's zone in the first month of its operations, August, 1944.[6]

By that time the authority of the provisional government had made itself felt throughout the liberated areas by the appointment of regional commissioners (*Commissaires Régionaux de la République*), who, under power conferred by the Laws of the State of Siege, had power to appoint and remove officials. The work of their appointees from the first was prevailing effective. "As the Third U.S. Army moved forward, increasing strength and better organization in civil government were found. Orleans and the surrounding area were ably administered."[7] The originally cordial relations with French officials were confirmed on August 25 by the "Revised Directive for Civil Affairs Operations in France," which made civil affairs policies conform with the agreements concluded by the United States and Great Britain with the provisional government and defined the powers of each in the zones of operation. In Lorraine, and particularly in Nancy, where the Third Army had its headquarters from October 1, 1944, to Jan-

[6]See below, page 157, for an account of the effectiveness of the control of civilian traffic on the French roads.

[7]*After-Action Report,* I, 37.

uary 3, 1945, the record of efficiency and cooperation on the part of the French with the American forces was outstanding. In part, the explanation lay in the friendliness of the regional commissioner, M. Chailly-Bert, and the prefect of Meuse-et-Moselle, M. Rébourset, toward the Allies. Both men were members of the medical faculty of the University of Nancy, and M. Rébourset had been an exchange professor at Harvard in 1937. Neither gentleman, however, allowed his friendliness for his liberators to interfere with his championship of French interests in differences of opinion over the billeting of troops, the determination of the claims of the army to fuel of German origin lying still unpaid for in the bins of French industrialists, and other questions arising out of the interest of the United Nations in captured and abandoned enemy property in France.

Abandoned enemy property was often a danger to good relations with the French. It was frequently a question of whether to insist upon the rights of the army under international law or to disappoint troops of the *Forces Françaises de l'Intérieur* or municipal authorities whose need often seemed to them greater than that of the Allies. In mid-August a directive was issued asserting the rights of the United Nations to certain classes of abandoned enemy property, but recognizing French claims to other classes and providing for prompt releases of all classes for French civilian use in emergencies. Some rather fantastic French claims were seriously put forward; in Montargis, for example, where all abandoned enemy property was described as having been officially bestowed upon the municipality by the departing Germans, and at Bar-le-Duc, where the prefect of Meuse insisted upon the claim of civilian hospitals to the beds in a German-equipped military hospital in use by the American forces. In resisting these and many more plausible claims, civil affairs officers usually succeeded in avoiding friction and strengthening their friendship with the French. A still broader foundation for enduring good relations with the French was laid by the traveling "claims teams" which worked out of SHAEF to assist local civil affairs officers in handling all kinds of private demands and grievances against the army or any of its personnel.

The case of the army against French civilians who stole military property or otherwise offended against it proved to be difficult to handle. From the outset the army was clear that it intended to avoid setting up military courts for the trial of civilians and that jurisdiction over them would rest with French tribunals. While the Third Army lay waiting to become operative in Normandy in July, 1944, Colonel Gaspar G. Bacon, Chief Legal Officer at Headquarters, G-5, visited several local courts and encouraged local police judges (*Juges de Simple Police*) in handling minor offenders against the army. In August he officially welcomed the declaration of the Commander of the Tenth (French) Military District, which asserted "the jurisdiction of the French over offenses which concerned the security of the Allied Forces."[8] In consistent practice the right and responsibility of the French courts to try offenders against the army was recognized. Yet until November, 1944, many French authorities were under the impression that the civil courts were under no obligation to punish offenders against the army either because it was supposed to have its own jurisdiction over them or because French military tribunals were supposed to have concurrent jurisdiction. The resulting confusion led to delays of justice and to "sentences incommensurate with the offence."[9] Conferences between the inspector of French military tribunals and civil affairs representatives resulted in a decision that French military tribunals sitting in the region should exercise sole jurisdiction over all cases involving the interest of the Allied forces. By publicizing trials and stiffening sentences the French finally helped to end the appearance of army rations and gasoline on the black market.[10]

Jurisdictional conflicts with the French were avoided on the administrative level no less successfully than on the judicial. The promptness of the provisional government in appointing regional commissioners and the promptness of the commissioners in naming local mayors in the opening weeks of the campaign mainly relieved divisional civil affairs officers of the responsibility of finding temporary officials in the towns that they uncovered. During the advance in Lor-

[8] *After-Action Report*, II (G-5 Section), 9, col. 1.

[9] *After-Action Report*, II (G-5 Section), 23, col. 1.

[10] Some areas, notably Paris, were less fortunate.

raine, which began on November 8, 1944, however, the situation was less simple. There, in many small communities on the front the *mayors* and many citizens were recent immigrants from Germany, and decisions about new officials had to be made immediately by divisional civil affairs officers with the advice of their French liaison officers. Sometimes the liaison officers themselves seem to have made the appointments. Later they were reviewed by the subprefects, who often made new appointments. There were occasional mistakes, such as the nomination of two men to be *mayor* of the same little group of hamlets by civil affairs officers attached to two rapidly moving divisions with a fluctuating boundary. "Some confusion" was reported by the 10th Armored Division as resulting "from the appointment of *maires* by French officials, other than those temporarily named by Civil Affairs officers, and the subsequent arrest of some of the latters' appointees by French Chasseurs without notice to the American officers."[11] However, such difficulties were easily disposed of by conferences among the various interested authorities.

Conferences between mayors and higher public officials and civil affairs officers at all levels were the key to much of the latter's success in France, Luxembourg, and Belgium. This statement is particularly true of the army's effort to control civilian traffic, from the farmer's roundup of his cows to the industrialist's trip to Paris. Before curfew and blackout were passably observed in Nancy, there had to be a conclave of local police officials with civil affairs officers from SHAEF and Third Army Headquarters on the importance and techniques of passive defense. Countless conferences with mayors and brigadiers of the gendarmery were needed before the resulting ordinances were observed in the industrial towns of the Meurthe and Moselle valleys.

Another illustration of the mutual understanding and confidence born of the conferences between civil affairs officers and public officials was the striking fact that no city where large numbers of American troops were quartered had a big fire or a serious air raid. Still more significant was the effect upon security of the constant,

[11]December Historical Report of Captain Leigh S. Plummer, S-5 with the 10th Armored Division.

zealous cooperation of the local police in enforcing pass regulations upon travelers. The mass of work involved in checking every train, car, and pedestrian on the roads was made more complicated by the frequently conflicting pass policies of American corps and divisions. Much credit for the final establishment of an essentially uniform pass system in the Third Army zone was due to the civilian police officials in Lorraine and Luxembourg.

The confidence of the French in their liberators and their willingness to cooperate in legal and administrative matters with civil affairs officers were to a considerable extent based upon the respect of the Allies for French money and banks. From the first landings on the Norman beaches it was the experience of the army that "money and banking required a minimum of aid and supervision."[12] In recognition of that fact, the army discontinued its proclamations imposing its franc as legal tender as of September 1, 1944, though of course the Allied francs continued to circulate just as they had done in the first two months of the battle of France. When monetary proclamations were required in Haut-Rhin, Bas-Rhin, and Moselle, they were issued in the name of the provisional government. When in December, 1944, and January, 1945, the redemption of German marks for French francs became necessary in those departments and difficulty arose over divergent values set upon the mark by the French and American authorities, civil affairs officers assisted in the actual exchange of money, in which many Allied soldiers were involved for at least small amounts. When rumors of counterfeiting of the Allied franc spread in Lorraine, civil affairs officers quietly arranged with bankers for the withdrawal from circulation of the denomination involved. The confidence which the French felt in the Allied franc was sedulously maintained by the respect of civil affairs officers for the prestige of their financial institutions.

Undoubtedly the most popular measure in the Allied financial policy was the decision to implement the provisions of the agreement between the French provisional government and the governments of the United States and Great Britain. On November 1, 1944, in Nancy, and generally throughout the regions under the control of

[12] *After-Action Report,* II (G-5 Section), 9, col. 1.

the Allied armies soon thereafter, the French government assumed the payment of wages at current, legal rates to all civilian labor in army employ. The result of this action was not only to eliminate the difficulty of recruiting labor which had sprung from the army's inability to determine and legalize civilian wage rates for its own purposes; the action also removed all real and apparent injustice in the army's demands for labor in a market where it was often at a premium, and it helped to consolidate the interest and policies of the provisional government with those of the Allies at the point where these policies touched most closely the lives of French wage earners as well as administrative officials.

Refugees and Displaced Persons

The fear that the first advances from the Norman beaches in June, 1944, might be embarrassed by refugees was ill-founded. Even in July the Allied forces encountered very few of them moving in either direction, and only toward the end of the month did *returning* refugees begin to appear on the supply routes. The first fugitives with whom the Third Army had to reckon in Normandy were homeward-bound residents of Cherbourg, and the first interference with its supply trains by refugees occurred at Gavray on August 6, when some seven thousand of them crowded onto the roads in an effort to go back to their homes behind the American lines. After causing serious confusion they were finally routed north over secondary roads.

Refugee routes were an obvious remedy for a problem which would soon threaten the entire Red Ball Supply Line, and on August 9 civil affairs officers of Third Army headquarters submitted to the G-4 convoy control officer their first map-overlay of secondary roads for the use of refugees. On August 11, a refugee route from front to rear was cleared with G-4, and G-5 was given permission to direct civilians over any road not included in the army's circulation map. On August 12, the main refugee routes were published to all civil affairs detachments, and their commanders became responsible for routing all civilian traffic onto nonmilitary roads. As soon as roadblocks could be established with local French authorities, gendarmes began to help military police in manning them, and hundreds of young Frenchmen, many of them from various resistance groups, were recruited to wear the brassard of civilian traffic police.

In Brittany elaborate overlays of refugee routes were prepared well in advance of the need for them. Though the plan of routing refugees over secondary roads parallel to military supply lines soon gave way to a "standfast policy," it fully justified itself with those who in the early phases of the fighting desire to *return* to their homes in rural areas behind the Allied lines. The morale of such returning groups was admirable, and they usually were zealous in obedience to all traffic officers.

Refugees in Brittany proved to be more formidable in statistics than in fact, but credit for the solution of their problem rested mainly with the French authorities. With an estimated total of 150,000, of whom 20,000 were released in a single mass at Brest on August 14, the three civil affairs detachments at Plabennec, Guingamp, and Rennes, on which responsibility for distributing relief supplies mainly rested, would have been overwhelmed. After visiting all active detachments in the peninsula on August 16, a civil affairs officer reported that everywhere the homeless were being housed by the French and fed in the main from local resources. Mayors reported "no suffering and no serious lack of food." Civil affairs officers provided two temporary shelters for refugees in Brittany, but the ready hospitality of the peasants spared the refugees from cantonment of any kind for more than a few hours. The only service required of civil affairs detachments seemed to be "coordination of the work of civilian authorities, to be sure that no need might develop beyond local means, instruction of local officials in traffic control, and provision of certain supplies not locally available."

Refugees from Paris began to embarrass the First and Third Armies when Le Mans and Orléans were liberated, and the first rumors of German withdrawal from Paris threatened a landslide in its direction. Though a standfast order had been published, and was finally broadcast by the French in a nation-wide radio appeal on August 26, it could not be severely enforced. At the moment there were 100,000 Parisians in the Third Army zone alone, most of whom seemed anxious to go home. In the end the situation was saved less by the measures taken to enforce the standfast order than by the sweep of the tide of war to the east and by the careful routing of civilian traffic over secondary routes.

On August 31 a civil affairs officer estimated that 500,000 refugees had been found in the army's various zones of operation. That number was probably greater than the totals in all other Allied operating zones combined. Thanks to the French authorities, it was possible to report very little suffering. Though "no facilities were set up under military administration, the French authorities, the *maires*, the *Secours National*, and the *Croix Rouge Française* functioned in so excellent a manner that no unmet needs were reported."[13]

Refugees in Alsace-Lorraine during the September advance were a diminishing problem, but in the drive which opened on November 8 they suffered much distress. Except in communities actually involved in the battle, the standfast principle was severely enforced. About 13,000 refugees were, however, evacuated from front-line towns in the XX Corps area, and a similar report came from XII Corps to the south. Divisional civil affairs personnel crossed the Moselle under fire with French liaison officers and women of the *Mission Militaire de Liaison Administrative* to assist villagers in no man's land, and sometimes to stay with them for over twenty-four hours before evacuation was possible. Morhange, Pont-à-Mousson, and some smaller towns on the edge of the battle became collecting points where "D" civil affairs detachments tried to care for sometimes as many as 500 persons with mainly locally recruited medical help and with no transportation except a single jeep and trailer.

In part perhaps because French hospitality now proved less responsive to the plight of refugees than it had in the earlier fighting following D day, and because representatives of the *Ministère des Réfugiés et des Déportés* and the local prefects waited for the actual need before moving to create the necessary centers for handling refugees and displaced persons behind the lines, there was a general desire among the former to go back to their homes in the battle area.

[13]Report of the Field Historian with Third Army Headquarters, G-5, for November, 1944, p. 15.

Though their wish conflicted with the army's determination to freeze civilian traffic at the Moselle, public opinion and the press supported the refugees, especially the farmers, whose crops were being lost and whose cattle were dying of neglect. On November 19, the regional commissioner in Nancy formally asked the commander of the Third Army to withdraw the no-passage line to the river Seille. Motives of security prevailed against the request, but its main object was gained by a compromise whereby carefully screened individuals, most of them mayors or leading farmers in the little communities beyond the Moselle, were escorted back to their homes by civil affairs personnel.

In the Battle of the Bulge in December, 1944, the standfast order for civilians suffered its toughest application and test. At first the Luxembourg government authorized the movement of a mass of fugitives from the threatened northern end of the Grand Duchy, but the movement was halted in deference to the Allied policy. Refugees in Belgium were handled by civil affairs officers of the VIII and III Corps in the summary way that the tactical situation imposed. In an official report, the situation was described as follows: "At the onset of the German offensive on December 16 it became apparent that refugee traffic would, unless ruthlessly controlled at the source, go quickly beyond control. Roving patrols of Civil Affairs personnel were organized soon after the first refugees started trickling onto the roads. The patrols quickly drafted additional auxiliary police from among civilians and diverted all fugitives off main roads and into the countryside communities where they could take refuge with the neighboring farmers."[14] The effective support given by the Belgian Red Cross in all stages of the December fighting contributed much to the clearance of military routes. Both the Belgian and the Luxembourg governments cooperated admirably in caring for their refugees and returning them to their homes according to a systematic plan which had the approval of the Allies in the first three months of 1945.

Displaced persons did not become a major problem in battle areas until after the invasion of Germany. In the zone of the Third Army

[14]*Monthly Historical Report of the A.C. of S., G-5, VIII Corps, December, 1944.*

in Lorraine from September to December, 1944, the number never exceeded 11,000 in any month. The French left their care and supervision mainly to civil affairs officers, assisted by the not always efficient local gendarmes and the usually very competent teams of social workers and nurses of the *Mission Militaire de Liaison Administrative*. Typical collecting centers were established in one of the great French military barracks at Verdun and in a number of the workers' communities of the *Petits Fils de François Wendel* around Briey, at Hayange, and elsewhere. Lack of essential train transportation and of definite policies for the displaced persons by both the French and their respective governments prevented the removal of the displaced persons from the collecting centers at a rate better than about five thousand a month. The story of their rearward movements by trainloads of a few hundred or a few score of passengers at a time in the autumn of 1944 is in itself an epic. The unfortunate groups who had to remain more or less indefinitely in the centers presented all the problems of feeding, clothing, and controlling a hunger-stricken, desperate, polyglot mob, most of whom were ignorant of American standards of sanitary discipline and were restive under the constraint of having to prepare their own meals from unfamiliar rations over captured German field kitchens in the open air, or in communal cookrooms. The fact that a minority had recently been fighting with the *Franc-Tireurs* and Partisans and gave up their weapons only under diplomatic pressure, if at all, added to the embarrassments of the supervising civil affairs detachments.

The full record of the repatriations with which civil affairs officers were finally concerned in France in 1945 can only be indicated in the statistics of the SHAEF Mission to France. It is estimated that from January 1 to March 31, 1945, approximately 1,000 Czechs, 5,000 Poles, 2,000 Russians, and 300 persons of other nationalities were repatriated from or through France. As the result of an inter-Allied agreement whereby Belgian and Dutch nationals were to receive parallel treatment with French displaced persons, approximately 50,-000 Belgians and 15,000 Dutch were brought into France from enemy territory in that period and staged there pending arrangements by their respective governments for their repatriation. For the following

nine months—April 1 to December 31, 1945—the following tabula-
tion is given:

Belgians	90,818
Czechs	9,722
Dutch	16,799
Germans	8,494
Greeks	732
Hungarians	6,870
Italians	50,498
Jews (to Palestine)	1,910
Poles	35,649
Russians	112,299
Yugoslavs	19,867
Danes	263
Norwegians	357
Swedes	5
Miscellaneous	1,969
Total	356,252

The miscellaneous category included Austrians, Brazilians, Chinese, Corsicans, Luxemburgers, and Syrians. It did not include a final
movement of approximately 1,500 Germans from an internment
camp in Spain to the American occupation zone in Germany early in
1946.

Relief Supply

Relief supply was a section of the civil affairs organization at army
and army group headquarters as well as on higher levels. Its job
was to maintain supplies of food, fuel, clothing, medical necessities
and everything essential for the maintenance of a decent, minimum
civilian economy throughout all zones of military operations. Though
its claims upon the quartermaster and the transportation corps
were subordinate to military needs, it drew upon army supplies in
emergencies during the initial phases of the battle of France, and—
beginning October 6, 1944, for the Third Army—there were systematic movements of relief supplies from the communications zone[15] to

[15]When the European Theater of Operations U. S. Army (ETOUSA) was organized
in London, some thought was given to a Civil Affairs Military Government Staff. A

the army's civil affairs depot. Its total issue to the French authorities in that month were

Food	129,680	pounds
Soap	10,080	pounds
Shoes	3,850	pairs
Gas, oil, and motor fuels	33,000	gallons
Clothing (undergarments)	2,546	each

In December the issues had grown to

Food	126,600	pounds
Soap	27,600	pounds
Clothing	10.52	tons
Blankets	15.33	tons

Gas, oil, and motor fuels totaled 2,811 gallons[16] in the region of Nancy alone, with proportionate allocations in the other large cities of the army zone.

In comparison with the stocks of relief supplies at the ports and with the 225,000 pounds for which requisitions were placed by the Third Army alone in September these issues seem small. That they were not larger was due to the prompt distribution of vast quantities of captured enemy material to local civilian authorities. In September the amount of captured bread, meat, grain, and other foodstuffs made available to the French was almost fifty times the quantity of such relief supplies which civil affairs delivered to them from the stocks of the Allied nations. The motor fuels so distributed tripled the contribu-

---

few officers were assigned to this work, but they later became a part of either the First U. S. Army Group (later 12th A.G.) G-5, or of the newly formed combined command staff. It was not until after D day and ETOUSA had moved to the Continent as Headquarters Communications Zone (Comm. Z.) that the G-5 staff of that headquarters assumed any great importance. Before going to the Continent the nucleus of the G-5 staff was organized; later, under operational pressure in France, the staff became quite large. It was organized similarly to other G-5 staffs with administrative and functional sections and in addition, along with the rest of Comm. Z., had a forward element known as Advance Section Communications Zone G-5 (G-5 Ad. Sec.). The main purpose of G-5 Comm. Z. and G-5 Ad. Sec. was to take over the control and administration of the civil affairs detachments when the tactical units moved on and a territory was declared to be out of the Zone of Action and under the jurisdiction of the Communications Zone.

[16] About 25 per cent of a standard tank car.

tions from Allied stocks. Captured cement, stoves, fire extinguishers, and household goods also went directly to many communities where war damage had been worst. The greatest single German cache to be uncovered was that near Tours, at Sinq-Mars, where over twenty-five miles of storage tunnels were crammed with German food and liquor rations. Though civilians and soldiers of both the American army and the *Forces Françaises de l'Intérieur* were helping themselves to these luxuries when a civil affairs detachment took charge of them, the depredations ended and the goods were distributed without friction through the proper channels.

In the distribution of captured supplies a balance had to be struck between civilians and the army, which, though it had first choice of everything, took far less than the lion's share. Conferences with both sides culminated at the highest level in an agreement on July 31, 1944, that delivery of imported relief supplies should be made only to departmental directorates of the General Food Administration. The centralized control helped the French rationing authorities, especially in the issue of gasoline, and enabled them to save the harvest in Brittany in August, and in Lorraine in September. With increasing confidence and knowledge of the situation on both sides, adjustments to emergencies became almost a matter of routine. During the harvest in October civil affairs arranged with the quartermaster for a daily issue of 1,400 gallons of gasoline to take care of essential civilian needs in the region of Nancy, and from captured stocks over 9,000 gallons of motor fuel were found for use on farms. When Metz fell in November and the exceptionally large influx of refugees there was in desperate need of food and clothing, several large captured stocks of food, including 150 tons of fresh beef and 650 tons of flour, were made available through the Communication Zone in less than a day. The need for clothing was met shortly afterward from civil affairs stocks of overcoats and blankets. In the general advance in November, divisional civil affairs officers took relief supplies into a number of small communities under fire.

The general supply problem in France was one of transportation and organization. In August, when demands upon the relief stocks of the Allied nations were almost negligible, civil affairs officers arranged a number of important exchanges of food against various other commodities among several cities. With the assumption of control of the country west of the combat zone in Alsace-Lorraine by the provisional government, the main initiative in the organization of internal supply services rested with the French authorities. Rationing of bread, meat, fats, and almost all other foods continued, and even in such agricultural provinces as Haut-Rhin and Bas-Rhin the situation improved only very slowly. Discussion of the situation by the press of all shades of opinion in France was gratifying disinclined to make the army a scapegoat for what was honestly regarded as essentially an administrative, civilian problem. The army was often mentioned as a factor in the shortage of fuel and the paralysis of transportation, but its concessions to facilitate the supply of the large cities by rail and truck were recognized and its contributions to victualing in the combat zone were at least locally appreciated. The press of both left and right prevailingly put the blame for shortages of supply upon the enemy and the war, the black market, the "selfish peasants" or the "greedy townspeople" in provincial cities in agricultural areas, but most of all upon the departmental and national authorities for failing to control the food markets and organize their supply.

Transportation, Public Utilities, and Communication

Shortage of transportation was the greatest single handicap under which civil affairs labored in France, and the net achievement in final service to the war-damaged economy and war-wrecked towns and to refugees and displaced persons was mainly due to the use of U.S. army equipment operated by army personnel and to the French troops of the Civil Affairs Transport Pools established in September, 1944. The original allotment of 390 vehicles to the approximate strength of 1,200 officers and enlisted men composing the civil affairs contingent of the Third Army allowed a standard organic allowance of only one jeep and one half-ton truck each to detachments, many of which were charged with an entire *arrondissement* or even larger rural areas. Much vital work by civil affairs officers at Third

Army Headquarters was done in captured or abandoned enemy vehicles in advanced stages of disrepair. Salvage usurped far too much of the time and strength of transport officers until late in September, and thereafter the jobs of maintenance and salvage by the Civil Affairs Transport Platoon, in charge of all repairs of civil affairs vehicles, including 100 one-ton trucks and their one-ton trailers driven by two companies of French troops, remained two of the hardest and humblest tasks in the service.

When the Civil Affairs Transport Pool was established at Verdun, on the arrival of the French drivers and their 100 trucks and trailers loaded with relief supplies, on September 22, all servicing of five displaced persons' centers in the army zone was being done by means of five salvaged German trucks. The newly established transport pool immediately began a service which, by December, 1944, had expanded to an average of over 258,000 miles of travel per month, short or long hauls of over 4,000 refugees and 20,000 displaced persons, and transport of over 5,331,000 pounds of Red Cross and United Nations relief supplies to various stricken communities, some of them under fire.

Railroads and rolling stock were found somewhat less damaged than was expected, and with the cooperation of the French they were made as useful to the army as possible. As mediator between military and civilian interests, civil affairs began in October to make a gradually increasing minimum of private travel possible between the provincial cities and Paris. With steadily increasing regularity, supply trains victualed the larger cities and in emergencies brought in lifts of food, clothing, and medical supplies. In December, in the Third Army zone alone, a total of 26,092 tons of food, 30,739 tons of hard fuel, and 15,168 tons of various merchandise was cleared by rail. At the same time permission was given to resume some suburban tram services, military trucks and military gasoline occasionally bore a hand in moving local stocks of vegetables, and everything possible was done to mitigate the war paralysis of transportation.

From the point of view of the small civil affairs detachment (C and D detachments) in the field, organic transportation was never adequate. To the end its shortage remained a prime handicap upon the work of civil affairs officers.

In the first phase of invasion, in Normandy and Brittany, all steam electric-generating plants were found damaged while hydroelectric plants were limited by low water and were at first under enemy control. On August 18, 1944, all the Breton power companies arranged a consolidated plan of control with army representatives and cooperated admirably with the army in repair of plants and high-tension lines. At the end of the month, however, the fuel shortage held the delivery of power to something like 5 per cent of 1939 consumption.

In September the movement of the army was too rapid for more than local concern about utilities and public works, and assistance by the army was mainly limited to efforts by civil affairs officers in the field to help civilian surveys of damaged water supplies and transmission cables. The amount of such damage was less than was expected, for German destruction of utilities did not become systematic until the retreat from Alsace-Lorraine in November and December.

The main limitation upon electric service throughout France remained the fuel shortage. With the help of civil affairs specialists, civilian authorities repaired damaged generators everywhere and in December were able to bring power to Metz, which had been cut off by enemy destruction of the lines between it and Kreuzwald. Repair of the generating plants at Kreuzwald, Carling, and Merlebach in December also made the resumption of coal mining possible in the area.

The comparatively limited damage to telephone and telegraph installations in Normandy and Brittany during the landings was undoubtedly in part due to organized French resistance. By request of General Koenig to the Supreme Commander[17] before D day, technicians of all kinds who supported the Resistance were to stand by their posts in order to thwart the German policy of the scorched earth, "and were to do everything possible for the hastening of the eventual re-establishment of public utilities." It was not surprising then that, although "inspections of the communications systems in the liberated areas showed that cables and wires had been cut by bombs and gunfire, the German plans for destruction had not been carried out."[18]

[17]Butcher, *My Three Years with Eisenhower,* p. 591.

[18]*After-Action Report,* II (G-5 Section), 5, col. 1.

In the initial phases of the fighting, it proved possible to save the Signal Corps much wire construction by promptly restoring civilian trunk lines from Avranches and Le Mans through Maintenon to Paris. In this and similar work all the way to the German border communications specialists had the help of officials of the Ministry of Post, Telephone, and Telegraph (PTT) who knew the German networks as well as the French, and were also familiar with the details of sabotage by the *Forces Françaises de l'Intérieur.*

With the stabilization of the fronts in September it was at first found necessary to use the army net for communication between civil affairs officers in Briey, Châlons-sur-Marne, Commercy, Nancy, St.-Dizier, and Verdun. Civil affairs officers also relied increasingly upon their very efficient courier service, and civilian couriers for strictly administrative use were authorized in France and Luxembourg. Local civilian labor of the PTT with civil affairs passes immediately began to repair the French telephone circuits, and in October their use by PTT officials was authorized to expedite the work. Twelve intercity circuits were restored in September, and the restoration continued at about the same rate throughout the autumn.

Though the claims of civilian administration and business upon telephone service were a potential threat to security, they were increasingly recognized. On September 9, civil affairs detachments, with the advice of Counter Intelligence Corps and French police officers, were authorized to admit civilians to intracity telephone communication as individual cases might warrant. By December, official intercity telephone circuits were in use between Nancy, Bar-le-Duc, Briey, Jarney, Pont-à-Mousson, and Toul. Several industries in Lorraine were enjoying telephone privileges. In November partial mail service for the general public began with intercity postal privileges limited to nonillustrated postcards and letters of less than twenty grams. In December this privilege was extended to the department of Meuse and all France was opened to correspondence with most of the Allied nations. Before the release of any impounded mail in November, Allied censorship officers and the French Technical Control Services undertook a complete check of all mail delivered.

Public Health

Although the sanitary utilities of many French cities had suffered during German occupation, no outbreak of epidemic disease occurred at any time during the campaign on a scale to threaten the armies or to cause any serious disturbance among civilians. In spite of a great increase of tuberculosis and venereal disease among the French during the war, and in spite of some malnutrition in the large cities, public health could usually be pronounced "satisfactory" by civil affairs officers. In part this surprising situation was due to the high sanitary standards of the Allied armies, but it may also have owed more than was usually recognized to the "standfast policy" in handling refugees, and to the sanitary precautions of both the French and the Allied authorities in handling displaced persons. It was also partly explicable by the fact that the Pasteur Institute in Paris had considerable stocks of biologicals ready for distribution through civilian channels and that there was never any shortage in the medical supplies which the Army Medical Supply Depot furnished on civil affairs requisition.

Malnutrition in Third Army territory in August and September was not a problem and was indeed officially declared nonexistent. In Paris it was from the first an increasingly serious problem, and in the larger cities in Alsace-Lorraine it was held at bay only by continued, though gradually relaxing, food rationing.

In the first phases of the campaign the army assumed the main responsibility for civilian wounded. In 1944, from August 1 to October 1, 1,374 civilians were admitted to military medical stations, and in later months the number continued to be almost as large, for civilians who were critically ill were also received. The most dramatic incidents of relief to wounded civilians occurred at Sarrequemines and Welferding in December, when public health officers took first aid and medical supplies, under fire, to several thousand French refugees in caves in no man's land.

With the help of public health officers several civilian hospitals which had been stripped by the retreating Germans were rehabilitated. Medical supplies were made generously available to the French authorities to enable them to take over the care of their wounded as soon as possible, and to encourage them to assume their responsibility for the medical care and supervision of displaced persons' centers. An Allied Relief Board basic medical unit, which was established in Metz to supply civilian agencies in the Moselle area, made a half ton of DDT powder available to them. Fractional basic medical units and DDT powder were made available in all localities where French civilian authorities were responsible for refugees and displaced persons. Though a survey in September indicated that only 3 per cent of all displaced persons in centers were lice-infested, and that communicable disease problems were negligible, the sanitary discipline of displaced persons and refugees was unsatisfactory and the need for vigilance by both French authorities and civil affairs officers never ceased to be stressed.

Conclusion

The mission, responsibility, and object of civil affairs were outlined on April 26, 1944, by the commanding general of the Third Army in these emphatic words:[19] "The sole mission of Civil Affairs Administration is to further military objectives. The exercise of Civil Affairs control is a command responsibility. The object of Civil Affairs is to assist in military operations." To this narrowly military objective civil affairs officers made a substantial contribution in France and the Low Countries. Indeed, in the control of refugees on the public roads the contribution to the success of the campaign was of very great importance. In the repair and control of civilian postal facilities, telephones, and telegraphs, in the protection and repair of public services, water supplies, power plants, and the like, jointly with the local authorities, and in the direction given to those authorities in reorganizing their police and fire brigades, their public health and hospital services, and their schools and churches a substantial contribution was made to the military goal as well as to the diplomatic one of good understanding between the Army of the United States and its Allies. Arts and monuments officers contributed to the diplomatic object

[19] *After-Action Report,* I (G-5 Section), 4.

both by providing materials and helping to secure labor for first aid to priceless public buildings, churches, and private residences of historic interest, and by tactfully protecting such structures against the indiscriminate billeting of troops. In the quiet intervention of an American officer to check the dilapidation of the shell-shattered University of Pont-à-Mousson, where Père Marquette and Lafayette were once students, was an example which might be multiplied many times over of the practical friendship whereby the army laid the foundation of a permanent, local appreciation of the people and government of the United States.

In the fields of legal affairs and public relations, also, the diplomatic work done by civil affairs officers served both the military objective and the diplomatic. The minor part played by G-5 in the guidance of war correspondents by the army was the least of its contributions to an understanding of the American people and the Allied armies by the French, and of the French by the Allied armies and peoples. The major contribution of G-5 was made by its careful study of the rising French press and of other sources of information about French public opinion and by the good relations it established with the French authorities and the French press. In the more delicate field of legal relations with the French, who were naturally restive under continuing short rations, blackouts, and restriction of traffic and communication in the autumn of 1944, legal officers tactfully performed the necessary minimum of intervention in the French courts and secured the support of the civilian authorities in prosecuting offenders against security regulations as well as against the property and personnel of the Army of the United States. Civilian supply officers also made a substantial contribution to good relations with the French, not so much by their large deliveries of food and clothing to regions of acute civilian suffering as by their constant study of the problems of railway transport of indigenous supplies and their assistance to the French authorities in the problem of organizing their own national economy.

Chapter VIII

American Military Government in Austria
May 1945–February 1946

GEORGE C. S. BENSON

The Problem

Most of the military government officers who came to Salzburg in May of 1945 had served in army or regional or provincial military governments for many months in Italy and carried vivid memories of towns which, like Ancona or Rimini, were mostly rubble or, like Naples, seemed in wartime to be mostly filth. A fortnight later, the first spontaneous, optimistic reaction to the new assignment had been reinforced by several circumstances. Not only had it become evident, after the German army surrender, that the anticipated dangers of mountain fortresses and "werewolves" would not materialize; it had also become evident that the Austrian officials would be considerably more alert, more intelligent, more honest, and more genuinely co-operative than the Italians with whom these officers had been working. In Salzburg an anti-Nazi city government had already been established before the American entry, and the formation of a *Land* (state) government was merely awaiting approval. The vigorous disavowals of Nazi sympathies seemed to be, on the whole, sincere; the Austrians were pleased to see the renewal of their ties with England and America, severed, of course, since the *Anschluss* of 1938 with Nazi Germany, and they were clearly delighted to be able to restore those portions of the Catholic establishment which the Nazis had shut down. Although they were realistic enough to recognize the economic difficulties in store for a small Austria, they enthusiastically supported the American program of establishing their country in a free and independent status.

It was naturally very helpful to have this favorable psychological setting. At the same time the task confronting military government officials was stupendous and unforeseeable in its magnitude. In spite of tremendous handicaps, such as scarcity of trained personnel, lack of adequate information, the administrative difficulties restricting quadripartite control and all the rest, the American military succeeded in re-establishing orderly government in the short space of nine months. The many shortcomings which will be discussed as the details of the story are told in the following pages must not allow one to lose sight of the final accomplishment.

Program

The uncertainty as to general policy declarations by the Allied Powers, the inertia of the staff of the Allied Commission for Austria during the preparatory period in Italy, the indecision as to whether the area would be under ETO or MTO—all help to explain why no clear-cut military government program for Austria was ever outlined.

In a general way, everyone agreed that Austria was to be treated more liberally than Germany. The handbooks prepared both in the European Theater and in the Mediterranean Theater, with the customary idealism and generosity of American foreign policy, made these assumptions:

1) Law and order were to be maintained.

2) No one was to starve.

3) Civilian governmental functions were to be re-established at an undetermined rate of speed.

4) An Austrian currency system was to be re-established.

5) Displaced persons were to receive special rations and to be favored in other ways.

6) Ardent Nazis were to be eliminated from public office, and all Nazis to be eliminated from top offices.

7) Captured enemy materials were to be turned over to the army.

8) Vigorous efforts were to be made to maintain price and ration controls. Wages and salaries were to be frozen.

9) Freedom of religious worship was to be re-established.

10) The armaments industry was to be eliminated but production for civilian purposes was to continue.

11) Democratic teaching in the schools was to be revived.

Obviously, detailed regulations were essential to implement these extremely general policy declarations. These regulations were established very belatedly by the Allied Commission for Austria. Fortunately, in the intervening period, utter chaos was avoided because most of the provincial officers, as a result of experience with a similar program in Italy, were capable of devising their own regulations. The most serious aspect of the entire situation was the continued failure to formulate a clear-cut decision on the crucial question of how rapidly governmental functions were to be turned back to the Austrians.

The points of the general program noted above fall roughly under six headings: denazification, handling of displaced persons, the complexity of law enforcement activities, re-education for democracy, re-establishment of Austrian government, control of economic life. This chapter will endeavor to cover only the most obvious parts of the action taken by military government in Austria during the period May, 1945–February, 1946.

The discussion of the work projected and the work accomplished will be preceded by a consideration of the staff and organization with which U.S. Military Government undertook its part in re-creating an Austrian nation.

Staff

In May, 1945, most of the 150 or so officers working in military government of the provinces and smaller units of government were men who had had similar experience for eighteen months in Italy. A large number had been selected because of their outstanding qualities, and the provincial staff was probably better than the average staff in Italy. Aside from their Italian experience, however, few of the men were any more suited in experience and training than the average American for the difficult and delicate task of re-creating a foreign country; unfortunately very few of the officers (or of the enlisted men) spoke German;[1] and the group could not be considered particularly international in outlook. Yet most of the men had the average American's adaptability and tolerance of other races—qualities which make for cooperative effort and internationalism of outlook.

The Allied Commission (Control Council) for Austria, American Element, which moved into limited operation in Salzburg in June and was established in Vienna in August did not contain as many well-qualified officers as the first group. There were far too many officers for the job. Some of the capable younger men were buried because they were outranked by older officers. Some members of the group had been "planning" for Austria for more than a year and were definitely stale.

The commanding generals seem to have lacked almost completely the ability to build the speedy, flexible type of organization needed to control a conquered country. In addition, the entire staff situation was complicated by bad planning of the problem of replacements. The American Element of the Allied Council was far slower in requesting civilian replacements from Washington for Austria than was Headquarters of Military Government, Germany, and the requests on file in Washington in March of 1946 were not well related to the needs. Moreover, officers who were entirely unnecessary were released very unwillingly.

Organization

Military government has always had to face the problem of shifting from a primarily tactical organization in the early stage of conquest to an organization based on the territorial units of government in the later stage when more nearly normal economic and political controls can—and must—function. After eighteen months of experience, a

---

[1] An effort of some of the more enterprising men to learn a bit of German while the group was "planning" in Naples had been suppressed by commanding officers.

reasonably satisfactory pattern for making this shift had been worked out in Italy.[2]

An account of the procedure in Austria will indicate that a not very sound pattern was employed in that country and that considerations other than good administration were dominant in the minds of the army officers who were setting up the organization.

In 1944 it had been determined that the Mediterranean Theater of Operations would administer the American part of Austria. Accordingly, early in 1945 the staff of the American Element of the Allied Commission, Austria (then known as the Group Control Council, Austria), and a portion of the so-called "task force" which was to fill up the provincial and lower unit military government teams were assembled at Allied Force Headquarters (Mediterranean Theater) in Italy. Some effort was made to work out joint planning at that time, but purely personal considerations interfered. Part of the time the "task force" was independent of the Group Control Council, part of the time it was subordinated to it.

When it became probable that American troops would first enter Austria from the north rather than from Italy, a portion of the task force was airshipped to Paris and turned over to the European Theater of Operations. The European Civil Affairs Division reorganized and re-equipped this group to fit its structure, and in a very leisurely way sent the teams down to Austria to report to the corps or division headquarters in the towns where the teams were to locate.

The relation between the territorial teams and the tactical unit G-5's was surprising to officers accustomed to the fairly simple pattern of military government organization which had been evolved in Italy. In Salzburg, XV Corps Headquarters G-5 maintained for about two weeks a territorial team which was intended for another type of area in Germany, which was too large for the city of Salzburg, and which was not in any way prepared for the provincial job. Meanwhile the teams designated for the Salzburg area were kept on the side lines during this most critical time. This situation continued until a critical article in *Time Magazine* forced the G-5 of XV Corps

[2]See Chapter VI.

to do what it should have done the first day, i.e., give exclusive jurisdiction to the territorial units designed for the area. In Upper Austria,
a different series of problems arose. There, two different corps headquarters and several divisions were trying to govern one province.
It was almost two months before the provincial team gained control
of its province and took over staff supervision of localities.

After the needless waste of time caused by the superabundance of
tactical unit G-5's in the ETO came a new type of problem. The
Allied Commission for Austria, American Element, was still in Italy
—still awaiting a view of the land for which it had been "planning"
so long. It was destined to wait even longer. When XV and other
ETO Corps Headquarters were ordered out, it was decided to turn
over the American zone of Austria to a new corps headquarters,
II Corps from Italy. At the time that this new arrangement went into
effect, in mid-June, part of the Allied Commission staff was brought
to Salzburg and rather vague arrangements were made for its working in a staff relationship to II Corps, while presumably the II Corps
G-5 staff supervised the provincial government teams. Since the staff
was small and knew little of the problems, the control was not very
effective.

By August, II Corps was moved out of action and control was
taken over by United States Forces in Austria Headquarters. This
body continued the organizational confusion with two new variations. First, it sent to Vienna its staff of Allied Control Council for
Austria. At the same time it maintained other parts of its headquarters
in Salzburg. When, after two or three months, the confusion became
too great, all of headquarters except G-5 was moved to Vienna.

In early November, United States Forces in Austria Headquarters
issued an order purporting to clarify relationships between G-5 and
Allied Commission. Staff supervision of Salzburg and Upper Austria
was assigned to G-5, but staff supervision of the American part of
Vienna was left to Allied Commission. The Allied Commission was
to prepare military government policies and to coordinate their execution within the American zone. The order did not help much. As
matters were allowed to drift an intermittent staff supervision was
exercised at times by G-5, at times by Allied Commission.

There was also the problem of the relation between military government and the tactical troops in the field. In Italy, tactical units below Army level had almost never been given authority over military government territorial units and never after the first months of occupation of a new area. Control of military government units by divisions and corps had been completely eliminated in Germany by winter. Yet in "liberated" Austria, where tactical unit control was presumably less necessary than in conquered Germany, a commander was permitted to subordinate territorial units to the different parts of the divisional staff long after the end of hostilities. An infantry division took over the military government of *Land* Salzburg in October, 1945. The experiment was unsuccessful and was abandoned in January, 1946.

The fact that the divisional staff lacked a detailed knowledge of military government problems and a balanced administrative approach to government situations was one of the disadvantages of tactical control after the combat period. Moreover, the chain of command through the tactical unit to military government higher headquarters caused an unnecessary delay, complicated the solution of problems, and resulted in a lack of coordination between the higher and lower levels. An added difficulty was the interference by the tactical unit with military government court procedures.

However, a few advantages of such an arrangement should be listed. First, it provided the assistance of extra staff, and the younger division officers were capable, hard-working men whose general ability compensated for their lack of governmental experience. Second, it facilitated the maintenance of law and order and the handling of displaced persons—joint problems of military government and the division. Thefts were greatly reduced. Since civilian authorities were charged with financial responsibility for imported goods, they were far more effective in stopping thefts than were military guards. In Salzburg thefts were reduced when GI guards were taken from the food warehouses and "off limits" signs were substituted. The GI's were too likely to take pity on some hungry Austrians and pass the food out on their own.

Although as far as organization is concerned, Austrian military government learned little from the experience in Italy, it did learn some important general lessons from the failures of military government in Italy, and especially from the failure to control inflation and black market there. All the directives prescribed strict price control in the American zone of Austria. Perhaps even more important than the directives was the fact that most of the officers had seen what lack of price control meant. Accordingly, the Austrian provincial and county control agencies were ordered to resume activity immediately after the American occupation—and to enforce the previous German price laws.

For several reasons this control proved surprisingly effective in the American as well as in the British zone. The Austrians, a relatively well-disciplined people, were accustomed to strict controls of the economy. Their administrators were able. Finally, the fact that the Allies were importing a large proportion of the food supplies made it possible to see that these supplies were distributed only through ration channels.

Such black marketing as existed came from three or four sources. The worst were the Displaced Persons camps referred to in a subsequent section. As a result of certain policy decisions, the DP's were maintained by the American army in an ideal position for black marketing and they did not fail to use their opportunity. Toward the end of the year the army began to police the camps and to conduct moderately successful "shakedowns."

Purchases by American military personnel presented a second difficulty. Although sharply worded orders prohibited the purchase of rationed civilian goods by military personnel, the enforcement of these regulations was in the hands of unit commanders who oftentimes did nothing and never did much when their attention was called to violations.

Despite lack of information on the entire labor program, a few comments can be made. The labor officers of the Allied Commission did excellent work in enforcing the wage freeze needed to supplement the price freeze. One employer who raised wages was tried before a military government court and given a moderately heavy sentence.

The labor officers set up and denazified the civilian labor agencies. Their knowledge of the general labor shortage in the community undoubtedly helped stir higher-ranking officers to another constructive step—the fairly rapid release of prisoners of war. The latter was essential to economic recovery, since a very large proportion of Austrian man power had been forced into the *Wehrmacht*.

Denazification[3]

This sore subject, much discussed in the press, has been given little fundamental consideration. Everyone agrees that the Nazi party led Germany, including Austria, into some of the foulest kind of crimes against civilization and that the persons who are responsible for these crimes deserve their punishment. It is also agreed that persons whose Nazi affiliations indicate that they are unsuitable for democratic government should not have an opportunity to lead the new Austria (or the new Germany) into a similar type of authoritarianism. At the same time it is fairly clear that any arbitrary elimination from any responsible professional or administrative work of all persons who belonged to the Nazi party or who held positions of confidence under the Nazi regime was impossible.

American policy on denazification in Austria, stated very summarily, is that persons who belonged to the Nazi party before *Anschluss* may hold no responsible positions in any phase of Austrian life. Those who joined after *Anschluss* may hold no positions in government and no top positions in business. Practice has wavered between arbitrary elimination of all persons and the elimination of only those who were guiltiest, but the tendency has been toward the former.

As a result of present denazification policies, anti-Nazi Austrians formerly sympathetic to denazification are now opposed to it. When the Americans arrived in Salzburg in May they found the Austrians had already established an anti-Nazi government and were enthusiastically firing Nazis. Yet, nine months later, a number of responsible anti-Nazi Austrian leaders felt denazification was the greatest

[3]For a fuller treatment of this topic, see below, Chapter XII.

mistake in American policy. In general their position was that judgments should be based on the guilt of individual Nazis and not on blanket proscriptions.

Moreover, the denazification policy was devised without careful consideration of its effect on the life of the community. At one time in Salzburg it was calculated that 60 per cent of the lawyers and 50 per cent of the doctors were not allowed to practice their professions because of former Nazi connections. At the same time the government was in dire need of men of administrative experience. The professions, which required long training periods, and the government, which required persons of experience and training, could not find replacements for their displaced Nazis and actually could not operate effectively. A belated recognition of this fact caused a change in policy permitting some reinstatements in Germany, but at the end of the year this order had not yet been copied in Austria.

The policy worked a serious injustice on individuals—and on governmental operations—in the case of lower-paid government employees who had joined the party as a result of ignorance or pressure, but who were, nevertheless, arbitrarily removed.

And finally, the denazification policy will almost undoubtedly result, as in Italy, in a reaction which will restore former Nazis to more authority than they would ever have attained had it been more reasonable. On March 4, 1946, USFA announced that it had arrested almost 11,000 people in the American zone of Austria up to February 10. This included 4,900 members of such formations as the Elite Guard and Storm Troopers, 3,100 Nazi officials and other party members, and 1,021 war criminals and similar persons. Most of these were arrested under the American policy of mandatory arrests of all persons in certain categories, e.g., all officers of the *Abwehr* (German County Intelligence Corps), and all men who were mayors of towns under the Nazi regime.

There is considerable doubt as to the wisdom of holding so many people on no formal charges. Presumably the intention is to query all those arrested as to their connections with war crimes. Unfortunately, the querying is proceeding very slowly and the Austrians are, not unnaturally, wondering about the purpose of the mass arrests. It is interesting to notice that as late as November 28, 1945, the Austrian bishops requested release of the three classes comprising prisoners of war, old and sick persons, and doctors.

Without slurring in any way the integrity or intelligence of counter intelligence staff members in Austria, the way in which their operations obstructed the long-range goal of military government should be candidly considered. The fullest possible sympathy for all victims of Nazi oppression need not blind one to the thought that such victims are apt to be swayed by strong prejudices, and that in so far as these prejudices were not shared by Americans generally, they misrepresented the United States. It must be borne in mind, of course, that the army was very short of personnel with satisfactory linguistic qualifications and found itself obliged to use personnel with such qualifications and trust to supervision to correct their bias.

The lack of organizational relationship between counter intelligence and military government damaged the effectiveness of both. For some time in Salzburg, an Austrian posed as the "government" on the basis of a Counter Intelligence Corps authorization, to the detriment of the organization that the military government had established. Although counter intelligence and military government worked together without friction, there never was a cordial exchange of information. The former probably thought the latter was too "easy," while the latter certainly thought the former was at times unreasonable in its demands. A typical example is that of an Austrian official interrogated lengthily and fruitlessly on four different occasions over four months on the basis of one ex-employee's accusation. Counter intelligence never checked with military government before an "investigation," although the province's slim food supply was largely dependent upon this officer's work.

The attitude of the Counter Intelligence Corps toward individual Austrians seemed rather arbitrary to military government public safety officers. Counter intelligence left large groups of individuals in jail for long periods, marking on their records "turned over to MG" with no word to military government and no offense stated on the record. In another section are indicated the flaws in the mandatory arrest policy.

In defense of Counter Intelligence Corps it should be observed that it would have been difficult to recruit an adequate German-speaking staff, capable of tracking down Nazis, without making great use of refugees. Probably some of the long confinements of innocent persons were a result of the lack of staff for prompt questioning. The conclusion is inescapable: the type of counter intelligence staff and its insufficiently close relationships to military government damaged American aims in Austria.

One of the happier and more constructive features of the denazification program was the fact that the political parties—including the conservative Christian Social party—displayed a tendency to put a considerable number of anti-Nazis in top positions. This was of course partly window dressing for the benefit of the occupation powers. Yet in Salzburg, where after the election military government did not interfere at all in governmental appointments, a considerable number of higher ups in both of the two leading parties had spent time as inmates of concentration camps. Naturally the infusion of this group into the government and the parties was an important phase of constructive denazification.

Displaced Persons

The problems of displaced persons divide themselves into two main operations. The first was largely in the initial three months of operation in which the main job was to get home as rapidly as possible those who wanted to go home. The second was the care of those who did not wish to go home.

The first job was the kind of hurry-up humanitarianism in which Americans excel. It was done excellently, chiefly by tactical units but usually under direction of corps and army G-5's, and with full cooperation from military government territorial units. Displaced persons were gathered together, fed and housed as well as possible under the circumstances, and rushed home by train, army truck, or any other conveyance available. Naturally there were differences of opinion as particular corps or army headquarters felt they were receiving more persons than they could handle. Freeze orders had to be put on movements to congested channels like the Brenner Pass. But good nature and patience prevailed and a first-class job was done.

The second task called for sociological analysis as well as technical efficiency. As a result it was almost as badly handled as the first was well handled. The talents of the American army are not sociological.

The basic problem was the care of scores of thousands of persons from Poland, the Baltic States, the Ukraine, Yugoslavia, or other areas now subject to Soviet control. These people did not want to go home, because they were opposed to the Soviet system on economic and political grounds, and as often because they might be subject to trials for collaboration with the Nazis. Where there had been such collaboration, incidentally, it was usually as picayunish as having worked for a German officers' mess.

Although a few serious Nazi collaborators hid themselves in the DP camps, there was not much evidence of strong pro-Ally or strong anti-Ally leanings. There was every evidence of strong anti-Soviet leanings.

Few readers will disagree with the humanitarian policy adopted by the American government: that it would not forcibly return these people to a homeland where altered political conditions gave them reason to think they might be maltreated. A policy of persuasion might have been adopted in the summer of 1945, but by fall these people were too well marked to be sent home unless they wished to go.[4]

By fall it had become apparent that the ultimate disposition of these people would leave some in Austria and Germany. Although France had offered to take Poles and Yugoslavs to work in her mines and the United States offered to admit some on quota, it was clear that a large number would have to remain where they were and that steps should be taken to fit them into the Austrian population.

Instead, the American Displaced Persons policy seemed to be pushing in exactly the opposite direction. A decision had been made early in the summer that "stateless persons" (which covered most of the

---

[4]No reference is made to the smaller number of Jews who presented a very different problem. The Jews were on the whole very well cared for with full agreement of the American army, military government, and the Austrian government.

White Russians) were to receive the preferential treatment accorded to "United Nations Displaced Persons." No account was taken of the fact that most of the "United Nations Displaced Persons" in Austria did not wish to return to whichever one of the United Nations they had come from. Instead, the preferential treatments were multiplied. An 800 calory bonus in the daily ration, extensive and often unneeded issue of American clothing, freedom from any financial payments, exemption from the compulsory work provision applied to all Austrians, extensive issue of American cigarettes, highly valuable in the black market, were the main parts of this preferential program.

The result was that these people began to view themselves as above and outside the Austrian state. Black marketing centered around Displaced Persons camps. Over a four months' period in Salzburg as much Black Marketing was committed by 30,000 displaced persons as by 300,000 Austrians. A large number of these irregularities could have been stopped by the simple procedure of putting the DP's to work and requiring them to pay for their food. This solution was rejected by the commanding general on the ground of political pressures from the United States. But little effort was made to inform public opinion or the Civil Affairs Division in Washington as to what the situation really was.

A logical result of this inept policy was an increase in the Austrian opposition to the displaced persons. With opposition, of course, came economic and other discriminations that boded ill for those who would eventually be absorbed by Austria.

Civil-Military Relationships and Law Enforcement

During Military Government's first nine months in Salzburg there were never any serious clashes or even disagreements between troops and population. There was some stealing of foodstuffs and personal objects in the early days by two combat divisions whose officers were unwilling to bring their troops under control. There were also a moderate number of "rape" cases reported to the police by Austrian

women. Both troubles largely disappeared when the combat divisions
left the province.

In general, it may be said that the Austrians liked the Americans,
and that the latter reciprocated. When "fraternization" was legalized,
chocolate bars and cigarettes became a more or less standard exchange
for feminine favors.

The Austrians found in many ways greater freedom under American military occupation than they had had as part of Nazi Germany.
So long as the latter memories were fresh, they were not likely to
resent the American occupation. Moreover, military government
officers, by acting as a sort of channel for justified civilian complaints,
did much to keep civil-military relationships smooth, especially in the
difficult problem of billeting. The third and most significant element
in the generally cordial relations between Austrians and Americans is
the average American soldier himself. Although since VE day and
more especially since VJ day, American troops have fallen off sharply
in discipline and appearance, with some consequent loss of respect
from the civilian population, and although a small fraction of officers
and men have been indifferent to the social consequences of publicly
indulging in liquor and of profiting from black-market activities, the
ordinary American soldier is one of the best arguments for democracy
that the Americans have brought into Austria.

Re-Education for Democracy

This, the most important of the American goals, was but partly a
responsibility of Military Government proper. Since, however, re-
education for democracy was so intimately connected with all American operations, it seems appropriate to discuss all the efforts made to
promote it. The general objective may be broken down into re-
education through democratic functioning of government, re-education through the schools, and re-education through channels of public
communication such as the press and radio.

In spite of the weaknesses already noted, considerable progress was
made in re-establishing habits of democratic thought in government.

Initial appointments of top officials were usually made only after consultation with a number of elements in the community. American authorities gave full freedom for party discussion and activity (except, of course, antidemocratic parties), encouraged an early election for national and state legislative bodies, interfered in no way with the conduct of the election, and interposed no difficulties in the transposition of authority from the officials they had appointed to those who were elected. The Americans also cooperated on the return to the democratic constitution of 1920 as amended in 1929.

It is only fair to say that responsible Austrians wished to take these steps and that the Americans went along with them. The Austrians, in fact, did a more thorough job of democratization than the Americans could have done. For example, the Bürgermeister of Salzburg submitted his budget for protests of individual citizens before it was passed, a bit of democratization which would never have occurred to the American finance officer. It should be remembered, however, that the presence of occupation troops probably ensured a much more orderly reinstitution of the democratic processes than would have occurred if the Austrians had made the restoration independently. The fact that the Americans were importing a small but adequate quantity of foodstuffs also contributed to the good order of these operations.

The excesses of denazification weakened the administrative functioning of some departments and, as pointed out above, may serve in the future to strengthen some kind of authoritarian movement. But for the immediate present, there can be no doubt that the broad scope of denazification and of the mandatory arrest program contributed to the strength of the democratic elements in political party life. But of the major parties, the *Volkspartei* (heirs of the old Christian Socialist party) and the Social Democrats were managed by democratic elements within their own membership.

Education officers in military government found three major difficulties in re-establishing the excellent Austrian school system—buildings, books, and staff. The first was probably the most difficult. A substantial number of buildings had been destroyed. Others were controlled by the American army, chiefly for the use of displaced persons. Supplies of coal for heating existing buildings were grossly inadequate. Despite these difficulties, enough space was secured to operate most of the schools somewhat intermittently during the winter of 1945–1946, the rationing of civilian coal for the schools being wisely left to the civilian rationing authorities to accomplish.

Temporary solutions to the textbook problem were found by using only books published in 1938 or earlier and by printing pamphlet materials. Since former party members had been rigorously weeded out, the staff problem was quite difficult, and it was found necessary to reinstate a number of those who had been dismissed.

The press, the radio, books, and the theatre, these fields of re-education were controlled by Information Services Branch (formerly Psychological Warfare Branch). The press was, on the whole, handled in statesmanlike fashion. It began with the issuance of a few news-papers by the staff of the Information Services Branch, of course with the aid of Austrian staff. These papers were largely factual, though there was initially some rather dull boiler plate about American in-stitutions. Comments that might tend to reflect against American troops were censored. Like most censorships this one was a bit wooden, and widely different standards prevailed between the Linz and the Salzburg papers, for example. In October, licenses were given to party papers to operate, and three of the American papers were taken over by nonparty groups. Local news coverage improved considerably in the Salzburg paper when it was taken over by the Austrians (with-out censorship) and the viewpoint continued to be democratic and anti-Nazi. Extensive coverage was given to the Nuremberg trials, for example. Almost no criticisms of Allied troops were made, although the paper did not hesitate to print criticisms of civilian governmental policies, which may have been backed by military government. There appeared to be some prospect that ISB might have introduced a non-party type of newspaper which would be very useful for Austria and which the Austrians might not have made for themselves.[5]

The radio was handled less imaginatively but fairly well. A small network—Red, White, Red, the Austrian national colors—was estab-lished in the American zone. Its program was supervised by Amer-

[5] *The New York Times,* March 19, 1946, "Austrians Snarl Free Press Plans."

icans but the basic preparation was carried out by Austrians. It did not particularly try to propagandize for democracy but the network broadcasted a good deal of Austrian music and many talks by Austrian officials and other leaders.

Failure to publish books and magazines was the glaring weakness in the ISB program. When the Americans entered Salzburg in May the bookstores were empty even of German classics, for the Nazis had used the printing presses solely for propaganda books. The Austrians were hungry for news and ideas from the outside world. A golden opportunity to bring them translations of Anglo-American literature and the German literature of Switzerland and of the exiles was lost. In February, 1946, the bookstores were as empty as they were in May, 1945. One copy of a sort of translated *Reader's Digest,* a translation of Robert Sherwood's "Tarawa," and a book of pictures of concentration camps made a pathetic showing.[6]

A structurally important point often overlooked is the fact that two vital parts of the general military government program were not, during most of the period of operation, tied in organizationally to military government below the theater headquarters level:

1) The denazification program was under the general direction of G-2.

2) The re-education for democracy through press, radio, and other general mediums of communication was a responsibility of Information Control Division (formerly Psychological Warfare Branch). Schools were handled by education officers of military government but military government had nothing to do with the general information field except as it was intermittently asked for advice by information control.

Establishment of Austrian Government

Re-establishment of the three local levels of government in Austria —the municipality (*Gemeinde*), county (*Kreis* or *Bezirk*), and the state (*Land*) progressed very rapidly. Most of the military govern-

---

[6]See article by Erika Mann on Germany's Books in Paris Edition of *New York Herald Tribune,* February 22, 1946.

ment officers in the field had learned by bitter experience in Italy that the only way to administer affairs was through indigenous government units. The Austrians facilitated the transition by accepting orders very readily and by eliminating on their own initiative most of the higher-ranking Nazis, those, that is, who had not already fled. The unwillingness of tactical unit G-5's to recognize the necessity of civilian organization was a stumbling block, but the previously referred to article in *Time,* coupled with the uneven distribution of food supplies, forced most of these tactical units to change their attitude in the first two months. Valuable time had been lost, but the ill effects were not too great.

More permanently serious was the failure to withdraw the *Bezirk* teams when their purpose had been served. If the Italian pattern had been followed, all such teams would have been withdrawn by the first of September. Even in Germany, where there was a much more difficult problem of denazification, such teams had been transformed into observers by the first of January, 1946. Their abolition did not begin in Austria until early April, 1946.

Reasons for abolishing the *Bezirk* teams were clear and convincing. The *Bezirk* governments were the logical executive agencies for Austrian provincial governments. Once the latter were firmly established, they needed full control over the former. Rationing arrangements, food movements, financial programs, the whole gamut of governmental activity had to be conducted on a consistent state-wide basis. Equally important from a different angle was the fact that the military government officers on the *Bezirk* level were, with a few exceptions, the weakest men in the field. Left in positions of undefined authority in smaller towns, they were exposed to grave temptations to misuse their authority.[7] Finally, in any serious attempt to show the Austrians that the American authorities valued their efforts to establish themselves as a democratic country, the removal of *Bezirk*

[7]The four potential courts-martial of officers in *Land* Salzburg MG, all for relatively petty offenses, concerned members of *Bezirk* teams. There were only five *Bezirk* teams, and the offenders were scattered through three of them. The same experience on a wider scale was reported in the bottom level of MG in Germany. See, for example, *Washington Star*, March 9, 1946, "AMG Indicates Probe of GI's in New Black Market Scandals."

teams was an obvious initial step: it was a step which would remove no important authority from American military government and which would yet serve the purpose of expressing confidence.

The establishment of an Austrian national government was initially delayed for reasons which do not reflect upon American military government leaders. Upon entering Vienna in April, 1945, the Russians had established a provisional government under Karl Renner, old-time Social Democrat who had figured prominently in Austrian affairs between the establishment of the Republic and the setting up of Austrian fascism in 1934. The other powers refused to concur in the establishment of this government until it had been somewhat broadened, but in October it was agreed that the authority of the revamped provisional government should be extended to the provinces. In November a new Austrian parliament was elected. The elections went off very peacefully, with no indication that any occupying power was attempting to influence the results. The Renner government was formally recognized by the United States on January 7, 1946. However, all of the government's laws were subject to approval by the Allied Commission, and individual commissioners were empowered to suspend the execution of such laws if they deemed it necessary. Several laws have indeed been disapproved by the Allied Commission, but of these, none, except possibly a law establishing a censorship bureau, were of great importance.

Under these conditions, a constructive military government policy would have commenced in October a gradual handing over of administrative authority to the Austrian government. Experience in Italy had clearly shown the value of a gradual transition process during which the reins of control were slowly loosened while the indigenous government was acquiring necessary background information, beginning to operate on the simpler tasks, and slowly finding out the capacities of its existing administrative personnel. In Austria it was especially important to have the central government start supervising the *Länder,* since the latter were always somewhat too prone to independent action. Yet most of the departments in the American Element of the commission had not delegated even the most minor administrative tasks to the Austrian government by February, 1946. A few had made plans to do so, but only in rare cases was there any sort of time program attached to those plans. The main task of establishing a free and independent Austria was being slighted on the administrative side while it was being pushed on other fronts.

This curious situation seems to have been largely the result of a negative general policy. Neither the American commissioner nor his principal subordinates had issued instructions to the divisions of the commission staff covering the use or nonuse of the Austrian government. As a result, each department did what it pleased.

Control of Austrian Economic Life

It has already been emphasized that the problem of Austrian economic life was the most difficult which military government had to face. The country, which had reached its highest standard of living and its greatest internal economic adjustment as part of two large empires, was now broken up into four zones administered by powers whose economic theories were poles apart. Russian claims for the confiscation of many Austrian economic assets under the Soviet interpretation of the Potsdam Agreement were a constant problem for American economic specialists in military government. Operations of these officers were further handicapped by the cycle of military government organizations to which they were subjected, and to which their special field of activity was more sensitive than was any other special field. It follows that many of the difficulties described below were more or less beyond the control of individual economics officers.

In Austria, as in many Central European countries, there was a form of semipaternal economy which, although far removed from the Soviet system of complete governmental operation of major industry, was still markedly different from the American system of almost complete freedom for private enterprise. To some extent the existing controls were inheritances of the National Socialist wartime system, but more often they merely continued older Austrian controls. Prices were completely controlled, as were wages. Businesses were privately owned, but permission to operate them or to secure essential materials came from governmental economic control agencies. Much of the rationing was conducted by Chambers of Food and Agriculture and of Commerce which, although formerly controlled by boards elected by the members, were now in fact officers subordinated to the provincial administration. The government also took substantial interest in the development of new lines of business, of handicrafts, of tourist trade, and of particular agricultural products. No effort was made by military government to alter this system.

So far as materials and markets were available, industry (other than armaments, of course) was allowed to operate fairly freely in the American zone. Since military government did not have control of billeting there was some difficulty in clearing troops from essential factories and warehouses, but by the end of the first six months enough troops had been evacuated so that the problem was not a serious one. There were labor shortages, but resourceful managers got around them without needing much assistance from military government. By February, 1946, perhaps 60 per cent of industry was operating at perhaps 50 per cent of capacity. The failure of the rest, which was very serious for the limited Austrian economy, was almost entirely a result of interzonal and international trade restrictions and of the European coal shortage.

In a small country like Austria the main task was, of course, to eliminate interzonal trade restrictions as rapidly as possible. The Economics Division of the Allied Commission, American Element, had worked seriously but ineffectively on this problem up to February, 1946. One main difficulty lay in the Russian attitude toward occupied countries. Since Russia desired to continue unrestricted requisitioning and export to Russia of commodities and materials within its own zone, military government officials of the other zones feared that freedom of trade between zones would mean, in effect, an increased loss of Austrian assets to Russia. Whereas there was some justification for this attitude it is only fair to admit that some of the American officers pushed their fear of "subsidizing" the Russian zone so far as to prevent natural exports to Vienna. Only after vigorous complaints from the Austrian government was a restriction on the sending of milk, vegetables, and wood to Vienna withdrawn.[8] It might be noted, incidentally, that *The New York Times* correspondent reported on March 17, 1946, some secret movements of machinery out of the Russian into the American and British zones.

Prior to the establishment of an all-Austrian economy, it was, of course, possible to establish international trade between the American zone of Austria and at least three other places: Italy, the American zone of Germany, and Switzerland. A special section was set up in the Economics Division to encourage and approve such trade. This section operated with only minimum effectiveness, partly because of inadequate and changing personnel, partly because of a misconception of its function. Originally convinced that its work was to be largely "control," the staff only very slowly learned that hard work and aggressive policies were necessary if Austria was to have any foreign trade to control.

Two problems presented themselves. The most serious was the refusal of American military government in Germany to permit any trade except for dollar exchange or to permit any travel of civilians for commercial purposes without its express approval. This policy was especially obstructive since repair parts for much Austrian machinery were to be secured only in Germany.[9] Perhaps because he viewed it as desirable to separate Austria from Germany economically, the American commissioner had up to February, 1946, made no protest on this point to the Civil Affairs Division in Washington.

A second major problem—or at least major delay—interrupted barter trade with Italy. For a period of several months it was impossible to secure from Counter Intelligence Corps passes for civilians to travel to Italy, even though the trade project on which they were working had been approved by both Italian and Austrian authorities. The result, an almost complete paralysis of Italian-Austrian trade,

[8]In some cases, the regulations of military government headquarters seem to have stemmed from nothing except an excess of paternalism. On January 19, 1946, for example, USFAHQ ordered military government in Upper Austria to deliver salt to Vienna.

[9]"Cutting of Austria from Germany Hit," *The New York Times,* April 18, 1946.

entailed considerable hardship to both countries. The Economics Division did assist in the negotiation of a very general Italo-Austrian trade pact.

Before being too self-righteous over the cavalier Russian attitude toward captured enemy materials in Austria and Manchuria Americans should remember that in Austria at least the American army policy, while irreproachable in theory, was often shockingly wasteful in practice. The basic principles were sound: first, that all captured *Wehrmacht* property belongs to the American army; and second, that it should be issued to the Austrian authorities on quantitative receipts, thus postponing the problems of pricing and of payment, if the American army or the displaced persons did not need it. The actual procedures were, however, less happy than the theories.

There was, of course, a tremendous quantity of captured enemy material. In its last few months the German army had requisitioned a substantial proportion of the normal industrial supplies and motor vehicles of Austria. All factories which had been used in war production were also counted as a part of captured enemy materials. Energetic divisional G-4's and supply services piled up vast masses of captured supplies in requisitioned warehouses.

Without release of some of these materials, civilian economic operations were practically impossible. The problem of captured enemy materials was, therefore, largely a problem of the method of release. Various corps officers, division MG's, commanding officers of small tactical units all assumed it. In more than one case *Wehrmacht* cars were "released" for a bottle of schnapps. By July, higher headquarters began to work out methods of control. The Salzburg economics officer suggested during the first conference on the subject in July that the army select what it needed and rapidly release the rest to civilians. G-4 of USFA, however, decided instead to inventory everything and to release to civilian authorities only on application. It was December before the impossibility of complete, current inventories was recognized and the decision reached to release supplies more freely.

There was a little unnecessary squandering of Austrian materials for somewhat questionable "military purposes" in the first few weeks of occupation, but it was speedily stopped. Any purchasing or requisitioning of rationed materials was prohibited by regulations which were enforced with relative strictness. Some of the earlier military units to leave Austria took materials with them, but this practice was soon put under control. As a general rule, military government officers called attention to the bad effects of such practices and higher military headquarters were quite cooperative in helping to stop them.

The problem of civilian supply was so "hot" that it could not be allowed to fall into all of the difficulties characteristic of the other aspects of economic controls. The attitude of military government was always generous. Imports of foodstuffs and of essential petroleum products for the civilian population were made by the army. More than six months before American troops entered Austria, it was recognized that the area which might be the American zone was far from self-sufficient in food supplies. Requisitions were made at that time by the Mediterranean Theater. It later proved necessary to secure supplies from the north, and inter-Theater difficulties delayed the arrival of substantial quantities for two or three months. During that time a good deal of scurrying around by civilian authorities and their military government sponsors kept people alive on an 800-odd calory. basis. When shipments began to arrive it was possible to raise the ration slowly to 1,500 calories a day, where it stayed until April of 1946.

Perhaps the most important administrative lesson to be learned from the Austrian experience in food supply was the usefulness of employing indigenous agencies entirely. Most of the provincial supply officers had learned from hard experience in Italy the desirability of turning foodstuffs over immediately to local authorities, thus avoiding the accounting and guarding responsibilities which come with operation of a military government warehouse. When carloads or truckloads of American supplies came to town, quantitative receipts were secured from the provincial government. No further action was necessary. The savings in staff and trouble over the methods first used in Italy where military government personnel received, handled, and accounted for all foodstuffs were incalculable.

Austria has now become a "self-governing" nation. While not yet technically "at peace," because of the difficulties of reaching agreement on certain peace terms, and while still occupied by troops of the four major allies, she has repaired her status as an independent nation sufficiently to have qualified as a "participating nation" in the Paris Conference which met in the summer of 1947 to develop plans for European reconstruction in response to the proposal of Secretary of State George C. Marshall made at Harvard, June 5, 1947. Military government in Austria is drawing to a close, but it will be some time yet before this experiment in "re-establishing democracy" will be completed.

Part III

*Descriptive Account and Evaluation of
Experience in Germany*

★   ★   ★   ★   ★   ★

Chapter IX

Organizational Evolution in Germany, 1945–1947

CARL J. FRIEDRICH

THE organizational evolution of government in Germany is composed of two intertwined parts: Allied and American authorities and German authorities. Some of their problems are, however, joint ones. The men engaged in the military government of Germany had to struggle from the outset against strong odds which were due 1) to the chaos created by the National Socialist government of Germany before its complete collapse and unconditional surrender, 2) to the contradictory policies of the Allies, and 3) to the American failure to crystallize clear-cut policies *before* the enemy's defeat.

It is often stated in informed quarters that American military government learned many lessons in Italy. While there is undoubtedly a good deal of resemblance in field operations on the administrative level, the political setting in Germany was so different that many of the lessons learned in Italy proved inapplicable. The main reason was of course that instead of the joint Anglo-American operation in Italy, there was set up in Germany a system of separate zones under a quadripartite Control Council. The jurisdiction of this Control Council was uncertain from the start. The legal problems involved have never been settled. Is the ACC the sovereign power as some would insist? Or is it exercising the sovereign powers while sovereignty remains in the German people? Or is it an international body composed of "ambassadors" which has a coordinating function implementing the actions of the zonal commanders who exercise the sovereign powers under international law on behalf of their governments? Or are they exercising these powers on behalf of the German people? If the last, are they exercising these powers on behalf of the entire German people, or on behalf of that portion which lives in their zone? Whom does the term "the German people" cover today? These and many related problems illustrate the complexity of the Allied occupation of Germany. "Unconditional Surrender" was so novel a concept and the total disappearance of established government from a territory containing tens of millions of people so unprecedented that organizational tasks were fraught with uncertainties.

But whatever may be the answer to these legal questions, there can be no doubt that beneath the quadripartite consultative structure of the Allied Control Authority the military commander of each occupation zone was in complete control, subject, of course, to his own government.[1] His power was explicitly described as "supreme legislative, executive, and judicial authority"; in other words, undivided, concentrated power such as is traditionally described by students of comparative government as autocratic or nonconstitutional.[2] Such power may be justified from a democratic and constitutional standpoint by the fact that it is of specified and limited duration, and that its purpose is the establishment or re-establishment of democracy in the Western sense. It was recognized even in Roman times that a dictatorship may be set up *rei publicae constituendae causa,* that is to say, for the purpose of establishing a constitutional system; and there can be no question that the American policy of military occupation in both Germany and Japan is directed toward that end. The official declarations are replete with references to this task.[3] It is very important for the student of military government to grasp this basic pattern of "con-

[1] See JCS 1067, p. 000. Compare also Harold Zink, *American Military Government in Germany* (1947), Chap. XX, and James K. Pollock, "Germany under Military Occupation" in a volume he edited, entitled *Changes and Crisis in European Government* (1947).

[2] See, e.g., John Locke, *Essays in Civil Government,* Vol. II, and the tradition following him. For modern statements, compare Charles H. McIlwain, *Constitutionalism, Ancient and Modern* (1940); Carl J. Friedrich, *Constitutional Government and Democracy* (1941), especially Chaps. I, VII, and IX, and for the problem of emergency powers, XV; as well as Frederick M. Watkins, "The Problems of Constitutional Dictatorship," in *Public Policy,* Friedrich and Mason eds. (1940), I, 361, 363.

[3] See Chapters I and II above.

stitutional dictatorship," for it carries with it the processes involved in "turning things over to the Germans," an objective that American military government has retained throughout the changes of official policy described in the next chapter.

Military Government Pattern, 1945

The organizational pattern in the summer of 1945 (see page 417 below) placed the military government field detachments under the G-5 divisions of the tactical units (army groups, armies, corps, and divisions) and thus into the tactical chain of command. The policy or directives formulated by the G-5 division of SHAEF, located at Frankfurt, were passed down through the complete tactical command channel, from the commanding general of SHAEF to the commanding general of the army group and so on to the army, the corps, the division, and finally the detachment. In addition to this, some directives reached the detachments from the European Civil Affairs Division. This system prevailed until a territorial organization was evolved and military government was given its own chain of command (January 1, 1946).

The general problems associated with the tactical pattern are outlined in Chapter III. This type of organization is poorly adapted to the needs of a military occupation after the cessation of hostilities. It was bound to be replaced by a pattern in which military government authorities are more nearly in accord with the pattern of the government of the occupied country, especially as far as territorial subdivisions are concerned. During the period of its use, the tactical pattern caused a large number of artificial problems for military government. Beside the problems of channel of command there was constant confusion of jurisdiction. Two or more military authorities of the same level might have joint responsibilities over units of government in the occupied territory operating throughout an area in which the several military commands had a share. These problems would have been very much more serious had a German national government continued to exist after unconditional surrender was accepted. As it was, the commanding general wielding sovereign power in his zone (within the framework of his general directives from his government) could, in theory at least, bring about that coordination of policy in military government through appropriate delegation of authority to his G-5. Such coordination of all military government action was, of course, subject to such further coordination at the national level as the Allied Control Authority wished to foster.

The Allied Control Authority

A great deal of sharp criticism has been leveled at the ACA, in Britain and in the United States. The unanimity rule has enabled the powers represented on the ACA—the Soviet Union, the United States, Great Britain, and France—to use the voting as a convenient opportunity for barter. During the fall and winter of 1945–1946, the three powers, the Soviet Union, the United States, and Great Britain, seemed pretty well agreed on economic unity for Germany, but could not overcome French opposition. It was generally believed and reported through various channels, including the French press, that the French were holding out for concessions on the Rhineland and the Ruhr, as well as on the Saar industrial region. They sought control of the latter, and an international regime for the former. Since any international regime would raise problems of control of a very complex nature, including the stalemates resulting from the rivalries of the Great Powers, these concessions were not made. The French opposition was believed by the Russians to be a screen for a British, if not an American, design to consolidate their position so as to prevent a Communist ascendancy in all of Germany. Among Americans and the British a corresponding belief was prevalent attributing French opposition in this matter to Soviet backing. It seems doubtful that either of these suspicions was well founded in fact. No such fanciful explanations are needed for a French policy so entirely in keeping with their past traditions and current situation. What is a fact, not yet adequately explained by anyone, is that the Soviet Union abandoned its previous position and began to throw every conceivable obstacle in the way of economic unification after about April 1, 1946. This turnabout occurred in connection with an agreement that had finally

been worked out for achieving over-all unity in certain central economic concerns delineated in the Potsdam Declaration, notably banking and finance, foreign trade, commerce, industry, and transport.
The Russian shift coincided with a number of developments, among
which one might mention a new wave of plant removals from their
zone, rapid progress in denazification and democratization in the
American zone, marked setbacks in Communist party support in
various elections, a sharpening of the conflict in Iran, and an inclination on the part of France to back down. It seems idle further to specu-
late on which of these factors, if any—or whether, perhaps internal
developments in the Soviet Union, including the initiation of the new
Five-Year Plan—were responsible for the sudden reversal of Soviet
policy.

In spite of all the criticism, the ACA has a certain substantial
amount of work to its credit.[4] That a quadripartite condominium
could not successfully govern a country in such a state of disorganization and exhaustion as Germany was in during 1945–1946 was a foregone conclusion. Even if the four occupying powers had been united
in general outlook and ideology, their divergent interests would have
prevented such an enterprise from being a complete success. What
amazes the student of government as he studies the work of the ACA
is not how little was done, but how much. Naturally, most of the
characteristic achievements of the ACA are on the negative and destructive side. Since the Allies had been united in their determination to defeat the common enemy, and had agreed to make sure that
he could never rise again to threaten the world with aggressive military designs, all policies pointed in this direction received a substantial
measure of common support and crystallized into laws, proclamations, orders, directives, and instructions. This work was accomplished
through an organization whose general outlines can readily be
gleaned from the chart appearing in the Appendix, page 422. The real
working parts of the ACA were, and are, the various directorates and
the committees, which in turn are implemented by subcommittees.

---

[4]The work of the Allied Control Authority in Germany is available in six stout
volumes (to June, 1947) compiled by the Legal Division of OMGUS, and entitled
Enactments and Approved Papers of the Control Council and Coordinating Committee.
It is divided into Proclamations, Laws, Orders, Directives, and Instructions.

The directorates correspond, as can be seen, to what would be the ministries or departments of a German government if there were one, plus a few others, such as reparations and restitution, resulting directly from the terms of unconditional surrender. The supreme authority, however, is lodged in the Allied Control Council, consisting of the four commanders in chief and meeting three times a month in Berlin. The council delegates a great part of its work to the Coordinating Committee, consisting of the deputy military governors, who are in fact directors of military government. The secretariat consists of four secretaries general, one from each of the four occupying powers, and attends to such matters as meetings, routing of council decisions to directorates and committees and the reverse, and so on. Most of its work is of a routine administrative nature.

A detailed analysis of the work accomplished by the ACA would lead quite far afield. Many of its decisions have proved unworkable, such as the law regarding the destruction of Nazi books and other publications, or the law requiring the destruction of all war memorials, both of which aroused a sharp debate in the House of Commons and in the British and American press. Many others have remained paper declarations, since the ACA is not provided with any inspectorate apart from the occupying powers themselves to ascertain whether its decisions are being carried out in the several zones, and if so, whether they are being carried out uniformly.[5] As a result all the major fields of Allied control activity have shown marked diversity in the four zones, demilitarization being probably the most uniform one, deindustrialization next, denazification and democratization least so. To any student of administration and the problems involved in law enforcement, it would be surprising, indeed, if great diversity were not found in four zones under a control setup such as exists in Germany today under the ACA.

[5]However, in 1947 a special inspection to determine how far the destruction of military installations had progressed was authorized.

United States Forces, European Theater and
the Office of Military Government, US

Formally, the direction of military government in Germany, as in Japan, is in the hands of the Commanding General of the United States Forces in the European Theater. Actually, a very large part of this responsibility devolved upon the deputy military governor, who for military purposes is commanding general of the military government setup, known as OMGUS (see Appendix, page 418). As can be seen from the chart, he has several advisers, including the political adviser who also has a direct relationship to the State Department. Ambassador Robert Murphy, who fills this post, had been an important leader in his role of political adviser to General Eisenhower. He heads the political division in OMGUS.[6]

As the two charts clearly show, OMGUS became an intermediate organization, one face turned toward the Allied Control Authority, into which its divisions are tied through the many committees; the other face turned toward Germany, where its authority is wielded through five territorial military government establishments, *Land* Bavaria, *Land* (Greater) Hesse, *Land* Württemberg-Baden, Bremen Enclave,[7] and the U.S. Sector of Berlin. There are also a number of special offices, such as the Denazification Review Board, and the Regional Government Coordinating Office (see page 424 in the Appendix). The *Land* detachments are in turn organized in a fashion roughly corresponding to the ministries or departments of their *Land* (see page 427), and in the course of operations direct contact has been developed between the divisions in OMGUS, Berlin, and at *Land* level. However, because there is no direct territorial contact between Berlin and the American zone, all communication having to traverse Soviet-

[6]This pattern was changed again when, on March 15, 1947, the then deputy military governor, General Lucius D. Clay, became military governor and commander in chief, Europe.

[7]Bremen, together with Bremerhaven, became a fifth *Land* in January, 1947. This settlement ended a complex arrangement under which the military government of the enclave, although staffed by Americans and subject to OMGUS in general policy, was also subordinate to British military government authorities of *Land* Lower Saxony, with seat in Hanover.

controlled territory, and on prescribed and rather circuitous routes, the working relationship between central offices and the field, proverbially beset by many difficulties, encounters many more obstacles.[8] These obstructions are becoming more troublesome as German governmental activity increases and supervisory functions call for frequent consultation. The cost to the American taxpayer in man-hours lost due to this treatment of American requirements by an ally and beneficiary under lend-lease runs into the millions. Yet only the governments at Moscow and at Washington could have changed these arrangements. This "minor" administrative issue well illustrates the cumbersome and inefficient nature of quadripartite machinery.

When, on March 15, 1947, General Lucius D. Clay, the then Deputy Military Governor, became commander in chief and military governor, the organization of military government was changed so as to enable General Clay to continue the active direction of military government. The headquarters of the CIC were transferred to Berlin, and an office was established for the CIC consisting of a group of overall advisers and coordinators. Personnel, budgetary and organizational control, intelligence, and certain other general activities were thus put into the position of relating the practices of the military government command to those of the occupation troops, more especially the constabulary and the military police. This constituted an important forward step, since divergencies in their respective approach to the occupation had been a cause of trouble.[9] In addition to the Political Adviser, the military governor established an economic adviser, a governmental affairs adviser, and a financial adviser to whom others were to be added as occasion arose. It was intended that these top-level policy advisers would assist the military governor and his two deputies, the commanding general of EUCOM and the commanding general of OMGUS, in coordinating the activities of subordinate units, including the divisions of OMGUS. The difficulty of such an approach lies in the fact that these advisers are outside the

[8]Besides the air transport connections, which are dependent on the weather, there are regular night trains from Berlin to Frankfurt and an *Autobahn* (speed highway) paralleling this railroad line. Both, as well as the air routes, necessitate time-consuming detours between Berlin and a large part of the zone.

[9]See above Chapter I, pages 12–14, for the issues involved.

chain of command, yet lack the unity of a genuine general staff setup. Yet it is generally agreed that perhaps the most important requirement of a long-range enterprise such as the American occupation in Germany is a staff of men who are in a position, because of background, experience, and education, to assist the military governor in preparing programs, plans, and policies for divergent trends and in reconciling policy decisions arrived at in Washington as a result of over-all national policy.

German Constitutional Developments

It has been American as well as Allied policy to foster democratization of Germany. The complete collapse of all existing German government machinery, while a handicap in many ways, had the advantage of allowing the building up of democratic support "from the grass roots," as the saying goes in America.[10] Elections were first called for in the smallest units and gradually widened in scope. National elections seem still a rather remote prospect, but elections have been held for constitutional assemblies in the three states of the American zone. (Strictly local elections have also taken place in the French, British, and Soviet zone for local legislative bodies.) These presumably will be followed by state-wide elections under the constitutions to be adopted by the people on the basis of drafts prepared by these conventions.[11] In the meantime, preliminary drafts, submitted to these conventions at the suggestion of American military government authorities by their minister-presidents, who had appointed commissions to prepare them, have been thoroughly analyzed in OMGUS by an interdivisional committee, and general lines of policy formulated with regard to a number of central points. On the eve of the meeting of the conventions, the military governor issued

[10]That all was not well with this formula is strongly suggested by the analysis in Chapter XI, especially page 246. However, American policy is now vindicating its dedication to this approach.

[11]Constitutions are also in the making in the two former states (*Länder*) of Hamburg and Bremen, the Hamburg one having been approved by British military government authorities. These constitutions were, however, drafted and adopted by councils appointed by military government, as was also the constitution of the city of Berlin, which is a regular city charter, without any reference to civil liberties or other basic matters.

a statement of general principles that could readily be interpreted as a guide for OMGUS as well as for the Germans. It implemented established policy by stating (1) the criteria for democratization, and (2) the criteria for decentralization (see Appendix, page 403). As these constitutions become law, American military government will be increasingly justified in adopting a policy of watchful vigilance, allowing the Germans to assume responsibility, but making sure that they stay within the general objectives of Allied policy.

The Council of States

The American initiative in requesting the Germans to enter upon the task of drafting constitutions was preceded by an important step for creating a measure of cooperation and unity within the American zone. This was an urgent, and unavoidable enterprise, because American policy needed to secure an equivalent to the unified German setup in the Soviet zone; yet it was also a very delicate enterprise, because American policy wished to avoid aggravating Russian suspicions that it was bent on creating a "Western capital."[12] One may doubt that the United States has been wholly successful in such efforts, and the use by former Secretary Byrnes of Stuttgart as a platform for delivering his historic speech surely reinforced such suspicions. But rather than appoint German officials to offices or departments having authority throughout the American zone, as the Russians had done in theirs, the United States created a Council of States (*Länderrat*) which is in effect a federation of the three states in the American zone through the office of their three minister-presidents. It follows a pattern familiar to the student of German constitutional history, for the *Bundesrat* in the empire and the *Reichsrat* in the Weimar Republic had each been composed of the heads of the executive establishments.[13] Like them, the *Länderrat* (see page

[12]The concern over a "Western capital" had been a factor in connection with USFET's use of Frankfurt as a headquarters, and the transfer of OMGUS to Berlin was to some extent a gesture in the opposite direction.

[13]For an analytical discussion of this curious pattern see C. J. Friedrich, *Constitutional Government and Politics,* Chapter XIII. See also Arnold Brecht, *Federalism and Regionalism in Germany* (1945), especially Chapter VI and Appendix D.

426) works mainly through a large number of committees in which the specialists from the three governments are able to discuss the proposed steps in legislation needed for the zone as a whole. Mention has already been made of the denazification law, but not only the large sphere of economic activities—potentially the task of central German agencies under Potsdam—but a number of other important matters, such as press and civil service legislation, have been the subject of extended discussion and eventual legislative drafting. It is not very easy to see how these activities are going to go forward, once constitutionally elected governments have superseded the appointed governments which collaborated in the council during most of 1946. Evidently such government will often be subject to different party controls. Another complication will arise from the establishment of bizonal agencies under the British-American merger, although for the time being it is planned to make the German delegates to the bizonal boards controlling these agencies report directly to the *Länderrat,* as far as the American zone is concerned.[14] Something akin to the Council of States may, however, emerge at the seat of the bizonal agencies —or the central German agencies if the other two powers join Great Britain and the United States—to counterbalance a directly elected German parliament, thus re-creating the traditional German federal structure in a new setting.

The importance attached by American military government authorities to this Council of States is attested to by the fact that a separate office was created known as the Regional Government Coordinating Office, whose director reports directly to the deputy military governor. Its first director was the architect of the council, and it is fair to say that central importance is being attached to the council as an instrumentality in the process of fostering constitutional reconstruction in Germany. The members of its staff participate in the numerous committee meetings, thus constituting an essential liaison link between the German activities and OMGUS divisions, especially the Civil Administration Division, which sends one of its staff members to the Coordinating Office for observation of *Länderrat* activities each week. As a matter of course, German zonal agencies for the

[14] See the reports by Dana Schmidt to *The New York Times* during August, 1946.

American zone have been placed under the Council of States and will continue in this relationship now that they are being merged into the bizonal agencies.

Bizonal Agencies

By July, 1946, American authorities both in military government and without had become sufficiently provoked by the failure of the ACA to authorize the establishment of central German agencies, as provided under the Potsdam Declaration, to propose to any of the occupying powers interested in such a plan the establishment of interzonal agencies forthwith. The British government accepted this proposal within a week, and the necessary organizational adaptations were being pushed vigorously all through the summer of 1946. It was the hope that both the other occupying powers would join in these interzonal agencies, but at the outset the hope for such a development appeared slim. Thus the proposal really amounted to an economic merger of the British and American zones. That such an economic merger would bring a considerable adaptation in its train on the side of government and administration was generally conceded as inevitable. The British had been progressing more cautiously in fostering self-government in those parts of Germany directly under their jurisdiction. One difficulty the British have had to contend with is the territorial complexity of their zone, containing the great rump of Western Prussia, with the relatively small enclaves of Hamburg, Bremen, Oldenburg, Braunschweig, Lippe, and so on. Attempts to simplify this structure encounter considerable opposition, and the British, traditionally more mindful of historical precedent, seem to hesitate to act decisively, as American military government certainly did when it merged the parts of Württemberg and Baden now within its zone (although the French did not merge theirs), and lumped into Greater Heese the South German Grand Duchy of Hesse with the Prussian province of Hesse.

Unlike the American practice of gathering zonal agencies in Stuttgart under the jurisdiction of the Council of States, the British scattered their zonal agencies and assigned them to different cities, with great resulting inconvenience of operation. In the beginning the bizonal agencies followed this pattern. The reason given was that it was desired not to raise the issue of a Western capital. The resulting inefficiency threatened defeat of the zonal merger. This view was reported to have been expressed by German authorities immediately.[15]

Conclusion

The complex organizational problems that have arisen in the military occupation of Germany have been much more perplexing than those in Japan, where the established government was allowed to transform itself and then continue, and where the United States has been carrying on the occupation alone, advised and at times criticized by an Allied commission, known today as the Far Eastern Commission. American military government has been trying gradually to resolve this within the limited framework in which it is operating. A measure of progress has been achieved, but it has not been possible to describe or analyze the underlying economic stresses and strains that have resulted from the slow pace of that progress. This situation is still too much in a state of flux to allow definitive treatment. Pessimists predicted economic disaster in Germany as well as death by starvation of a large part of the population during the winter of 1945–1946. While starvation was very real, death from it was kept within limits. In spite of an exceptional harvest in 1946, the food deficit in the British and American zones continues to be very serious. Even the maintenance of a ration of 1,550 calories which prevailed again in the fall of 1946 presumably called for imports amounting to between $300,000,000 and $400,000,000, and a subsistence ration of 2,200 would more than double that amount. According to a report made by General Lucius D. Clay in mid-November, 1946, it was hoped that the two zones can be made self-sustaining in three years by

[15]The bizonal organization has been completely revamped since the Moscow Conference failed to bring agreement on German unity. Its component units are now consolidated, with headquarters at Frankfurt. On the German side two coordinating bodies, with representative equality, have been established: the Bizonal Economic Council, composed of representatives elected by the *Land* legislatures, and the Bizonal Executive Committee, composed of representatives of the *Land* cabinets.

a capital investment of $1,000,000,000. There certainly is a substantial amount of unused plant capacity and man power in Germany today, but whether this reservoir can be effectively tapped for international trade remains to be seen. That this view of the situation is not motivated by a sudden inclination to be soft with the Germans, but by the general recognition of the desperate necessities of the European economy as a whole, hardly needs to be stressed.[16]

[16]See the Revised Directive below, Appendix B. The requirements indicated in the text are at present being revised to fit in with the "Marshall plan."

Chapter X

Conflicts over Planning at Staff Headquarters

DALE CLARK

Introduction

Eᴀʀʟʏ in the course of World War II, elaborate preparations were undertaken to select and train military government officers, to develop a control organization, and to define and strengthen the American concepts and techniques for dealing with liberated and conquered peoples. Military government experience growing out of World War I was reviewed and analyzed by military government officers with a view to avoiding mistakes made in the Allied occupation of the Rhineland. One basic defect of that occupation, the segmenting of the occupied area into relatively independent spheres, was given particular attention.

The early philosophy which emphasized constructive measures and unified control organization was further developed during the planning operations conducted in England by the German Country Unit, SHAEF during the spring and summer of 1944. Under vigorous leadership a plan for Germany was prepared and officers were selected to take over strategic positions controlling German administration as soon as the enemy forces should collapse. Officers had been selected and trained for control positions at the German central ministerial level as well as at 237 key regional control points designated in what now compromises the American, British, and French zones. The central and regional control offices of this inclusive organization were to have been drawn together from top to bottom and operated in a coordinated manner. This phase of the planning was known as "laying the carpet." Early plans assumed that the Russians would yet join in a coordinated allied control of all Germany.

The policy handbook that had been prepared in England was based upon the traditional concept of "firm though just treatment" and it envisaged laying a groundwork for reconstruction in a devastated Europe. The policies and plans produced in the summer of 1944 by the military government planning organization were considered by many to be superior to later policies and plans.[1]

With the announcement of the so-called "Morgenthau plan" and the issuance of JCS 1067, which embodied features of this plan, the approach to military government planning changed direction. The German Country Unit of SHAEF was liquidated. New officers arrived with instructions to implement plans that virtually partitioned Germany, blocked earlier designs to reconstitute German central organization or integrated regional organization, paralyzed trade and industry, nullified the effectiveness of four-power control machinery in Berlin, and segmented the control organization in Germany even within the American zone.

How was it possible that an essentially sound approach which had been recommended on the basis of experience in World War I and which is now the object of belated efforts of restoration was defeated in the first place?

Three main forces contributed to the revolution in American military government policy:

1) The rising tide of wartime hate and emotion, always a threat to postwar rehabilitation, was allowed to overflow the barriers that civilization erects and to submerge temporarily national ideals and interests. Already it begins to seem unreal, but men in positions of influence could advocate a "Carthaginian peace" and sanction chaos as an instrument of national policy. There were many who became insensitive to the moral bankruptcy of the doctrine that we should do to the Germans as they had done to others. "The best way to kill rats,"

---

[1] See page 36. This chapter was written before Hajo Holborn's competent *Military Government Organization and Politics* (1947) appeared. But Holborn does not deal with the problems overseas which are here analyzed; hence the book and this chapter implement each other well.—ED.

said one disciple of the "hard peace" school of thought, "is to burn down the whole house." "When we go into Germany," said another official who held a key position, "this will be our policy: Germany will be in flames. We will be the fire department and we won't turn on the water!"

2) Competition arose for control of the organization of military occupation. Should Germany be governed by the tactical military forces which occupy it or by a specially constituted organization composed of men experienced in civilian administration? This question and also the question of the relative power to be given to various military commands resulted in deadlocks. Each party to this struggle tended to become the protagonist of a philosophy of military government which favored its own institutional interests, and objective analysis became subordinated. An organization designed for the purpose of winning a war is apt to be very different from an organization required for establishing the peace. It may differ in its structure, procedures, attitudes, and criteria for leadership. It is, however, extremely difficult to transfer leadership from the hands of tactical military leaders to a corps of administrators even though the latter may have been placed in uniform. The "regulars" of the victorious military organization are at the height of their prestige; they are a "going concern"; and they arrived on the scene first. It is not in the nature of power to abdicate.

3) Unrealistic conceptions about the early policy of the Soviet Union contributed to the present situation. By concentrating on the evils of Nazi Germany, Americans lost sight of the potential dangers in the structure and policy of the Soviet Union. In those days it was popular to say: "We must get along with Russia at any cost," and the costs were not calculated. American policy allowed Russia to entrench herself in Central Europe.

In some Marxist thinking and Communist practice, a condition of chaos precedes revolution and ushers in Communism. In democratic thinking, stability and prosperity go hand in hand with democratic development. Early punitive policies tending toward economic stagnation in Germany produced a feeling of frustration in conscientious officers. Many shared the cynical conviction that a politics of planned chaos was being instituted in Germany and that the Soviet Union would be the beneficiary.

To depict the conduct of preliminary planning operations for American military government for Germany against this background of conflicting factions, interests, and ideologies is the purpose of the following sections of this chapter. Discussion will be focused on the impact of high policy, particularly JCS 1067, on the development of plans for Germany, and on the policy conflicts that plagued successive phases of military government planning operations.

First Planning Staff in England

To understand some of the basic conflicts it is necessary to sketch the beginnings of American military government in World War II. In the winter of 1943–1944, military government officers destined for Germany were being assembled in England. A training center was established at a former British army post at Shrivenham for the purposes of interim training, organizing, and waiting.

Initial planning operations for military government had been undertaken in London at Supreme Allied Command (predecessor to SHAEF) and at lower military echelons in London. It was an unproductive period for military government planning mainly because the organization was being adapted primarily to the tactical operation. There were frequent organization changes, distractions, inadequate basic data on Germany, and lack of policy.

A decision was made to reorganize military government planning activities. Within SHAEF there would be "Country Units" that would work up plans with the British for the occupation of specific countries.

SHAEF Missions

An important organizational device was developed for the purpose of preparing for the entry into Allied countries. In order to have a combined planning staff for each of the countries of Europe there were organized in England early in 1944 what came to be known first as Country Units, and later, during the operational phase, as SHAEF Missions. With the exception of a few months (January—April, 1944) the Country Units, composed of British and American officers, were located in London, where they prepared detailed plans for civil affairs operations in each of the countries of Northwest Europe—France, Belgium, the Netherlands, Luxembourg, Denmark, and Norway.[2] For technical direction these units were attached to the operations branch of the G-5 division of SHAEF. Later they also came under the administrative control of SHAEF and were part of the SHAEF table of organization. Organized on functional lines with sections for supply, legal affairs, finance, displaced persons, and so on, the units maintained liaison with corresponding sections of the exiled governments located in England. In conjunction with these governments the British and American officers prepared plans in the form of operational handbooks, directives, and proclamations to be used in the countries when they were liberated.

From the first it was planned that the SHAEF Missions would work with the top level of the restored governments of the countries of Northwest Europe. They would form the necessary liaison group with the top officials in each office. Therefore, as soon as a central government of the liberated country was organized, the SHAEF Mission for that particular country moved into the country as near the headquarters of the central government as possible. The SHAEF Mission to France, the largest of the Missions, set up its headquarters at the Trianon Hotel in Paris soon after the city was liberated. The last of the Missions to go in were those for Norway and Denmark. Both accompanied the task forces into the countries after the German surrender.

The Missions had two chief aims: to secure from the government of the liberated country the services, supplies, and property that the country could furnish for the use of the Allied armies; and to handle the negotiations for the movement of supplies that the Allied countries furnished for rebuilding the nation and feeding the population. In one way the Missions were carrying on some of the work of the

[2]During the summer of 1944 the Norwegian Unit moved to Edinburgh, Scotland, in order to be near Scottish Command, the army command scheduled for Norway.

embassies and other diplomatic agencies until these could be re-established. Indeed, when the Missions left the country, and they were usually the last army unit to leave, some of their remaining functions and personnel were transferred to the American and British embassies. On the whole, the Missions were made up of officers technically well fitted for their jobs. Most of them were specialists in their fields and had held key positions in civilian life. As units through which all dealings between the army and the central government officials were carried on, they successfully accomplished their assigned tasks.[3]

Up to that time there had been no policy, no plan, no effective organization. The job now was to produce all three. Under vigorous leadership the group responded to the challenging situation. Whereas some 125 skeptical British and American officers had left London on this expedition to Shrivenham, it was a cohesive organization that returned in June, 1944, some three months later. Organization of the officers into divisions corresponding generally to the German ministries began as soon as they boarded the train for Shrivenham. The colonel temporarily in command went from one train compartment to another, checking on the aptitudes and preferences of officers for various assignments.

The preparation of the *Basic Handbook for Military Government of Germany* was begun almost immediately upon the arrival of the group at Shrivenham. An Organization and Personnel Planning Section began the preparation of the over-all control organization and planned the disposition of military government teams for the post-hostilities phase. There were many headaches, and many sections of the preliminary drafts were inadequate. But the pressure was on. The control organization was being created. As policy plans and a control organization came into being, they brought a sense of confidence and exhilaration.

Essential features of the organization plan were these:

1) In regard to the organization of Germany itself, zones would exist for purposes of garrisoning troops of the occupying powers and for the handling of supply and special problems of military occupa-

[3]The essential material for these paragraphs on SHAEF missions was furnished by Lt. Col. Robert H. Slover.

tion. It was hoped that the Soviet Union would agree that the Allied administration of Germany would be joint and centralized, and that Germany would be administered as an "integrated" unit. The Russians had been invited to participate in the planning program and preparations were being made for the expected arrival of U.S.S.R. military government officers. The French, still under German domination, had not yet been allocated a zone of occupation.

2) The Allied control organization to be superimposed on German organization would be closely coordinated from the center so that the policies would be uniform; lines of control would extend from the central control agency to subordinate units, not through military tactical channels but through technical military government channels that conformed to German political organization.

In order to secure this vertical cohesion, the next step, after providing for a ministerial planning organization, was to prepare in advance for military government organization at the regional level.

ECAD (European Civil Affairs Division), which was also at Shrivenham, had jurisdiction over the necessary "bodies," as personnel was then described. They were assembled at ECAD in preparation for the tactical operations. The proposal was made to "borrow" officers temporarily from ECAD regiments to be earmarked and trained for eventual duty at key control centers in Germany, such as provincial capitals and important cities. After the training period these officers were to rejoin their military government detachments under ECAD for their assigns in the invasion through France and Germany during the mobile combat phase. In case of the sudden collapse of the enemy, which was then considered a possibility, there would be in readiness a skeleton organization of specialists for Germany around which completed staffs could quickly be built. Officers would move to predetermined cities and occupy positions for which they were prepared. In the post-hostilities period the designated officers would in any event be sent to their specified control points for which they had been "pinpointed" on the administrative map of Germany.

The officers designated in advance for key control points in Germany were assembled at the Regional Staff Program at Manchester, England, on July 4, 1944. They were to be welded into an organization framework covering 237 key control points in western Germany and to begin the preparation of more detailed plans for this level. Planning conferences were conducted on the basis of functional and areal interest. A transportation specialist was, for example, destined for the railroad center of Nuremberg. He participated in area planning conferences with economists and other specialists on the Nuremberg team, or those designated for Bavaria. He also met in transportation conferences with transportation men of all areas, and with transportation officers in the U.S. Group Control Council intended to be set up in Berlin. Those intangible and informal relationships that make for smooth operations in organization were being encouraged by pre-invasion planning contacts among central staff and regional staff officers.

The planning enterprise had a distinctly civilian character during this phase. The inherent conflict that had existed since the beginning was now brought to a head, showing American military government to be indeed a "house divided." The most apparent conflict developed over the question of who would gain control of the organization. Would it be the regular military, or an organization dominated by civilian administrators recruited for the job such as the German Country Unit?

The collision on this point came at Manchester, England, on July 3 and 4, 1944, when the organization plan of the German Country Unit was being presented at the opening meeting of the Regional Staff Program. The regional specialists from ECAD presented conflicting concepts. They were told they would be linked up by direct connection to Berlin in an organization conforming to German political organization. However, the new commanding officer of ECAD reversed the policy of his predecessor and announced that they were to be part of a military organization "in the true sense of the word." The temporary gains of German Country Unit's conception of a political "chain of command" were being challenged.

The question of who would occupy the dominant position in military government engaged the attention of several military commands who recognized the opportunity for service, power, and preferment.

Leading contenders besides the German Country Unit of SHAEF were the U.S. element of G-5, SHAEF, European Civil Affairs Division, and for a time the 12th Army Group.

The announcement of the zone boundaries and the decision to locate Theater headquarters at Frankfort opened the conflict as to the allocation of functions between Berlin and Frankfort. The army tactical commands stressed the importance of decentralizing authority to the zone where, it was convincingly argued, the main job would have to be done.

The unfortunate results of the internal maneuvers for power emphasize the danger of embarking on an extensive program without clarification of policy in Washington. At their best the various commands were all trying to carry out their assignments while vigorously striving to assume leadership. At their worst they were competitive contenders in a struggle for control. In some cases they duplicated planning, hoarded and raided personnel, monopolized documents, sabotaged their rivals' efforts, and maintained veritable espionage systems against one another.

By July, 1944, the German Country Unit had completed a preliminary plan for the military government of Germany and its concept was winning out. At a meeting of General Eisenhower's staff the plan was presented. General Eisenhower stated that it met with his approval and directed that steps be taken to implement it. In August, 1944, the U.S. Group Control Council was organized, taking over the American personnel of the German Country Unit almost intact. The British set up a parallel organization and hopes were revived that the Soviet Union would send a Russian Group Control Council in order that closely coordinated planning could be carried on by the three powers. In order to provide adequate facilities, the newly formed U.S. Group Control Council was moved from Prince's Garden to Bushy Park, a suburb of London, which before the invasion had been main headquarters of SHAEF. Thereby a splendidly functioning joint U.S./British organization was taken apart in order to allay any suspicions of the Russians that the United States and Britain were presenting a united front. It was hoped, however, that an enlarged control organization would be created at Bushy Park that would include the Russians on an equal basis and would reflect Allied solidarity.

It was in Washington that the fate of American policy on Germany was to be determined. The plan of the German Country Unit had been received in Washington and brought to a head the fundamental conflict in policy. The basic question was how the victors should treat the vanquished. Should plans be directed primarily toward the destruction of the enemy nation or destruction of the will to war? Can victors win the enemy to a lasting peace while destroying her immediate war potential? Should the occupation be punitive? Should the policy be constructive?

A copy of the German Unit's plan for administration of Germany as a unit had been forwarded to the Secretary of War by the colonel in command of the German Country Unit. It was considered "constructive" and it was hoped that proponents of constructive policy would prepare the ground for Washington's approval of its basic concepts. But a copy of an earlier preliminary draft of the plan had been transmitted directly through private channels to the Secretary of the Treasury. Officers of the military government planning staffs who had eagerly awaited major decisions from Washington clarifying policy were to receive in the fall ominous signs of things to come. Newspaper reports informed them that the Secretary of the Treasury had laid before the President a copy of the military government plan for Germany. Certain passages in the plan had been marked for special scrutiny and reportedly had called forth strong presidential censure.[4] The opponents of constructive policy had taken the initiative in Washington in discrediting the planning that had been done in England.

---

[4]After Mr. Morgenthau had submitted to President Roosevelt the preliminary draft of the policy handbook for Military Government of Germany proposed by the German Country Unit, President Roosevelt wrote Secretary of War Stimson a letter highly critical of the planning undertaken in England. "It gives me the impression," President Roosevelt wrote Stimson, "that Germany is to be restored just as much as the Netherlands or Belgium, and the people of Germany brought back as quickly as possible to their pre-war estate."—*PM*, December 2, 1945, p. 10.

A Reversal of Planning: The Morgenthau Plan

When President Roosevelt departed for the historic conference with Prime Minister Churchill at Quebec in September, 1944, he was provided with a memorandum: "Program to Prevent Germany from Starting a World War III." This memorandum summarized the "Morgenthau plan" for control of Germany.

The plan called for removal or destruction of "key industries which are basic to military strength," and for "new boundaries of Germany," "partitioning of new Germany," internationalization of the Ruhr and the closing of mines and removal of "all equipment," restitution and reparation "by forced labor outside Germany," and a twenty-five-year control of German "foreign trade and industry" by the United Nations designed to prevent in the newly established (German) states the establishment or expansion of key industries basic to the German military potential and designed further to control other key industries.[5]

Mr. Morgenthau has issued a statement on what transpired at Quebec:[6]

At the Quebec conference in September 1944, the President raised with Mr. Churchill this question of the treatment of Germany. He invited me to Quebec to join in these conversations. At the conclusion of the discussions on this topic a memorandum of agreement was dictated by Prime Minister Churchill to his secretary and was then read and initialed by him and by President Roosevelt. Because I feel that it may be helpful for the record, I am going to quote this memorandum:

"At a conference between the President and the Prime Minister upon the best measures to prevent renewed rearmament by Germany, it was felt that an essential feature was the disposition of the Ruhr and the Saar.

"The ease with which the metallurgical, chemical, and electric industries in Germany can be converted from peace to war has already been impressed upon us by bitter experience. It must also be remembered that the Germans have devastated a large portion of the industries of Russia and of other neighboring Allies, and it is only in accordance with justice

[5] A statement by Mr. Morgenthau on how the policy for Germany was evolved is quoted in Chapter II, page 36.

[6] Henry Morgenthau, Jr., "Postwar Treatment of Germany," *The Annals of the American Academy of Political and Social Science* (July, 1946), p. 126.

that these injured countries should be entitled to remove the machinery they require in order to repair the losses they have suffered. The industries referred to in the Ruhr and in the Saar would therefore be necessarily put out of action and closed down. It was felt that the two districts should be put under some body under the world organization which would supervise the dismantling of these industries and make sure that they were not started up again by some subterfuge.

"This programme for eliminating the war-making industries in the Ruhr and in the Saar is looking forward to converting Germany into a country primarily agricultural and pastoral in its character.

"The Prime Minister and the President were in agreement on this programme."   (Intd.) O.K.
                                                         F.D.R.
September 15, 1944   (Intd.) W.S.C.

Basic provisions of the memorandum which Morgenthau had drawn up for the Quebec Conference, including the plan for reducing Germany to an agricultural country, suddenly emerged as Allied policy. A matter of crucial importance in both foreign policy and military operations had been formulated without either the Secretary of State or the Secretary of War being present. The announcement of the decisions at Quebec signified a rupture in planning in the U.S. Group Control Council, successor to the German Country Unit. These plans had been directed toward a more constructive military occupation in Germany. Newspaper comment on the Morgenthau proposals revived the controversial discussion of "How to treat the Germans." In discussions of this subject among military government personnel there was nearly always a division between those advocating constructive measures and those who argued for a punitive program. Until now those favoring a constructive peace had generally kept their hand at the helm.

It was a strategic time to push for a plan aimed at the destruction of Germany. The capture of Roetgen, first important German town to surrender, was announced on September 24, the same day as the story of the Morgenthau plan became public. The war was moving into the last phase, and war emotions stiffened the American attitude. With the prospects of a collapse of the German armed forces, the U.S. Army "regulars" would move into the controlling positions of the military government organization. The Control Council was then being built up and there was still time for corrective personnel appointments.

Despite its announcement at Quebec and widespread press comment on the Morgenthau plan, responsible persons refused to believe that such a destructive plan would be seriously contemplated. Many regarded it as an extreme proposal that public opinion and the exercise of good judgment in administration circles would defeat. The reaction of American public opinion to the Morgenthau plan gave encouragement to this view. It was widely resented as a breach of military secrecy that immediately placed in the hand of Nazi propaganda a weapon of great value. *The New York Times* editorially attacked the plan on the day following its announcement, pointing out its fallacies with respect to the destruction of industry and the consequent abandonment of reparations. Five leading American engineering societies, through a joint report issued by their presidents, promptly predicted that "we must recognize that the German nation cannot arbitrarily be kept in economic and industrial subjugation. . . . Recovery cannot come about through an economy wholly agricultural, even if that were practicable; or without industry to produce both for German needs and for the reconstruction of other nations of Europe; or without markets."[7]

The plan was also attacked in the House of Commons, where a storm awaited Mr. Eden's return from Quebec. After putting questions as to the position of His Majesty's Government and as to why Secretary of State Hull and Secretary of War Stimson did not take part in the discussion, Mr. Stokes (Laborite) asked: "Is my Right Honorable Friend aware that if the Morgenthau plan is carried out it will lead to a general lowering of the standard of living throughout Europe and, in the view of a great many people, to another war?"[8]

The reaction of the press indicated that the American people were strongly divided over it. Under this pressure, President Roosevelt

[7]This report was entitled "Program for Industrial Control of Postwar Germany." The presidents of the five engineering societies which now comprise Engineers Joint Council completed this report on September 29, 1944, and submitted it to the State Department a few days later.

[8]*The New York Times,* September 29, 1944.

publicly stated that he had not endorsed the Morgenthau plan. This statement was regarded as a hopeful sign by military government officers. As events showed, however, it was merely an evasive statement, while policy followed the "Quebec plan."[9] The new plan continued to guide policy through the "top secret" channels of the army.[10]

To put through a policy that encountered so much opposition required consummate skill in the manipulation of power. That the men who accomplished this feat were not mediocrities is revealed by the details of their skillful performance. The secrecy surrounding military planning was a factor which aided in the instituting of a policy which appeared to be out of harmony with American practices and interests.

Setting the stage for the pattern of military government, a group of officials in the Treasury and others near the Secretary of the Treasury had actively participated in the military government planning to the point where officials in the State Department and officers in the Civil Affairs Division, War Department, were complaining of the necessity for clearing papers with the Treasury. A former Treasury official who occupied a key position as Director of the Finance Division of SHAEF was commonly referred to in London as a Treasury representative in uniform. Contact with his former chief, the Secretary of the Treasury, and thence to the White House, gave him a pronounced advantage in negotiations in England. Furthermore, he could draw on the work of the dependable staff from the Treasury Department and he was able to have many former Treasury employees attached to his office. Research units in Washington, such as the Board of Economic Warfare and the Foreign Economic Administration, had worked on elaborate planning projects from the early days of the war. They helped developed the case and provided a background of facts and figures. Secretary Morgenthau, because

[9]Morgenthau himself claims in the article cited above, page 221, that Roosevelt was in fact strongly in favor of it. Holborn, *op. cit.,* page 40, rejects this opinion. See also Fainsod, above, page 37.

[10]It is curious that Harry C. Butcher, in his *My Three Years with Eisenhower* (1946), makes no mention of this whole development, and even in speaking of the Quebec Conference merely speaks of its discarding General Eisenhower's recommendations for continuing a joint operation through SHAEF.

of his personal relationship with the President, was thus the effective spearhead of an organized effort.

In order to put into effect the military and foreign policy sponsored by the Secretary of the Treasury it was necessary to secure the rejection of the draft directives prepared by the European Advisory Council in London. The planning done by SHAEF's German Country Unit and of its successor, the U.S. Group Control Council, was largely discarded. Significant personnel changes were effected. State Department policy negotiators who favored allowing a higher level of industry for Germany found their work obstructed.[11]

A reversal of the earlier policy was achieved when essential provisions of the Quebec agreement were written into JCS 1067.[12] The document as a whole reflected a change from positive to negative policy. The new emphasis was; "The Germans shall be made to feel the full consequence of their defeat." Under the heading, "their war-making potential shall be destroyed," not only demilitarization and denazification but deindustrialization and decentralization (which some interpreted to mean virtually partition) were strongly emphasized.[13]

The effect of JCS 1067 on military government organization was immediate. It led to several main lines of attack that changed the basic pattern at the U.S. Group Control Council: reorganization, replacement of key personnel, reinterpretation of the directives, and reformulation of concepts about the purpose and functions of military government. Finally, there was a temporary immobilization of the U.S. Group Control Council (which later was renamed OMGUS) by the U.S. element of SHAEF.[14]

The reorganization of the U.S. Group Control Council proceeded

[11]Morgenthau has indicated that disagreement existed in the Cabinet Committee composed of the Secretaries of State, War, and Treasury. He asserts that the President's decision did not differ significantly from his own views. CF. *Annals, loc. cit.,* pp. 126 ff.

[12]For the provisions of JCS 1067, see pages 381–402. Holborn, *op. cit.,* takes a different view. In his discussion of the background of JCS 1067, he admits, however, that the economic sections were new, and that "denazification" was "broadened."

[13]"Decentralization," a familiar word in democracies, for some policy makers actually stood for permanent partitioning of the country, regardless of the wishes of the population.

[14]This element later became USFET (United States Forces, European Theater).

rapidly on the basis of the new policy interpretations. The existing command was dissolved and a large part of its central planning staff transferred to other positions. The Chief of the Finance Division of G-5, SHAEF was given the additional assignment as Director of the Finance Division of the U.S. Group Control Council and many new recruits for his office arrived from the Treasury Department. Several officers who had been in the Finance Division requested transfers in protest at the new policies being developed.

A number of Regular Army officers were assigned to the organization at this time. They succeeded in gaining greater emphasis on the use of Regular Army procedures and channels than before. Unfortunately, many of the new officers who arrived had no particular aptitude for or interest in military government work. The parade of transient appointees from other military staffs began to pass in and out. The U.S. Group Control Council went into a state of readjustment and transition from which it never emerged until it was dissolved and succeeded by OMGUS (Office of Military Government for Germany, U.S.).

Through JCS 1067 many features of the Quebec plan had become the basis of planning of the U.S. Group Control Council, albeit in a somewhat attenuated form. However, those who believed in a sterner approach toward Germany naturally sought to interpret JCS 1067 in the light of the original Quebec policy. A close reading of 1067 readily shows that it was a compromise and as such capable of different interpretations. The consequent divergencies were great.

The more important controversies were those which centered on seemingly contradictory provisions of JCS 1067. For example, there was the general provision: "It should be brought home to the Germans that Germany's ruthless warfare and the fanatical Nazi resistance have destroyed the German economy and made chaos and suffering inevitable and that the Germans cannot escape responsibility for what they have brought upon themselves."[15]

Another basic provision of JCS 1067 was "the preparation for an eventual reconstruction of German political life on a democratic basis." These provisions of JCS 1067 could be used respectively by

[15] The full text appears in the Appendix, pages 381–402.

those who advanced the policy of retribution and those who believed that a constructive program was a necessary prelude to democracy in Germany and security in Europe.

JCS 1067 also directed the commanding general to impose such controls "as may be essential to protect the safety and meet the needs of the occupying forces and assure the production and maintenance of goods and services required to prevent starvation or such disease and unrest as would endanger these forces." This clause could be used as authorization for socially constructive aims.

The section of the directive on economics provided that no steps be taken (a) looking toward the economic rehabilitation of Germany or (b) designed to maintain or strengthen the German economy. Nevertheless, it also directed that specific steps be taken which would strengthen the economy. "You will urge upon the Control Council that uniform ration scales be applied throughout Germany," and further that "the Control Council should adopt such policies as are clearly necessary to prevent or restrain inflation of a character or dimension which would definitely endanger accomplishment of the objectives of the occupation."

The most disputed issue at this time had to do with the structure of the Allied Control organization and the German governmental organization. In regard to the latter the basic directive stated that "the administration of affairs in Germany shall be directed towards the decentralization of the political and administrative structure and the development of local responsibility." This same paragraph continues: "The Control Council may . . . permit centralized administration or establish central controls of a) essential national public services such as railroads, communications and power, b) finance and foreign affairs and c) production and distribution of essential commodities." In regard to commerce, the commander in chief is directed to "take steps to provide for the equitable interzonal distribution and the movement of goods and services. . . ."

That these provisions relating to the problems of "federal structure" and "interstate commerce" caused a great deal of contention will be no surprise to those familiar with the same issues in American constitutional development. In the deliberations in the U.S. Group

Control Council there were those who interpreted the directive to mean virtually partition, and others who argued that the control authorities should utilize carefully staffed central German agencies to accomplish Allied objectives more effectively.

In respect to these points of controversy most of the Division Chiefs of the U.S. Group Control Council, almost without exception, opposed the negative interpretations pursuant to the Quebec doctrine that were being supported from Washington.

Written comments which were submitted by all division chiefs of the U.S. Group Control Council while at Bushy Park in October, 1944, generally pointed out that an unduly repressive policy would paralyze the economy and lay a basis for chaos, discontent, and political radicalism. It would create a political vacuum that undemocratic forces would fill. It would make uniform standards of administration impossible among the zones and would discredit the American system of control. It would give the Germans an opportunity to play one of the Allies against another and foster disunity. It would cause a breakdown of administrative controls, such as price control and rationing. It would complicate the problem of denazification, reverse the natural and universal trend in government toward greater integration, and even violate the principles of military necessity and enlightened self-interest because it would threaten famine and disease and thereby endanger the health and morale of the occupying forces. As events have shown, these apprehensions were not without foundation.

So well recognized was the "revolt of the division chiefs" against the spirit of Quebec embodied in JCS 1067 that measures were taken to bring them into line. A memorandum was issued by Headquarters, U.S. Group Control Council to the various divisions and offices, calling attention to the basic policy and demanding conformity. Officers were reminded in staff meetings that JCS 1067 was in the category of military command. Several visiting officials from Washington came to observe and report on compliance.

Plans were rewritten, each division again submitting that section pertaining to its responsibilities. The revised plans were still not regarded as drastic enough by the program review committee of Headquarters, U.S. Group Control Council. It was directed by Headquarters that plans be further revised by the respective divisions to make them conform to the "spirit and letter" of JCS 1067.

What is the spirit of JCS 1067? Officers began to ask if JCS 1067 enacted the Morgenthau plan. It was apparent to many that its premise was to transform Germany into an agricultural country and that this could be done by paralyzing her intricate economic and administrative system by partition and allowing her to disintegrate industrially. Whereas the earlier plans in the *Handbook* had provided for utilizing the services of reorganized central German agencies, the official interpretation now being given to JCS 1067 was essentially in line with the original Morgenthau memorandum which had said: "The military administration in Germany in the initial period should be carried out with a view toward the eventual partitioning of Germany."[16] The fact that the rupture of a system of highly interdependent economic and political controls would paralyze industry was regarded as in keeping with the original Quebec policy of deindustrialization and pastoralization, that is, of forcing greater reliance on agricultural subsistence. What if the application of these extreme measures should result in mass starvation, disease, and death through exposure?

Some argued that the Allied authority which would assume the powers of the former German government and control its institutions would also have to assume the responsibility for the results of these measures. But this view was not accepted by all. Some held that no responsibility for the results of the proposed drastic policies was being assumed. The argument that a proposed measure would result in starvation and suffering was met by the counter argument that not we but the Germans were responsible. The Germans had started the war and according to JCS 1067 they should be made to feel the consequences of defeat. Officers at U.S. Group Control Council agreed vehemently in behalf of the traditional American concept of responsible military government. They argued that JCS 1067 need

[16]This memorandum summarizing the Morgenthau plan, which President Roosevelt took with him to Quebec in September of 1944, is reproduced in the form of a Photostat on special pages preceding the table of contents of Henry Morgenthau, Jr., *Germany Is Our Problem* (1945). The paragraph referred to is item 7 of the memorandum.

not be interpreted to imply such irresponsibility. But the new line, which was frankly attributed to Washington, was tenaciously held. Its key exponents at headquarters, who claimed to be accurately informed regarding high policy decisions, repeated concepts and even phrases which could be recognized when the secret Morgenthau memorandum for Germany was later made public.[17]

The basis for this new approach which seemed to foster chaos and deny responsibility is seen in Mr. Morgenthau's provisions aimed not only to destroy industry but also to "dismiss all policy making officials of the Reich government and deal primarily with local governments."[18] At the same time "The Allied Military Government shall not assume responsibility for such economic problems as price controls, rationing, unemployment, production, reconstruction, distribution, consumption, housing, or transportation, or take any measures designed to maintain or strengthen the German economy, except those which are essential to military operations. The responsibility for sustaining the German economy and people rests with the German people with such facilities as may be available under the circumstances."[19]

To many the new policy seemed to absolve the occupation authorities from the responsibility of administering efficiently or well.

An official interpretation of the decentralization provision of JCS 1067 was prepared at headquarters and issued to the divisions as Planning Directive No. 7. The restoration of central German controls was virtually prohibited to the various divisions which hoped that central German agencies might be established through which they might administer their respective functions. Control would now be exercised primarily by Regular Army units in the American zone. The role at Berlin was minimized. This almost amounted to Ameri-

[17]That the Morgenthau plan was the basis not only of JCS 1067 but also of the Potsdam Declaration is evident on comparison of the three documents. Mr. Morgenthau states: "Since that [Quebec] conference, it is worth noting, the basic principles of the program have represented the official position of the United States Government. It is obvious that in the Potsdam Declaration signed by President Truman, Prime Minister Attlee and Marshal Stalin, the three principal allies were seeking to carry out the objectives of that policy."—Morgenthau, *Germany Is Our Problem,* p. xii.

[18]"Program to Prevent Germany from Starting a World War III," Item 7a. Reprinted in *Germany Is Our Problem.*

[19]*Ibid.,* Item 8.

can sponsorship of the policy of dividing Germany into four different countries.

Such a division of the American command in Germany signified a victory for the retributionists. It was preferred by many officers in army tactical commands because under such a plan they would be able to operate in the zone as directed from headquarters in Frankfort, with a minimum of interference from Berlin. It was also a policy favorable to effective Soviet control in that zone of Germany. It was a rejection of the policy of a joint, unified, indirect system of controls which the British and American military government officers had jointly worked out at Shrivenham.

Many say that the difficulties later encountered by military government in Germany today are evident only through the advantage of hindsight. In fact, however, these consequences were largely foreseen and were put on the record during "the battle of Bushy Park." There the American military government officers who had been selected and trained for military government for the purpose of bringing professionalism to the problems of military occupation had stated their case.

Problems of Indoctrinating Men and Officers

A well-integrated organization, like a well-integrated individual, possesses attitudes that harmonize with central objectives and is equipped with the techniques to achieve them. After the change in policies in the Control Council, its attitude and outlook also changed. The "personality" of the control organization became noticeably harder after the spirit of JCS 1067 became injected into U.S. Group Control Council in the fall of 1944.

The program to condition the minds of American servicemen presents an interesting subject of investigation for social psychologists. One might assume that the natural resentments and hatreds caused by fighting would cause the soldiers to favor a stern occupation policy. However, the experience in Germany at the close of World War I revealed that many of the occupation troops, including combat troops, had been friendly and popular with the German population.

It was recognized in World War II that proper orientation was needed to prevent the American GI from becoming too sympathetic. Attitude tests conducted among troops by the Psychological Warfare Division confirmed this suspicion. The American GI was not proving to be a good hater. Despite the "This is the enemy" propaganda, he was surprisingly free from hatred. It seems ironic that GI's who fought without hating should have been the object of patronizing concern by observers who hated without fighting.

The doctrine that "there is no such thing as a good German" was for a time encouraged. Whereas the occupation soldiers in World War I had been quartered with German families, an arrangement which led to much friendly understanding, the policy in World War II was to order German occupants to evacuate their dwelling to provide army billets, often within two hours. American personnel were directed not to return the salutes of Germans. This prohibition applied to the newly appointed German policemen who snapped to attention and saluted as the conquerors walked stiffly by, ignoring icily or sometimes betraying uncertainty or embarrassment because of this reversal of normal conduct. Some U.S. military personnel were disturbed by the contrast with the Russian policy, which officially did not adopt this behavior. The Russians returned salutes and placarded Berlin with statements of Russian leaders in which the distinction was made between tyrannical Nazi leadership and the rank-and-file Germans who had been liberated and who could now look with hope to a decent future. The antifraternization policy, which served to isolate servicemen from the German population, aroused a great deal of controversy behind the scenes. Many regarded it as a corollary of the Morgenthau plan, an obstacle to efficient administration as well as a bar to the return of good will. It was contended on the one hand that the order would eliminate contacts that were open, normal, and harmless, but could not prevent undesirable association. The order was defended on the grounds that, aside from the security aspects, the American GI should be protected from contamination by German ideologies.

The spirit of these efforts in reorientation was evidenced in a mimeographed reprint of "Fourteen Rules for the Occupation Of-

---

ficer in Germany," from an article by Emil Ludwig which was distributed to servicemen. Some excerpts follow:

You are entering Germany, not as a liberator but as a victor.

Do not keep smiling. Never offer a cigarette to a visitor whom you do not know well, nor offer him your hand. The Germans will respect you as long as they see in you a successor to Hitler, who never offered them his hand.

Forget the American habit of meeting everyone in an open way. Distrust everybody who has given you no proof of his honesty.

Always wear a uniform, never wear civilian clothes.

Never give way. Anything that is granted as a favor will be regarded by the German as his right, and he will subsequently demand twice as much. He thinks fair play is cowardice.

The only way to get along with the Germans is to make them respect you, to make them feel the hand of the master.

Advice on "how to act around Germans" had been frequently given to military government personnel but was unnecessarily involved and mainly fruitless. Taken altogether it was not worth one simple slogan: "Act like an American."

The new orientation made visible headway, engendering disillusionment and resentment among those officers who saw the American ideal being blotted out. A feeling of irresponsibility was encouraged. An incident may illustrate this situation. At one of the field headquarters a large group of military government officers was being oriented to the new plans and policies under JCS 1067 prior to its entry into Germany. After pondering the implications of the new directive, one thoughtful officer asked, "Doesn't this mean that it will be impossible to do a good job of administration in Germany?" The lecturer was temporarily stumped until someone hit the keynote. "Does it really matter if we do a good job of administration?" "That's it," responded the lecturer. "After all, isn't it true that what the Germans need is a good dose of bad administration?"

Many feared that the then existing policies were well designed to fulfill this requirement. One scarcely need comment on what becomes of the morale and tone of an organization that officially disclaims moral purpose and that has a sense of power and privilege exceeding its sense of responsibility.

The Struggle for Control

Officers of the U.S. Group Control Council would generally be inclined toward a moderate interpretation of JCS 1067 and try to avoid the more extreme aspects of the Quebec doctrine. Indeed, many officers still believed that American military government would somehow enter Germany with a more constructive policy. This issue was intertwined with the issue of centralized versus decentralized control. The U.S. Group Control Council was a logical place to develop affirmative, over-all plans for Germany, if indeed there were to be any. This organization was destined to go to the seat of central German administration and, it was early assumed, participate in the administration of Germany as an integrated unit under the supervision of Allied agencies. It became evident, however, that the U.S. Group Control Council would hesitate to carry out fully the spirit of JCS 1067.[20] The so-called "revolt of the division chiefs" had made this clear.

Developments were soon under way which limited the importance of the U.S. Group Control Council and shifted the center of power to the U.S. element of G-5, SHAEF (later absorbed by USFET with headquarters at Frankfort). The U.S. element of SHAEF had a different orientation from that of the U.S. Control Council. The case for integrated control of Germany from Berlin and the case for virtually independent zonal control from Frankfort had their protagonists in U.S. Group Control Council and G-5 SHAEF, respectively. Besides this basic difference, G-5, SHAEF was not so encumbered with "civilian" administrators and planners; its concern was the "military show"; its focus was on operations within the zone, not over

[20]Mr. Morgenthau has written of his dissatisfaction with the planning for Germany that had been done by this organization (under the earlier name, "German Country Unit"). It placed "too great a share of the responsibility for rebuilding Germany on the occupying forces" and not enough emphasis "on the task of destroying Nazi influence and eliminating Germany's industrial potential for war." He continues: "In any event, it was clear that these were important issues of national policy which ought not to be decided at a technical military level."—*Annals, loc. cit.,* p. 126.

matters affecting Germany as a whole; it thrived on decentralization.
There were other consequences of SHAEF, G-5's more typically military point of view. The military is accustomed to its standard pattern
of organization and visualizes military government in terms of a
military hierarchy rather than in terms of channels of government
and administration. The doctrine that the army commander is supreme within his own area gave support to the idea of a decentralized
or divided Germany in which there would be no higher echelon at
Berlin staffed with numerous civilians which could send down orders
through governmental channels. The demand for maximum authority for the future USFET was based upon the contention that
there would be no central German government and hence there
would be little for the Allied Control Council to do. The U.S. element (OMGUS) would function merely as a sort of legislative or advisory committee. The real business of government would be carried
on through army echelons in the zone. The hope became essentially
the reality.

Until the U.S. Group Control Council became an element of the
Allied "supreme authority" for Germany in Berlin, it was to be controlled by the U.S. element of SHAEF, G-5, an organization that
presumably would not exist in the post-hostilities phase. This arrangement was formally worked out in an administrative agreement
dubbed the "Treaty of Bushy Park."[21] It gave a veto power to G-5,
SHAEF over actions of the U.S. Group Control Council. SHAEF
was in a strategic place anyway to institute its favored policies and
block tendencies of the U.S. Group Control Council. Because of its
predominant position during the combat phase, it might set the tone
and pattern of military government. SHAEF and not the European
Advisory Council or the U.S. Group Control Council should occupy
the controlling position during the crucial initial phase following
cessation of hostilities. The U.S. element of SHAEF began writing
its own handbook for a post-hostilities, pre-armistice period, when

[21]This was an administrative agreement clarifying relationships between the U.S.
Group Control Council and the U.S. element of G-5, SHAEF. This "treaty" provided
that before any policy could be negotiated by the U.S. Group Control Council with the
British counterpart, the concurrence of the U.S. element of SHAEF on matters of policy
was essential.

it would be in command in the areas of Germany occupied by American troops.

It is unfortunate that a constitutional struggle resembling that of the American Civil War had to be waged among U.S. Army organization planners for military government in Germany. Conflict, however, was inherent in this situation, where potential power was not defined.

Conclusion

The collapse of German resistance in April and May of 1945 was accompanied by a collapse of morale among officers in the U.S. Group Control Council. At the very time that there should have been enthusiasm at the beginning of their job there was a disillusioned feeling that their battle for a creditable occupation of Germany had been fought and lost. Many officers had been training and planning for military government for two years. Early conceptions of the function of military government had been rejected. The plan which embodied these concepts in a program of integrated control had been superseded. There was to be no military government setup, relatively autonomous and removed from the control of the military. At the same time their basic recommendations for American policy had not been accepted but had been attacked and replaced by the Quebec doctrines. The U.S. Group Control Council had been rendered impotent during the later planning stages, and policies had been adopted that would cripple it during the operational stage. The basis had been set for a paralyzing jurisdictional conflict between American authority in Berlin and Frankfort. The military government organizational plan incorporated features that tended toward the division of Germany which aggravated economic chaos, political unrest, and international complications.

With the surrender of the German *Wehrmacht,* the three-year period of preparation and planning was concluded. But the organization was still described as being in a "state of transition." Essentially, there was no clear-cut plan. When it was declared at Yalta[22] that

[22]"American Organizational Plans for Military Government of Germany," released May 11, 1945. Reprinted in *The Axis in Defeat.*

Germany would be governed through a Control Council on which each of the four powers would be represented, the stage was set for the difficulties that have marked American military government operations ever since the day of the surrender.[23]

[23]Eventually, the balance of control was radically redressed, and OMGUS emerged as the dominant control group. (See Chapter XI.) Likewise, the ideas of the "German Country Unit" reasserted themselves in The Revised Directive to the Theatre Commander, issued in July, 1947. Cf. Appendix B.

Chapter XI

The Three Phases of Field Operations in Germany, 1945–1946

CARL J. FRIEDRICH

Introduction[1]

THE sharp cleavages between conflicting approaches on higher planning levels which have been treated in the two preceding chapters left field operations without guidance on many important questions which the *Field Manual* raised rather than settled, such as the employment or dismissal of Nazis, the handling of displaced persons, and the restitution of looted property. Field officers of military government had been left to struggle with these matters as best they could until some dramatic mishaps forced policy decisions upon those in higher authority.

A detailed history of field operations in military government will be produced eventually from a mass of field reports now being assembled by official historians. But field reports will not always give an exact picture of conditions at the lower levels, because the practice has been to consolidate reports going up from lower echelons to higher echelons. In this process much valuable data has had to be eliminated. Anyone who has been privileged to peruse some of these records, as well as compare experiences with fellow officers, comes away impressed with the vast mass of specific experience that awaits

[1]In preparing this chapter the writer utilized valuable material from a number of army officers among whom special mention should be made of Lt. Col. Robert Slover, Maj. Richard Eaton, and Lt. Solomon Lebovitz.

integration, analysis, and eventual formulation into new and better regulations for the field operations of military government.

It is, however, possible at the present time to sketch certain general aspects and to mark out certain phases of this gigantic undertaking, in the course of which American army units took over nearly half of Europe's most advanced industrial nation and established military government at the moment of its nadir of disorganization and collapse. For western Germany, U.S. Military Government had teams developed as early as 1944 for various *Stadt* and *Landkreise,* as well as for Berlin. This process was called "pinpointing." In the course of the German collapse, other teams, many of them provisional, were established. Many of the officers participating in this enterprise have stressed the failure of planners at the staff level to deal adequately with the "eclipse" phase of military occupation of the enemy's land. It is undoubtedly true that training in the army's schools at Charlottesville and Fort Custer and at the universities' CATS (Civil Affairs Training Schools) had overstressed the combat phase of military government, whereas the special problems presented by a total collapse of the enemy's resistance and government had received scant attention. Because of a failure to perceive the true conditions resulting from an enemy's total rout, there was likewise a tendency to be rather unrealistic about the post-collapse phase of military occupation. Too much emphasis was placed on the Rhineland occupation after the last war as a precedent for the task ahead, and too little on the American Civil War, in which Sherman's march to the sea had produced conditions more nearly resembling those faced in Germany in the spring and summer of 1945. It would be unfair to blame the military authorities exclusively or even primarily for these shortcomings. The failure lay with the political leadership, which failed to grasp—or at any rate failed to impress upon the military—the essentially revolutionary task in which the American forces were engaged, and the comprehensive military government tasks resulting from such a total collapse as the avowed destruction of the Nazi regime implied. The uncompromising formula of "unconditional surrender" should have served as a clear indication of what was ahead, but it was treated as a rhetorical formula by many responsible persons. The dangers which this lack of foresight was bound to cause once Germany was entered were heightened further by a lack of insight into the true nature of the Nazi dictatorship, with its terroristic methods of repression which kept all German opposition at bay. When Secretary of State Cordell Hull was reported in the press to have said, after the so-called generals' *Putsch* in July, 1944, that Americans were not in the least interested in the fate of the conspirators, that they hated them as much as they did the Nazi regime, the full measure of blindness of political leadership was revealed. But the remark went unheeded and military government teams were allowed to stumble forward, groping in the dark for some signposts that might guide them in dealing with the morass of Aachen, Cologne, and a procession of other large German cities. Their principal task was the problem of keeping civilians from interfering with the tasks of the advancing army. This task the military government teams did well.

From what has been said it is clear that a realistic analysis discloses at least three phases of military government operations: 1) the combat phase, 2) the phase of collapsing enemy organization, and 3) the phase of building a new government. The last of these may again be subdivided into three phases: (a) the phase of building anew by the Americans alone, (b) the phase of building anew jointly with the allies, and (c) the phase of supervising the Germans' building anew under American and Allied supervision. It is not easy to fix dates for these phases, since they imperceptibly merge and overlap, but those who participated in the work will readily recognize the several steps which these phases suggest, for each had its high-water mark in field operations which may be roughly delineated as follows: (1) winter, 1944–1945; (2) April—May, 1945; (3-a) July, 1945; (3-b) winter, 1945–1946; (3-c) summer, 1946. This chapter will deal primarily with phases (1), (2), (3-a), and (3-b), while (3-c) has received some attention above in Chapter I. Even within these limits the present chapter does not pretend to be complete, let alone exhaustive, but will describe some of the more important operations.

The Combat Phase[2]

The combat phase of military government operations in Germany differed from preceding operations, such as that in Italy, primarily by the fact that the Allies came into enemy territory with the avowed aim of conquest rather than liberation. Troops had been indoctrinated in an unqualified hatred for the German people, who were very largely being identified with the Nazi regime and the revolting crimes which the troops continually uncovered as they advanced further into enemy territory.[3] Military government officers had to fight continually against the suspicion that their concern for the populace was the result of "softness." They encountered the familiar technical problems of water, electricity, and the other public services wholly or partly disrupted by fighting and the scorched-earth policy of the retreating enemy. For even in Germany proper, the more fanatical Nazi formations, especially the SS, regardless of the misery caused their people by such procedures, destroyed roads, bridges, factories, and other installations that might facilitate military government operations. They also committed atrocities which caused American troops to take measures of retaliation, such as the total destruction of the city of Bruchsal. Consequently, a very considerable amount of military government effort had to be directed toward the establishment of essential public services. All this was in keeping with orthodox military government rules. The reports sent home by officers are replete with sentences such as "Water supply still only half of normal, but will be nearly normal in another week, my engineer reports," or "With water supply largely gone, civilian population has been securing the most essential supply by forming bucket lines leading from remaining wells and waterholes." On the whole, technical engineering problems were solved well, and thanks to the American capacity for improvising under unexpected conditions, a heritage of pioneering days, military government was saved from many a desperate situation.

But two tasks presented extraordinary difficulties, although on a

[2]Cf. Chapter 7 in Harold Zink's *American Military Government in Germany* (1947).
[3]Cf. the discussion in the preceding chapter, pages 232–234.

much smaller scale. These problems—"displaced persons" and "denazification"—had arisen elsewhere.

The vast number of foreign laborers that the Nazi regime had imported into Germany to assist in industrial operations—tens of thousands of nationals of the United Nations, Poles, Russians, Frenchmen, Dutch, Belgians, Norwegians, Czechs, Greeks and so on—left their places of confinement and began to roam the countryside. These displaced persons, or DP's, became the immediate charge of military government officers. They had to be housed, fed, counted, and provided eventually with opportunities to return to their homeland. A total of 2,500,000 such DP's had been uncovered by May 25, 1945, of whom 23 per cent were French, 14 per cent were Poles, and 40 per cent were Russians.[4] In their deep hatred of their German oppressors, these DP's frequently engaged in wholesale looting, raping, and other kinds of activities which under ordinary conditions would be considered criminal. An official report rendered in May puts it cautiously thus: "In the initial phases of occupation some looting and pillaging and other disorders have taken place. This was the result not only of the natural exuberance of liberation among the displaced persons themselves but of the necessity of not delaying military operations. . . ."[5] It was the task of military government (in collaboration with the United Nations Relief and Rehabilitation Administration) to get these people under control with a minimum of harshness. In retrospect it is astonishing to what an extent this problem was handled successfully. Yet, at times, serious breakdowns occurred, and some of the incidents were widely publicized, creating the impression that military government failed in dealing with displaced persons. Some of the great difficulties arose from the division of responsibility between military

[4] See "Displaced Persons in Germany, Present Operations," released May 25, 1945, and reprinted in *The Axis in Defeat*, p. 83. This document notes, interestingly enough, that this figure was substantially below the original estimate of 4,400,000 on which planning had been based. It also states that the problem has been handled as a command responsibility, and that "where consistent with military operations, combat units have been utilized to care for and control displaced persons." Considering the amount of work occasioned by these DP's for military government teams throughout the American zone, one would judge that their handling by combat units was not too often "consistent with military operations" during the collapse phase.

[5] *Ibid.*

government and UNRRA. UNRRA ran the camps once they were established, and military government provided liaison and assistance.

Denazification presented an equally difficult and novel obstacle to smooth military government operations. The fixed over-all policy of removing all Nazis from positions of influence has been dealt with elsewhere in this volume, and there is no need to repeat the directives here.[6] It may, however, be relevant to quote a passage from an officer's report to illustrate the task with which military government was faced.

Theoretically we are supposed to augment our number by requisitioning German help, but it is a slow business to find anti-Nazis, especially when the rules ordain that the government officials who are "party" men must be removed from office. This I must do myself. [The writer was heading his detachment.] I chucked the *Oberbürgermeister* [city manager] and *Landrat* [chief county executive] the second day. Have been taking a flier on an acting burgo, and will probably make a choice of a new acting *Landrat* tomorrow. Most of the department heads are now fired, and I am going to pick a few top ones myself to give balance to the new crowd so as to prevent the promotion of a Tammany Hall or cliques of friends of the new burgo. After that is done, I'll let him fill up the vacancies in the more important departments. . . .[7]

Julian Bach, Jr., in his level-headed discussion of this topic, emphasizes the size of the job as one reason why denazification did not at once succeed in getting rid of all Nazis.[8] After remarking that it inevitably resulted in inefficiency, he claims, on the basis of extensive observation in the field, that "many Americans fought de-Nazification at the time. . . . Their view was: Get this trolley line operating first, get the milk supply flowing again, get roofing materials turned out again, and *then* de-Nazify." Since there was marked disagreement among military government officers on this issue, there was a considerable diversity of treatment. One town would be recovering rapidly from the worst difficulties and develop a measure of new life

[6]See Chapter XII.

[7]From a letter by Major Richard Eaton, who served in military government.

[8]Julian Bach, Jr., *America's Germany* (1946), Chapter VI. See also the next chapter, especially page 258.

under business leadership that was fairly intact because only the most extreme Nazis had been removed, while another town would be languishing in virtual stagnation because every Nazi supporter had been removed without regard to consequences. The root of the trouble was that denazification as an over-all policy called for a complete revision of the planning of military government operations, since the traditional policy of utilizing existing native personnel was largely rendered impractical by a forceful denazification policy. Military government officers in the field were suspended between the Nazi devil and the deep blue sea of economic and social disorganization. The immediate concern of military government teams, both urban and rural, was to re-establish essential services. Military government laid stress not on the discretionary removals but upon the mandatory ones.

One problem which had been regarded as a possible source of great trouble turned out to be a very minor one—the Nazi underground, and general resistance by the German populace. Although military government officers had an occasional case of individual violence on their hands, there was very little trace of any underground guerilla warfare. The Nazi element itself was probably too much disorganized, and the hostile elements of the population were too much on the alert for the formation of an organized movement. The Public Safety officers' big problem was the DP's.[9] The much-publicized Werewolf and Edelweiss organizations did not give any appreciable trouble, since Counter Intelligence Corps was well organized and able to secure aid from German opposition elements.

The Phase of Collapsing Enemy Organization

The problems just outlined as characteristic of the combat phase continued well into the collapse phase. Indeed, some of them belong as much in the latter as in the former phase. But when fighting ceased, military government should have been in the position to move into high gear. Unfortunately, neither the trained man power nor the tables of organization under which to secure it were at hand. As a result of hurried efforts to set up "training programs" for combat

[9]See *The New York Times,* February 13 and March 24, 1945.

officers, hundreds had to be trained in a few days to handle military government. The pattern of military organization, with troop commanders in charge of small batches of territory, created endless difficulties for military government operations, especially in the larger towns. Some of the higher-ranking officers evidently thought that, with the war won, military government officers should devote themselves to the task of providing various necessities from water to toilet soap. Hard-pressed military government officers were indignant. And yet, if they wanted to get on with their job, they had to attend to these matters, and usually did. The continual conflict of jurisdiction caused great difficulties both during operations and in the static stage. These difficulties arose from the fact that whereas military government teams arrived and remained at their assigned posts, the tactical troops kept shifting and moving over various areas. Hence the local military government team would receive a succession of directives from the G-5 sections of the different tactical divisions that passed through the area. At times an officer might have on his desk SHAEF, army, corps, and division directives all at the same time. Whoever was the highest ranking officer among the military units in a town would become the town commander. Too often the military government commanding officer was outranked by one of the commanding officers of troop units and friction would inevitably result. When the separate military government channel was finally established, with command going from the *Land* level down to the *Kreis* level, a great many of these difficulties disappeared.

One of the most important and difficult tasks of military government, and one which loomed especially prominent after the collapse of the German government, was the problem of contact with civilian petitioners. The flood of specific requests for information and assistance made it necessary to develop machinery for sorting the important from the unimportant, and to ensure that military government officers would have at least some time for the performance of their duties. On the basis of available evidence, and in the light of later development, it seems fair to conclude that the most satisfactory arrangement provided that military government would consider only requests from the populace certified to it by the appointed German local authorities.

But practice varied and at least in the early period, even though these petitions were supposed to go through German channels, petitioners could not be kept from coming to see military government officers.

With the collapse, political problems forced themselves to the fore. In quite a few towns, groups of opposition elements had become organized as the Nazi organization fell apart and the secret police terror became sporadic. These groups were composed of various elements of the right and left, but under a SHAEF directive they had to be disbanded. It is difficult to assess the wisdom of this policy, which certainly nipped in the bud such revolutionary inclinations as the German population may have had. As a result, military government officers obliged to enforce the directive often found themselves accused of various kinds of political bias. American journalists picked up these German reactions from time to time and made them the basis of political criticism of military government officers. At times these critics were justified; more often they were not. In a number of important centers, the anti-Nazi organizations, variously called Antifascist Fighting Organization (Düsseldorf and Hamburg), Fighting Association against Fascism (Bremen), Anti-National-Socialist Movement (Halle), rapidly increased in size immediately after the collapse (3,000 in Leipzig, 4,000 in Bremen, to mention only two cities occupied by Americans). These organizations had engaged in sabotage and were ready to furnish American authorities with information on the whereabouts of Nazi leaders and on the location of their stores and archives. Some of these groups sprang up in the big plants and established factory committees. They considered themselves to be on the American side, and many military government reports speak of the "valuable assistance" rendered to them and to Counter Intelligence Corps by such groups. But under the directives they could not be officially recognized. In spite of this, several carried on, built organizations, and attempted to hold public meetings. Some military government officials suppressed them; others merely reprimanded them. The controlling influence of Communists in a number of these organizations disquieted some of the officers responsible for security. It is difficult to say in retrospect what might have happened had these organizations been permitted to undertake a large-scale program of

self-determined activities. There are people who believe that a revolutionary movement would have swept Germany and rebuilt its
foundations on a democratic basis. Others, and they are in the majority, are very skeptical. A few thousand men in a city of approximately
a million seem to them a feeble basis for comprehensive operations.
In any case, the task of military government was to hold these groups
at bay under the directive against party activities already cited. In
due course, during the next phase, parties were authorized.

The Phase of Building a New Organization[10]

Building anew alone and jointly with the Allies are two aspects of
the post-collapse phase prior to the last phase, when the Americans,
reluctantly followed by their Allies, turned the government over to
the Germans. It is possible to speak of two somewhat distinct phases
because joint operations with the Soviet Union were very slow in
getting under way, there having been no joint staff planning during
the war. As far as the British and the French were concerned, a measure of joint effort had been made, accompanied by friction and complications.[11]

During this third phase, denazification moved into high gear in all
military government jurisdictions, at least in the American zone. On
July 7, 1945, USFET issued a more detailed directive concerning denazification, as a result of which a considerable number of German
officials were dismissed during August and September. This was followed during October by a similar wave of dismissals in business and
other private organizations under Law No. 8.[12] When military government personnel found itself deprived of the administrative business leadership upon which it was relying to carry it through the
difficult months ahead, these dismissals aroused much irritation and
indignation.

The "Patton Incident," which occurred at this time, was widely
misunderstood in the American press, and the impression it created

[10]Cf. Zink, *op. cit.*, Chapters 8 and 9.

[11]For a more complete discussion of the problems of joint Allied effort see Chapter
VI, especially pages 115–118.

[12]For a more practical discussion see Chapter XII, pages 262–268.

was entirely misleading. The incident was interpreted to mean that denazification was lagging, at any rate within Patton's own command. Actually denazification had progressed so far that all but a very few Nazi party members had been removed from public employment.[13] The incident showed a certain lack of grasp of the realities of military government by the American press correspondents who reported it. It also revealed how limited was General Patton's own knowledge of what had been going on under his command in the post-collapse phase of military government with respect to denazification. He did, however, state in a subsequent interview that "there are no outstanding Nazis whose removal has not already been carried out." He evidently did not realize that a very much more thorough cleansing had been taking place throughout his command, although it was by no means completed. All through the following fall and winter, more questionnaires were gathered, analyzed, and made the basis of mandatory removals, especially in business, under Law No. 8.[14]

While this work was going forward, an increasing amount of the time of military government officers in the field had to be devoted to building the basis for a democratic reconstruction in Germany. As parties were being recognized in September and October under USFET directives, their organization and growth became a matter of concern to local detachments. Questionable individuals continued to come to the fore, such as Bavarian monarchists and nationalist reactionaries, subversive elements on the extreme left, and occasional Nazis. Military government detachments had to watch for such developments through their Public Safety officers, who, in close cooperation with the Counter Intelligence Corps, would ascertain the background of such individuals and have them removed. Each such case involves a great deal of work, and may produce a setback in democratic reconstruction; it needs to be handled with care.

By November, 1945, local elections were being called in counties throughout the American zone. In this phase, the elections were an-

[13]For a discussion of the state of denazification at the time of the "Patton Incident" compare Bach, *op. cit.,* pp. 178 ff.

[14]See Chapter XII below, pages 262–268 and the discussion in Bach, *op. cit.,* pages 18 ff.

other problem for the military government detachments, but the German population was too apathetic and confused to create any serious disturbance.

A considerable majority of military government officers have expressed the opinion that serious difficulties arose from time to time in connection with American troops. This is partly an organizational problem,[15] and partly a problem of attitudes. The kind of indoctrination suitable for battle conditions left in the simpler minds the residue of a desire to fight the Germans which it is hard to work off under such conditions as military government was charged with establishing in occupied Germany. Actually, the troops who came to occupation duties from combat proved less a problem than new recruits and replacements who had not had their share of the fighting. The servile and terrorized attitudes of the German population, and the mercenary conduct of a substantial percentage of German women, variously estimated at from 10 per cent to 20 per cent, tended to reinforce a contempt for the "Nazis" as many American officers and men continued to call all Germans—when they did not call them "Krauts." To an ardent anti-Nazi, the designation "Nazi" is, of course, extremely offensive, and the bitterness caused by this carry-over from the war propaganda hindered the military government officer bent upon re-establishing law and order.

Time and again an experienced military government officer would find, upon moving into a new assignment, that the German civil administration was badly disorganized, because whenever any troop unit wanted a building, or a piano, or anything else, it would demand that immediate attention be given to this requirement, without any regard for how much of the work of the city departments might be disrupted. The first task of such an officer would then be to make it quite unmistakably clear to all concerned—and that is not easy when the man in charge of the military government detachment is a field officer, and the man he has to talk to is a general officer—that it is the function of the military government detachment to provide the liaison between the tactical troops and the civil administration, and that all requests ought to be channeled through that detachment. As one of

[15]See Chapter VIII.

these men described it later: "I told General —— that I should be very glad, of course, to take up with the Krauts any requirement that he might have, but that I should also inform them that any requests addressed to them directly should be referred to me, and would be disallowed." Grinning, he added, "Within a week the city administration had improved a hundred per cent, and the non-coms were coming to me instead of upsetting the Germans."

Within the changing pattern of the over-all organization discussed in Chapter IX, military government detachments were slowly evolving toward the supervisory, as contrasted with the operational, functions. In this connection, steady cuts in personnel were effected. The numerous technical specialists that any operational responsibility calls for under modern industrial conditions were gradually withdrawn, and what remained was essentially a small core of administrators. For an urban county of approximately fifty thousand such a detachment might not by the end of 1946 number more than three officers and perhaps two to three enlisted men. The ratio of military government team personnel to the local population often fell far below this. It is obvious that such small teams would of necessity be seriously overburdened with responsibility. Moreover, the demobilization and discharge policy adopted by the War Department had a most unfortunate result for military government. Large numbers of men especially trained for the assignments returned home, along with those whom they had in turn trained through practical field experience in joint detachment operations. Thus men who often had spent a year in training for military government sometimes served in the field precisely six months. Because of their length of service in the army, they were entitled to discharge. The resulting turnover in military government personnel made an effective and smooth supervisory relationship to German authorities almost impossible. However, it was the delay in granting civilian status to military government personnel, together with the delay in bringing in further civilian employees, that caused the greatest trouble.

The supervisory approach to military government requires that the supervising officer know the officials who do the actual administering and be able to assess their personal and professional limitations.

Furthermore, the widespread unfamiliarity with the German language proved a much greater handicap after the supervisory approach was adopted. Again the reasons are not far to seek: when instructions are issued in the form of commands, it is up to the subordinate to understand what has been said to him; a supervisor, on the other hand, must be able to understand all that is going on, ask questions, and catch the precise meaning of replies. An interpreter is of only limited value, and may in fact be responsible for serious misunderstandings.

In order to supplement the small local detachments with the many types of special knowledge required in a functioning military government setup, the device of "specialist teams" was adopted in this period (and has been carried forward since). From their headquarters in one of the *Land* capitals, these teams of men with special knowledge, say, in banking or in public health, would move around their *Land*, much like circuit judges, visiting cities, towns, and counties and rendering whatever assistance might be required by local teams. The work they did was valuable, but "specialist teams" looked better on paper than in reality, and the shortage of personnel, especially in such specialties as law and public health, made these teams less effective than was originally hoped for.

An aspect of military government work that has been universally criticized by officers in the field is the multiplication of reports of every sort and description. In their desire to maintain some kind of live contact with field operations, headquarters, at *Land* level, at zonal level, and at theater level, required one report after another, with different divisions calling for reports in their own specialties, and all without regard to the total load thereby created. The burden thus built up over the months during the third phase eventually reached such proportions that officers in the field who made reporting a conscientious duty found little time for any other work.

Conclusion

The third stage of the third phase of military government in occupied Germany is still in the process of unfolding and is bound to be the longest and in many ways the most difficult. Although fewer men of high qualities of judgment and discrimination are needed, they will be increasingly difficult to find. Some broad general aspects of this final stage have been dealt with in a previous chapter.[16] As the Germans build governments of their own, under constitutions fashioned by themselves within the limits set by Allied policy, the function of military government will negatively be that of watching that the Germans do not overstep the boundaries prescribed to prevent the renascence of German militarism and Nazism. On the positive side, it will call for constant encouragement of the feeble forces of democracy. This will mean a great deal of direction in the field of economic reconstruction. Allied cooperation will remain an issue of primary concern. By the end of 1946, it had become clear that possibly the entire basis of our economic policy would have to be revamped.

[16]See Chapter I, page 21.

Chapter XII

Denazification, 1944–1946

CARL J. FRIEDRICH

Introduction

"THE German people must recognize that the basic cause of their suffering and distress is the war which the Nazi dictatorship brought upon the world," Secretary James F. Byrnes told them in his Stuttgart address. He made the same point at least three times in that same speech, which he concluded with another appeal to "the German people." Throughout the message a clear and dramatic distinction is drawn between the German people and the Nazis who "tortured and exterminated innocent men, women and children and sought with German arms to dominate and degrade the world." This distinction has always been part of American policy, but during the fighting it could not be an effective and practical one. Germans, whether Nazis, anti-Nazis, or just plain folks, were so completely intermingled as to form one turbulent and inchoate mass which Americans spoke of as Nazis or Germans more or less at random.

The separation of Nazis from Germans is the main part of the great enterprise that goes under the name of "denazification." Denazification comprises a number of other activities, such as the purging of the laws of Nazi ideas, the cleansing of school curricula and textbooks, and the removal of Nazi literature from public libraries. But the core of it all is the job of getting rid of the Nazis.

Our efforts in this direction also served the vital purpose of convincing many Germans of the sincerity of the whole American program. Since we could not hope to demonstrate the blessings of democracy under the conditions that the Nazis had left behind we needed a visible symbol of our democratic convictions. Denazification has served as such a symbol. And when American officers became at times too tolerant, the discovery of another Nazi atrocity or concentration camp fanned their flagging spirits. It was impossible for any man of sensitiveness and decency to visit these scenes of indescribable horror without becoming filled with zeal for eliminating, from all share in public life, the men and organizations responsible for such outrages. The elaborate rituals which the U.S. Army staged for the burial or reburial of the victims of these atrocities may have been hard on the nerves of the participants, as well as on those of their German collaborators, but the sincere anti-Nazi German welcomed such opportunities for cleansing out the Augean stables of guilt and crime.[1]

There have been three distinctive phases in the American denazification program from 1944 to 1946 and each of them merits some attention. The first of these phases was the predominately military one, when before and after VE day American troops occupied Germany, and proceeded to get rid of many Nazis as a matter of military security. This phase lasted to the fall of 1945. The second phase consisted of an abortive effort to bring about a genuinely joint Allied policy under an Allied Control Authority directive. It lasted through the winter of 1945–1946. The third phase of denazification did not end in 1946; it presumably will last for some time. In this phase, German authorities are carrying forward, or rather are taking over, the job of denazifying the German people in the American zone under American supervision and control.

In all three phases, there have been marked differences between American policy and that of the other Allies. A good deal has been said about this aspect of the matter in the American press. Parts of these stories are highly misleading, are compounded of rumors and political distortions, and are not based upon any detailed examination of the facts. But the stories are true in at least one respect—the divergence between the policies of the several occupying powers. Nor is this

[1] See Zink, *American Military Government in Germany,* which is good on our early planning, or lack of it. See also Holborn, *American Military Government, Its Organization and Policies.*

divergence surprising. Each power has carried out denazification in line with its over-all approach to the German problem. It is always dangerous to generalize too broadly. But if one were to characterize the three other powers' denazification policy in very general terms, he would, on the basis of observation and factual analysis put it thus: each of these policies is tied in with the national and party prejudices of the occupying power. The Communists were most ready to get rid of those Nazis, especially business and professional leaders, who fitted into their idea of Hitler as the last-ditch defender of dying capitalism. The French were guided by the idea that a Nazi who was willing to collaborate with the French was all right; he knew how things were run and if he became discredited in the process, so much the better. The British inclined toward seizing the criminal element among the Nazis, and the more radical groups who would disturb their efforts at economic reconstruction. After all, Germany was Britain's best customer. We Americans had no such "realistic" signposts to guide us in developing our policy. If we had one, it was the idea of getting on with the job of establishing democracy in Germany, a rather idealistic undertaking which many abroad and at home regarded as destined to fail. But whatever one's estimate of that matter, in the task of denazification we were the St. George, riding the shining white steed with spear in hand, ready to slay the Hydra-headed dragon of Nazidom. How did we go about it?

The Military Phase of Denazification

In the early military phase, denazification of a drastic type ran counter to traditional military government policy. It had formerly been the view of liberal-minded men that "the existing laws, customs and institutions of the occupied country have been created by its people, and are presumably those best suited to them." The American Military Government *Field Manual* stated it this way, following a famous memorandum written by Francis Lieber in Civil War days. Surely, this was a principle which could not be applied to the Nazis in defeat, even by those who were most firmly convinced that the Hitler outlook and conduct were a distinctive German creation.

Americans were fighting the war to rid themselves of the Nazis, and to free the Germans in the bargain. In short, Americans were quite clear about their belief that "existing law, customs and institutions were *not* those best suited" to the Germans. But while the official *Field Manual* was amended in the course of the war, and a revised edition was published in 1943 (see Chapter II), the basic principle of "economy of effort" remained dominant. According to this principle, military government was to be conducted in such a way as to leave as much as possible of the government to the native population. However, in the days of the Nazi collapse—the eclipse phase, as it is at times called—Americans were entering a country whose economy had been completely disrupted, and whose government had disappeared on all levels. American policy insisted on organizing and governing the country without using any of the men who had taken part in governing it during the preceding twelve years. Anyone who had prominently participated in Hitler's regime became tabu under the general policy of denazification.

A great deal of uncertainty and controversy had beclouded our military government policies on denazification during the early months after our entry into German territory on September 11, 1944. In the absence of top-level policy decisions in this field, directives had to be issued by SHAEF, 12th Army Group and other units, some of which directives are found in the SHAEF handbook. It should also be remembered that denazification problems were somewhat eased during the combat phase by the fact that many of the leading National Socialists fled or committed suicide. Yet uncertainties remained until JCS 1067 was issued (see Appendix). An introductory statement which the State Department issued later frankly admits that General Eisenhower was "directed to urge the (Allied) Control Council to adopt these policies for enforcement throughout Germany." It implies that the United States was unsuccessful, since we are told that the meeting at Potsdam took place, "before this directive was discussed in the Control Council," and that the directive should therefore be read in the light of the Potsdam policies.[2] That Americans

---

[2]*The Axis in Defeat,* p. 13. For a concrete illustration of how this worked, see the next chapter, especially pages 276–279.

hoped, when JCS 1067 was issued, to secure reasonable uniformity is clear from what the document itself states as an anticipation: that substantially similar directives would be issued to British, Soviet, and French Commanders. There can be little question that Americans provided the driving force behind explicit denazification policies.

Germany, the commander in chief was told, will not be occupied for the purpose of liberation, but as a defeated enemy nation. And the first essential step on the road to realizing the principal Allied objective of preventing Germany from ever becoming again a threat to the peace of the world was denazification, or, to use the directive's own words: "the elimination of Nazism and militarism in all their forms." Consequently, a whole section of the directive deals with denazification, the dissolution of the Nazi party and all its formations, the abrogation of all specifically Nazi laws, and the elimination of all Nazis from any positions of influence. "All members of the Nazi party who have been more than nominal participants in its activities, all active supporters of Nazism or militarism and all other persons hostile to Allied purposes will be removed and excluded from public office and from positions of importance in quasi-public and private enterprises." The latter were described as including civic and labor organizations, industry, commerce, agriculture and finance, education, the press and publishing.[3]

Clearly, when the manner in which we defined the "more than nominal participants" in Nazi party activities and the "active supporters of Nazism and militarism" is fully appreciated, it is no wonder that military government officers in the field felt time and again that the job was impossible. Under the directive, all men and women who had held office in *any* Nazi organization whatsoever were included, all "avowed believers" in Nazism or militarism, all those who had given voluntary support, whether moral or material, or political assistance of any kind to the Nazi party or its leaders. In view of the extent to which the Nazi revolution had swept away former officials and had terrorized and forced all the more prominent men in public life into participation in the manyfold organizations, such as professional and commercial associations under Nazi labels and controls,

[3]Cf. Alfred Nagts, *Hitler's Second Army* (1943).

the stigma of Nazi affiliation applied to nearly everybody in local and provincial government, business administration, and professional life. A substantial portion of the men who had fought these pressures, who had defied the terror and resisted all efforts at coordination, had been killed in concentration camps, had been driven into exile, or had committed suicide when faced by the *Gestapo*. No wonder that military government field detachments faced extreme difficulties in carrying out their heavy assignments.

In order fully to appreciate the disgust frequently felt by field officers at over-all denazification policies, one must try to recapture the facts as these officers faced them. Wherever they came, they found the same general picture of governmental chaos, economic paralysis, administrative collapse. Hence the military authorities went ahead on their well-tried dogma of "economy of effort" and "employment of the native population," while the political program veered toward an ever more severe policy of "getting rid of the Nazis." When a military government detachment came into a town or city, almost its first task was to remove all Nazis from office, and to bring in new men. These were hard to find, harder to evaluate, and to watch. Time and again, after a search by military government had yielded a new city manager (*Bürgermeister*) or district administrator, the counter intelligence investigated the man and demanded his removal. It was inevitable that different men would act differently under such conditions. Some would curse the brass hats and leave in office men who looked good to them, calling them "nominal Nazis," while others would remove the same man, calling him an "active" one. Sometimes this strict interpretation of the "rules" was carried to absurd extremes. But seen in the perspective of eventual democratization and pacification of Germany, this removal of all Nazis should be considered part of the war. There can be no question that a return toward normal conditions was slowed in the American zone as a result of the rigors of denazification. But eventual success in getting German administration going and in "turning things over to the Germans" was likewise made possible by this initial effort.

The Attempt at Uniform Allied Denazification

The combat-conquest phase of denazification changed imperceptibly into that difficult and abortive phase during which the United States tried once more to secure a uniform application of our general principles to all of Germany. Having secured the inclusion of the basic ideas of its general policy directive into the Potsdam Declaration, American policy makers hoped that uniform practices would be adopted by the Allies to carry out these broad principles. In this they were sadly disappointed. Clearly, it was the American intention and avowed purpose to eliminate virtually the entire German "ruling class" whether in favor of National Socialism, or against it, provided they were "hostile to Allied purposes." Presumably this was true of all Germans in positions of leadership, except the few men who possessed the boldness of spirit to dissociate themselves from the war effort and commit acts of sabotage in favor of the enemy. Only those men and women were exempted whose hostility to the National Socialist party and its activities was so fierce as to persuade them that even high treason was an allowable weapon to be used against the Hitler government.[4]

Each of the Allies had a different conception of what these general principles implied. Quite naturally, each linked denazification to over-all policy regarding Germany. The French, who were not a party to the Potsdam Agreement, felt that they were entitled anyway to pursue a policy of their own. Even when the Allied Control Authority, with French assent, adopted a law comparable to, and implementing the Potsdam Agreement,[5] the French nevertheless proceeded, at least

[4]A remarkable group of books has recently been published in which these activities of the German underground are described. Most authoritative is Allen W. Dulles, *The German Underground* (1947). See also the official publication of the United States Strategic Bombing Survey, entitled *The Effects of Strategic Bombing on German Morale* (1947). The document notes that in 1944, "Approximately one of every 1,200 German adults was arrested by the Gestapo for political or religious offense," p. 2. Cf. also the details in Chapter 7, entitled "The Control of Subversion and Opposition."

[5]See Control Council Directive No. 24, "Removal from Office and from Positions of Responsibility of Nazis and of Persons Hostile to Allied Purposes," Berlin, January 12, 1946.

in Württemberg South, to leave the matter entirely to the German authorities.

The Russians since the beginning have employed denazification for the purpose of forwarding the reshaping of German society along the lines of Soviet policy. Already in midwinter 1945–1946, the Soviet-controlled radio was broadcasting appeals to the "little party member" (*kleine Pg*) to have no fear—that any convincing proof of a change of heart, such as joining the Communist party (later the Socialist Unity Party) and loyally cooperating with the Red army would be sufficient to reinstate him as an equal citizen in the Soviet zone of Germany. Posters like that reproduced in *The New York Times*[6] showing a big street poster, citing Stalin and reading, "The experience of history proves that Hitlers come and go, but the German people, the German state remain," are part of a continuing Soviet appeal to German mass sentiment which contrasts oddly with their victory monuments in Berlin. But in fact both are part of the same pattern of saying to the common man of Germany: "We came to help you, to liberate you from your Fascist capitalist oppressors, honor us and follow us. The guilty Nazis are not those many men who believed in the Nazi creed, but the members of the ruling class, whether Nazis or not."

The British have concentrated their punitive action upon the criminal element of the Nazi movement: the concentration camp personnel, the secret police agents, and some of the more ruthless exploiters of power and privilege. But they were eager to make very sure that businessmen and other professional people whose service might be vital to their efforts at reconstruction would be thoroughly investigated at once and, if possible, cleared of the more serious penalties of complicity in Nazi activities. It has often been alleged, and in the author's opinion quite rashly, that the British let many Nazis continue in high posts. Such statements originate in quarters which are not and cannot be familiar with the elaborate secret service investigation and hearings which the British authorities have used to ascertain the actual facts. There are men who fought the Nazis from within the party or from a government office. Admittedly, such cases are

[6] See *The New York Times*, September 12, 1946.

comparatively rare, and many Germans now pretend to have been much more courageous than they were. Men of this type were often exonerated by the British authorities after several days of careful cross-examination by secret service men and then released for return to their work. Unfortunately, such secret investigations did not convince the public, and an impression was created that the British were "soft" on Nazis. The only basis in fact for this accusation is that the British definitely made every effort to salvage trained personnel wherever they could.

The American Enforcement Effort

While seeking Allied agreement under the Control Council, American military government proceeded to apply its interpretation of the Potsdam Agreement. A very comprehensive questionnaire (*Fragebogen*) was being distributed which contained approximately 150 questions and covered in considerable detail the background and life history of each of the million or more Germans under investigation.[7] These questionnaires, described by some German officials as a "statistical masterpiece," soon became a source of considerable merriment among the populace, who could not but reflect that the red tape (*Amtsschimmel*) of by-gone bureaucratic days had returned with a vengeance. One feature of American policy particularly disturbed the well-intentioned Germans, and that was our making May 1, 1937, the dividing line for determining whether party membership was to be regarded merely with suspicion or was criminal and hence ground for mandatory dismissal. Perhaps the publication that year of the National Socialist Civil Service law, which made it obligatory for any new civil service appointee to become a party member, caused the selection of that date.[8]

The cleansing of other fields of "private" business was undertaken

[7] As of February 15, 1946, American military government authorities had received 1,304,000 completed questionnaires (*Fragebogen*) required of all persons appointed to, or continued in office or important positions.

[8] The Civil Service Act was actually published on January 26, 1937, entitled *Deutsches Beamtengesetz*. Cf. K. Loewenstein, *Hitler's Germany* (1940), p. 174.

in the much-criticized Law No. 8 issued September 26, 1946.[9] It specifically provided for the elimination of all businessmen from their supervisory or managerial posts if they had been members of the Nazi party or any of its affiliates. Under this law it became a criminal offense for any man to employ a party member and for any party member to take such employment. An appeal procedure was set up so that any aggrieved person, e.g. a former member of the party, could plead that he had not been actively engaged. In order to prevent any substantial number from escaping the punitive provisions of this law, active support was, as before, defined to include "avowed belief in Nazism, or racial or militaristic creeds," as well as "political support of any kind" to either the party or its leaders. It is not definitely known how many persons sought to secure a review through such an appeal, or how many were actually cleared through it. The number of persons who lost their jobs under Law No. 8 presumably was considerable. During the spring of 1946, complaint was loud among both Americans and Germans that economic activity in the American zone had been severely handicapped as a result of its rigid application.

The American program of vigorous denazification had covered a great deal of ground by the end of January, 1946. Including the people in business and the free professions, 1,103,000 persons had been investigated by questionnaire and otherwise, and of these about 260,000 or 25 per cent had been adjudged active Nazis and militarists and removed from important positions, including about 15 per cent from the public service.

Leading anti-Nazis in positions of influence under our military government who were and are strong believers in denazification have sharply criticized our procedures, because they are both *too* harsh and *too* soft. The blanket rule about Nazi party members had quite often the most bizarre results. From among many, two cases were cited by a long-time Socialist inmate of a concentration camp—an anti-Nazi, if there ever was one.[10] His first case was that of a leading lawyer

[9]For this law, see German Denazification Law, OMGUS, Bavaria, p. 204, June 15, 1946.

[10]See the article "Denazification" (with a foreword by Alvin Johnson) in *Social Research*, XIV (March, 1947), 59 ff. For the two instances, see page 68.

who in a number of instances had committed acts of political black-mail, extortion, and denunciation in order to secure private and per-sonal advantages. But the man was not a party member and in the summer of 1946, he was still a member of the judiciary because all efforts to convince American military government authorities of the need of eliminating him had failed. In the second instance, a local judge had as late as March, 1945, become chairman of a summary tribunal, and in that capacity had condemned a man to death because he had committed an act of sabotage in an effort to aid the Allies. The latter had been a party member and so was removed from his position; whereas the judge has remained in his post. It was inevitable that a law with results as awkward as these could not command the full support of those Germans whose support we ourselves desired.

In spite of these great divergencies in the several zones, or perhaps because of them, the Allied Control Council finally adopted a unify-ing set of guiding principles in Directive No. 24, which was issued on January 12, 1946. This directive reinforced the broad conceptions of the Potsdam Agreement, but implemented them by a list which classified as major offenders and offenders a large number of German higher officials, as well as functionaries of the Nazi party and its far-flung network of affiliate organizations.

The German Phase of Denazification

Basically, the entire American denazification program had been carried out as if it were a military security measure, justified by the anticipated fight against the Nazi underground and guerilla warfare of the "Werewolf" type. A real purification of German political life, it was felt, must be undertaken by the Germans themselves and carried through by them. As early as November, 1945, certain German high officials had begun work on legislation by Germans for Germans in the field of denazification. The Ministers of Justice in the several states of the American zone—Bavaria, Württemberg-Baden, and Greater Hesse—had drafts prepared initiating such legislation. It is not possible to examine these drafts in any detail here. There are, however, some interesting contrasts between these drafts and the legislation adopted later. The German drafts were designed to catch the big fish rather than the little ones and tended to define the Nazi more narrowly as an active participant in the Hitler tyranny. However, the Germans themselves were rather sharply in disagreement with each other as to what was needed. Military government authorities requested that they jointly develop a uniform law for all three states through the Council of States.[11]

After an extended period of negotiation and discussion, the Germans through their Council of States came forward with a draft "Law for the Liberation from National Socialism and Militarism" which our military government authorities rejected. Without going into the details of this rejection, it is enough to say that it was based upon the conviction of American officials in military government that the draft law contravened basic policy objectives in Germany. There can be little question that the Germans had eliminated some of the favorite American approaches. They did not propose to remove from their positions of leadership in German life all the categories we had originally included under the broad conception of the denazification program. They especially objected to the inclusion of certain categories of civil servants, judges, and professional men. But it would be quite erroneous to assume that such objections are meant to "soften" denazification.[12] To illustrate, one might mention two well-known features of the original draft law which the Germans were, and are, quite keen about. One is the size of the monetary penalty to be collected from so-called followers, merely passive members or supporters of the party in business and other walks of life. The Germans wanted to go at least as high as 50,000 marks ($5,000) on the theory that a well-to-do business or professional man ought to be fined in accordance with his ability to pay, and to the point where it hurt. We have insisted that the limit be 2,000 marks. An explanation is hard to find, and the only one stated, both officially and unofficially, is that such men could be put into a category calling for a more severe penalty.

[11]See above, pages 206–208.

[12]This "explanation" of German criticism has been an overworked, because convenient, alibi for resisting their views. See the article quoted above in footnote 10 for further detail.

But this expedient is not only unjust but impracticable. It is like having a penal code provide a nominal penalty for manslaughter, and then defending such an arrangement on the ground that the jury can find for murder. The other controversial feature of the German draft—provisions which were intended to check the flood of denunciations and false witnesses—provided severe penalties for such conduct. These provisions were rejected by American military government because it was felt that they would undermine the system of informers and confidential agents. It is not without interest, perhaps, that denazification in the French zone of South Württemberg, which took the form of a purely German law entitled "Ordinance for a Political Clean-up" (May 28, 1946), established no limits for monetary fines; this law also made it a criminal offense to allege that someone was a Nazi or had committed any of the reprehensible acts the ordinance sought to punish when the informer knew, or could know, the contrary to be the truth. The original drafts of Greater Hesse also contained a similar provision. Significantly the author of the German ordinance in South Württemberg is a leader of Social Democracy in South Germany and an ardent anti-Nazi. His ideas may therefore be assumed to be those of German democrats.

It is clear, then, that the disagreement between the Americans and the Germans as to what constitutes a good denazification law was not that between advocates of a soft and of a harsh policy. Whatever the merits of the controversy, it was quite unfortunate that American authorities should have found it necessary to reject the German draft. The rejection caused many Germans to feel that this was *not* essentially a *German* law. American authorities had very much hoped that it would be so considered and have continued to maintain that it *is* a *German* law.

For better or worse, the "Law for the Liberation from National Socialism and Militarism" went into force on March 10, 1946. What then are the provisions of this law? It can be said that in general they follow the pattern of American denazification policy but modified by experience and German legal traditions. The law recognized at the outset the superior authority of Control Council Directive No. 24 and that of our Law No. 8. It proclaimed that "liberation from national socialism and militarism is an indispensable prerequisite to political, economic, and cultural reconstruction," because "for twelve years national socialism and militarism have carried on in Germany their tyranny, have committed most serious crimes against the German people and the world, have thrown Germany into distress and misery and destroyed the German Reich." Even this preamble suggests that the law is at least in part a German law; for it puts the crimes against the German people first. Furthermore, in its "principles" it states a more universal ground than hostility to Allied purposes as the basis for adjudging a man subject to the punitive provisions of the law. All those "are guilty" who have "violated the principles of justice and humanity" or have "selfishly exploited the conditions" created by the Nazi tyranny. Everyone who shared this responsibility is to be called to account, yet he will be given an opportunity to vindicate himself. In keeping with this approach, the law insists upon the *individual's* responsibility for his actual conduct, and it rejects the "outward indications" such as membership in the party, as decisive criteria of responsibility. The law also provides that Germans who were not members of the party may be adjudged Nazis.

The law undertakes to describe in considerable detail four classes of Nazis and militarists which in the order of decreasing responsibility are called 1) major offenders, 2) offenders, 3) lesser offenders or probationers, and 4) followers. The offenders are further subdivided into (a) activists, (b) militarists, (c) profiteers. These wrongdoers are described in terms of the offenses committed, such as "anyone who, in Germany or in the occupied areas, treated foreign civilians or prisoners of war contrary to international law" (a major offender); or "anyone who, through national socialist teachings or education, poisoned the spirit and soul of youth" (an activist); or "anyone who made disproportionately high profits in armament and war transactions" (a profiteer). These phrasings are merely samples of the catalogue of offenses used by the law to outline what misdeeds each category of Nazi offenders is to cover. There also was recognized a category 5) of exonerated persons, men and women who on investigation turned out not to have been Nazis at all. This approach was not deemed adequate by American authorities, who insisted that the lists of officials and organizations appended to Control Council Directive No. 24 must be used. The Germans objected. The matter was finally compromised by adding an appendix to the law which is stated to be "based on Directive No. 24 which is binding on the German governments and the German people." But the minister-presidents did not sign this appendix, of which they disapprove, with the awkward and legally absurd result that a "law" refers to an appendix which those making the law reject as unsound. This accounts for the Germans' insistence that this law is American, while we take the opposite view.

Why did the Germans protest with such sharpness against the appendix? The appendix contains long lists of officials and organizations which are classified into two groups, one I) containing the major offenders, and the other II) the offenders and covering the three groups under category 2) of the German law. Upon inspecting the list, we find that Class I comprises not only the key Nazis, such as party leaders and Gestapo, but ambassadors, chairmen and presidents of economic associations, high-ranking judges, to mention only a few. It was urged by Germans that such lumping together of key Nazis with other leaders of German life, though the latter admittedly share responsibility, exculpates the Nazis by putting them into the same class with men who are often entitled to a measure of respect in spite of their weakness in supporting the Hitler regime. This argument holds even more true of the Class II category which treats lower Nazi officials on the same plane with executives of economic groups and officials of the Foreign Office. No one reading this list of offices and persons enumerated in the appendix can help feeling that the men responsible for it sought a wholesale indictment of the German ruling class in all its branches.

Denazification has been spoken of as a cold, bureaucratic revolution—and in a certain sense it is—but not even the Communists among German parties wholly approve of it. The leader of the Communist party in one of the states in the American zone at one time stated quite blandly that he felt the only clear indication of a man's repentance was his willingness to join the Communist party. At the same time he cited the letter of an SS man who wrote him that he had seen the errors of his ways, and now realized how right the Communist party had been in opposing the Nazis from the start, and that he was quite willing to join them, and even to go to the devastated areas to help rebuild, in order to release a Communist prisoner of war. It was this party leader's opinion that a man like that should not be deprived of his voting right under the denazification law.[13] A more usual criticism, prevalent among Social Democrats, has frequently been put forward: many bourgeois middle-class Germans with nationalistic convictions did not join the party because they were not under pressure to do so; former Social Democrats in the lower ranks of officialdom, such as letter carriers and railroad employees, did join because they claimed for themselves the fundamental right of not having to be heroes. If, besides joining, a little party member had collected contributions to the National Socialist Welfare Fund, he is, under the lists, deemed to have been an official of the Nazi party, and hence adjudged an offender; whereas the bourgeois nationalist goes scot-free.[14] It will be noted that in both cases the German critics of the law—and they are presumably avowed anti-Nazis—object to the law because of the appendix and its lists which make it difficult for those administering the law to render justice.

If German criticism was sharp and continuous, American criticism was not lacking. Businessmen especially objected strongly to making people responsible for purely business activities, on the ground that they somehow or other aided the Nazi war effort. Their viewpoint is well stated by Lewis H. Brown, who, while accepting denazification as "imperiously demanded by the conscience of the world," nevertheless insists that "the process has gone to destructive extremes." He, too, would readily punish the Nazis, but not the "millions of Germans who were forced to cooperate or merely climbed on the bandwagon of a winning party as men do everywhere." Brown urges that it was "impossible for anyone in wartime Germany to be skilled

[13]No German party ever officially approved of the law, though the Communists came closest to it. It is a fair surmise that any party doing so would lose greatly at the polls. Even the Communists, who at one time tried to use the law to carry through a policy similar to one their party had developed in the Soviet zone, became critical.

[14]See "Denazification," Social Research, XIV, 72. This criticism neglects the provisions about militarism under the law—a common error among Germans.

or competent without being assigned some post under the Nazis." He wants to rescue the "brains and competence of Germany" for peacetime reconstruction. He therefore recommends that the status of denazification be settled at once by "A. stopping all future indictments. B. Reclassifying as nominal all party followers . . . unless a court has determined otherwise. C. Granting the right to return to work of all except Category I, this right subject to revocation if later determined by a court. D. Setting a definite date for the termination of the trials by the denazification courts, except those in Category I."[15]

The organization for enforcing the "Law for the Liberation from National Socialism and Militarism" is, of course, entirely German, except for the American supervisory personnel. The law provided for a special ministry of liberation in each state, whose head is a member of the cabinet. The real responsibility for the enforcement of the law was put, however, into local quasi-judicial bodies, called *Spruchkammern,* which resemble the local draft boards in the United States in that they are drawn from the local citizens. More than three hundred of these local tribunals or boards had to be organized to handle the more than three million people chargeable under the law. It is obvious that considerable variation would develop between the decisions of these boards, and since the jurisdiction was quasi-criminal, such variations caused bitter resentment and rapidly discredited the law. The difficulty of enforcement would have been lessened if Germans had been ready to serve on these tribunals. What happened should have been anticipated: even proven and well-known anti-Nazis have hesitated to serve. Those ready and eager to go on the boards were at times undesirable elements who wanted to abuse the board for political purposes (both reactionary and Communist). The rub in such situations is that neighbor is to judge neighbor. Even in a working democracy, such as the United States, difficulties were encountered with locally recruited OPA boards as soon as the fighting was over and the patriotic impulse rapidly declined. Within the German village or town, not only was there lack of the democratic spirit of public service, but much terror of the Nazi years of oppression lingered, re-

---

[15]See Lewis H. Brown, *Report on Germany* (1947), pp. 36, 63, 86. The actual reform as reported in footnote 22 is along these lines, though more moderate.

inforced by the fear of a return of these men to power. Remarks currently heard brought this out: "These men are my neighbors"; "I shall have to live with them for the rest of my life"; "I'll be living here long after you Americans have gone home"; "Yes, you are right, the job must be done, but why not have it done by professional judges?" Why not, indeed? The lack of trained judicial personnel was one of the main reasons for trying this system of *Spruchkammern*. The majority of judges were disqualified by Nazi affiliations and could not be employed until tried themselves. Eventually, however, all the tribunals were fully manned, and some have done an outstanding job in clearing up their assignment. Others have been a complete failure. A contributory cause for widespread failure in enforcement has been due to the procedure under which cases may be appealed to one of the eight appeal boards or tribunals. A further unanticipated difficulty has been caused by the millions of expelled Germans from the Eastern provinces, the Sudetens from Czechoslovakia, and the numerous German-speaking minorities, such as the Moldavians from Rumania and others from Hungary, Austria, and Yugoslavia. Although substantial numbers of these people were undoubtedly Nazis of various degrees of enthusiasm, they were not known to the local boards. In regard to all these persons—and in many communities they number 50 per cent and over of the population today—the idea broke down that a local board would be better able to assess the personal background of the accused.

When responsible officials in the Ministries of Liberation (and of Justice) began to estimate the amount of time involved in bringing to trial all those chargeable under the law they arrived at staggering totals. Various estimates ranged from ten to twenty and even fifty years. Clearly, the urgent task of denazification could not be thus jeopardized. What to do? It was decided, since no one chargeable under the law could be employed as anything but a common laborer, that the *Spruchkammern* should try first of all to handle the mass of followers, the little party member or Pg (pronounced Paygay), and after imposing the small fines involved enable them to return to their jobs. But this procedure had two serious disadvantages: 1) it kept many valuable professional and managerial people out of

work, and thus prevented them from contributing their share to reconstruction, and 2) it left those most deserving punishment free
to go about, unless they were kept under arrest in camp, where many
of them were better off than the starving civilians outside. In order,
therefore, to get on with the denazification of those for whom the law
was really and primarily intended, American military government
authorized two sweeping amnesties. The first of these applied to very
young former party members whom it was felt could not be held
personally responsible, since they were fourteen years or younger
when the party came to power (ex-Nazis born after 1920). The second, also known as the Christmas amnesty, pardoned former Nazis
in the lowest income group (earning less than RM 3600 in 1943) if
they were followers or lesser offenders. This latter provision of the
amnesty, however, necessitated bringing to trial many borderline
cases to determine whether a particular man should be put into these
lower categories of the law.

A serious administrative problem occurred in connection with all
those not chargeable under the law. Since it had been provided that
every German voter (adult) would fill out a general questionnaire,[16]
large numbers of persons had to be notified, after the questionnaires
had been examined, that they were not chargeable under the law.
The number of such persons ran into millions. It eventually required
very strong pressure from American military government to clean up
this side of the law's enforcement, and thereby allay the anxieties
caused to hundreds of thousands of innocent citizens who had remained in suspense as to what was happening to their questionnaires.

Perhaps the most problematical aspect of this law in the eyes of
Americans and Germans alike is its apparent *ex post facto* nature.
One writer recently put the problem thus:

Law and justice are being compromised. . . . From ages past, society
has developed the idea and form of criminal procedure for the purpose
of prosecuting individual and specific crimes. In this we have at our disposal the wisdom and the experience of thousands of years. . . . The idea

[16]These questionnaires were called *Meldebogen* to distinguish them from the
Fragebogen originally required of all persons holding positions of influence when the
military administered denazification.

of putting an individual on trial on the ground of membership in a ruling, and *de facto*, mass party, or to prosecute him for activities which in themselves had no illegal content . . . is not altogether new. What is new, however, is the clothing of this process in the garb of a government of law and thus giving it the appearance of democratic and independent administration of justice.[17]

On the face of it, the Liberation Law looks like such a law, indeed. People are being punished for past deeds which were not subject to a penalty under existing law when committed. Two answers can be given to this objection. First, it can be argued—and is so argued by many German advocates of denazification—that this law is not a criminal law in the strict sense, but a law for expiation and atonement. The law itself speaks of reparation, rather than punishment. The criminality of the entire National Socialist movement was such that its supporters have become responsible for the damages it brought upon the German people and can justifiably be asked to "repair" that damage. They may also justifiably be excluded from German public life, having demonstrated their political immaturity, if nothing worse. The more effective argument is the second one that during the Hitler regime there was no genuine law in operation at all, and the many novel crimes committed by and on behalf of the National Socialist party and its formations cannot therefore be allowed to go free of punishment. These criminal acts ought not to be protected by a legal rule applicable only under lawful and constitutional governments.

The problem of *ex post facto* legislation had to be faced when the constitutions in the several states of the American zone were being adopted (see above, Chapter I). For as is traditional under modern constitutional government, each of the constitutions undertook to outlaw *ex post facto* laws. But in each constitution, the "Liberation Law" itself, as well as later laws directed toward the same purpose, is exempted from these and other provisions of the constitution. The preambles of these constitutions reject explicitly militarism and Na-

---

[17]See "Denazification," cited above. Even more sharply critical are the articles by Max Rheinstein, "Renazifying Germany," *University of Chicago Magazine*, April, 1947, and "The Ghost of the Morgenthau Plan," *The Christian Century*, April 2, 1947. It should be noted that the so-called "Morgenthau plan" did not deal with denazification.

tional Socialism as undemocratic, and each contains a number of specific provisions for the protection of the constitution against anti-constitutional acts and movements such as wrecked the Weimar Republic.[18]

Experience in trying to enforce the "Law for Liberation" eventually proved the soundness of a good part of the criticism of the law. Various proposals have been formulated by German and American enforcement officials, but no revisions were in fact adopted during the first year of the law's existence. Top American officials, including General Clay himself, felt that a serious effort must be made first to carry out the law. International complications, such as the Moscow Conference, also played their part in causing hesitancy about revising it. Of course, this resistance to amendments of the law proposed by German authorities further strengthened the conviction that this was in reality an American and not a German law. When popularly elected legislatures in the several *Länder* informally put forward suggestions for change, they at first met with little response, and they resented it as any democratic legislature would. But while these arguments were batted about, the enforcement machinery organized by the law kept grinding on.

The supervisory machinery of American military government has operated on all levels of denazification. In the local communities, a member of a local military government detachment has ordinarily been assigned to the one or more *Spruchkammern*. Unfortunately, the recurrent reductions in such local personnel have made this phase of supervision increasingly perfunctory. On the level of the *Land* government, where the appeal tribunals and the ministry operate, the so-called Special Branch of Public Safety has carried the burden under the general direction of the Land Director of Military Government. At the headquarters of OMGUS, in Berlin, Public Safety has

[18]Thus the Bavarian Constitution provides in Article 184: "The validity of any laws aimed at National Socialism and militarism or which are intended to eliminate their consequences are not affected or limited by this constitution." The corresponding article in the Constitution of Hesse is 158; in Württemberg-Baden, 104. In the latter two constitutions, the validity of such remedial legislation is limited to January 1, 1949. See the official translation contained in *Constitutions of Bavaria, Hesse and Württemberg-Baden*, OMGUS, Berlin, Germany, February 15, 1947.

likewise been the primary administrative authority, but implemented by a Denazification Review Board set up directly under the then Deputy Military Governor, General Clay.[19] This board has kept in constant touch with the work in the field through its executive, Dr. Walter Dorn, who, as Special Adviser to the DMG on denazification, has played a decisive role in the shaping of recent American policy in this field. Both *Land* and OMGUS officers are aided in their supervision of the enforcement of the law by our intelligence units.[20]

It is far too early to assess accurately the success or failure of American denazification policy. As one competent student of American military government in Germany has recently remarked, "if one were to select the single item which received the most attention from military government officers of the United States in Germany, stirred up the widest controversy, occasioned the greatest perplexity among British, Russian and French Allies, and gave rise to the most widespread publicity in the United States, it would without much question be the denazification program."[21] The intense interest in denazification possibly has focused too much attention upon this phase of our occupation policy. This argument is often heard among American military government officials. To this writer, it seems untrue. Inquiries among anti-Nazi Germans have disclosed no detailed, workable plan for effective action in the field of denazification. Quite a few German officials of intelligence and probity believed in the summer of 1946 that the "Law for the Liberation from National Socialism and Militarism" could, in spite of its shortcomings, be carried out. It is too often forgotten that Hitler and his followers, by the very thoroughness of the destruction they wrought, created this extremely difficult problem for those who took over after the regime's collapse. As was observed at the outset, denazification, with all its shortcomings and inadequacies, was yet an intrinsic and necessary part of American policy in Germany. Neither the democratization nor the

[19]Since March, 1947, this board is directly under the Military Governor, thus demonstrating General Clay's continuing intense personal concern with denazification.

[20]The sharp rebuke which General Clay addressed to the Council of States (*Länderrat*) on November 9, 1946, was, of course, based upon the concept of active supervision described above.

[21]Zink, *op. cit.*, p. 130.

reconstruction of Germany could be countenanced by responsible
American authorities until everything possible—nay, even the impossible—had been done to rid German life of the Nazis. In the long
run, it was more excusable to err on the side of trying to remove too
many than too few. Perhaps American military government first, and
the German democratic governments who took over afterward, went
too far and included too many. But whatever the mistakes, the job
had to be undertaken.

Finally, it is important to bear in mind that there will be Nazis in
Germany for many years to come. No mistake would be more fatal
than to assume that the procedures adopted (or any others that might
have been followed) could have prevented this from happening. Besides punishing the guilty and restraining the recalcitrant, the practical political problem after a great revolutionary upheaval of this
kind is to keep sympathizers of Hitler from occupying positions of influence and power. Even the moderate must sincerely hope that this
will be done. If it is, we have, after all, reason to be satisfied, for it was
the primary and original objective of the Combined Chiefs of Staff
to accomplish "the destruction of the National Socialist party and
the removal of all active Nazis from positions of authority."[22] Perhaps it would have been well, if American military government policy
had remained restricted to this limited, conservative objective.[23]

[22]Holborn, *op. cit.*, pp. 36–37.

[23]Since this was written, American military government authorities have accepted
basic modifications in the law. As reported in *The New York Times,* October 5, 1947,
the amendments 1) make the trial of lesser offenders and followers discretionary
with the prosecutor, 2) permit lesser offenders and followers to take jobs higher than
ordinary labor, but not positions of influence such as public office, and 3) make the
period of probation discretionary. The American press did not mention the fact that
this action was precipitated by a unilateral action of the Soviet authorities who, after
holding up proposed uniform Control Council legislation as agreed upon in Moscow,
suddenly in July 1947, promulgated their Law 201, which presumably freed all but
the most incriminated Nazis from further prosecution.

Chapter XIII

Information Control in the American Zone of Germany, 1945–1946

JOSEPH DUNNER

INFORMATION control policy received its first test during the occupation of the Rhineland by the Allied Expeditionary Forces. Making full use of the practical experience gained during the initial penetration of German territory in the West, Supreme Headquarters of Allied Expeditionary Forces (SHAEF) established policy directives in the spring of 1945 with regard to information services in Germany. These directives may be summed up as follows: 1) The Nazi propaganda machine is to be destroyed; filling the void thus left, Allied services were asked 2) to tell the Germans in straightforward language of the disappearance of the Nazi order, and 3) to provide them with a demonstration of what a factual information service means. It was stipulated that the media to be used in this first phase of Allied occupation would be mainly press and radiobroadcasting. Both media were to be operated by military government.

It was during this first phase of military occupation that Law No. 191 concerning the control of publications, radiobroadcasting, news services, films, theaters, and music was issued. This law really constituted an elaboration of the directives just described. The leading objective of the law was, of course, stated as "ensuring the security of AEF" and the "achievement of the objectives of the Supreme Commander." Since the provisions of this law became the basic framework within which all information control work was developed, its primary provisions will be summarized.

First, the law prohibited virtually all communication and entertainment activities, enumerating them all in an exhaustive catalogue, extending from the printing of newspapers to the production of operas and other performances of any kind. Hereafter, any and all of these activities could only be carried on "as authorized by military government." Second, the law prohibited the exercise of any and all functions of the former Ministry of Propaganda. In other words, military authorities claimed the sole right to exercise these functions of information control, including review, approval, or authorization. Naturally, the law also placed under military government all the funds, property, equipment, accounts, and records of the Goebbels ministry. Third, the law proposed to compromise within this prohibition and suspension all the subsidiary, affiliated, and controlled organizations, such as the Reich Chamber of Culture. Fourth, the law gave military government courts jurisdiction over all offenders, and authorized them to inflict any "lawful" punishment, including death, without specifying what violations would be punished by what penalties.

Regulation No. 1, implementing this law, has further provided that all the various activities whose free undertaking had been prohibited could be carried on if the person had either secured a license or registered at the Office of Military Government. The licensing was required of the key production control activities: the publication of newspapers, magazines, periodicals, books, posters, pamphlets, printed music, and the like; the operation of a news service, news or photographic agency, radiobroadcasting or television station, and so on; the production of a film, or the production and presentation of a play, concert, opera, fair, circus, carnival, and the like. Registration was asked of those who distribute, sell, lend, or print such publications, who work for show producers and similar enterprisers, and who process or print motion pictures, or distribute, sell, or lend recordings commercially. From these stringent requirements of licensing and registering were exempted only music incidental to religious services, and entertainment music at restaurants, inns, and the like. Again, discretionary "lawful" punishment by a military government court was provided in this regulation.

The policy directives described in the beginning of this chapter looked forward to the time when the military situation would permit the reconstruction of democratic German information services. At that time, the information control offices of SHAEF were to devote themselves to the re-establishment of German information services. Such a re-establishment was to proceed under Allied supervision, but with German personnel in all functions, provided the German staff members were not Nazis. Such supervision was also to be directed toward the elimination of all remainders of Nazi and militarist ideology.

It is clear that the program envisaged for information control in occupied Germany called for far-flung activities, since it required a complete taking over and eventual rebuilding of the media of press, radio, and entertainment for a people of well over sixty million, a people who possessed a deep-rooted native culture in all these fields, but especially in music. True, this culture had been perverted by the Nazi ideology and propaganda, but with these corrupting influences removed, it was bound to reassert itself powerfully and hence would call for exceptional skill, tact, and firmness on the part of foreigners seeking to control and guide it effectively for some time.[1]

Functional Plan

While SHAEF reserved for itself the right to enunciate further basic directives, it entrusted the carrying out of these directives to the Psychological Warfare Division. After the dissolution of SHAEF into its American and British components and the creation of separate zones of occupation, the Psychological Warfare Division, with headquarters in Bad Homburg, changed its name into Information Control Division of the U.S. Forces, European Theater (ICD-USFET). This division in turn comprised three information control units attached to the two American military districts and the American sector of Berlin: 6870 DISCC, with headquarters in Munich; 6871 DISCC, with headquarters in Wiesbaden; and the information con-

[1]The preceding section of this chapter has been rewritten by the editor from the legal material furnished by the author. The same is true of the conclusion.

trol section of the Office of Military Government, United States (OMGUS), in Berlin.

Each information control unit in the American zone of occupation was subdivided into a Plans and Directive Section, coordinating the work of the media sections, and maintaining liaison with divisional headquarters and other military units, an administrative section for the internal administration of the unit, the media sections, and an intelligence section for the purpose of assisting the media sections with respect to intelligence on facilities and personalities in each medium.

The tasks of an information control officer in any of the information media consisted of a variety of activities.

He was to report to the public safety officer of military government in a given locality violations of any basic or current policy instructions. Germans who, without a license, engaged in activities in the information services that according to Information Control Regulation No. 1 required a license, were to be prosecuted by the public safety officer with the assistance of the information control unit.

Although property of the German state and the Nazi party was normally frozen under Military Government Law No. 52, the information control officer for district information control purposes was authorized to demand the requisition of property belonging to German individuals or corporations. Since in the reconstruction of democratic information services it was necessary to rely on Germans who, as a rule, were unable to purchase the required property, the information control unit provided for the use of confiscated or requisitioned properties. The licensees were to pay into a blocked account, under the jurisdiction of the military government property control officer, a fair rental value for the use of nonconsumable property and a fair value for consumable property.

The main concern of the information control officer was to find suitable personnel for the German information services. In view of the enormous influence exerted on the public by persons engaged in creative or managerial functions in the information media, an exhaustive scrutiny of potential licensees had to be conducted.

The Examining of German Licensees [2]

In general, the methods that information control officers applied in judging a candidate's suitability were these:

The applicant's name was checked against the "white," "gray," and "black" lists compiled by divisional headquarters on the basis of information given by prominent anti-Nazis, certain public sources, and interrogators of German prisoners of war. "White" were anti-Nazi and non-Nazi Germans who, according to this information, had in no way ever compromised with the Nazi regime. "Gray" connoted non-Nazi Germans who, though not zealous supporters of the Nazi regime, had rendered it some measure of service. "Black" was reserved for Nazis, German militarists, and ardent Nazi sympathizers. Only persons who were on the "white" lists or who were judged "white" by the control officer could become licensees.

The candidate's military government questionnaire, containing 131 questions as to his educational background, income, and political and religious affiliations, was reviewed.

In a personal interview the candidate was encouraged to tell his life story. (The press control section for Munich and Upper Bavaria asked its applicants to write a short autobiography and to answer in essay form these two questions: "Why are you opposed to the Nazi regime?" "What is the function of the newspaper?")

The reliability of the applicant's statements was thoroughly checked.

Other military government units, particularly the Counter Intelligence Corps, were consulted.

Broad criteria governed the selection of applicants for licenses as newspaper or book publishers, and managers of theater, film, or music companies. They had to be politically suitable. They had to have sound business judgment and the ability to select subordinates capable of doing their part of the job. Above all, the licensees had to be capable of recognizing and suppressing Nazi or other undesirable

[2] For the general background of this section, compare Chapter XII on denazification, especially the section entitled "The Military Phase of Denazification."

political elements so as to prevent these from penetrating their operations.

As to the political suitability of a candidate, an over-all judgment would usually rest on his former political and organizational affiliations. It was somehow assumed that Germans with democratic convictions were before 1933 affiliated either with parties or with religious, cultural, and sport associations opposed to Nazi and Pan-German teachings.

Another factor was the candidate's record under the Hitler regime. In general, anyone was suspect who in the years from 1933 to 1945 had succeeded in improving considerably his career and income. Individuals who before 1933 had occupied important positions and continued in them in order, as they claimed, to use their "sobering" influence on the Nazis, and such "time servers" as "unpolitical" civil servants were also viewed with less favor than people who had opposed the Nazi regime to the extent that they lost their jobs or were persecuted for their convictions.

Of greater importance than formal political affiliations were, of course, the genuine attitudes of a candidate toward crucial political issues as revealed in his answers to certain key questions presented to him: "Who is responsible for the war? What did you like or dislike about National Socialism? What do you think of the Jewish problem? Was Hitler justified in liquidating all other political parties in 1933? Do you believe that Germany had too little 'living space'? When did you feel for the first time that you were a Nazi? Or a non-Nazi?"

At a special screening center for potential licensees in Bad Orb in the fall of 1945 an interesting attempt was made to check the veracity of a candidate's statements as to his political background and convictions and to judge his general character and personality. Since a large number of bona fide anti-Nazis who had been mistreated in prisons and concentration camps were found to lack the emotional stability to fulfill the functions expected of them, the Bad Orb faculty was evenly divided into political experts and psychiatrists. The candidate stayed at the center for two days, in which he went through a number of different tests. An essay on the subject of denazification was followed by an essay on "My feelings and state of mind during the Hitler regime." The third test consisted in setting up a series of criteria that might be used to differentiate Nazis from non-Nazis. The fourth test was a completion test of forty items designed to reveal political attitudes. In the course of the fifth test, an informal discussion during which the candidate met with the members of the screening staff and other candidates, he was requested to recount an interesting episode in his life history, while the other candidates were encouraged to ask him questions. The sixth test consisted of a political interview conducted by one of the political experts on the staff. The last test, the Rorschach test,[3] was administered by a psychiatrist to evoke spontaneous reactions revealing the candidate's thought patterns. On the basis of this test the psychiatrist probed into the candidate's life story. He generally assumed that a man with normal reactions, reflecting no particular emotional instability, would probably not have been a militant anti-Nazi, but rather one who had been able to make some kind of adjustment to the Nazi regime. The psychiatrists on the Bad Orb staff believed they found the typical pattern of events in the life history of the actual anti-Nazi that led him to throw his weight against the dictatorship. These factors, called deviation data, included, among others, a strong maternal influence, the absence of an authoritarian father, being the favorite or only child, leaving one's church.

Experience showed a close interrelationship between political and psychological interviews. For example, one candidate, who denied any Nazi affiliations, was able to give the political interviewer few details of his experiences during the Nazi regime. In tests conducted by the psychiatrist it was revealed that he was an immature exhibitionist who would lightly surrender his personal convictions and make any concessions for success. This finding led to the suspicion that he had actually compromised with Nazism. A more intensive interrogation finally brought out the fact that he had been a member of the Nazi party.

[3]The Rorschach test comprises a series of ten standardized ink blots of various forms and colors. The responses by a candidate as to what he sees on presentation of each figure constitutes a form of free association of ideas considered as an index of his mental and emotional state, his personality make-up, and his character.

Once the results of all investigations proved a candidate suitable for the position of a licensee in the information services, the information control officer would recommend to the commanding officer of the information control unit the granting of a license. While from April to August, 1945, licenses had to be issued or revoked by a special licensing board, consisting of representatives of the Information Control Division and the American political adviser, it eventually became the practice for the commanding officer of the information control unit to issue the license in the name of U.S. Military Government and merely inform the divisional headquarters of the accomplished fact.

The Press

In the area of the press, army newspapers like the *Aachener Zeitung*, the *Frankfurter Presse*, and *Die Neue Zeitung* in Munich filled the news vacuum created by the suppression of the Nazi press. Of these army newspapers, only *Die Neue Zeitung* survived the SHAEF phase. It is today the official German-language paper of the American occupation authorities for the entire American zone, published weekly with the aims of informing the Germans of American policy and the American way of life, and of presenting them with a model of journalistic practice. In the spring of 1945, it was being published in an edition of 1,590,000 copies, or one copy for each fifteen persons in the American zone and the American sector of Berlin.

Die Neue Zeitung was perhaps the single most successful venture of ICD in Germany. Even its huge circulation could have been doubled if newsprint could have been made available. The average German reader has been lavish in his praise, clearly preferring it to any other paper published in the American or any other zone. The main reason given was that it concentrated on *news* as contrasted with editorial comment. Naturally, *Die Neue Zeitung* has also had its critics, especially among its less successful competitors among the German licensees. The very name *Die Neue Zeitung* ("The New Newspaper") seemed to be unfortunate, since the licensed German papers were also new newspapers. Having at the start better publishing facilities, ample paper and newsprint, international contacts, and a large guaranteed income, *Die Neue Zeitung* was for a time considered an unfair competitor for the licensed papers. Another criticism was that it did not satisfactorily project life in America and the American point of view. Two out of five readers failed to realize that *Die Neue Zeitung* was sponsored directly by American military government.

With the exception of *Die Neue Zeitung,* all army newspapers were replaced by papers published by licensed Germans. There are today over fifty such newspapers in the American zone. Their names have deliberately been held innocuous: *Tagesspiegel* (Berlin), *Frankfurter Rundschau, Marburger Presse, Süddeutsche Zeitung* (Munich). These German papers received their physical equipment from the production officers of the information control units. While in the beginning of Allied occupation a London news file of the Psychological Warfare Division was made available to the first licensed papers by radio transmission, the licensed press during 1945 and 1946 relied for the coverage of world and German news, and for special feature and picture services as well, on DANA (*Deutsche Allgemeine Nachrichten-Agentur*), a monopolistic news service originated by the Psychological Warfare Division and now in German hands. DANA's operations, like the operations of all licensees in the information services, are predicated upon a number of general "negative directives": the licensees may not propagate National Socialism, racism, and race hatred; they may not propagate militaristic ideas, Pan-Germanism, and German imperialism; they may not attempt to create divisions between the United Nations or foster disrespect for any of the Allies; they may not criticize military government officials and military government acts. In fact, they are not to interfere in any way with military government operations. Although there is an exchange of newspapers of the various zones of occupation, non-German papers have so far been excluded from the German market. A German editor in the American zone therefore does not receive *The New York Times* or any other newspaper published in the United States or in Great Britain or in any other country outside Germany.

At first it was planned that all German papers in the American zone would be subjected to a preproduction scrutiny. This plan was never put into practice; instead, a postproduction scrutiny has been conducted by special scrutiny officers in the divisional headquarters. They have reported violations of the "negative directives" to the information control units, which in turn enforce respect for these directives by reprimanding the licensees or, in severe cases, by revoking the licenses.[4]

The general level and journalistic style of the licensed papers vary in accordance with the caliber of the licensees and their editorial staff. The papers were urged to be nonpartisan and unbiased. The platforms and proclamations of licensed political parties must be given equal and fair treatment. To ensure impartiality, editorial talents and licensees are drawn from all or most of the political parties active in the community.[5]

Book Publishing

Up to the end of January, 1946, 130 books and pamphlets and 35 periodicals had been published in the American zone. Upon applying for a license, publishers must submit a program of the works they intend to print. The publisher having received his license, the main restriction imposed upon him is that he must not publish any material violating the "negative directives." Because of the paper shortage, originally only 5,000 copies of any book could be printed unless the publisher could demonstrate that the book in question was of very exceptional interest. These restrictions are gradually being relaxed. The first licensed publishing house in Bavaria published in December, 1945, the following books: *Dies Irae* (poems) by Werner Bergen-

[4]Such a case occurred in Bavaria in the summer of 1946 when the *Münchener Zeitung* was punished by military government authorities for printing a story stating that the editor had received many letters complaining of the condition of evacuees arriving from the Sudeten district in Czechoslovakia. Since this was held to be a violation of the military government regulation forbidding German papers to criticize any of the Allies, the paper was reduced from eight pages to four for a month.

[5]Sharp criticism, however, was leveled by both Americans and Germans at the fact that only *one* newspaper is available in each locality and that these papers therefore enjoy a monopolistic position not justified by their quality. This situation is slowly being remedied, as the newsprint situation permits re-allotments.

gruen, *Die Jerominkinder* (a novel) by Ernst Wiechert, and also by the same author, *Rede an die deutsche Jugend 1945; Die Rumpelhanni* (a novel) by Lena Christ; *Oil for the Lamps of China* (in German translation) by Alice Tisdale Hobart; *The Good Earth* (in German translation) by Pearl S. Buck; and a pictorial calendar.

Of the two illustrated periodicals published in the American zone, one called *Heute* is an American army publication in German. Its aim, like the aim of the *Neue Zeitung,* is to explain the United States to the German reader. A number of American book titles selected by the Office of War Information and the Psychological Warfare Division are available in American libraries, established in the larger cities of the American zone.[6]

The Radio Control Section of ICD has been operating stations in Frankfort, Stuttgart, and Munich. The editorial and technical personnel of these three stations consists of Americans and carefully screened Germans. Programs for German audiences are arranged and executed by Germans under the supervision of the control section. In addition, the "Voice of America," orginating in New York and broadcast in German, is relayed. The following program of Radio Stuttgart of February 20, 1946, can be called typical for the winter of 1945–1946.

10:00	*Schulfunk* (School of the Air)
10:30	*Nachrichten* (News)
10:45	*Musik*
11:00	*Suchdienst* (Search for Missing Relatives and Friends)
11:30	*Musik*
11:50	*Haus und Heim* (House and Home)
12:00	*Nachrichten* (News)
12:15	*Musik*
13:15	*Stimme Amerikas* (Voice of America)
14.00	*Schulfunk* (School of the Air)
18:00	*Nachrichten* (News)
19.00	*Aktuelle Stunde* (Special News Hour)
19:30	*Fragen, die allen angehen* (Everybody's Problems)

[6]An increasing number of American best sellers, both fiction and nonfiction, are now being printed and distributed by ICD, and are greatly appreciated by Germans of all stations. It was gratifying to find the table of a famous scholar at Heidelberg laden with these books, including Emery Reeves' plea for world government.

20:00 *Nachrichten* (News)
20:15 *Nürnberger Prozess* (Nuremberg Trial)
20:30 *Schlager Cocktail* (Hit Parade)
21:00 *Hörspiel* (Drama)
21:45 *Musik*
22:00 *Stimme Amerikas* (Voice of America)

Theater, Music, Films

By the end of January, 1946, ICD reported that 164 licenses in theater and music had been granted. Two American plays, "Thunder Rock" and "Our Town," have been produced in the American zone with great success. The concert, opera, and theater programs of the larger centers included symphony concerts of practically all classic composers, "Madame Butterfly," "Tosca," "A Midsummer Night's Dream," Molnar's "Spiel im Schloss," Sutton Vane's "Überfahrt," "Candida," and several Shakespearean plays.

By the end of January, 1946, 347 cinemas were in operation; of these, 130 were located in the area of 6870 DISCC, 168 were in the area of 6871 DISCC, and 49 were in the Berlin district. Exhibitions in the cinemas were then exclusively American productions, chosen from a list of 49 features made available by the American motion-picture industry to ICD.

Shown with all features is always the joint British-American newsreel, "Die Welt im Film." The features were "I Married a Witch," "Young Edison," "Abe Lincoln," "It Happened Tomorrow," "You Were Never More Beautiful," and the like. All cinemas in the American zone had to show for at least one consecutive week "The Mills of Death," produced jointly by OWI, ICD, and the British Political Intelligence Division, depicting the atrocities committed by the Nazis in the concentration camps.

Conclusion—An Evaluation

The Nazis had constructed the most elaborate network the world outside of Soviet Russia has ever seen for influencing the mind of a people. They had changed the entire basis of the informational services. Instead of being media of free intellectual expression, these services had become powerful instruments for the propaganda of a totalitarian regime.

Guided by the principle that every propaganda campaign should be aimed at specific targets, and that the human target should be made an active participant in, rather than a mere passive recipient of, propaganda, the activities of the Reich Ministry for Enlightenment and Propaganda, the Reich Chamber of Culture, and similar agencies had embraced virtually every aspect of the life of the German nation from the instruction of the public at home and abroad to the arrangement of fairs and exhibitions and the control of the tourist traffic.

Aware of the tight controls of the information services under the Nazi system, American policy makers should have formulated a program tending toward the loosening of these controls and the liberalization of the creative spirit. Instead, ICD, with its subdivisions, neatly replaced the Reich Chamber of Culture, with its seven chambers of press, literature, radio, film, theater, music, and art. For four crucial months following the collapse of the Nazi regime anti-Nazi Germans longed in vain for the message of democracy and their own chance to re-create it in Germany while their creative democratic elements were busy answering questionnaires and complying with a plethora of other formalities. American army broadcasts and American army newspapers, indifferent toward the psychic needs of the German masses, coupled poorly written, factual news reports with cheap sensationalism: for example, the story of Hitler's marriage to Eva Braun, and the ever-repeated question of whether Hitler was dead or alive. It must be emphasized that the Hitler legend was created by American journalists and broadcasters, not by the Germans, whose democratic elements were only too anxious to put an end to all Nazi mythology.

In the press field, DANA became the substitute of DNB (*Deutsche Nachrichten Bureau*), the latter an agency of the Propaganda Ministry that monopolized all news services and dictated the character of the news. Before 1933, news, editorials, features, and illustrations were supplied by literally hundreds of agencies in Germany, many of which asked for licenses, for they could have resumed their activities if the American directives had been more flexible.

It was decided to ban American newspapers and periodicals from the American zone in Germany. The reason offered was that Americans, a free people, would be undisturbed by many news items and editorial comments which would cause trouble in Germany. Many questioned the validity of this reason, believing that the disadvantages outweighed the advantages of such a restriction. Probably the frequent and often sharp criticisms of the Allies appearing in the American press made this decision advisable in the early period.

Apart from a few first-class productions, American films shown to the Germans thus far have been technically, as well as from the point of view of context, inferior to the standard films produced in Germany before 1933. Although Germans flocked to the motion-picture houses as to any place promising entertainment and a temporary escape from reality, the subdued criticism of the licensed press and the more articulate criticism of motion-picture audiences left no doubt as to the general disrespect for Hollywood's glamorous fairyland. By contrast, the Swiss production, "The Last Chance," made a deep and favorable impression on the few Germans who were allowed to see this simple and realistic film about the refugees from Hitlerism and Italian Fascism.

One of the fallacies in the reasoning of those who selected films, books, and magazines for dissemination in Germany was their emphasis on dull neutrality, their fear of controversial subjects. Because of this way of thinking, valuable time was lost during the period between the collapse of the Nazi propaganda machine and the final licensing of responsible Germans in the information fields.

The effect of the Nazi policy on the various information media was a continuous stream of propaganda and the resulting obedience to authority. The effect of ICD's failure to cut loose from this totalitarian policy was the substitution of American for Nazi authority and the widespread belief that "everything is now American propaganda." The idea of a purified atmosphere in which people may read and see only what the group in power wants them to read and see is a totalitarian and not a democratic concept.

Ideally, government, as we know it in the Western democracies, puts the highest value on the life, dignity, and happiness of every person equally. This concept, to be realized, requires a great deal of publicity regarding all public affairs, irrespective of whether this publicity stirs up controversy or not.

It would not be fair, however, to blame an executive branch of the army, like ICD, for mistakes inherent in the American general de-nazification policy and the unfortunate formula of "unconditional surrender." Indifferent to or unaware of the strength of anti-Nazism inside Germany, American policy makers imposed on the Germans a totalitarian regime, more benevolent, to be sure, than that of the Nazis but giving little consideration to the best in German tradition and to the legitimate wishes of those men and women who had not accepted totalitarian methods.

Measures that concentrated on the negative aspects of denazifica-tion, on the punishment of the leaders of the Nazi party, and on the removal of its members from office were insufficient support for the struggling prodemocratic elements in the German population. Fail-ure to recognize the fact that the Nazi movement, like all political and psychological mass phenomena, was the product of highly un-satisfactory social, economic, and psychological conditions meant fail-ure to recognize that the task of re-education called for aiding the Ger-mans to achieve a social order that would help the bulk of the popula-tion to resist totalitarian ideologies. Too little differentiation between Nazis and anti-Nazis had the effect of compromising anti-Nazis by identifying them with Allied-controlled operations. At the same time these anti-Nazis were denied a chance to exert their free and full influence on the community.

Americans spoke of the American way of life but failed to trans-late this into terms comprehensible to the Germans. The American failure to permit the Germans practice in democratic procedures is un-doubtedly responsible for the success that the Communists have had in the American zone. However, it should be noted that members of the Communist party, completely out of proportion to their numerical strength among the German population, have been appointed to key functions in the information media by control officers who either were prejudiced in favor of Communism or perhaps lacked maturity of judgment. Upon the advice of 6871 DISCC, three out of the seven licensees composing the editorial board of the *Frankfurter Rundschau* were chosen from the membership of the Communist party. For a time, this paper, with an edition of close to 500,000, was the largest licensed paper in the American zone. The Communist influence in this paper's editorial staff could easily be recognized by its frequent front-page appeal to Social Democrats and Communists to join the Communist-dominated United Socialist party functioning in the Soviet zone since 1946, the SED, or Sozialistische Einheitspartei Deutschlands. It was eventually so recognized by military government when they found it necessary to remove the Communist editor in chief, Herr Carlebach; they made it clear that "for two years Herr Carlebach has run his paper along strictly party lines."[7]

The Information Control Division, one of the leading American agencies entrusted with the re-election of the Germans in the American zone, has like other American agencies been handicapped by the instability and the vacillation of America's general policy. Like its predecessor, the Psychological Warfare Division, the Information Control Division, was composed of military and civilian personnel. The latter recruited from the Office of War Information and the Office of Strategic Services. Unfortunately the majority of the information control officers had little or no training for their functions, and very few had a fluent command of the German language, a basic requirement in information control services. Even smaller was the number of those who had some knowledge of German history, tradition, politics, and personalities. Considering these shortcomings in basic policy and personnel, it is remarkable how well the ICD has performed its major functions. With numerous papers and magazines established throughout the zone and Berlin, with book publishers bringing out an increasing number of significant fiction and non-fiction works, the most serious obstacle to the re-establishment of full freedom of the press remains the paper shortage. As long as this shortage continues, artificial controls will have to continue in effect.

[7] See *The New York Times,* September 6, 1947. Another instance of radical leftist influence was revealed recently, when the editor of the American-sponsored magazine *Heute* was not reappointed. See *ibid.,* September 17, 1947.

Part IV

*Military Government Organization and
Experience in the Pacific*

★　　　★　　　★　　　★　　　★

Chapter XIV

Experience in the Pacific Islands as Illustrated by Guam

EDWARD G. LEWIS

Introduction

N AVAL military government for Guam was planned concurrently with the military phases of the operation, and was intimately linked with them, particularly with regard to availability of supplies. The occupation of Guam, together with that of Tinian and Saipan, was the Navy's first large-scale military government experience of World War II. Although the small number of people involved in these earlier experiences was unrelated to the size and scope of later military government activities, the activities of the first military government teams in the Gilberts and the Marshalls were followed with avidity by the officers responsible for planning the Guam occupation. They realized that such an occupation was military, and that it must proceed in accordance with the wishes of the military commanders, men who might be guided by the advice of civil affairs officers, but who obviously would not be ruled by it; men who were understandably more concerned with the progress of the battle than with the vicissitudes of the civilian population. The good military government officer was one who could care for the needs of the island people and prevent them from being a problem to the men whose full time was taken with fighting the war.

At the beginning, a small team of officers was to plan for the military government of Guam. These men were attached to the staff of

the prospective island commander with rank equivalent to that of t[
standard staff branches. As the size of the problem became manife[
more officers were added to the military government staff, divid[
into assault and later echelons. The structure of the government d[
signed by these officers envisioned several standard departments. T[
headquarters was commanded by a marine colonel, the deputy chi[
civil affairs officer, who was responsible through the chain of com[
mand to the Commander in Chief Pacific Ocean Areas, who in tu[
was the military governor. The headquarters supervised the prepar[
tion of plans for a governmental structure, based in large part on t[
previous government of the island. Officers appointed to head t[
projected departments elaborated their own responsibilities, the[
man power needs, and their supply requirements. These individu[
departmental plans were discussed with other officers concerned, an[
a more or less integrated plan for the future government of the islan[
was developed.

Information on the previous governmental structure was obtaine[
primarily from the reports of the prewar Navy government of Guar[
supplemented by comments on the actual functioning of that go[
ernment as described in the *Guam Recorder*. Lists of names of in[
portant Guamanians were compiled, and included information abo[
people who could be useful after the occupation began.

The crucial part of the advance planning concerned supplies. T[
functioning of every prospective department depended upon certa[
materials: not only office supplies but food, shelter, clothes, and oth[
necessities of life. It was realized that total destruction might exi[
on the island and that every essential item of civilian life might b[
needed. Appropriate military channels for the procuring of such su[
plies must be opened. Shortages in critical items, which developed i[
the early stages of the occupation, could be accounted for in near[
every instance by the naturally low priority of civil affairs supplie[
Materials for the battle itself, of course, took precedence over thos[
planned for civilian rehabilitation.

Another phase of advance planning was that dealing with the a[
sault units for such civil affairs work as became necessary durin[
the assault on the island. Official orders and proclamations were pr[

red, setting forth the fact of occupation, defining war crimes, and
aling with the requisitioning of civilian property, the operation of
labor pool, and a notice to the people, who were to be placed in a
otective compound during the actual hostilities. It was planned that
e compound for the protection of civilians should be the responsibil-
y of the military units; however, in actual operations, this responsi-
lity devolved upon the civil affairs units, an arrangement that pre-
rved continuity of policy with the later island command phase.

Originally, the civil affairs function was thought to be on the staff
ther than on the operating level, but as the invasion grew nearer, it
as found that civil affairs, of necessity, should be an operating
ency because of the specialized nature of the work. Enlisted men
en selected to take an active part in the organization were given a
ort course of lectures on the particular problems of military govern-
ent. Had there been time, a more adequate preparation for this
oup would have been desirable; however, their value cannot be
verestimated.

The Situation during the Assault Phase

On one of the landing beaches, civil affairs officers and men went
hore on the first day of the assault; on another, they landed on
e third day. On both beaches, the situation was the same. Until
vilians began to appear, military government units, except for the
osting of proclamations of occupation, did very little except keep
emselves alive. Within a few days, however, civilians began to come
ithin the lines, and three protective compounds were soon estab-
shed. Two of the small camp areas were replaced speedily with
rger sites as the size of the problem became manifest. At Agat, for
xample, about a dozen men, outfitted in navy dungarees, constituted
e first camp. To preserve their area it was marked with a single
rand of discarded telephone wire. The men were sheltered, fed, and
othed by the military units. Soon afterward a larger camp was hur-
edly selected, and within a week it held 800 civilians. The supply
eeds were partially alleviated by the discovery of large hoards of
panese food, which were turned over to military government. This

captured food helped greatly until American supplies arrived in su[fficient] quantities.

The compounds protected the people from any more contact wi[th] actual hostilities than was absolutely necessary, segregated the loy[al] from the few disloyal, made the feeding, sheltering, and caring f[or] the refugees more convenient, and established a labor pool so that [as] many service men as possible could be kept on the fighting line.

The camps were similarly run. The officers and enlisted men co[n]stituting the guiding agency were assisted in the actual work by th[e] people, who were placed on a pay roll, to be met later when cash f[or] that purpose should become available. One camp, for example, w[as] divided into areas, each presided over by an enlisted man and a[n] appointed civilian leader. Mass feeding was necessary at first becau[se] of the lack of cooking utensils. As opened cans became more nume[r]ous more enterprising civilians preferred to do their own cookin[g] thereby taking some of the burden from the hard-pressed communi[ty] kitchens managed by a handful of service cooks and worked by e[x]perienced civilians. Guamanian stewards' mates and cooks who ha[d] previously seen naval service were of great help. After some expe[ri]mentation, a system of three meals a day for laboring men and two f[or] the rest was worked out. The diet consisted largely of various sorts [of] rice dishes, supplemented with such canned meats, vegetables, an[d] fruits as were discovered in any quantity in Japanese caches.

Dispensaries were established in each of the camps. Navy docto[rs] and corpsmen performed heroic works under the most difficult an[d] primitive of conditions. Malnutrition was so general that resistanc[e] was low, and large numbers of people were found to have yaws an[d] tropical ulcers. The sanitary inspections carried out daily by the corp[s]men in each of the areas revealed that health habits strongly estab[]lished during the previous American regime had broken down durin[g] the Japanese occupation and that the sanitary inspectors had to b[e] vigilant in their work. The galley and water supplies were frequentl[y] inspected by the medical branch, in order to guard against the dang[er] of epidemics. Sick call daily produced long lines of patients. The ligh[t] of a kerosene pressure lamp served at the delivery of many a bab[y] and often shone at night burials.

The spiritual life of the people was helped by Catholic chaplains, who came to the camps when time permitted to say masses, to baptize babies, and to bury the dead. Sacristans of former times saw to the building of rudimentary altars and the preservation of the holy objects.

A small squad of marines, together with the former local policemen, acted as guards for the camps. At one camp Japanese snipers were active as part of several efforts made by the Japanese to get at the food stocks of the camp. In the camps could be found guides for marine and army patrols in the backwoods areas and for military government and supply officers in search of hidden stores of food.

Shelter differed markedly at the different camps, depending upon available supplies of building scraps. At one camp, shelter halves, tarpaulins, and tents were supplemented by such little tin as could be found. At another, near the ruined city of Agana, where galvanized iron roofs and structures had been plentiful, the people constructed long community houses. At a third, the prevailing house style was that built out of indigenous materials (woven coconut palm fronds and the like), as directed by the Japanese when the area had been set up as a concentration camp just before the American reoccupation began. Nevertheless, the morale at each of the camps was uniformly excellent in spite of hardship. It was touching indeed to hear the people singing, when first gathered into American lines, a ballad composed during the Japanese times, "Uncle Sam Please Come Back to Guam." Equally moving was their singing of "America" as the Stars and Stripes rose over the different camps.

In spite of the assistance of military units in providing partially or fully for civilians in their employ, the officers and men in the military government headquarters found the supply problem a difficult one. Salvaged Japanese food was collected in a centralized depot, conveniently located in a bombed-out, reinforced concrete mansion which the Japanese themselves had used partly for food storage. On a day-to-day, hand-to-mouth basis, food was collected. For emergency feeding, military storage depots had made excess C and D rations available in limited quantities. As more and more Japanese rice was found, the supply depot became a mound of rice in various stages

of freshness. Supply officers salvaged Japanese supplies wherever the
could be found, using the captured Japanese trucks made available
the civil affairs officers. In addition to the salvage operation, t
supply personnel at the central supply dump distributed other e
sentials to the various camps. Because of the bad weather and t
heavy military traffic, the road at one camp soon broke down so com
pletely that supplies were sent for the last mile to the camp by carab
cart. At another camp, off the main road, the supplies were regular
brought in by the same method. It was to the great credit of the supp
department that, although the supplies had mostly to be gathered
the hat-in-hand begging system from the military units, at no tim
did the people go hungry.

The Function of Military Government after the Assault Phase

During the assault phase, most of the military government office
were attached to the various camps, but after the island comman
phase opened, personnel was transferred from the camps to head
quarters to assume the planned military government functions. B
the early part of September, slightly more than a month after the a
sault, the various branches of the full-fledged military governmen
were in operating condition.

As was originally intended, the function of the headquarters b
came that of directing and coordinating the growing activities of t
different departments. Headquarters remained the channel to high
authority, preparing the never-ending reports required by high
echelons, and disseminating policy decisions made at a higher level
well as those made internally.

Although not originally provided for, a Native Welfare Depar
ment was established within a few months and was later known
the Welfare and Education Department. Its welfare function was di
ferent from that usually connected with the term in military parlanc
Instead of morale building through recreational activities, the depar
ment acted as the channel for the enforcement of decisions affectin
the people. The enforcement was accomplished through civilian con

issioners in each of the communities, men of local prominence who
were appointed by the military government and also had the dual
function of making the wishes of the military government known
to the people and the people's desires known to the government. During the first part of their monthly meeting, held in the capital, the
commissioners attended the regular staff meeting of the military government officers, who presented current problems and advised on the
method of solution. During the second part of their meeting the commissioners met with the head of the Welfare Department and presented problems of less general interest. Individual department heads
sometimes instructed commissioners on forthcoming orders and
asked their advice on particular problems. It was at this point that
such democracy as could exist in the military government expressed
itself. Most certainly there was not full self-government, nor could
there be in wartime, but the people of Guam had an institution
through which to express their wishes; and, even though they were
usually reticent about mentioning their problems, the commissioners'
meetings provided one of the sources of legislation.

Another function of the Welfare Department was the relocation of
civilians, made necessary by the land requirements of military installations. These military requirements forced a change in the people's way of life, since most of the desirable flat land was requisitioned.
For those civilians who cared to take the opportunity, transportation
was provided to ready-built houses in villages constructed by the
engineering department of the military government. The eviction
procedure became standardized with the passage of time. In the event
that the family did not want to go to the village provided, as was
frequently the case, transportation elsewhere was made available
when possible. No labor was furnished for the reconstruction of the
shelters of people who preferred not to live in one of the new villages.
The objections to the new villages became gradually evident. The
homes were closer together than the prewar small farmhouses had
been. The largest new village was established near the site of one of
the old villages that had had an unsavory reputation, and this reputation unfortunately was transferred to the new area. Necessary sani-

tary regulations in the new villages tended to become onerous. On the other hand, many conveniences were available in the new village so that in time they came to be more desired.

As the island came more and more to resemble one large militar camp, the places left for civilians became fewer and fewer. A militar area assignment board allotted some specific areas for independer civilian colonization. The problem became one of requiring, as nearl as possible, that the civilians who did not move into the new villages e tablished their new homes in set areas. Because the military goverr ment controlled the transporting of civilians, it was not difficult to se that construction materials were taken only to suitable places. Occa sionally, civilians who had received removal notices would mov themselves and their goods without any supervision from military go ernment, but since such unauthorized moves were generally to lan reserved for military establishments, they were usually impermanen Nevertheless, in the hundreds of relocations made necessary, only tw or three families objected to the necessity of moving. It is to the lastin; credit of the civilians that they regarded the misery of moving as price to be paid for advancing the cause of the war.

Because of its participation in this relocation work, the Welfar Department became the agency for controlling the new villages a they were built. The regular commissioners or their assistants, in act ing for the Welfare Department, assumed a role not unlike that o the mayor of an average small town.

If the compounds were to be closed by returning the people to thei own houses, food must be available in sufficient quantity in the town to lure the people from the available food supplies of the camps. Re lief supplies were distributed to the different communities as the began to be occupied by their inhabitants. A diet of essential food re quirements was worked out, based upon a scientifically planned die and modified by the actual food supply available. Because of the con ditions on the island, armed guards were sent with each relief truck and frequent deliveries made it unnecessary to store large quantitie of food in the communities. Native commissioners were responsibl for local distribution of the supplies and for all food delivered them For a short period outlying communities relied heavily on the ra

ion delivery trucks as a means of communication: the trucks carried
ivilian patients to the central hospital and brought mail to and from
he military personnel of civil affairs in the field, notices and orders
rom headquarters, supplies from the agriculture department to
he farmer, oil drums for sanitary purposes, and anything else which
equired transportation from one place to another.

In its early stages the program should be described as one of ra-
ioning rather than relief, for no money was available, no stores were
pen, and individual farms were the only unofficial sources of food.
The issuance of subsistence rations was abruptly stopped during
October on the date fixed for the opening of trade stores. Thereafter
t was resumed on a much smaller scale and for relief purposes only.
The number of people on relief was reduced very rapidly as more employment opportunities were opened on the island and as people re-
urned, where possible, to their normal peacetime occupations.

In the original planning, arrangements were not made for the immediate supply of clothing to the population. There was, however, a
considerable clothing shortage on the island, because the Japanese
had not lately imported clothing materials in any quantity. Through
he generosity of the American Red Cross nearly one hundred thousand articles of clothing were prepared for shipment to Guam via
naval channels. Upon the arrival of the first shipment of clothes, a
voluntary unofficial Red Cross committee of Guamanians was formed
for the sorting and initial distribution to the commissioners. The
latter were not uniformly happy at the prospect of having to distribute desperately needed clothes, far too few in number, to the people in their communities. They had no particular problem in the
distribution of food rations—there was enough for an equal sharing.
However, in the matter of clothes, the situation was quite different.
The majority of the people were frantic to receive what shoes were
available, since the cure for the widely prevalent hookworm included
wearing shoes in order to eliminate the usual means of infection,
through the bare feet. As long as shoes were rationed in the United
States, the purchase of suitable small-sized civilian shoes in sufficient
quantities remained difficult.

The general clothing situation eased after subsequent shipments from the Red Cross and other benevolent organizations, and as limited amounts of clothing materials became available in civilian stores. When the United States post office opened parcel-post channels to the people, mail-order houses in the United States had many a Guamanian as a customer.

Coincident with the opening of the trade stores, the Relief and Education Department was amalgamated with the native Welfare Department. For a short period the Education Department had a separate existence, but it too came to be included under the welfare function as a part of the Welfare and Education Department.

The Resumption of Education

As the relief function of the Relief and Education Department diminished, the organization's emphasis shifted to the educational needs of the people. A preliminary meeting of the available former teachers was held in early September to explain the scope of the educational program and the emergency conditions under which the schools would have to be opened. Five schools were opened in early October in the building least damaged during the assault on the island. A small number of textbooks saved from the Japanese, often at considerable personal risk, were for a time the only texts available, but they were supplemented as far as possible with mimeographed materials. Paper, chalk, and pencils were furnished in quantity to each school as it opened.

The former civilian Superintendent of Schools became a member of the education office, as did also the former chief clerk of the department. Through the action of the superintendent and his assistants, the former teachers living in each community were located and assembled under the leadership of a principal. Each principal exercised his own ingenuity in outfitting the school beyond the essentials of paper, pencil, chalk, and teachers. In one instance each child brought his own packing box as a seat. In another, the building was floored by the students, each of whom brought one board. Gay flowers filled formerly deserted buildings and the schools assumed the lively air of a reviving community. They suggested a return of some sort of normal life after the immediate horrors of warfare passed.

In areas which had seen much hard fighting and heavy bombardment, the opening of schools involved the building, at first, of temporary structures, crudely constructed out of coconut palm logs and covered with tarpaulins or roofed with woven coconut fronds. The normal warmth of the climate made such structures possible as makeshift schoolhouses. In some of the smaller communities the people were told that if they would build suitable school buildings, the Department of Welfare and Education would staff and supply the school. Several schools were thus opened earlier than would otherwise have been the case. In the newly constructed villages, schools were included as a part of the community plan. In fact, school buildings and dispensaries, as well as public safety patrolmen's quarters, were constructed at the same time as the houses. Gradually, as the temporary buildings began to disintegrate, more permanent schools were built as the military logistic picture improved.

As the schools quickly approached their prewar status recreational programs were developed. Equipment was ordered, and many military units adopted different schools to supervise their sports and other activities. Curriculums in step with equivalent school programs in the United States were developed under the auspices of the department. A working library was assembled for teachers and students. In institutes held during the summer months teachers were informed about world events since the Japanese occupation of the island.

One of the important functions of the high school in Guam was the training of future teachers. In the midst of war shipping-shortages it was not possible to contemplate sending potential teachers to any of the teacher-training institutions of collegiate level in the United States. Under an interim plan possible future teachers were instructed in elementary teaching techniques in their last year in high school. Their training also included supervised teaching in the different schools of the island under the guidance of the local teachers and the supervising principal.

Within a few months after the opening of schools vocational education was provided on both the high school and the grammar school levels. Local handicraft techniques were taught, particularly in those

areas noted for their handicraft excellence. School gardens, in som
instances, were productive as well as instructive. In the high schoc
the vocational students at first were apprenticed for a half day at
small wage to the various skilled craftsmen in the military goverm
ment shops, with a rudimentary supervision by the education o
ficer. Later a vocational course was developed whereby the student
were to work at their vocational training five days a week and go t
school on the sixth day.

In contrast to the practice under the former naval governmen
of peacetime Guam, the educational office was headed by officers wh
had had considerable civilian professional experience with education
rather than by members of the Chaplain Corps of the Navy.

The welfare work of the department included the encouragemen
of athletic and recreational activities. One of the most important o
the recreational activities was the re-establishment of the boy scou
and girl scout movements on the island as part of a program to de
velop a true community spirit in contrast to a strongly exclusive fam
ily community. Under the expert, voluntary leadership of member
of the armed forces who had been active in scout work, scout troop
were formed throughout the island. Community interests were als
fostered by the revival of the parent-teacher associations of the variou
schools on the island.

The Welfare and Education Department acted as intermediary be
tween the various other departments of military government and th
people. When difficulties or controversies not of a legal or crimina
nature arose, it was to the Welfare Department that the civilian came
The department was also a liaison between the civilians and othe
military units, although it must be admitted that it was not possibl
for any one department of military government, or for military gov
ernment as a whole, to control completely the myriads of contact
between civilians and the military.

The Legal Functions of Military Government

From the earliest planning phase, provision was made for the crea
tion of a Legal Department. Its first important work was the drafting

f proclamations to be posted on the island to acquaint the population
gally with the existence of the fact of military government. The
otices were to be posted when a substantial number of civilians came
ithin the American lines or when towns were retaken by the troops.
he first proclamation stated the circumstances of the occupation
nd declared that all powers of government rested with the
Commander in Chief Pacific Fleet and Pacific Ocean Areas
(CINCPAC&POA) as military governor of Guam. Japanese pow-
rs, laws, and regulations were rescinded. The people were told that
heir customs, religious beliefs, and property rights would be re-
pected, subject to the exigencies of military security; and that, subject
o war conditions, people would be permitted and expected to resume
heir normal occupations. The ordinance power was declared to exist
vith the military governor, and the people were enjoined to observe
he proclamations, orders, and regulations so issued. All administra-
ive, police, and judicial officials and employes of Japanese nationality
r sympathy were removed from office. All others, saving those removed by the military governor, were required to continue their ac-
ivities subject to those deputed to act for the military governor, and
he operation of local courts was temporarily suspended. Aside from
he minor judicial powers held by the commissioners just prior to the
apanese occupation, the laws previously in force were restored, except
s modified by later orders which were legally enforced. Only au-
horized political activity would be permitted.

The second proclamation was, in effect, an ordinance defining
a number of war crimes, and followed loosely the pattern set forth
n the War Department *Military Government Manual,* FN27–5.

As the legatee of the former naval government's Attorney General's
Department and Justice Department, the Legal Department concerned itself with the drafting of such orders and proclamations as
from time to time became necessary. Also, it successfully recovered
copies of the pre-occupation Civil Code, Penal Code, Code of Civil
Procedure, and Probate Code and civil regulations having the effect
of law. Gradually it employed civilians who formerly had been connected with the two appropriate pre-occupation departments. These
employees served as living repositories of such local customs as had

provided the background for the various codes. In the assault stages with the courts closed, summary justice for minor offenses was dispensed at the protective compounds by the camp commanders, who were assisted by Chamorro enlisted men in the United States Navy

In addition to the legislative drafting service performed by the Legal Department—if the term "legislative" may be applied to the ordinances and proclamations issued in the name of the island commander by the military government—the department was the focal point for the various courts established as the need for them became evident. At the island command level there was created the Exceptional Military Tribunal, whose function was the trial of those accused of treason or exceptional collaboration with the enemy. The many meetings of this body were reminiscent of the war crimes trials being held elsewhere in the world. Officers were detailed to act as judges, as prosecutors, and as defenders. The old island court system, staffed entirely with Guamanians and with parallel jurisdiction, was gradually restored.

The number of cases arising in the criminal courts was extremely small. Far more numerous were minor infractions of various military government orders, resulting from the necessary stringency of wartime regulations in conflict with some of the normal peacetime behavior patterns.

A further function of the Legal Department was the custodianship of enemy property. The property custodian was the deputy chief government officer. His assistant in the Legal Department was empowered to immobilize or operate property needed for military use, to maintain complete records, and to return private property to legal owners when ownership was established and it was no longer required for military purposes.

Problems of the Island Economy

The problem of devising a suitable control for the economic life of the island was one which required a certain amount of trial and error. It was thought at first that the most suitable device would be an Economics and Labor Department, which would combine the functions of the former Executive and Agriculture Departments. Whereas there had been no need for rigorous economic controls in peacetime, the situation was radically altered by war.

The Economics and Labor Department was set up shortly after the assault phase because of the demands from various military units for local civilian labor. In each of the refugee camps it had been necessary to create a labor section to centralize the handling of labor requisitions. These labor sections were subordinated as soon as possible to the Economics and Labor Department so that the labor resources of the island could be put under a coordinated control.

The labor sections in refugee camps, following directives, conducted a survey of the available labor in the camp. Persons available for assignment were registered and were gathered together in groups, generally of twenty-five, under the management of a foreman, who was in turn responsible to an enlisted man sent out with each labor team. For the assault phase, workers were taken out each morning from the various protective compounds. Their noon meals were provided by the unit employing them, and they were brought back to the compounds in the evening.

For a period of time, a certain amount of labor was hired directly by the military units without clearing with the military government. Under this method of hiring, one unit frequently competed with another by offering higher wages, or higher classifications of skill, or better rations. The labor situation on the island thus tended to become highly fluid. To remedy this situation, it was ordered that all civilian labor be cleared through the appropriate military government department.

Partly to economize on the use of transportation equipment, and partly to save time, a few of the largest employers of civilian labor were encouraged to set up housing and rationing centers for their laborers and families. An effect of the establishment of these areas, which gave promise of developing into villages, was to reduce markedly the number of civilians in the refugee camps.

As the work of the Labor and Economics Department increased in complexity and volume, it became necessary to establish a separate Labor Department. This new department, operating by October,

1944, maintained a register of all available civilian labor, including such female labor as volunteered for work. As military construction on the island increased, the need for civilian labor became critical. So difficult was the task of allotting labor priorities that a Priority Board was established. The major military units were represented on this board in order to coordinate the labor requirements with the general problem of island development. Once the priority had been assigned, it was the task of the Labor Department to find the necessary labor until the civilian labor pool was completely exhausted. Several traveling labor recruiting parties were sent by the department throughout the island to make certain that all available labor was registered and at work. It was further found necessary to define exactly the duties of farmers so that only full-time farmers would be left on the farms. The peacetime farmer did not always put the majority of his time on his farm. In fact, many an agriculturist cultivated just enough for his own immediate needs. With labor urgently needed in order to build a mighty base, it became necessary to alter this pattern of life to obtain the maximum number of laborers.

The Labor Department was also responsible for the establishment of a committee regulating wages and hours and standards of pay. The earlier classification of laborers into skilled and unskilled, and into the various artisan classes, had been adequate for the assault and early phases of government, but as the economic structure of the island increased in complexity, and as the civilian economy became a money economy, it became necessary to coordinate the different wage levels with the different types of work. Such problems as fixing professional salaries at such a scale that professional and administrative workers could afford to remain at their posts rather than turn to manual labor in order to increase their standard of living were considered. The prewar naval government's pay-scale distinction between federal civil service positions and naval government employees was abandoned so that all of the Guamanian employees of the military government, as well as those working for different military units, were placed on a uniform pay scale. Elaborate rules became necessary with regard to promotion within the pay scale in order to prevent labor pirating between units. The employment office function of the Labor

Department became that of keeping a record of each individual laborer rather than that of finding work for the unemployed. Every man and woman who desired work was working.

The Commerce and Industry Department, like the Labor Department, was at first a part of the Economics and Labor Department. This section began its work with a study of the possibility of reviving normal commercial life on the island. It evolved, in consultation with the Supply Department, a modified commercial distribution system which operated through civilian wholesalers, carefully selected by the military government on the basis of their experience in the field. At first two private wholesale companies were established, empowered to purchase on credit supplies from the government for later sale to retail outlets. Retail outlets were established in each community. Because of the inevitable shortage of supplies, it was not desirable to permit more than a limited number of retailers on the island as a whole. Accordingly, it became the difficult task of the commerce and industry section to decide which of the many applicants for retail stores should be allowed to operate. The basis for the selection was generally the prewar experience of the applicant in so far as his occupation record was free from known collaboration. The retailer was issued commodities on the basis of the number of people whom his store served. In October, with the splitting of the Economics and Labor Department, the Economics Department took charge of the merchandising problem. Within three months of the assault, commercial activities were restored on a rudimentary basis. The department kept a close watch on the financial position of the private dealers, and as their position became stronger, more and more of the normal charges of business were assessed to them, thereby taking the load off the military government.

One of the functions of the Economics Department was ordering, through military government supply channels, the stock requested by the private merchandisers. Had commercial shipping been available during the war years in the Pacific, such controls would not have been necessary. As it was, with all shipping under military control, no other channels for the purchase of material were available.

From the beginning, the shortage of supply and the ready availability of purchasing power made it necessary for the department to establish price levels on all commodities. Likewise, the prices of civilian services, such as laundry and tailoring, were fixed. Critical items were placed on a ration list, the amounts in no case exceeding similarly rationed articles in the United States. Infractions of the ceiling price or rationing regulations were subject to court action.

At a later date the department made efforts to stimulate the soap and tile industries on the island. It was also the function of the Economics Department to stimulate the re-establishment of private markets for agricultural producers. Again with no vehicles privately owned, the transportation was furnished by the military government. Many of the citizens of the capital city could obtain fresh fruits and vegetables only through these markets, whose surplus products were sold to military units. A civilian representative of the Economics Department acted as the manager of the market.

A particularly thorny problem of the Economics Department was the control of the sale of handicraft products. The market for these items was mainly the military units, for servicemen were anxious to purchase these products as souvenirs. Stringent regulations were enforced against the purchase of any items by military personnel from the trade stores. With respect to the handicraft materials, the problem was to regulate the distribution of the limited production as fairly as possible. From the first, an elaborate black market flourished although serious efforts were made to control it. It was finally arranged that the scarce shell purses and woven products be purchased from the Economics Department by the retail stores of the various military units. What happened to the products after their transfer from the military government was not its responsibility.

The original Economics and Labor Department included an agriculture section which, in October, 1944, became the Agriculture and Fisheries Department and still later—in the third major revision of military government in April, 1945—became a part of the Commerce and Industry Department. It was not until the assault phase had passed that the work of this section could begin in earnest. Its over-all objective was to raise the agricultural production of the island to a level of food self-sufficiency. Considering that the staple starch of the people was rice, and that the island had not in its past history been a large rice-producing area, the basic objective was extremely difficult to accomplish. Moreover, two major military necessities on the island prevented the increase of agricultural acreage for civilian use: the enormous military expansion, which required ever more land; and the Foreign Economic Administration, which, in extending its activities to Guam, established large-scale farms whose products were available to the military units but not to civilians. Thus the total arable land available for civilian use was considerably reduced. It was not possible, in these circumstances, to consider a program of basic food self-sufficiency for the civilians, whose economy, as has already been mentioned, increasingly became a money economy based upon their working for a military unit or the military government and upon their purchasing necessities from trade stores stocked by the military supply services.

Within this limited framework, the agriculture section endeavored to encourage agricultural activities. Not long after establishment, the agriculture section hired agricultural experiment agents whose functions included the management of small modern farms, the testing of the most efficient methods of work and of new plants and seeds, and the encouragement of efficient animal husbandry. The difficulties ecountered by the agents on Guam were not unlike those found by similar agents elsewhere. Many a farmer was loath to adapt himself to new methods. What had worked best for his father was likely to work best for him. Why should a man use a tractor to help plow the land when he had a carabao which could pull the plow for him? Gradually, however, as more tractors were put into use on the Guam farms, the agents arranged that maximum use be made of those available.

Encouraging the farmer was difficult in the face of the setbacks to which the enterprising planter was subjected through no fault of his own. Shortly after people began moving out of the refugee camps and back to their small farms, the farmers began planting their crops with seeds they had saved from previous crops or had obtained from military government's agriculture section. Too often, however, no sooner had the seeds begun to germinate than the land was requisitioned by the military units for air fields, rest camps, training grounds, storage areas, or other uses. In very few sections of the island could the farmer pursue his normal occupation without fear of future interference.

Another function of the agriculture section was the encouragement of fishing on a commercial scale. The objective was, again, increasing the local food supply so as to reduce the importation of food. Within a few months after the assault, fishing was in operation on a scale nearly equivalent to that of prewar days. While it can be said that the fisheries unit of the agriculture section increased fishing activities, it was unable to stimulate mass commercial fishing because the customs and experience of the people ran in the direction of small-scale subsistence fishing.

With a view to the improvement of the local breeds of livestock plans were advanced for the importation of breeding animals, and a number of goats were shipped to the island. Under military government guidance, veterinary work was undertaken. The inspection of freshly slaughtered animals was required, but so depleted was the stock as a result of the Japanese occupation and the hostilities attendant on the reoccupation that it was necessary to prohibit the slaughter of cattle for food unless the animals were too old to be useful for breeding purposes. The enforcement of the nonslaughter rule was particularly difficult because of the lack of other fresh meat for the civilians.

The Functions of Finance and Supply

The Finance Department, shortly to become known as the Supply Department, was constructed out of the former customs and immigration, records and accounts, bank and supply sections. Reference has already been made to the enormous work of finding supplies for military government during the earlier phases of operation. That work continued. In so far as to the demands made on the department corresponded to those of a normal naval supply office, naval procedure was followed. For the rest, the former naval government structure was restored. The Supply Department carried on banking functions to a limited degree prior to the re-establishment of the Bank of Guam. In this connection, the process of redeeming Japanese yen was a difficult and complicated one. The department collected the yen and gave receipts for it. The amount to be paid back in United States currency was to be determined later by the United States Treasury Department.

Other Functions of Military Government

The Public Health Department carried on the functions of the former Department of Health. Its head was a United States Navy medical officer, who was assisted by other medical officers and by corpsmen. Guamanians who had been connected with the prewar department were rehired whenever possible. In the camp phase, the seemingly endless work of the department centered in the camp dispensaries. After the assault phase, the old naval hospital was reconditioned for use as a civilian hospital.

The public health work was widespread. Dispensaries were established in each of the villages under the direction of navy corpsmen assisted by Guamanians. The more serious cases were sent to the civilian hospital. The standards previously enforced by the naval government had fallen during the Japanese occupation, and the dislocations caused by hostilities had destroyed most of the sanitary facilities, with the result that much work had to be done. A campaign for improved public health was pushed throughout the school system, and vaccination and innoculation programs were carried out all over the island. The Public Health Department also established a school for the training of local civilian nurses and later expanded the program to train nurses and to provide additional native medical practitioners for the whole island area.

The old Department of Industries was originally established as the Engineering Department but was later renamed the Public Works Department. Besides re-establishing villages throughout the island the Department maintained machine shop and construction divisions.

Furniture was built for administrative offices, desks and tables for the schools, and prefabricated sections of houses for more speedy village construction.

The Public Works officers were also responsible for the maintenance of the transportation pool equipment of the military government unit. The problem of transportation was particularly difficult. Neither motor vehicles nor fuel was available to civilians, whose ox and carabao carts were such a menace to safety on the roads that they could not be encouraged. Since the majority of the trips that civilians wished to make in government vehicles could not be considered official, the solution was to create an island utilities organization which, in addition to other activities, ran daily bus trips between important centers.

A Public Safety Department, set up with a native police force under the leadership of marine corps personnel, directed the usual police activities and the important police patrols. Because of their wide knowledge of the island and their enthusiasm for this task, native patrolmen were particularly effective in rounding up enemy stragglers left on the island.

During the assault phase, military government included an Intelligence Department which conducted a census of civilians on the island. It carried out preliminary investigations, in many cases, of civilians suspected of having been collaborationists. The later intelligence function, with respect to Japanese citizens, was performed by higher echelons.

Conclusion

As has been indicated throughout this account, the over-all organization of military government on Guam underwent several modifications. In nearly every instance, however, the same functions remained, although they were arranged in different patterns of coordination. Combination of like functions, mainly with a view to reducing the size of the policy-forming staff, accounted for at least two reorganizations.[1] As the operation shifted from the assault phase

[1] After more than a year of operation, military government was cut away from the regular staff divisions of island command. It became subject to the Staff Division as

to the rear area phase, and as the emphasis on certain civilian problems also shifted, the departmental structure—but not the over-all structure—of military government underwent some change. For example, as its work was completed, the Intelligence Department went out of existence and the census-taking function was transferred to the Records and Accounts section of the Finance Department. As the refugee camps closed or were turned into villages, their operation was transferred from camp commanders to the control of the respective functional departments of the central military government. In this manner the military government kept itself abreast of the changing situation and adapted its organization to the solution of the problems which arose during the military reoccupation of Guam.

---

a separate unit. The change made little difference in the operation of the various military government departments.

Chapter XV

American Military Government Experience in Japan[1]

ARTHUR D. BOUTERSE, PHILIP H. TAYLOR, and ARTHUR A. MAASS

THE story of military government and civil affairs in the Pacific is the story of thousands of American men thrown into strange surroundings to undertake new and unfamiliar tasks. Faced first with the necessity of bringing government to sparsely populated islands that had known little or no previous government (one dislikes calling colonial exploitation "government") and progressing through the Philippines, whose nation birth pains had hardly yet reached world attention, military government reached a climax in the task of directing and controlling the collapsed empire of a proud and superstitious race.

In World War II American youth gave re-expression to its almost forgotten capacity for quick adaptation and startled its older leaders and more cynical members by showing that democracy does breed among its offspring an alert and intelligent ability to govern. The eighteenth century offered proof that men with little previous experience can govern themselves ably and well. World War II demonstrated that the eighteenth century's great-great-grandchildren can do as well when the task involves the direction of others.

Nowhere in the world was America faced with a greater variety of circumstances under which government must operate than in the

[1]This chapter is primarily concerned with the administration and operation of military government in Japan, and not with any thorough analysis of the substance of occupational directives.

Pacific Ocean areas. The European problem was complex and beset with certain difficulties which never confronted military government personnel in the Pacific. But from Tarawa to Tokyo the strange and unexpected became commonplace. The best of blueprints and plans became obsolete before they could be used. Or, as was too often the case, the plans of military government personnel were disapproved or ignored by the tactical command.

That they were often ignored is not surprising when one remembers the military man's traditional lack of concern for the civilian during combat. The lessons of the Rhineland occupation were remembered by some specialists in the American army, but the efforts of a few farseeing men in Washington to train personnel to handle war-ravaged civilians indeed seemed futile when trained military government detachments in the Philippines were reassigned to combat duties. But the tactician is adaptable. Those detachments were quickly reassembled when it became evident that modern war does not allow an army to ignore the inhabitants of the land through which it passes. Not a few military government officers and enlisted men suspect, however, that to the bitter end the combat soldier and tactician gave small support to the theory that civilians should be handled by men trained to do the job.

The complete story of Pacific military government cannot yet be told by one man. The area of activity covered so many millions of square miles, involved so many commands—marine, navy, army— and continued for so long (from 1942 to the time of this writing in the fall of 1946), that all of the pieces cannot yet be gathered into one place. But before mellowness softens too many vivid experiences and impressions, a beginning should be made. No apology is offered for lack of perspective, for conclusions based on inadequate knowledge, or for personal opinions. The future historian can judge for himself how well the story fits the documented account.

To understand how General MacArthur's dual commands, AFPAC (Army Forces in the Pacific) and SCAP (Supreme Command for the Allied Powers), accomplished the military government tasks requires a detailed study, including an examination of the trained military personnel available to these commands.

Personnel for Military Government

When Japan offered preliminary surrender terms on August 10, 1945, military government personnel in the United States specifically trained and available for duty in Japan included over 2,000 army and navy officers, of whom more than 1,000 were at the Civil Affairs Staging Area (CASA), Monterey, California, some 500 in Civil Affairs Training Schools (CATS), and 250 at the School of Military Government (SMG). About 4,000 enlisted men in all grades, with more or less special training, had been designated for military government duty in Japan.

All of the officers and some of the enlisted men had been carefully selected on the basis of general background, training, or technical specialty. Very few officers had been commissioned directly from civilian life, in marked contrast to the early selection program for military government officers sent to the European Theater. Many officers destined for the Pacific Theater had seen combat service in one or both World Wars. The vast majority had been in the armed services for some years.

During the week of August 18–25, 297 military government officers were rushed from CASA to Manila on A-1 air priority. From this group and from the Philippine Civil Affairs Unit (PCAU) pool at Antipolo, 227 officers were at once assigned to the Sixth and Eighth Armies and XXIV Corps. From the remainder, about 75 administrative officers and military government technical specialists were assigned to the Military Government Section, GHQ.

The month of September found nearly 800 Military Government officers and 900 enlisted men in the Pacific Theater with 1,250 additional officers and over 3,000 enlisted men ordered or enroute. By October 11, 1945, a detailed breakdown of military government personnel allocations showed 155 officers and 200 enlisted men in Military Government Section, GHQ; 150 officers, 180 enlisted men with the Sixth Army; 125 officers, 60 enlisted men with the Eighth Army and 350 officers, 465 men with the XXIV Corps. Those assigned to the tactical troops included ten organized military government companies, two provincial groups and several provincial companies. Of

those ordered or enroute, 310 officers and 85 enlisted men were assigned to the Military Government Section, GHQ, 450 officers and
1,575 men (including 2 military government groups and 9 military
government companies) were assigned to XXIV Corps. In addition,
approximately 375 officers were held in the reserve pool in the United
States. The grand total of Military government personnel available
for duty in the Pacific theater on October 11, 1945, was approximately
2,400 officers and 4,200 enlisted men.

Two events brought about a reshuffle of military government personnel in the latter half of September. The hearty Japanese cooperation with the Sixth and Eighth Armies eased the demand for military
government units in the home islands. On the other hand, the unexpectedly tense political situation in Korea coupled with the lack
of qualified Koreans for Governmental positions greatly increased the
need for military government officers and specialists in the XXIV
Corps. A number of military government groups and companies
were reassigned to the XXIV Corps and were diverted enroute to
Korea.

The training of the military government officers had been extensive. Special materials were prepared for use both in training and in
operating military government in Japan. Eighteen Civil Affairs
Handbooks (Army Service Forces Manuals 354–1 to 354–18) covered
such subjects as transportation, agriculture, industry, money and
banking, communication, political institutions. Forty-eight prefectural manuals, prepared at Monterey as a joint CASA–OSS project,
contained available factual material on each Japanese prefecture. At
the time of Japan's capitulation, thirteen of these manuals (covering
Kyushu and Tokyo and its surrounding prefectures) had been completed and sent to Washington for reproduction. Many other factual
summaries and many sample directives, instructions, and policy statements prepared at CASA and at the various CATS had been mimeographed. Thousands of beautifully colored and detailed maps covering every major phase of Japanese activity had been prepared by OSS.
In short, tons of useful material were available, practically none of
which ever reached Japan, although it was used in training. This
unfortunate circumstance can be attributed to poor planning at CASA

and in Washington and to the AFPAC dictum that all available shipping space be used for "bodies not books."

Early Planning

The sequence of events leading up to the occupation illustrates the difficulties faced by military planners. The invasion of Japan was scheduled for November, 1945, and in April General MacArthur was given command of the United States Army Forces, Pacific and ordered to direct the operation. On July 26 the Potsdam Declaration was issued; on August 9 the Soviet Union declared war on Japan; on August 10 Tokyo made a qualified peace offer; and on August 15 unconditional surrender was accepted. The impact of the rapidly changing situation on the military government organization was no less severe than it was on the combat units. Faced unexpectedly with a completely altered program, the army was without clear-cut direction. The tactical command quickly adjusted its plans to meet new circumstances, but the rapidity of events left the military government organization stranded.

Much confusion of thought has become evident concerning the planning phases of the Japanese and Korean occupation programs. Magazine articles and newspaper stories published during the early months of the occupation alleged that General MacArthur had been ill advised to reject carefully laid plans for military government in Japan and had preferred a "soft" regime. The decision to deal with the existing government and to retain the Emperor, and General MacArthur's estimate of the relatively low number of American troops likely to be required for police duty were sharply criticized. The American public was led to believe that the occupation was based upon a do-nothing plan and that General MacArthur had rejected carefully laid alternative proposals.

Planning for the occupation of Japan and Korea was by no means the responsibility of General MacArthur alone.[2] Initial policies were developed by the State-War-Navy Coordinating Committee and were

[2]Merle Fainsod, "Military Government and the Occupation of Japan," *Japan's Prospects,* Chapter IX.

submitted to the President for his approval. The Department of State through its Far Eastern Affairs office, the War Department through the Civil Affairs Division, and the Navy Department through the Military Government Section in its Office of Naval Operations worked jointly in assisting the Far Eastern subcommittee of SWNCC in this task. The Joint Chiefs of Staff contributed military policy as it affected the occupation problem and served as the channel for issuing SWNCC directives to the Supreme Commander for the Allied Powers. The representations of foreign powers were made first through the Far Eastern Advisory Commission and later through the Far Eastern Commission and the Far Eastern Council. Directives issued to General MacArthur covered basic policy. Methods of implementing policy and the development of administrative machinery for occupation duties were the responsibility of the Supreme Commander.

Wide discretionary powers were delegated to General MacArthur, and the exercise of his responsibility involved the drafting of a complex and minute administrative and operational blueprint. The control of civil government was only one of many aspects of the job. The landing of a relatively small force in an area where several million well-armed troops were still firmly in control posed a security problem of the first order. The purely military phases of the peaceful invasion were almost as complex as a combat landing would have been. In addition, the whole problem of political and economic policy had to be faced and decisions reached on the thousands of administrative details necessary to its solution.

Soon after General MacArthur's appointment as commander in chief, Brigadier General W. E. Crist, chief military government officer for Okinawa, was placed in charge of military government matters. General Crist's task was to form a military government organization for Japan and Korea and to undertake the necessary planning. At the time of his appointment in the summer of 1945, there was little or no inkling of the urgency of his task. The Okinawa campaign was officially completed and Pacific war prospects were encouraging, but all plans indicated that a six months' period of preparation would precede the occupation of Japan.

One of General Crist's first moves after his appointment was a hurried trip to Washington to begin a badly needed coordination of Civil Affairs Division plans with those of the theater. A notably weak aspect of early plans for the occupation of Japan and Korea was the lack of clear-cut military government liaison with the theater. The carefully developed officer-training program was not adequately interpreted to General MacArthur or to his advisers, although he had probably learned useful lessons in the Philippines and at Okinawa which demonstrated the soundness of the War Department's personnel training plan. General Crist attempted to fill the liaison gap quickly and to acquaint himself with available personnel resources. Conferences with Civil Affairs Division leaders and with the command at the California staging area resulted in plans to move available personnel forward to a Philippines base and to perfect the proposed organization and detailed plans in the theater.

Most of these decisions were made during July, with five months still supposedly available for planning. At that point time ran out. August events quickly made obsolete the decisions of July, and military government was left suspended in the torrid summer atmosphere of the Pacific.

One casualty of the swiftly changing scene was the planning unit which had been operating at the Civil Affairs Staging Area (CASA). During the spring and early summer of 1945, a special division had been established at CASA in anticipation of the theater's need for occupation plans. One hundred and fifty officers began the planning task in May and by mid-July had developed the principal features of an occupation blueprint. This effort apparently was not officially recognized either by Washington or by headquarters in Manila. General Crist was informed of it soon after his appointment, but both he and the Civil Affairs Division in Washington appear to have evaluated the effort primarily as a training aid. However, plans were developed at the staging area which were basic to the occupation problem whether it developed under combat or peaceful circumstances. The assumption was, of course, that the November invasion of Kyushu would set the stage for the military government organization. Not only the planning division but the entire training program at the staging area operated on that assumption. When military government personnel were brought forward from California to Manila, the CASA planning unit was disbanded.

Organization of Military Government Section, AFPAC

On August 5, 1945, the Military Government Section of General Headquarters, United States Army Forces, Pacific (AFPAC) was formally activated in Manila by General Order No. 92. This order, however, did not assign the section specific duties or functions, or give it authority to act. From the beginning General MacArthur and his closest general staff advisers opposed the establishment of a G-5 section on the general staff to assume responsibilities in the field of military government as had developed in the European Theater. Instead, it was provided that for the conduct of military government, Military Government Section and other special staff sections would function directly under the Chief of Staff, with coordination as necessary with general staff agencies.

Initially it was contemplated that the Military Government Section of GHQ would advise General MacArthur concerning the control of the civil government and population of the occupied territories. Under such plans the Military Government Section would have been responsible for the issuance of appropriate instructions to army and corps commanders to ensure adherence to the general policies and directives effecting control of the civil government and people of Japan. This procedure was never put into practice, and the repeated attempts to establish direct channels for even technical civil matters between the specialists in the Military Government Section of GHQ and the military government officers in the field were opposed by the Chief of Staff.

Thus, when military government personnel were assigned to the armies and to XXIV Corps, the Military Government Section lost all control over them. All communications, regardless of their nonmilitary character, had to follow the tortuous established channels from GHQ, AFPAC down through army, corps, and division with the general staff officers at each echelon assuming very real concern over the appropriateness of their content. It was apparently supposed that there would be no direct military government in Japan, and that the tactical commanders, having been given full responsibility over definite areas, would oppose any interference on the part of any outside agency and would prohibit communications with subordinate elements of their command by other than regular military channels.

The Military Government Section, set up with other GHQ staff sections in the City Hall, Manila, was in full operation by the third week in August. Without clear authorization and, at this stage, lacking any form of directive, it proceeded to function as the civil affairs section of a theater staff according to paragraph 22, FM 27–5.[3]

The Military Government Section, GHQ, AFPAC performed such duties as the following:

a) Preparation of proclamations, orders, directives, regulations, operating procedures, technical bulletins and instructional manuals which might be of use by, or for the guidance of, military government officers in the field.

b) Preparation of table of organization, allowances and equipment for military government units; determination of supplies required for military occupation and for emergency relief to recovered nationals, displaced persons, and, where necessary to prevent disease and unrest, the native population.

c) Preparation of plans to impose such controls over the Japanese Government at both national and local levels as would ensure enforcement of surrender terms and all promulgations of the Supreme Commander for the Allied Powers, including:

1) supervision and control over financial institutions, currency, credit, foreign exchange, public finance, taxation, freezing of assets, government budgets and fiscal records;

2) control over disease among civilian population and supervision of the distribution of welfare supplies;

3) supervisory control over the operation of refugee camps and the transfer or repatriation of displaced and recovered persons;

4) surveillance of police and fire departments, and prisons;

5) direction, within adopted policy, of courts and law procedures,

[3]For this see above Chapter II, especially pages 31–35.

including recommendations for removal or appointment of judicial officers, and the provision for trial of civilians before military courts;

6) encouragement of essential production of consumers' goods and the restoration of industry and commerce with a view to minimizing the need for imports;

7) control over wages and prices, and close supervision of rationing; the procurement of labor;

8) supervisory control over educational and religious institutions, the press, radio, and motion pictures; and the preservation of works of art;

9) regulation of government agencies concerned with public works, utilities, transportation, communications, and buildings; assisting the appropriate agencies of the occupation forces in adapting these facilities to military requirements;

10) formulation of ordinances and enactments, later, directives and instructions to the Japanese government to effectuate or implement the above.

To accomplish the objectives outlined above, the Military Government Section was organized internally into divisions as shown on the chart in Appendix D, page 425.

The Civilian Advisers or Policy subsection included representatives of the State Department, the Treasury Department, the Foreign Economic Administration, and other similar agencies in Washington. The Public Affairs Division was further subdivided into a Legal Branch, a Public Safety Branch, a Civil Government Branch, and an Education Branch, the latter having religion, arts, and monuments within its jurisdiction. The Economics Division contained branches on Commerce and Trade, Agriculture and Forestry, Fisheries, Labor and Wages, Natural Resources, Industry and Manufacturing, Price Control and Rationing, Salvage and Priorities, and Engineering. The titles of the other divisions adequately describe their major activity. All the divisions were staffed with well-qualified individuals who were often recognized experts or outstanding authorities within their fields.

Activities of the Military Government, AFPAC

The unconditional surrender of the Imperial Japanese Government on August 15, 1945, automatically made obsolete much of the elaborate preparations for military government based upon an invasion of Japan. Yet uncertainty remained as to what conditions military government might have to cope with or how the Japanese would react. With no directive to guide its activities, the Military Government Section had to plan for at least two possible situations: satisfactory compliance; and inefficiency or resistance, open or underground, by the people or by governmental agencies. To meet these exigencies, alternative approaches called Phase A and Phase B were drawn up for all comprehensive plans prepared by the divisions.

The situation was clarified to a considerable extent by the basic decision to allow the Emperor to retain his position and to use the Japanese administration intact at all governmental levels. A definite statement of policy by General MacArthur and the first military government instructions to army and corps commanders were contained in the Government Annex of August 28. The following excerpts indicate its importance:

Military control of Japan will be established by the Commander-in-Chief as the Supreme Commander for the Allied Powers.

The Supreme Commander for the Allied Powers will exercise control over Japan and the Japanese, to the greatest practicable extent, through the Emperor and the various instrumentalities of the Japanese Imperial Government which prove suitable for this purpose.

The Commanding Generals, Sixth and Eighth Armies and XXIV Corps, will supervise the functioning of those agencies of the Japanese Imperial Government within the areas of their commands in accordance with this and other directives issued by the Supreme Commander for the Allied Powers.

The Supreme Commander for the Allied Powers will issue all necessary instructions to the Japanese Emperor or to the Imperial Government and every opportunity will be given for the Government and the Japanese people to carry out such instructions without further compulsion. If necessary, however, the Supreme Commander will issue appropriate orders to the Army and Corps commanders indicating the action to be taken by them to secure the obedience by the agencies of the Imperial Government or Japanese people within the areas of their commands. In other words, the occupation forces will act principally as an agency upon which the Supreme Commander may call, if necessary, to secure compliance with his instructions to the Japanese Imperial Government.[4]

Verbal interpretation of the written instructions emphasized that unit commanders and their staffs were to avoid any attempt at direct civil government and were merely to observe and report to GHQ such developments as were pertinent.

These basic decisions of occupation policy were released to the public by President Truman on September 22.[5] This release stated that it was the objective of the United States to prevent Japan from again becoming a menace to the United States or to the peace and security of the world, and emphasized that in bringing about the "eventual establishment of a peaceful and responsible . . . and democratic self-government . . . it is not the responsibility of the Allied Powers to impose any form of government not supported by the freely expressed will of the people."

Particularly pertinent to the administrative pattern of the occupation was the following passage of the policy statement:

In view of the present character of Japanese society and the desire of the United States to attain its objective with a minimum commitment of its forces and resources, the Supreme Commander will exercise his authority through Japanese governmental machinery and agencies, including the Emperor, to the extent that this satisfactorily furthers United States' objectives. The Japanese government will be permitted, under his instructions, to exercise the normal powers of government in matters of domestic administration. This policy, however, will be subject to the right and duty of the Supreme Commander to require changes in governmental machinery or personnel or to act directly if the Emperor or other Japanese authority does not satisfactorily meet the requirements of the Supreme Commander in effectuating the surrender terms. This policy, moreover, does not commit the Supreme Commander to support the

[4]Annex 8, dated August 28, 1945, to Operating Instructions No. 4, August 15, 1945.

[5]For the official version see the *Department of State Bulletin,* September 23, 1945, pages 423–427. The quotations in this text are from Fainsod, as quoted above. For the general issues of democratic foreign policy involved here, compare Chapter I above.

Emperor or any other Japanese authority in opposition to evolutionary changes looking toward the attainment of United States' objectives. The policy is to use the existing form of government in Japan, not to support it. Changes in the form of government initiated by the Japanese people or government in the direction of modifying its feudal and authoritarian tendencies are to be permitted and favored. In the event that the effectuating of such changes involves the use of force by the Japanese people or government against persons opposed thereto, the Supreme Commander should intervene only where necessary to insure the security of his forces and the attainment of all other objectives of the occupation.

The Advance Echelon, GHQ, including many key men of the Military Government Section, left Manila for Japan during the last few days of August. Their departure slowed up work considerably in Manila, since consultation between the two echelons was necessary on many vital issues. In Japan organization of the Military Government Section had to remain indefinite until it had become clear what type of control structure was required. Meanwhile personnel kept moving up from Manila throughout September.

Regardless of these conditions, the section was able to make some worth-while contributions to the nonmilitary phases of the occupation of Japan and Korea. The armies of occupation were given essential military government personnel before entering their respective areas, and a vast amount of staff work was accomplished.

The three basic proclamations on 1) general provisions, 2) crimes and offenses, and 3) currency were prepared by the coordinated work of several divisions of the Military Government Section. Besides the English text for both, they were printed with a Japanese translation for the proclamations destined for Japan, and with both Korean and Japanese texts for those to be posted in Korea. However, following the surrender ceremonies and as a result of conversations with high Japanese officials, the Supreme Commander decided that it would not be expedient to use the proclamations in Japan. If the Supreme Commander was going to use the Japanese Emperor as the mouthpiece for his orders to the Japanese government and people, a direct order from the Supreme Commander to the Japanese nation would compromise the Emperor's authority at the start. Hence, the contents of the three proclamations were given to the Emperor, who issued them as his orders for Japan.

In Korea another kind of difficulty arose. Some 50,000 copies of each proclamation were printed in Yokohama and made ready for use by the troops entering Korea. Several hundred were actually posted by the first troops to land. In preparing the translation great care had been taken to use the correct characters for the words of the Cairo Conference: "In due course Korea shall become free and independent." However, a number of Koreans interpreted the Korean translation to mean immediate independence in a matter of days. To prevent additional complications in an already difficult state of affairs, it was decided to withhold further publication of the documents and to employ other means of transmitting to the Koreans the orders they contained.

Although the legal subdivision had prepared a complete set of procedures and forms for the establishment of military occupation courts, they were considered unnecessary so long as the Japanese government proved able and willing to maintain order and administer justice in cases involving United Nations nationals. Occupation courts were to have been an instrument of the Supreme Commander's authority, and the offenses to be tried were to be established by the Supreme Commander rather than by Japanese law. Since an ordinance establishing these courts would have to be addressed by the Supreme Commander to the Japanese people, such an ordinance might have been considered as an unjustified step toward direct military government at a time when the Japanese government had demonstrated complete cooperation. It was therefore decided that the interests of the occupation forces and United Nations nationals could be safeguarded by requiring the Japanese government to have its judicial agencies notify the Supreme Commander of all cases involving the occupation forces or United Nations nationals or property. A directive specified that his permission was to be secured before such cases could be tried, and reserved his power of veto over the decisions.

Numerous proclamations, ordinances, notices, and memoranda were prepared in Manila. While these were not always issued as prepared, they provided the contents of a variety of directives issued to the Japanese government by authority of the Supreme Commander. Among these were the memorandum on supplemental military yen currency marked "B," as legal tender, issued September 6 and 10; that on production in nonwar plants, of September 15; on the surrender of arms by the civilian population of Japan, of September 16; on the release of surplus Japanese army and navy medical supplies for civilian use, submitted September 20 and sent out October 3; on the protection of property of friendly nations and their nationals, of September 22; on public health measures, of September 22; on the voiding of promotion of civil service officials in Korea, of September 29 and October 2; and the far-reaching four-point order of October 4, called the "Bill of Rights" directive, which ordered the release of political prisoners, the abolition of the secret police and allied agencies, the dismissal of the Home Minister and all top officials having to do with "thought control," and the abrogation of all laws and ordinances denying the people free exercise of their political, civil, and religious rights.

One of the section's most valuable contributions was the proposed Directive No. 3, a most comprehensive order covering nearly all phases of Japanese public affairs. It was never issued as such, but from it was taken the substance of economic Directive No. 3, of September 22, 1945, as well as that of projected Directive No. 4, which was published in the form of a series of specific instructions to the Japanese government.

Many of the memoranda prepared by the Finance Division at Manila were issued by the Supreme Commander as directives to the Japanese government. These included directives on control of financial transactions and controls over exports and imports of gold, silver, securities, and financial instruments. A recommendation on closing institutions which had financed Japan's war and expansionist efforts and which were unnecessary for her internal economy was accepted and carried out by an order of September 30, 1945. Many other specific recommendations in the financial field were held for consideration or later action.

Another comprehensive memorandum prepared by the Military Government Section was the draft (dated September 16, 1945) of a

Standing Operating Procedure, Instruction No. 6, Military Government Procedure in Japan. This document was held pending the establishment of the special staff section of GHQ, SCAP.

Because of the absorption of the functions and personnel of divisions of the Military Government Section by new or existing special staff section toward the end of September, much of the work done by the Military Government Section was incorporated in the actions and memoranda of these special staff sections.

Move to Tokyo and Deactivation of the Military Government Section

Two airborne detachments and a waterborne detachment of military government totaling 8 officers, 11 enlisted men, 3 interpreters, and a civilian employee arrived in Yokohama on August 31 and September 1, 1945. There the advance echelon of the Military Government Section, GHQ was established on the first floor of the Customs Building. Following the ceremonies attendant upon the signing of the Surrender Document aboard the U.S.S. "Missouri" September 2, this nucleus of military government officers remained in Yokohama for two weeks.

This period was the critical one for the success of the entire occupation mission. The surrender, coming with unexpected suddenness, left not only a fully equipped defense force in the four main islands but a producing armament industry. An early report that the Japanese armies in the islands were short of equipment and ammunition proved to be completely unfounded. Huge stores of food and munitions for military use were uncovered shortly after the American army landed. Despite heavy bombings industrial production was at 66 per cent of peak capacity.

General MacArthur's immediate task was to release and evacuate American and other Allied prisoners of war and to make the islands secure for American occupation by disarming the Japanese troops. This job, neither political nor economic, was strictly military in nature and was properly placed in the hands of the tactical command. Inspection and search parties of American troops began the seizure and destruction of armaments immediately upon arrival in their assigned zones. Military precautions were the first order of the day, and the bulk of the early general headquarters directives covered military subjects.

It was quickly evident, however, that economic and political problems had a direct bearing upon the security of American troops, and that the implementation of high policy demanded the making of speedy and far-reaching decisions. At the time of the first landings, the economic and political situation was already becoming acute. Even before the formal surrender, the Japanese government had begun the resettlement of Koreans to the mainland of Asia, and, with the declaration of the end of hostilities, thousands of Koreans and Chinese stopped work on their forced-labor jobs and demanded immediate freedom from Japanese control.

The problem of the control of devastated areas, the feeding of millions of unemployed persons, the care of friendly foreign nationals in Japan, the seriously disrupted system of commodity distribution, and countless other problems could not long be ignored by the occupying army. The moral collapse of the Japanese government accentuated the need for American direction. The decision to allow the government to continue its normal functions under the policy direction of General MacArthur unquestionably reduced American personnel requirements, but the immediate need for informing the government of specific policy requirements in dozens of governmental areas was a difficult and time-consuming task. In the preparation of directives and proposals on policies to advise the Supreme Commander the Military Government Section played a significant role.

On September 17, the advance echelon of Military Government Section, GHQ, which had grown to 15 officers and 20 enlisted men, moved from Yokohama to Tokyo. Here it established its offices in the Forestry Building, immediately behind the Dai Ichi Building which housed GHQ.

Beginning about September 18, 76 army and 23 navy officers and 76 enlisted men departed by air and water transport from Manila, all reaching Tokyo before October 1. Other arrivals from CASA brought the total personnel of the Military Government Section in Tokyo as of October 21, 1945, to 144 officers and 134 enlisted men. There remained 12 officers and about 70 enlisted men in Manila. The organization of the Military Government Section which had been in Manila remained substantially unchanged during and immediately after the movement to Tokyo.

General Order No. 92 of August 5, which authorized the organization of the Military Government Section, GHQ, was never implemented to define its duties. The Standing Operating Procedure, Instruction No. 6, Military Government Procedure in Japan, was not approved and accordingly was never published. This situation, in which the Military Government Section had no clearly defined functions, was bound to create a considerable degree of uncertainty within the section and in its contacts with other sections of GHQ. The main difficulty arose from the fact that the role of military government had been planned in terms of an invasion, or at least in terms of the assumption of direct control of the Japanese governmental machinery at all levels. The surrender terms, which allowed the Emperor to remain as head of the Japanese state, and then the initial demonstrations by the Japanese government of its willingness to cooperate fully in carrying out the orders of the Supreme Commander, made it clear from the start that some fundamental changes in the previously conceived functioning of military government in Japan would be necessary. During the last week of August and the first two weeks of September all those concerned with the occupation of Japan were necessarily feeling their way. The decision regarding the ultimate organization for the control over Japan and Korea to be exercised by SCAP depended upon a number of intangible factors. The plans could not, or at least should not, have been drafted in haste.

The first official act pointing to the probable dissolution of the Military Government Section, GHQ, AFPAC was General Order No. 170, dated September 15, 1945, establishing the Economic and Scientific Section as a special staff section, GHQ. The duties of this new section were to advise the Supreme Commander on economic, industrial, financial, and scientific policies to be pursued in Japan and Korea, in order to implement the Potsdam Declaration. The effect of General Order No. 170 was to remove from the Military Government Section most of the functions and personnel previously under the control of the Economics Division and the Finance Division.

The functions of the Military Government Section were further curtailed by General Order No. 183, dated September 22, 1945, which created an additional GHQ special staff, the Civil Information and Education Section. The stated purpose of this section was to advise the Supreme Commander on policies relating to public information, education, religion, and other sociological problems of Japan and Korea; in effect, it absorbed the functions of military government in these fields.

Lieutenant General R. K. Sutherland, Chief of Staff, addressing the Military Government Section assembled in the Dai Ichi Theater, September 26, 1945, said, in brief, that 1) there would be no military government as such in Japan; 2) the Military Government Section would be discontinued; 3) the majority of military government headquarters personnel would be assigned to the XXIV Corps in Korea, where there was a very real military government job to do; 4) the remainder of the personnel would be assigned to GHQ special staffs, already established or to be established, in Tokyo. This was the first official announcement of the expected discontinuance of the Military Government Section, GHQ, and the absorption into other agencies of the activities and personnel for military government in Japan.

The Military Government Section went out of existence by General Order No. 224, GHQ, AFPAC, dated October 4, 1945.

Organization of Special Staff Sections

Under GHQ, SCAP General Order No. 1, dated October 2, 1945, stated, "General Headquarters of the Supreme Commander for the Allied Powers is to be established with station at Tokyo, Japan." Transfer of military government functions to SCAP was accomplished by a series of general orders published during the first two weeks of October, but all dated October 2, 1945, which established the following ten special staff sections. Their principal duties, or the subject fields on which they were charged to advise the Supreme Commander regarding policies, are stated. The last four sections listed were activated several months later.

Special Staff Sections
GHO, SCAP

(1) *Economic and Scientific Section:* Economic (trade and commerce), industrial, financial and scientific.

(2) *Civil Information and Education Section:* Public information (press, radio, motion pictures, theater), education, religion, and arts and monuments.

(3) *Natural Resources Section:* Agriculture, forestry, fishing, and mining (including geology and hydrology).

(4) *Public Health and Welfare Section.*

(5) *Government Section:* Military government in Korea and Civil Government in Japan.

(6) *Statistical and Reports Section:* Preparation of data and reports concerned with nonmilitary phases of occupation in Japan and Korea.

(7) *Civil Communications Section:* Use and rehabilitation of civil communication in Japan and Korea.

(8) *Legal Section:* Advice on general questions and procedures; supervision of prosecution of war criminals.

(9) *Civil Intelligence Section:* Civil public safety agencies investigating noncompliance with directives and instructions to the Japanese government.

(10) *The Office of General Procurement Agent:* Coordination and control of procurement of supplies, equipment, materials, services, and real property by forces of the Allied Powers.

Sections established later were

(11) *International Prosecution Section:* Preparation and prosecution of cases before the International Tribunal.

(12) *General Accounting Section:* Financial accounting and maintenance of records.

(13) *Property Control Section:* Procedures concerning management and disposition of properties over which SCAP exercises control.

(14) *Office of Civilian Personnel:* Civilian personnel program.

The Government Section, more than any other section of SCAP, embodies the normal attributes of civil affairs or military government in occupied areas. Its primary functions are twofold: 1) in regard to Korea "to maintain close liaison on matters of military government with the United States Army Forces in Korea"; also to "advise the Supreme Commander for the Allied Powers on the development and progress of military government in Korea and recommend action in furtherance of the occupation mission"; and 2) in regard to Japan to "investigate, study and advise the Supreme Commander in general with respect to the structure of civil government in Japan and in particular with respect to: (a) relationship of civil government to military affairs and control of military forces; (b) relationship of Imperial Japanese Government to subordinate agencies or subdivisions . . . ; (c) relationship of Imperial Japanese Government . . . to the people; (d) relationship of government to business. . . ."

In general the special staff sections appear to be so organized as to provide the Supreme Commander with one or more staffs of advisers on every phase of activity—political, economic, and social—of the Japanese people. A question might be raised as to why a general accounting agency and a property control section were not established until six months after the occupation commenced. And it is difficult to explain why, in comparison with the extensive functions of other sections, civil communications alone warranted a separate special staff under a major general. It is also hard to believe that in the entire GHQ there was no one responsible for public utilities until February, 1946, when the public-utilities desk in the Industry Division, Economic Section, was filled. Although the critical food situation was largely a matter of distribution, a half year of occupation passed before any comprehensive data were collected on which to formulate policy concerning rail, motor, and water transportation.

The Relation of Special Staff Sections
to the General Staff

The general staff sections retained their usual military functions and in addition served as the channel through which recommendations made by special staff sections were forwarded to the Chief of Staff and General MacArthur. Proposed instructions and memoranda to the Japanese government, prepared by special staff sections in their particular fields of responsibility, usually required the concurrence of a general staff section chief before submission to the Chief of Staff. This practice, a part of the usual military staff pattern, placed the real control over policy decisions in the hands of General MacArthur's military advisers, to the frequent disadvantage of his civil affairs specialists.

In early 1946, G-3 proposed to formalize the procedure for clearing all special staff recommendations through the general staff prior to submission to the Chief of Staff. Under this plan, G-1, in addition to its duties, would clear all matters relating to the supervision and control of Japanese civil and criminal courts and the health and welfare of United Nations nationals. G-3 would review the decisions of special staff experts concerning the following subjects, among others: the dissemination of democratic principles and the strengthening of democratic processes among the Japanese people, the advancement of the four freedoms, the control over communications, and the supervision of education. G-4 would clear all policies for the entire national economy of Japan and Korea and for the preservation of works of art.

Considerable opposition to this plan developed among the special staff sections. Counterproposals were made and in April, 1946, an important change in Special Staff—General Staff relations was promulgated. A Deputy Chief of Staff for Civil Affairs was assigned the responsibility for "top side" consideration of all civil affairs matters. Instructions and directives prepared for the Japanese government by the special staff sections were at long last permitted to by-pass the general staff and go directly to the Deputy Chief of Staff for Civil Affairs for final staff action.

Relations between special staff and general staff sections were further complicated, however, by the interrelation of the two commands, SCAP and AFPAC. SCAP is only a headquarters organization and exists solely to "advise the Supreme Commander." It must rely on GHQ, AFPAC for orders, pay and quarters, and also for cooperation and action in the execution of any policies. This situation is simplified in that both commands have the same commanding general, the same chief of staff, and the same general staff.

However, below the general staff the two headquarters have little in common, and many special staff sections of GHQ, AFPAC duplicate functions of roughly corresponding sections under SCAP. Continual and often difficult coordination became necessary. The Civil Communications Section of SCAP must coordinate with the Chief Signal Officer, AFPAC. Constant assistance by AFPAC Provost Marshal and Chief Counter Intelligence Officer is essential to the operations of the Civil Intelligence Section, SCAP, as well as to the Legal Section. This necessary cooperation carries through all activities: Economic Section, SCAP—Chief Engineer, AFPAC; Public Health and Welfare Section, SCAP—Chief Surgeon, AFPAC; Civil Information Section, SCAP—Army Information Services, AFPAC; and so on. It is a little more difficult to understand why the General Procurement Agent and the General Accounting Section are in GHQ, SCAP while the Fiscal Director remains in GHQ, AFPAC, or why the SCAP monthly report, prepared by a SCAP staff section must be approved by the AFPAC Public Relations Officer before publication for the War Department.

The Relation of SCAP to the Japanese Government

The White House policy statement had summarized the instructions under which General MacArthur was to operate. Specific objectives were to include limiting Japan's sovereignty to the four main and the numerous outlying islands; disarming and demilitarizing the nation completely; stimulating the Japanese people to develop a desire for individual liberties and a respect for fundamental human rights; encouraging them to form "democratic and representative organizations"; and affording the Japanese people an "opportunity to develop for themselves an economy which will permit the peaceful requirements of the population to be met."

Other political aims included the apprehension and trial of war criminals; the dissolution of nationalistic associations and societies, with their attendant teachings of race superiority and glorification of the military; religious freedom; abolition of political, religious, and other discrimination; the reform of judicial, legal, and police systems. Economic policy aimed to destroy Japan's war potential by limiting its heavy industries and removing its armament shops; to encourage labor, industry, and agriculture to organize on a democratic basis; to dissolve the big business trusts; to promote landownership by resident farmers. The Japanese authorities were to be required to develop programs: "(a) to avoid acute economic distress (b) to insure just and impartial distribution of available supplies (c) to meet the requirements for reparations deliveries agreed upon by the Allied governments (d) to facilitate the restoration of the Japanese economy so that the reasonable peaceful requirements of the population can be met."[6]

In enforcing and interpreting these policies to the Japanese government, the Supreme Commander had at his disposal the general headquarters organization previously described and the Sixth and Eighth armies, with their tactical units and military government sections. (In January the Eighth Army, assisted by a small contingent of British troops, assumed all occupation duties.)

Procedures were established which provided for issuing directives to the Imperial Japanese Government by the Supreme Commander through a central liaison committee composed of Japanese officials, appointed by the Prime Minister, and American officers, assigned by general headquarters. General headquarters section chiefs, who actually prepared the various directives (officially entitled "memoranda"), were permitted to confer with Japanese officials only by arrangement with the central liaison committee. In theory, no contact between staff personnel and the government was permitted except by such formal clearance with the committee.

[6]*Ibid.*

All memoranda prepared in general headquarters and approved by the Chief of Staff and the Supreme Commander were issued over the signature of the Adjutant General "to the Imperial Japanese Government, through the Central Liaison Committee." Delivery was then made to the proper Japanese ministry. Acknowledgment of receipt of memoranda was made by the committee, and replies from the Japanese government were routed through it to the proper staff section of SCAP.

Japanese prefectural governments were notified through Japanese governmental channels of action required by the Supreme Commander. Army commanders of lower echelons were not permitted to issue instructions to municipal or prefectural authorities without express authority from general headquarters.

Operation of occupation machinery can be illustrated by a brief description of the activities of the Public Health and Welfare Section of general headquarters. This unit was established early in October following the official decease of the Manila-born Military Government Section. Divisions of the section were organized with special functions in preventive medicine, nursing affairs, medical supplies (including narcotic control), hospital administration, veterinary affairs, dental affairs, and public welfare.

Within a few days after the arrival of the staff in Tokyo, a directive was issued through the central liaison committee requiring the Japanese Ministry of Health and Social Affairs to submit a complete report of the medical and welfare situation in Japan. Army commanders were notified of the desire of general headquarters for a first-hand survey of health conditions and report on the probable requirements for food and medicine. Conferences were scheduled between the various division chiefs under the chief of the section and the appropriate bureau personnel in the Japanese ministry.

Within a month after the section was organized it had assumed control of medical, dental, food, and other supplies which had been stockpiled by the Japanese army and navy and had returned them to the Japanese government for civilian distribution under regulations established by the section; undertaken a study of regulations governing the manufacture of serums and vaccines; rigidly implemented narcotic control; directed the registration of all cases of communicable diseases and the reporting of preventive measures; initiated a weekly report of hospital beds available; ordered the control and reporting of animal diseases; supervised the inspection of meats and dairy products; surveyed the social insurance system; undertaken to raise the professional standards of all medical and welfare personnel.

By the end of December, personnel in the section had a sufficiently clear grasp of the problem of implementing policy to have ordered the organization of a national relief program for unemployed and destitute persons, to have directed proper health and welfare precautions in the handling of Korean, Chinese, and Japanese repatriates, and to have begun the democratization of health and welfare administration. Hospitals formerly administered exclusively for the military were transferred to civilian uses, the abolition of veterans' preference in welfare and pension services was ordered, and action was taken to prevent the emergence of militarist figures in Red Cross and other welfare agencies.

The measures taken by the Public Health and Welfare Section and all action relating to civil government by general headquarters were limited, however, to directives issued to the national government. No implementation of headquarters policy at lower levels was instituted.

Relationship between SCAP and Military Government throughout Japan

This discussion has been primarily concerned with the organization and operation of military government in Japan on the national level. To complete the picture it seems desirable to point out some of the relationships between GHQ and its subordinate elements and to describe the manner in which policies determined by SCAP are executed or enforced by military government officers in the field.

The military government responsibilities of the occupation forces were set forth in the Eighth Army Annex No. 8 (Military Government) to Administrative Order No. 19. The occupation forces were to act solely as an agency for *observing, investigating,* and *reporting* compliance with the instructions of the Supreme Commander for the Allied Powers to the Imperial Japanese Government. Direct military government would under no circumstances be inaugurated except on direct orders from higher headquarters. Except in emergencies, the issuance of orders to, or the direct operation or supervision of, any Japanese governmental agency by subordinate commanders would not be undertaken unless specifically authorized by higher headquarters. Removal and appointment of Japanese officials would be effected only by Japanese agencies.

Aside from this directive, most tactical commanders and military government personnel received no instructions in the early and crucial months of occupation. Although they were ordered to observe, investigate, and report compliance with the instructions of the Supreme Commander for the Allied Powers to the Imperial Japanese Government, the responsible officers often never received copies of the SCAP directives. Incredible as it may seem, there was no adequate or reasonably prompt distribution of SCAP directives to military government personnel throughout Japan until May, 1946—eight months after the first one had been issued.[7] During this period the Japanese officials at prefectural and local levels received directives from their own government based on original SCAP directives often before the responsible army officers at the same level had in any way been informed of the nature of the SCAP directives. Fortunately, the fact that the English-language *Nippon Times* printed most of the SCAP directives enabled the officers in the field to learn of SCAP policies. For months in almost any subordinate headquarters throughout Japan one would invariably find an English-speaking Japanese girl carefully clipping the *Nippon Times* to inform the American officers what their Supreme Headquarters wished to have done.

By the middle of May this situation was remedied, and now directives are sent directly from the Eighth Army to all military government outfits. As a further assistance to both the staff and the occupation forces, the Statistical and Reports Section, SCAP finished, in the

[7] The SCAP Public Health and Welfare Section had initiated a more direct distribution of only its own directives prior to this date.

early spring, the chronological numbering of all directives and an index, alphabetically arranged by subject fields, called SCAPIN. This
belated but welcome service is maintained by issuing to all headquarters bound volumes of the directives and each month a current
and complete index.

Not only did they receive no information as to policy in the early
and crucial months of occupation; the tactical commanders received
no instructions as to the use of military government personnel and
units assigned to their commands. The result was the development
of varying practices by military commands. For example, one division
commander utilized his military government specialists to form an
active general staff section (G-5), whereas the corps commander to
whom he was responsible assigned his military government officers
to a subsection under G-1. Some units undertook little or no activity.
Others, by a broad interpretation of the "emergency" clause of the
Eighth Army directive, participated directly in military government.
The trained military government specialists were reluctant to be idle
witnesses to the confusion of increasing migration from rural urban
areas and the problems resulting from bombings, insufficient food,
unemployment, Korean and Chinese unrest, and the widespread inability of the local Japanese government to meet critical situations. A
few divisional and corps military government chiefs actively directed
the distribution of food to refugees, controlled incoming and outgoing repatriates, directed the care of foreign nationals, surveyed and
ordered the disposition of industrial equipment, issued permission
for renewal of manufacturing, and attempted to solve labor problems.

The lack of uniformity and central direction may be illustrated by
the activities of two members of the military government team assigned to Kanagawa Prefecture, South of Tokyo. Upon his arrival at
the prefectural capital in Yokohama in November, 1945, the military
government public education officer undertook a systematic inspection of the several hundred schools of the prefecture. For some time
he was unable to learn what directives SCAP had issued to the Japanese government on educational policy. However, despite his inability to obtain all of the directives in the course of several trips to
SCAP headquarters in Tokyo, and from an avid reading of the

Nippon Times, this officer undertook to inspect the schools for compliance with what he thought should have been the SCAP directives. The reports of his examinations were carefully filed on 3 x 5 index cards in his desk, and a wall map indicated by colored thumbtacks the progress of his inspection trips. With one exception[8] he was neither directed nor authorized to report his findings to any higher authority. His commanding officer had told him to collect as much information as he could so that if higher headquarters ever asked for it, he would be well prepared. (Higher headquarters had not asked for it by spring.) He knew that the Counter Intelligence Corps in Yokohama had undertaken to supervise the Japanese prefectural committee set up to screen teachers. But the CIC was singularly uncommunicative as to its work, and the officer knew only that very few teachers had been dismissed by the Japanese government.

In contrast to the military government public education officer in Yokohama, who by the nature of his duties was wholly dependent on higher authority for direction and for permission to take any direct action, certain military government officers in the same prefecture were actually "operating" in respect to local matters under a broad interpretation of the "emergency" exception to the occupation directive. For example, the military government port liaison officer for Yokohama and other ports of the prefecture—a naval officer attached to the army but trained by military government—performed the following, among other, specific tasks: granted permits to Japanese vessels to tie up at, and use the handling equipment of, port facilities under control of the army; instructed and supervised the Japanese Lighthouse Bureau in restoring lighted aids to navigation in Tokyo Basin; upon request of the Japanese, obtained permission of the United States Navy for the tow of lumber through restricted seaplane area; worked directly with Japanese authorities in attempting to speed up salvage work in debris-filled waterways of Yokohama and Kawasaki; instructed Japanese police to clear certain water areas of Japanese vessels so that army and navy could operate therein.

After several months of occupation, the Eighth Army issued a

[8]The exception dealt with arms and munitions found in the schools.

directive on "Military Government Organization and Administration." This directive stated that commanding generals of corps and USASCOM-C were not to delegate their responsibility for military government; specially trained military government teams would be utilized for the administration of military government within the respective areas of responsibility; trained military government companies were to be attached for the purpose of administering the functions of military government in one or more prefectures; trained military government personnel would not be used for other than military government assignments without special permission in each instance. Although this directive clarified several matters relating to the use of military government personnel, it did not provide any unity in military government operations, and the varying practices discussed above continued.

Intelligent drafting of directives and instructions to the Japanese government in Tokyo required the prompt receipt of detailed reports from the field. The Eighth Army military government annex provided for weekly reports on military occupation activity from all headquarters, consolidated at each major echelon, division, corps, and army before forwarding to GHQ. Little attention was given to the form, content, or submitted dates of these reports. Many headquarters chose to limit their contents so sharply as to render them of little use. An example of this limitation is the military government public education officer for Kanagawa who was authorized to report only on the arms and ammunition found in school buildings. Consolidation of reports at higher headquarters resulted in unfortunate delays and often in the elimination of pertinent information.

During the spring of 1946, eight or nine months after occupation, an earnest attempt was made to consolidate all really significant data into a few reports on standardized forms to be received at definite regular periods. Since the early summer of 1946, under a new operations instruction, reports from all headquarters have been sent directly to the Military Government Section of the Eighth Army. Here they are combined under appropriate subject headings and, without change or even editing, forwarded to GHQ in Tokyo, where they are immediately distributed to the special staff sections concerned. Some special reports and those of an urgent nature may be sent directly to SCAP from the originating field officers.

The difficulties in communicating instructions to military government officers and in receiving information from them could have been avoided in part by initially authorizing communications both ways between the experts on the GHQ staff and the military government officers in the field for all technical nonmilitary or civil affairs matters. Such a technical channel of communication is a well-established army technique.

Tactical vs. Territorial Organization for Military Government

The requirements of military government in Japan today, however, indicate the need for more than a technical channel of communication; they appear to indicate the need for a territorial form of civil affairs organization. The existing tactical unit type of control, under which all military government personnel are attached to tactical commands and most military government business is conducted, is the accepted method of organization in combat and in highly unsettled areas of control. However, where settled conditions prevail, this form of organization has several distinct disadvantages: 1) "such [combat] commanders are apt to overlook the importance of civil affairs duty . . ."; 2) combat "units are generally subject to frequent movement, resulting in repeated changes in the personnel assigned to exercise control over local officials, with consequent variations in policy. Only to a limited extent can this disadvantage be minimized by the retention in the area of civil affairs officers formerly on the staff of the outgoing unit"; 3) "combat commanders and their staffs are usually untrained in civil affairs work"; 4) ". . . the control of civil affairs by military commanders takes their attention from the training of their men for combat and from other strictly military duties, which should engage their whole time and energy."[9]

Where settled conditions prevail, a different type of organization has been approved by the War Department and has been adopted

[9]FM 27–5, Para. 17.

in every country occupied by American forces except Japan. This is
the territorial form of civil affairs organization under which "a separate civil affairs organization is created under the direct command
of the theater commander or under a subordinate commander. The
line of communication within the organization is direct from higher
to lower civil affairs officers. Local civil affairs officers are not responsible to operational unit commanders stationed in the area with regard to administration of civil affairs, but report directly to higher
civil affairs officers."[10]

An outstanding fallacy in the occupation of Japan is the assumption that control of the Emperor and the national ministries is the
only essential requirement; that by directing determined policies in
the form of SCAP directives to the Imperial Japanese Government
the mission of the occupation forces is accomplished. The Imperial
Japanese Government in Tokyo is not primarily an operating agency.
In most cases it translates the directives it receives from SCAP into
government orders which are issued to prefectural and local administrators for compliance. Regardless of how nicely a Japanese minister
in Tokyo bows and avows compliance with SCAP decrees, the test
of enforcement rests with the forty-seven Japanese governors who
administer national policies and ordinances throughout their prefectures. Under the American occupation some of these governors
have become increasingly independent of the Home Ministry, to
whom they are normally responsible. They fully appreciate that the
occupation forces in their areas are limited to *observation, investigation,* and *report,* and that methods for reporting are such that failure
to comply on their part will seldom result in any reprimand, and
when it does, the time lapse will have been so great that the particular
condition complained of may well have changed.

If occupation forces are to be strictly limited to observation, investigation, and report, then the only way to ensure any considerable
degree of compliance of the Japanese at the local level with SCAP
directives is to ensure that the military government teams—the eyes
and ears of SCAP—are so closely integrated with the Supreme Headquarters that they are at all times aware of all civil affairs policies and

[10]*Ibid.,* Para. 16.

interpretations thereof and are continually reporting local conditions to headquarters. Such close integration appears to call for the territorial organization of civil affairs.

If, on the other hand, occupation forces are to be assigned a more active role in supervising at the local level compliance with national directives, then certainly the territorial form of organization is indicated. Whether or not a more direct supervision is required depends on the degree of compliance obtained under an efficient system of observing, investigating, and reporting. No such system is in effect in Japan today.

Law and Order vs. Democracy

Despite all criticism of the administration and operation of military government in Japan—constructive criticism, it is hoped, for only in this spirit has it been presented—the outstanding fact about the occupation of Japan is the unexpected success of the entire operation. That a large part of the credit for this success belongs to General MacArthur no one who has been in Japan any length of time could deny.

However, the two factors largely responsible for this success to date threaten the realization of the long-term objectives of military occupation—"eventual establishment of a peaceful and responsible . . . and democratic self-government."

It may be said that the success of the occupation to date is largely attributable to the complete and wholehearted cooperation of the average Japanese citizen. (The lack of complete cooperation by a few of the national and prefectural government authorities, even though it may assume some significance in the future, does not represent the general pattern.) This cooperation by the average citizen continues to astound every soldier on occupation duty in Japan. It astounds Westerners because they are unable to understand the force which invokes such unpredictable behavior. That force is the will of the Emperor. The Emperor made known to his people, prior to the entry of Allied forces, that it was his will that the people cooperate fully with all directives of the occupation troops. His people have complied, not with malice, nor with resentment, but with wholehearted co-operation.

Although the occupation thus owes its success in large part to the fact that the Japanese have obeyed the dictates of their ruler to co-operate, the establishment of a responsible and democratic self-government among a people who react in this manner to the dictates of a single divine man may prove to be impossible. The prospects of ultimate democracy in Japan might appear brighter, as a matter of fact, if the occupation were not going so well from the point of view of order, if there were some opposition to the dictates of the divine ruler, if there were any evidence that the people are willing to take this opportunity to think for themselves and act accordingly.

Legal changes in the institution of the Emperor, such as those included in the new Japanese Constitution, will not effect any fundamental change in the conduct of the people. Their conduct has a social base and is not derived from an understanding of constitutional principles. In fact, in Japan today many people worship General MacArthur as a "divine occupier," and not long ago a Japanese newspaper shocked the whole of Japan by daring to suggest that the General be regarded as something less than divine. Although it is true that Japanese emperor-worship dates only from the Meiji period, when it was purposefully developed as a method for achieving complete adherence to the new Japanese state, there is nothing to indicate that a state of mind which produces such complete adherence to the dictates of a single individual is in any way a temporary or unstable factor in Japanese society.

The second consideration is that the occupation troops throughout Japan have relied heavily upon the Japanese police for the maintenance of order and the execution of nearly all of their directives. The Japanese police have responded admirably to this responsibility and a large part of the success of the occupation can be attributed to this fact. But it is not an oversimplification to describe Japan as fundamentally a police state. The police are direct representatives of the Emperor and exercise a control over all aspects of the life of the average citizen. The average Japanese lives at all times in mortal fear of the police and never challenges their authority. The "establishment of a peaceful and responsible and democratic self-government" for Japan would seem to require, then, a radical change in the attitude of the people to the police and of the police to the people—a planned destruction of the police state.

However, quite to the contrary, the occupation forces have relied heavily on the Japanese police. Despite the fact that SCAP has ordered the abolition of thought control by the police, despite the fact that SCAP has ordered the Home Ministry to democratize its police force, despite the fact that GI's have on occasion publicly degraded Japanese policemen, the average Japanese lives today in just as great a fear of the police as he did before the occupation. He knows that the police are supported by the occupation troops.

This reliance on the police is readily understandable. The occupation forces, even those carefully trained, do not really understand the Japanese people nor their language well enough to rely entirely on their own men for enforcement of directives. And the Japanese police are cooperative and extremely effective in doing the job. A single experience of the military government port liaison officer for Kanagawa prefecture may help illustrate this point.

The limited dock facilities at Yokohama were filled with ships discharging cargo and numerous other ships were waiting in the stream. The army planned to commence working some of these ships by discharging their cargoes into lighters, which then would make for a filled-in landing beach within the harbor. At this beach the cargo would be transferred to a temporary storage area. Although Japanese fishing boats and canal barges were then tied up at the beach, the Port Command wanted to commence operations by noon the next day.

Inspection of the area revealed that many of the fishing boats were not in use and that most of the markings did not yield the necessary information to the American Nisei interpreter. The military government officer proceeded immediately to the nearest police station, ordered the first policeman he saw to hop into the jeep, took him to the area, and ordered him to have all of the boats and barges out by noon the next day, but to take care that, where the owners did not move their own boats, they were informed as to their new locations.

At the designated time the Japanese boats were out and the Port Command commenced operations. Had the officer tried to do the job without the Japanese police, and without using American harbor craft and equipment, many of the boats might still be there. This is an example drawn from a very low level of military government operation; but if at that level the military government officer was compelled to rely so heavily on the Japanese police, one can imagine how much more intensified is the dependence of the army commander—directly responsible for the order and security of a large area and with a relatively small detachment of troops at his command—on the cooperative and effective Japanese police.

To date action by SCAP to "democratize" the Japanese police force has been unsuccessful. And in view of the dependence of the occupation troops on the police, this failure is not difficult to understand. Later SCAP issued an order to the Home Ministry, requiring the ministry to present a plan for democratizing its police force. The plan presented was wholly inadequate. As described in the Japanese newspapers, one of the major provisions of the plan called for revising the uniform of the police to provide sleeve stripes rather than the existing shoulder boards.

General MacArthur sent for Lewis Valentine, a former police commissioner of New York City, to serve as consultant on police affairs. Mr. Valentine's recommendations were primarily concerned with methods for improving the *efficiency* of the Japanese police—cars, radios, roving patrolmen, and so on. However, it is not primarily in efficiency that the Japanese police are lacking; it is rather in any understanding of civil liberties. The police of the average Japanese city have more thorough control over the population of that city than Mr. Valentine ever had over the population of New York City. The fact that they use old police techniques rather than the mechanized techniques of modern police administration is really not of great concern. If the Japanese police system is in need of an expert to improve it, that expert should be a civil liberties lawyer, not a police administrator.

Conclusion[11]

The greatest task which faces those responsible for the Japanese occupation is the task of ensuring that the two factors largely responsible for the success of the occupation to date—complete Japanese cooperation with the occupation forces, brought about through obedience to the will of the Emperor, and the American reliance on the Japanese police system—are not allowed to become obstacles in the path of achieving the long-run objective of the occupation: a peaceful, responsible, and democratic government for Japan.

[11]This chapter was completed in the spring of 1946. [Ed.]

Chapter XVI

Military Government Experience in Korea

Part I

ADMINISTRATION AND OPERATION OF MILITARY GOVERNMENT
IN KOREA

PHILIP H. TAYLOR

THIS is essentially a story of improvisation. Korea, the one country in the Pacific Theater over which a real military government was established, was the only important area occupied by American troops in the Pacific for which some study or preparations had not been made.

Saipan, Tinian, Guam, the Philippines, Okinawa—for all of these operations military government plans had been prepared in advance Even with the short notice before the attacks upon Saipan, Tinian, and Guam, military government instructions and policies were published; trained and qualified marine, naval and army officers were briefed for their assignments; essential equipment, supplies, and personnel were made available to the military government units.[1] For the Philippines, considerable planning was accomplished in the United States and at the Civil Affairs Camp near Buna, New Guinea; Philippine Civil Affairs Units (PCAU's) were organized and their duties and functions defined; general civil affairs instructions were issued prior to invasion; and a Civil Affairs Division of GHQ, USAFFE (United States Army Forces Far East) was well staffed.

In the case of Okinawa, the first major operation of military govern-

[1]See Chapter XV above.

ment over a large Japanese-populated area, planning began as early as August, 1944; operational directives, technical bulletins, and military government logistical data were published; a sufficient number of trained military government officers were organized; and a military government section was established on the GHQ of the newly organized Tenth Army. The training and planning of military government officers for Japan have been described in Chapter XV.

In marked contrast, there was almost a complete lack of training and preparation for military government for Korea. This is not the place to inquire what dictates of high policy in Washington repeatedly prohibited the study of Korea in army schools. The fact is that only a few military government officers were given any appreciation of conditions in Korea, and they were trained in the last two classes at the School of Military Government, which began two months after the Japanese surrender. Policies and plans for the occupation of Korea were not available when the time came to act. The sudden collapse and surrender of Japan, not altogether unforeseen, did not explain the absence of comprehensive plans for Korea—the most important Japanese territory beyond the home islands.

And yet, in spite of this situation, and in spite of other occasional handicaps greater than those in any occupied Pacific area, a sound and rather efficiently functioning military government organization was established. So many other factors are involved that it would be unfair to suggest that lack of training and preparation is in any way the cause of better administration, but the evidence is certainly striking.

When the XXIV Corps, part of the Tenth Army on Okinawa, was designated the Occupation Force for Korea, it had no directives, no plans, no trained military government personnel, and less than a month to prepare for the accomplishment of its mission. Conditions to be faced upon landing on Korea were unpredictable—these included the actions of the Japanese forces, the reactions of the Korean people, the relations with the Russian forces. Necessarily, top priority in planning was given to preparing the tactical troops to meet any eventuality, but military government and the administration of civil affairs, although secondary at this stage, were not overlooked.

The commanding general of the XXIV Corps appointed the commanding officer of the Tenth Army's anti-aircraft command to be his deputy for military government. With a dozen of the officers from his command—all professional soldiers and none with any training or experience in civil affairs—the latter set out to organize and prepare for the military government of Korea. This small group was soon joined by about twenty experienced military government officers of the Tenth Army. These officers, though they had had no training in the problems of Korea, had gained valuable experience in operating without decisive direction in the thoroughly confused situation at Okinawa. This experience may account in part for the more expeditious methods adopted for Korea.

With little help from Washington or Manila, except for brief and often contradictory radio messages from the War and State Departments passed on by AFPAC, this group of officers set out to plan military government operations for Korea. With no statements of policy or directives from higher authority to guide them, they made full use of all of the material available: War Department field manuals, the Cairo Declaration, the Joint Army-Navy Intelligence Survey on Korea (JANIS 75) and Field Manuals FM 27–5, "Military Government and Civil Affairs," and FM 27–10, "Rules of Land Warfare," which set forth the basic principles for the organization of military government in occupied areas. The Cairo Declaration provided the only statement of high policy available at the time, the single sentence: "The aforesaid three great powers, mindful of the enslavement of the people of Korea, are determined that in *due course Korea shall become free and independent.*" From the JANIS document the officers gathered what facts they could as to the actual conditions in Korea. However, as these Joint Army-Navy surveys were designed in large part for use in planning tactical offensive operations rather than occupation operations, they did not provide the required data on social, political, and economic conditions which had been included in the earlier and discarded surveys of the War Department Military Intelligence Service or the Office of Naval Intelligence.

But among the fine maps and detailed descriptions of targets in the JANIS document, some useful facts were found. For example, the thirty-eighth parallel roughly divides Korea's 85,000 square miles in half but gives about 17,000,000 of Korea's total population of 28,-000,000 to the southern (American) zone. (By the summer of 1946 this figure was nearing 20,000,000, for practically all of the 1,500,-000 slave-labor repatriates from Japan remained in the South, while thousands escaped each week from the northern [Russian] zone.) Most of Korea's mineral resources, industries, and hydroelectric power—two thirds or more—are located north of the thirty-eighth parallel. While two thirds of the farms and the great rice bowl are in southern Korea, that area's worn-out soil is dependent upon fertilizer, the Korean production of which is concentrated in the north. Korea stands very high among the states of the world in its extensive fisheries, and, as in Japan, fish is second only to rice as the staple food. Since their annexation of Korea in 1910, the Japanese had made every effort to weaken the will of the Koreans to regain their independence. Korean industry was operated by the Japanese, and the country's trade and commerce were controlled in the primary interests of Japanese profits. Japan had imposed a most autocratic rule that permitted no pretense of self-government, and filled with its own nationals practically all except the most subordinate government positions.[2]

At the very end of August, 1945, as its members were preparing to embark for Korea, the military government section of the XXIV Corps did receive copies of Annex 8 to AFPAC's Operations Instruction No. 4 dealing with military government. This was more confusing than helpful, for it placed the XXIV Corps in Korea in the same position as the Sixth and Eighth armies in Japan by instructing them to *"supervise the functioning* of those agencies of the Japanese Imperial Government within the areas of their commands." If AFPAC in Manila (almost exclusively concerned with plans for Japan) did not realize that there would be little if any actual functioning of Japanese government agencies in Korea, the XXIV Corps came to appreciate that fact soon after occupation. Even if the American occu-

[2]The difficulties sketched in the above paragraph with reference to adequate material high light the frequent failure to utilize readily available studies which have application to the particular field of operations. Reference should have been made to A. J. Grajdanzev, *Modern Korea* (1944).

pation forces had been able to keep Japanese administrators in their posts (many of them had absconded with official funds and records), the Korean people would have refused to submit peacefully to their continuance in office after Korea had been supposedly "liberated." Based on the information obtained from the sources discussed, the headquarters staff of the military government group prepared its own Annex 7 (later 8), Military Government, to Field Order No. 45 of the XXIV Corps.

The occupation of Korea south of the thirty-eighth parallel by divisions of the United States Army belonging to the XXIV Corps began on September 8, 1945. Although Korea had not been bombed and had not suffered perceptible war damage, many critical situations called for prompt and wise decisions. The generally tense and uncertain conditions were complicated by the presence of thousands of Japanese soldiers and Korean collaborators, both intensely hated by the majority of Koreans; by the expectation of many Koreans that they would be given independence almost immediately and that all Japanese-held property would be liquidated; by the confused political situation involving dozens of parties with widely conflicting views and a broad split between radical and conservative elements; and by the artificial division of Korea along the thirty-eighth parallel, which forcefully separated the industrial north from the agricultural south and divided the nation between Soviet and American troops. Armed road blocks on the Russian side prevented communication and effectively stopped the free passage of people, goods, and information.

The scarcity of qualified Korean officials or administrators untainted by Japanese collaboration, and the absence of any political party or coalition truly representative of the Korean people, made it necessary to decide whether to continue a Japanese administration or to establish direct American military government. The first alternative would have been strongly resented and resisted by the Koreans. According to a proclamation of General MacArthur dated September 7, 1945, all governmental authority in southern Korea was to be assumed by the United States Army. The commanding general was to retain over-all responsibility for the occupation, but his deputy for military government was appointed the United States military governor for southern Korea.

During the first two weeks the occupation forces were engaged in maintaining law and order, disarming the Japanese troops, and assembling all Japanese nationals preparatory to their repatriation. A SWNCC (State, War, Navy Coordinating Committee) directive, stating the "United States Policy for the Administration of Civil Affairs in Korea," approved by the President, was received. With this clear and complete statement to guide them, the American forces were now ready to work toward their objectives: to separate Korea completely from Japan, and to pave the way for the early establishment of independent Korean governmental, economic, and social institutions. In the accomplishment of this mission the American military government has for the most part received the free support and voluntary cooperation of the majority of the Korean people south of the thirty-eighth parallel.

During the latter part of September, a new military governor was appointed. He immediately assumed a more close direction of military government operations. Military government, with its offices in the beautiful and modern marble capital building at Seoul, was organized to correspond to the existing central government organization in Korea, called the Government General. In other words, the United States military governor acted as governor general of the Korean Government General.

To assist the military governor, a civil administrator coordinated the activities of the secretariat and of the various bureaus with the staff of the military governor. The chart on page 419 gives the eight sections which initially made up the secretariat and names the nine bureaus. It should be noted that the personnel section had to do with the Korean Civil Service. The other titles are self-explanatory.

Although the bureaus were headed by military government officers, they were mainly staffed with Koreans. These bureaus were the operating agencies of the Korean central government. The directors of the bureaus and the civil administrator constituted the cabinet of the governor general. The normal procedure was for matters of policy to be submitted by the various bureaus to the appropriate sections of the secretariat for study before they were placed before the civil administrator for his consideration.

Gradually more and more authority was given the military governor. In all civil affairs matters he was granted a larger degree of discretion, so that he was required to clear fewer types of policy decisions with general staff officers on the headquarters of the XXIV Corps. During the last three months of 1945 several minor changes were made in the make-up of the secretariat and bureaus, but none of noteworthy significance.

Generally speaking, American military government south of the thirty-eighth parallel functioned fairly satisfactorily on the national level and in and around Seoul. The greatest weakness lay in the ineffective direction of civil affairs at provincial and local levels due to the continuance of the tactical unit type of control.

During the first phase of the occupation, military government teams were attached to the tactical troops that entered the three principal cities of Seoul, Fusen, and Jinsen. As more military government teams arrived directly from the United States or were reassigned from Japan, they were deployed throughout southern Korea. Within a month or two each provincial capital had a military group, and the larger cities or counties had military government companies. But they were all attached to, and under the command of, the tactical unit in whose military administrative area they were located. To complicate matters rapid demobilization reduced the number of army divisions in Korea until one combat division might become responsible for several Korean provinces, and yet, in some cases, two divisions might overlap in the same province.

Regardless of this situation, the chief obstacle to the most efficient administration of civil affairs was the requirement that communications from the national government to the military government teams in the provinces go through the tortuous army channels.[3]

By the end of 1945, direct channels were being employed, albeit unofficially, on technical matters, between the military government officials on national and local levels. Although technical matters can be interpreted broadly, this was neither sound practice nor a satisfactory

[3]See the chart on page 419.

solution to the problem. The situation was generally analogous to that in Japan, which has been discussed in more detail in Chapter XVII. In Korea, however, the decision in favor of the obvious solution was not long delayed.

On January 4, 1946, the United States Army Military Government in Korea (USAMGIK) was established by General Order No. 1, USAFIK (United States Army Forces in Korea). On January 14 the control over all military government units passed from the tactical troop commanders to USAMGIK. This immediately increased the authority and enlarged the position of military government in Korea and, at the same time, provided for much closer coordination. It established military government on a territorial basis consonant with the political and administrative subdivisions of the occupied area. The shortened channels of communication between national and local governmental levels furnished highly desirable and more direct control over all phases in the administration of civil affairs.[4]

The reduced and weakened combat troops could now concentrate on their primary duty, training for battle. The tactical unit commanders were relieved of their previous responsibilities over nonmilitary activities, and the administration of civil affairs was placed squarely in the hands of the trained military government officials where it had always belonged. Instead of being held accountable for nonmilitary activities, the tactical commanders were charged with assisting the military government units in accomplishing the mission of the occupation forces.

In keeping with the above fundamental change, a provincial affairs section of the secretariat was established in January to improve the coordination of local government matters handled on the national level. This section was charged with the review of provincial budgets, the examination of local ordinances, and the supervision of local elections.

During the remainder of the first quarter of 1946 the further changes in the organization of military government in Korea were minor in character, but there was a vast improvement in sound ad-

[4] See the chart on page 420. Compare also the general discussion of this problem in Chapter III, pages 61–65.

ministrative functioning. The Provost Marshal General was appointed military governor of Korea.

In April, 1946, a reorganization of USAMGIK took place. All bureaus were renamed departments, sections of the secretariat were redesignated as offices, and the officials in charge were titled directors. These were changes in nomenclature, but some sought to use the fast-dwindling military personnel more efficiently and to extend greater responsibilities to the Korean officials. To achieve this, the Office of General Affairs was abolished, its Administrative Division was transferred to the new Office of Administration, which also took over the Office of Accounts, and its Legal Division was transferred to the Department of Justice. The Police Bureau was withdrawn from the National Defense Department and made a separate department. The Provincial Affairs Office was dissolved and its activities were taken over by the various offices or departments on a functional basis. Finally, all the offices and agencies responsible for "housekeeping" and military government personnel were organized separately under a chief of staff. These changes are shown in the chart on page 420. They represent, if not the last, the latest organization of United States Army Military Government in Korea.

In conclusion, we may ask why, with no advance training and planning for Korea, and with occupation problems often more difficult to handle than those of other occupied Pacific areas, such a sound and efficiently functioning military government organization evolved. One of the primary reasons, certainly, was the placement of the administration of civil affairs squarely in the hands of trained military government officials. To be sure, these officers had not been trained for Korea, but they had been trained in fundamentals of occupation policies and techniques. Placing civil affairs responsibility in the hands of military government officers was accomplished first by the appointment of a single military governor; second, by granting the military governor more and more responsibility over all civil affairs matters; and third, by the establishment of USAMGIK with direct control of the local military government personnel and operations by the military governor. A comparison of military government operations in Japan with those in Korea may seem to indicate that direct military government is easier to establish and administer than indirect control. This, however, is only a conjecture. More time and a greater perspective are required in order to know the answer.

Part II

FIELD EXPERIENCE IN MILITARY GOVERNMENT: CHOLLA NAMDO PROVINCE, 1945–1946

DONALD S. MCDONALD

American Military Government of Korea is of very special interest at the provincial and local levels, for it is here that Americans have had direct charge of detailed government operation and have dealt constantly and closely with the native population. Events in Cholla Namdo, southwest province of Korea, from VJ day to the observance of its first anniversary, provide a useful sample of the military government procedures followed, the progress made, and the reactions of the Korean people.

Cholla Namdo is mainly an agricultural province, producing a large food surplus. Its 3,000,000 people live in a country of hills interspersed with small valleys where rice grows in summer and barley in winter. There are textile mills at Kwangju, capital of the province; chemical and other industries are at Mokp'o, an important Yellow Sea port. Both cities are of 100,000 population, and represent the principal urban portion of the province's inhabitants, though there are several large towns.

Under a comparatively enlightened Japanese regime, the province had a governmental structure consisting of a provincial headquarters, twenty-two counties, and the two cities. Bureaus of Home Affairs, Agriculture and Commerce, Mining and Industry, Finance, and Police were each headed by a chief who reported to the provincial governor. City mayors and county chiefs reported to the Home Affairs Bureau, which was responsible for supervising local government and for controlling all government expenditures and property. There were twenty-two police districts, coextensive with counties, each under a district chief independent of county government, who reported to his provincial chief. Various agencies of the national government maintained offices in Kwangju; courts and prisons were national agencies independent of the provincial government. There were some complicated quasi-governmental associations for savings and loans, irrigation of rice fields, and so on. A provincial council existed, appointed from the local population to advise the governor, but its never very extensive functions had been largely curtailed during the war.

The Coming of Allied Troops

On August 15, 1945, the Korean people heard that their masters of thirty-five years had been defeated. Mindful of the Cairo Declaration that Korea would in due course become free and independent and realizing that peace and order must be maintained until Allied armies arrived, a group of thoughtful Korean citizens organized a "Committee of Preparation for Korean Independence" at Seoul and in each of the provinces. Originally this committee (known as the "People's Committee" was set up to prevent disorder and to supplement the remaining Japanese government, whose authority and prestige counted for little. In Cholla Namdo especially, a more radical group in the committee wished to take over the government by whatever means necessary and present the entering Allied armies with a *fait accompli* upon their arrival, hoping for official sanction and continuation in power. This radical group had far more capable organizers and rabble rousers than the idealistic but inexperienced intellectuals, aristocrats, and professional men in the original committee. American forces on their arrival found the committee, now calling itself the People's Republic, operating a *de facto* government of Cholla Namdo. It was supported by contributions of the citizenry—voluntary or otherwise—and reinforced with vigilantes and Youth Corpsmen (called "white-shirts" because of their uniforms made of expropriated unbleached cotton). The white-shirt chief in Kwangju even had a goon squad and trigger men in the best Chicago tradition. Japanese officials and their Korean underlings huddled in government buildings or in their own homes, afraid for their lives. The *de facto* government nevertheless maintained some degree of peace and quiet and property protection for the two months before military government arrived.

First Allied forces in Cholla Namdo were tactical troops of the 40th and 6th Divisions, fresh from combat in the Pacific, who arrived in late September. They made no attempt to meddle with civil government so long as there was no outward evidence of disease or unrest. Military police patrols were set up in Kwangju and Mokp'o. Officers in charge of MP's also supervised operations of official police, white-shirts, or both, according to local circumstances. Roving MP patrols covered all towns of the province accessible by road.

On October 23, 1945, the first military government units[5] arrived (via Korean railroad) to take over the government of Cholla Namdo. They were about as well equipped for the job as Washington's Continentals at Valley Forge. Officers had been trained for months in Japanese language and government, but knew absolutely nothing of Korea. Enlisted men had little training or experience of any sort. There were no interpreters. Except for the enlisted men's duffel bags and officers' haversacks, the units had no equipment—no cooking utensils, no stoves, no blankets, no typewriters or paper. (What government can be run without typewriters or paper—especially carbon paper?) Tactical forces provided food, quarters in schools and Japanese geisha houses, and bedding of one sort or another. During the first hours, crowds of people gathered around to watch every move—there was considerable enthusiasm, in those days, at the Americans' arrival.

The 6th Division, Military Government Section, had worked out the disposition of military government units. The group headquarters and 33d Company were jointly to operate provincial government headquarters, the group commander being designated provincial military governor. The twenty-two counties and two cities were

[5] The Headquarters and Headquarters Detachment, 101st Military Government Group, and 53d, 55th, 61st, and 69th Military Government Companies. The 33d Military Government Company, formed in the Philippines from experienced Philippine Civil Affairs personnel, had arrived the day before via train with most of its organic vehicles and equipment and two Nisei interpreters. The 45th Military Government Company arrived a month later; the 59th Military Government Company reached Cheju-Do, an island of 250,000 souls off the south coast of Cholla Namdo, in November.

grouped into four areas[6] and one of the military government companies was placed in charge of each, with headquarters at the most important city or town of its area.

The Problems of Military Government

The group headquarters began its operations with a general conference in the Japanese provincial governor's office. All Japanese (or Korean) bureau and section heads were introduced to all officers of the group headquarters; following the initial meeting, each military government officer started conferences of his own with his Japanese "opposite number." There was some confusion in pairing off, for the Group Table of Organization was totally unrelated to Korean government structure. No interpreters (except the 33d Company's two Nisei) were available at first, and junior officers who had taken their language study seriously were used as ineffective substitutes. Eventually some English-speaking people were produced by the Japanese from their own community, and things went a little better. Even when interpreters were found, however, progress was very slow, particularly until the various participants in the conference grew accustomed to one another's manner of speech. Technical terms were always a stumbling block.

Within a few days, the Japanese governor, vice-governor, and bureau chiefs were removed, and Americans installed in their places, directly in the government hierarchy. In two weeks, all Japanese officials—including those in local government—were removed, and the senior Korean government employee in each office was temporarily appointed to replace his Japanese superior. A few Japanese were retained in an advisory capacity for a matter of days or even months, according to the amount of technical detail they possessed. Except for certain technical personnel and hardship cases, all Japanese were on their way to their devastated homeland by December. Many did not want to leave. At a meeting of all Japanese police headquarters personnel, when the public safety officer told them they were relieved of

[6]Later six areas, after the arrival of 45th and 59th Military Government Companies in November.

duty, several of them shed unashamed tears—Oriental reserve not-withstanding—to hear pronouncement of this end to long careers.

After removal of the Japanese, control of the People's Republic became the most pressing problem. For the first weeks the *de facto* government continued without much interference while military government personnel studied and organized the governmental structure. But it soon became evident that a choice had to be made: either the whole provincial government had to be turned over to the Republic, or its control had to be broken. The conclusion finally reached was to use the Japanese framework of government and incumbent lesser officials as a basis, and to staff it with Korean key officials as rapidly as suitable leaders could be found. The People's Republic lost out as a group because, in spite of its good work, it had much too strong a gangster element, and there was grave doubt as to whether, deprived of its economic hold and its strong-arm men, it could command support of a popular majority. Accordingly, the white-shirt leader in Kwangju was turned down as provincial police chief—a post he coveted. The white-shirts were ordered to disband; and the Provincial Committee of the People's Republic was reduced to the status of a political party. The Republic's supporters were keenly disappointed at this turn of events, and the *de facto* government did not die easily. Posters appeared condemning and threatening Koreans who served the military government. Republic sympathizers subtly resisted military government efforts at organization. Some of the leaders, who attempted to continue Republic control while paying lip service to military government, were finally tried by provost court and sent to prison. While this expedient was necessary, the court proceedings often were mere travesties of the much-vaunted Anglo-Saxon principles of justice, and caused considerable disappointment and distress among Koreans. The white-shirts in Kwangju continued to parade around for a time; the provincial military governor enlisted their services to clean up the front yard of the capitol building, and that expedient effectively and permanently dissolved the organization.

Organization of the provincial government into an effective mechanism was the next job tackled, beginning with headquarters at

Kwangju. Some semblance of order had to be produced out of the immense confusion resulting from the removal of the Japanese. Each American bureau chief was allowed some freedom, and he exchanged views with the rest of the staff at brief daily meetings held at the beginning of the working day.

When bureaus had been organized and were functioning, changes in the Japanese pattern were made better to meet local conditions and to parallel as closely as possible the national government structure. Police organization was radically altered so as to be more democratic. A new Bureau of Public Health and Welfare was organized, as had been done at the national level, to put more emphasis on these activities (which had been handled by the police before). A Transportation Section was established in the Home Affairs Bureau to operate provincially owned vehicles and to supervise public carriers. Education, a Home Affairs function under the Japanese, was scheduled for elevation to a separate bureau. Other miscellaneous shifts, expansions, and consolidations were accomplished from time to time.

Early in the course of government reorganization, a Korean counterpart was appointed for each American in the provincial government. From then on the American and Korean occupied the position together, each consulting the other on all matters of major policy. While the American remained the final authority, each Korean counterpart was given more and more responsibility and latitude for decision. Eventually, as the Koreans took the main work load, it became possible to reduce the number of Americans.

Reorganization of Local Government

While the group headquarters and 33d Company were organizing provincial government, the companies in the field were reorganizing local government. For the first two months these groups were on their own. In nearly every county, a People's Republic group was in control when military government arrived on the scene, and the official government was either absent or in a state of utter confusion. In the majority of cases, local People's Republic groups were temporarily appointed to government posts and given a chance at administration.

Usually they failed. Partly the failure was for internal reasons: their police were incompetent and venal, their head officials were too anxious to take care of themselves and their friends; their political opposition was dealt with in much too high-handed a fashion. But local Republic groups were handicapped, for county government did not have the benefit of close American support and supervision except in places where the companies had their headquarters, and Republic personnel got less than no cooperation from the conservative Korean group at provincial headquarters.

In one urban area, the People's Republic ran the government for some time with full military government cooperation, but the senior military government officer there decided in January of 1946 to put an end to their regime, which he believed on the basis of CIC and other intelligence reports was getting out of hand. As a result of simultaneous raids made at several places suspected of illegal activity and illicit financial dealings with government officials, military government officers and enlisted men and Korean police, organized into raiding parties, arrested a total of forty-six people. Those arrested were not sure of the charges against them, and the raiding parties were not always sure of the identity of the persons apprehended—some turned out to be innocent bystanders. Most serious evidence picked up was an unworkable Japanese machine gun. The men arrested were tried by military provost court; their conviction was a certainty in advance, regardless of the evidence introduced. This incident left a bad taste in Korean mouths.

American personnel had two kinds of problems to overcome in organizing the province: they had to fight continually against their own internal inefficiency and inadequacy; and they were faced with a civilian group, disorganized, inexperienced in government, and speaking a different language.

Additional Problems to Be Met

Basic military government organization was poor. The positions on the table of organization of a group headquarters bore little relation to the provincial government organization; moreover, the headquarters strength of fourteen officers and twenty-six enlisted men was very inadequate—especially since the unit was usually much under-manned. The use of the 33d Company to supplement the group head-quarters was a good stopgap measure but created numerous problems of internal administration. Grouping of cities and counties into ar-tificial areas in order to apportion them among military government companies created great confusion, because civilian officials at pro-vincial headquarters communicated directly with city and county of-ficials, while military channels from Kwangju ran through an addi-tional echelon—the military government company headquarters. As a result channels were short-circuited, conflicting orders were issued, and much confusion and official unhappiness ensued.

Lack of communication, transportation, and supply added to the problem. The 69th Company, for example, had its headquarters 65 miles from the provincial capital, and supervised five counties, aggre-gating around 500,000 people; one county seat was 60 miles from com-pany headquarters. To cover this area the company had five jeeps and four trucks. Civilian transportation and communication facilities were of little value; military telephone was uncertain. During the first months particularly, supplies for all military government units were impossible to obtain through official channels and difficult through unofficial ones.

One problem serious in other areas—cooperation with tactical troops —was nonexistent in Cholla Namdo, where relations were unfailingly excellent. In the early stage, the group headquarters and each of the companies were attached directly to the 6th Division for supply and administration. For a time the colonel who commanded the 20th Regiment—tactical unit in the province—held nightly meetings of all key military government officers, at which the problems of the day were discussed. Very wisely, the colonel let the provincial military governor and his staff do the actual work; the meetings were mainly for information and coordination.

The ever-present language barrier slowed up work even with the best interpreters, prevented the sort of personal contact needed for proper personnel evaluation, and placed military government officials at the mercy of the native interpreters—some of whom charged fees

on the side for allowing Koreans to speak to Americans and mis-
translated to favor themselves or their political or social ideas. Moreover, interpreters were perpetually in short supply, and few of them
were really fluent in both languages. Military government was termed
by one Korean as "government of, for, and by interpreters."

It was very difficult to find, among a people who had not governed
themselves for thirty-five years, men who had at once honesty, executive ability, and willingness to serve military government. Early selections were made on the advice of CIC agents, recognized community
leaders, the Catholic priest (who had spent the war in Korean prisons,
and was loved and respected by Koreans and Americans alike),
Japanese officials, and those Koreans already chosen for government
service. Later, after the Advisory Council had been set up, it passed
on military government selections and in some cases suggested candidates. Eventually the Korean officials selected their own personnel,
subject to military government approval.

American unfamiliarity with the mechanics of Korean government
added to the confusion. As late as July of 1946, an American officer
prepared an elaborate directive setting up a provincial gazette for
publishing ordinances and regulations, only to discover that the
Japanese had issued a directive almost exactly similar to it in 1911,
which the Koreans were following.

The dead hand of Japanese ideology lay heavily upon Korean officials' thought processes—particularly on men who had served under
the Japanese. Police, for example, continued for many months a
watered-down version of the secret "thought police," which under the
Japanese had sent thousands to jail for their political beliefs or for
criticism of the government. Their activities in the first months of
occupation were actually responsible for much of the undue repression and persecution of left-wing groups—in some cases by torture—
which went on without the knowledge of Americans struggling for
impartiality. There was also the feeling of most government officials
that they were absolute rulers of the people, rather than public
servants. This sort of thing constantly had to be guarded against:
democracy cannot flower in such soil.

However carefully chosen, and however hard working and well

intentioned, Korean officials rarely displayed initiative in organizing or administering their departments. This was particularly true of those who had served under the Japanese. Like bureaucratic underlings the world over, they had been following orders from on high and making reports in quintuplicate for so long that they were lost without their traditional routine. They wanted specific directives for everything, and spent much valuable time splitting minute procedural and jurisdictional hairs, rather than driving toward accomplishment of the tasks before them.

By December, 1945, an advisory council at the provincial level was functioning. Its members were partly appointed by the national government and partly elected from the counties. A sort of initial experiment in democracy, the council was useful as a sounding board for public opinion, and had some value in the selection of key personnel, though it had few original ideas to offer. Initially the council's prestige was carefully bolstered by the Americans, who referred key personnel appointments and some policy matters to it for recommendation. But when the council developed the annoying habit of opposing everything the military government offered for approval, it had to be soft-pedaled and in some cases by-passed—an outcome to be expected when a quasi-democratic body and an authoritarian regime (as both Japanese and American governments were) tried to operate together. The council never wholly disappeared, but its importance and prestige dwindled. Councils at lower echelons were often more successful, and in some cases a working basis for cooperation between military government and the local council was reached and maintained.

Most controversial of all military government activities was its handling of enemy property. Much of the wealth of Korea—art treasures, bank deposits, automobiles, villas, houses by the thousand, immense farmland and forest holdings, factories, stores, army matériel—belonged to Japanese individuals or corporations or to the Japanese government. All such property was frozen when military government first arrived in Korea. Alien property custodians were designated in all military government companies and group headquarters to collect and catalogue alien property, store it, and issue movable items to American military units, Korean government agencies, and welfare agencies. Authorized sales were handled by a government corporation. Real estate (except farmland) was turned over to American military units for billeting, or leased to Koreans on a short-term basis. A government corporation administered from Seoul was placed in charge of Japanese farmland. Tenants continued to work such land in the same way as under the Japanese, rent being collected in grain, which was distributed in food-shortage areas. About the beginning of 1946, title to all Japanese property was vested in the United States government. This announcement caused much clamor from the public, which was hoping for land reform and the distribution of large estates to the tenants. Up to September, 1946, only movable property and certain types of industrial properties had been authorized for sale. Nothing had been done about land distribution, and the United States itself had more tenants than any other landlord in Korea.

Alien property custodians usually did the best they could with a very difficult job. The property was hard to locate, and sometimes had to be forcibly taken from Koreans who had filed "moonlight requisitions" for it. The records were in a foreign language. Warehousing, leasing, and issue necessarily were handled largely by Koreans, who were often tempted by the sight of plenty in the midst of famine. In a few instances, property custodians kept choice items for themselves, or, when it came to distributing home leases and other desirable property items, favored Korean friends who furnished company and entertainment. A very few such cases were enough to cause public resentment.

On January 14, 1946, a reorganization of military government placed all military government units in a single command grouping —United States Military Government in Korea—commanded by the military governor of Korea. The tactical divisions no longer had military government jurisdiction. The new setup was much more logical from an organizational standpoint: military channels now paralleled civilian ones, and the group headquarters was given full command and administrative jurisdiction over all military government units in the province. But USAMGIK was a mixed blessing in that it brought centralization of governmental functions. No longer could the provincial teams consider themselves the authority on provincial affairs; more and more the major decisions came down from Seoul, and the provincial military governor and his staff became field representatives of the national government.

The most drastic centralization was in the police force. The provincial police chief was made responsible, not to the provincial governor, but to his department chief at Seoul; all police in the country were integrated into a single machine, equipped with United States Army vehicles, Japanese Army rifles, bayonets, and machine guns, and their own private telephone and radio network—potentially a grave threat to a Korean democracy yet unborn.

Other Occupation Controls

After the first few weeks of occupation, commerce and trade were handled on a national basis; hence the subject is beyond the scope of this discussion. A brief summary, however, will round out the picture of the provincial situation. In the beginning, all Japanese market restrictions were lifted and a wholly free market was proclaimed. A government corporation bought and sold rice at fixed prices, but sale of rice to the corporation was not mandatory. The free market continued through most of the winter. Owing to the shortage of all consumer goods and to the hoarding of food stocks to sell at higher prices, it became apparent that the economy would soon break down. Controls were therefore reimposed; price ceilings and rationing programs were set up, and restrictions and priorities established on critical items such as coal, petroleum, lumber, and textiles. After controls were reimposed, an enormous black market was established. The only really successful solution to the problem, short of dictatorial government control and drastic policing, will be rehabilitation and expansion of indigenous consumer goods' industries and resumption of foreign trade so that the law of supply and demand can make a free economy successful.

Toward the end of the first year of American administration, the government of the country and province had become reasonably well organized, and was functioning largely by Korean direction, with less and less American interference. As a measure of this trend, three military government companies in Cholla Namdo had been de-activated and a fourth reduced to a skeleton force by September, 1946. Yet tension existed under a calm surface, evidenced by rumors, police reports, and occasional small-scale violence. The storm broke in Cholla Namdo on August 15—anniversary of VJ day and of so-called Korean liberation. Police gathered positive evidence of a planned and organized leftist[7] offensive against the government that was to begin with attacks against small police stations, work up to bigger ones, and thence move against the government itself. This particular offensive did not occur as scheduled because of preventive measures taken; but as a result of riots at several places two persons were killed and several badly injured. A force of one thousand miners from the near-by Hwasun coal mine marched to Kwangju to stage a parade, having refused to join the official celebration; they attempted to force their way through police and United States Army roadblocks, using locked-arm tactics and other maneuvers apparently well rehearsed. A small group did get through; with some of their comrades in Kwangju they double-timed in step through the city streets, shouting as they ran, and tried to break up the official parade as it passed the reviewing stand. A number of leaders were arrested and given prompt provost court trials at which several men were acquitted. On this occasion, the police were enthusiastic in subduing the leftists but on August 29, members of a rightist political group staged a similar, though much smaller, demonstration. It was equally illegal; yet the police merely stood by watching the fun until American officers forced them to break up the affair and arrest the leaders.

The contrast in attitude on the part of the police is an illustration of the official Korean partiality, which is one cause of public discontent. Other causes are dissatisfaction with the sorry economic condition of the country, resulting from extreme scarcity of basic consumers' goods and poor distribution; enforced government collection of barley (which the Japanese never collected); discontent over the

[7]By *leftists* are meant the political groups who stand for land reform, elimination of Korean government officials formerly associated with the Japanese, and more or less outspoken opposition to military government.

American land policy, or lack of it; and leftist agitation, spearheaded by competent rabble rousers who find ready ears among the poor and uneducated tenant farmers and unemployed. Another contributing factor is the fact that many trained and experienced military government officers are going home when they are still needed and are to be replaced by men who have not had their training or background.

Conclusion

Notwithstanding its difficulties, frictions, and disappointments, military government in Cholla Namdo made much progress in the first year. The native government became well organized and capable of functioning without American interference, at least on routine matters. Supervisory officials were growing more competent at administration. The government attitude—and that of the police, which was more important—was visibly more democratic, and police third-degree techniques had been largely eliminated. The schools were opened, minus the Japanese language and "morality" courses. Cities were cleaned up and epidemics controlled. Medicines and vaccines were distributed. Roads were repaired; transportation and communications were largely restored; beginnings were made at restoration of normal commerce and trade. Although food distribution was inefficient and inequitable, starvation was avoided.

Should such an occupation of a foreign country again become necessary, American experience in Korea indicates that the following steps taken in advance of the occupation would contribute immensely to its success: 1) preparation of unit tables of organization related to the government structure of the country to be occupied; 2) selection of both officers and enlisted personnel on the basis of their personality, beliefs in democratic government, and personal integrity, as well as training and experience; 3) thorough training of personnel on the area to be occupied and its people; 4) language training and provision of a sufficient number of good interpreters; 5) provision of adequate initial supply, especially vehicles, radios and telephones, and office equipment; 6) a military government chain of command paralleling that of civilian government.

Appendices

Appendix A

JCS 1067[1]

OCCUPATION
GERMANY
DIRECTIVE TO COMMANDER IN CHIEF OF
UNITED STATES FORCES OF OCCUPATION
REGARDING THE MILITARY GOVERNMENT
OF GERMANY

April 1945

(Released October 17, 1945)

It is considered appropriate, at the time of the release to the American public of the following directive setting forth United States policy with reference to the military government of Germany, to preface the directive with a short statement of the circumstances surrounding the issuance of the directive to General Eisenhower.

The directive was issued originally in April 1945, and was intended to serve two purposes. It was to guide General Eisenhower in the military government of that portion of Germany occupied by United States forces. At the same time he was directed to urge the Control Council to adopt these policies for enforcement throughout Germany.

Before this directive was discussed in the Control Council, President Truman, Prime Minister Attlee, and Generalissimo Stalin met at Potsdam and issued a communiqué setting forth agreed policies for the control of Germany. This communiqué was made public on August 2, 1945. The directive, therefore, should be read in the light of the policies enumerated at Potsdam. In particular, its provisions regarding disarmament, economic and financial matters, and reparations should be read together with the similar provisions set out in the Potsdam agreement on the treatment of

---

[1]Reprinted from *The Axis in Defeat*. Department of State Publication 2423.

Germany in the initial control period and in the agreement on reparations contained in the Potsdam communiqué. Many of the policy statements contained in the directive have been in substance adopted by the Potsdam agreement. Some policy statements in the Potsdam agreement differ from the policy statements on the same subjects in the directive. In such cases, the policies of the Potsdam agreement are controlling. Where the Potsdam agreement is silent on matters of policy dealt with in the directive, the latter continues to guide General Eisenhower in his administration of the United States Zone in Germany.

DIRECTIVE TO COMMANDER IN CHIEF OF UNITED
STATES FORCES OF OCCUPATION REGARDING THE
MILITARY GOVERNMENT OF GERMANY

1. *The Purpose and Scope of This Directive:*

This directive is issued to you as Commanding General of the United States forces of occupation in Germany. As such you will serve as United States member of the Control Council and will also be responsible for the administration of military government in the zone or zones assigned to the United States for purposes of occupation and administration. It outlines the basic policies which will guide you in those two capacities after the termination of the combined command of the Supreme Commander, Allied Expeditionary Force.

This directive sets forth policies relating to Germany in the initial postdefeat period. As such it is not intended to be an ultimate statement of policies of this Government concerning the treatment of Germany in the post-war world. It is therefore essential that, during the period covered by this directive, you assure that surveys are constantly maintained of economic, industrial, financial and social conditions within your zone and that the results of such surveys and such other surveys as may be made in other zones are made available to your Government, through the Joint Chiefs of Staff. These surveys should be developed in such manner as to serve as a basis for determining changes in the measures of control set forth herein as well as for the progressive formulation and development of policies to promote the basic objectives of the United States. Supplemental directives will be issued to you by the Joint Chiefs of Staff as may be required.

As a member of the Control Council you will urge the adoption by the other occupying powers of the principles and policies set forth in this directive and, pending Control Council agreement, you will follow them in your zone. It is anticipated that substantially similar directives will be issued to the Commanders in Chief of the U.K., U.S.S.R. and French forces of occupation.

PART I

General and Political

2. *The Basis of Military Government:*

a. The rights, power and status of the military government in Germany are based upon the unconditional surrender or total defeat of Germany.

b. Subject to the provisions of paragraph 3 below, you are, by virtue of your position, clothed with supreme legislative, executive, and judicial authority in the areas occupied by forces under your command. This authority will be broadly construed and includes authority to take all measures deemed by you necessary, appropriate or desirable in relation to military exigencies and the objectives of a firm military government.

c. You will issue a proclamation continuing in force such proclamations, orders and instructions as may have heretofore been issued by Allied Commanders in your zone, subject to such changes as you may determine. Authorizations of action by the Supreme Commander, Allied Expeditionary Force, may be considered as applicable to you unless inconsistent with this or later directives.

3. *The Control Council and Zones of Occupation:*

a. The four Commanders-in-Chief, acting jointly, will constitute the Control Council in Germany which will be the supreme organ of control over Germany in accordance with the agreement of Control Machinery in Germany. For purposes of administration of military government, Germany has been divided into four zones of occupation.

b. The authority of the Control Council to formulate policy and procedures and administrative relationships with respect to matters affecting Germany as a whole will be paramount throughout Germany. You will carry out and support in your zone the policies agreed upon in the Control Council. In the absence of such agreed policies you will act in accordance with this and other directives of the Joint Chiefs of Staff.

c. The administration of affairs in Germany shall be directed towards the decentralization of the political and administrative structure and the development of local responsibility. To this end you will encourage autonomy in regional, local and municipal agencies of German administration. The German economic structure shall also be decentralized. The Control Council may, however, to the minimum extent required for the fulfillment of purposes set forth herein, permit centralized administration or establish central control of (a) essential national public services such as railroads, communications and power, (b) finance and foreign affairs, and (c) production and distribution of essential commodities.

d. The Control Council should adopt procedures to effectuate, and you will facilitate in your zone, the equitable distribution of essential commodities between the zones. In the absence of a conflicting policy of the Control Council, you may deal directly with one or more zone commanders on matters of special concern to such zones.

e. Pending the formulation in the Control Council of uniform policies and procedures with respect to interzonal travel and movement of civilians, no civilians shall be permitted to leave or enter your zone without your authority, and no Germans within your zone shall be permitted to leave Germany except for specific purposes approved by you.

f. The military government personnel in each zone, including those dealing with regional and local branches of the departments of any central German administrative machinery, shall be selected by authority of the Commander of that zone except that liaison officers may be furnished by the Commanders of the other three zones. The respective Commanders-in-Chief shall have exclusive jurisdiction throughout the whole of Germany over the members of the armed forces under their command and over the civilians who accompany them.

g. The Control Council should be responsible for facilitating the severance of all governmental and administrative connections between Austria and Germany and the elimination of German economic influences in Austria in its efforts to effectuate these purposes.

4. *Basic Objectives of Military Government in Germany:*

a. It should be brought home to the Germans that Germany's ruthless warfare and the fanatical Nazi resistance have destroyed the German economy and made chaos and suffering inevitable and that the Germans cannot escape responsibility for what they have brought upon themselves.

b. Germany will not be occupied for the purpose of liberation but as a defeated enemy nation. Your aim is not oppression but to occupy Germany for the purpose of realizing certain important Allied objectives. In the conduct of your occupation and administration you should be just but firm and aloof. You will strongly discourage fraternization with the German officials and population.

c. The principal Allied objective is to prevent Germany from ever again becoming a threat to the peace of the world. Essential steps in the accomplishment of this objective are the elimination of Nazism and militarism in all their forms, the immediate apprehension of war criminals for punishment, the industrial disarmament and demilitarization of Germany, with continuing control over Germany's capacity to make war, and the preparation for an eventual reconstruction of German political life on a democratic basis.

d. Other Allied objectives are to enforce the program of reparations and restitution, to provide relief for the benefit of countries devastated by Nazi aggression, and to ensure that prisoners of war and displaced persons of the United Nations are cared for and repatriated.

5. *Economic Controls:*

a. As a member of the Control Council and as zone commander, you will be guided by the principle that controls upon the German economy may be imposed to the extent that such controls may be necessary to achieve the objectives enumerated in paragraph 4 above and also as they may be essential to protect the safety and meet the needs of the occupying forces and assure the production and maintenance of goods and services required to prevent starvation or such diseases and unrest as would endanger these forces. No action will be taken in execution of the reparations program or otherwise which would tend to support basic living conditions in Germany or in your zone on a higher level than that existing in any one of the neighboring United Nations.

b. In the imposition and maintenance of such controls as may be prescribed by you or the Control Council, German authorities will to the fullest extent practicable be ordered to proclaim and assume administration of such controls. Thus it should be brought home to the German people that the responsibility for the administration of such controls and for any break-downs in those controls will rest with themselves and German authorities.

6. *Denazification:*

a. A Proclamation dissolving the Nazi Party, its formations, affiliated associations and supervised organizations, and all Nazi public institutions which were set up as instruments of Party domination, and prohibiting their revival in any form, should be promulgated by the Control Council. You will assure the prompt effectuation of that policy in your zone and will make every effort to prevent the reconstitution of any such organization in underground, disguised or secret form. Responsibility for continuing desirable non-political social services of dissolved Party organizations may be transferred by the Control Council to appropriate central agencies and by you to appropriate local agencies.

b. The laws purporting to establish the political structure of National Socialism and the basis of the Hitler regime and all laws, decrees and regulations which establish discriminations on grounds of race, nationality, creed or political opinions should be abrogated by the Control Council. You will render them inoperative in your zone.

c. All members of the Nazi party who have been more than nominal participants in its activities, all active supporters of Nazism or militarism and all other persons hostile to Allied purposes will be removed and excluded from public office and from positions of importance in quasi-public and private enterprises such as (1) civic, economic and labor organization, (2) corporations and other organizations in which the German government or subdivisions have a major financial interest, (3) industry, commerce, agriculture, and finance, (4) education, and (5) the press, publishing houses and other agencies disseminating news and propaganda. Persons are to be treated as more than nominal participants in Party activities and as active supporters of Nazism or militarism when they have (1) held office or otherwise been active at any level from local to national in the party and its subordinate organizations, or in organizations which further militaristic doctrines, (2) authorized or participated affirmatively in any Nazi crimes, racial persecutions or discriminations, (3) been avowed believers in Nazism or racial and militaristic creeds, or (4) voluntarily given substantial moral or material support or political assistance of any kind to the Nazi Party or Nazi officials and leaders. No such persons shall be retained in any of the categories of employment listed above because of administrative necessity, convenience or expediency.

d. Property, real and personal, owned or controlled by the Nazi party, its formations, affiliated associations and supervised organizations, and by all persons subject to arrest under the provisions of paragraph 8, and found within your zone, will be taken under your control pending a decision by the Control Council or higher authority as to its eventual disposition.

e. All archives, monuments and museums of Nazi inception, or which are devoted to the perpetuation of German militarism, will be taken under your control and their properties held pending decision as to their disposition by the Control Council.

f. You will make special efforts to preserve from destruction and take under your control records, plans, books, documents, papers, files, and scientific, industrial and other information and data belonging to or controlled by the following:

(1) The Central German Government and its subdivisions, German military organizations, organizations engaged in military research, and such other governmental agencies as may be deemed advisable;

(2) The Nazi Party, its formations, affiliated associations and supervised organizations;

(3) All police organizations, including security and political police;

(4) Important economic organizations and industrial establishments including those controlled by the Nazi Party or its personnel;

(5) Institutes and special bureaus devoting themselves to racial, political, militaristic or similar research or propaganda.

7. *Demilitarization:*

a. In your zone you will assure that all units of the German armed forces, including para-military organizations, are dissolved as such, and that their personnel are promptly disarmed and controlled. Prior to their final disposition, you will arrest and hold all military personnel who are included under the provisions of paragraph 8.

b. The Control Council should proclaim, and in your zone you will effectuate, the total dissolution of all military and para-military orzanizations, including the General Staff, the German Officers Corps, the Reserve Corps and military academies, together with all associations which might serve to keep alive the military tradition in Germany.

c. You will seize or destroy all arms, ammunition and implements of war and stop the production thereof.

d. You will take proper steps to destroy the German war potential as set forth elsewhere in this directive.

8. *Suspected War Criminals and Security Arrests:*

a. You will search out, arrest, and hold, pending receipt by you of further instructions as to their disposition, Adolf Hitler, his chief Nazi associates, other war criminals and all persons who have participated in planning or carrying out Nazi enterprises involving or resulting in atrocities or war crimes.

b. All persons who, if permitted to remain at large, would endanger the accomplishment of your objectives will also be arrested and held in custody until trial by an appropriate semi-judicial body to be established by you. The following is a partial list of the categories of persons to be arrested in order to carry out this policy:

(Note: There follows at this point in the directive a detailed list of categories of Nazi war criminals and others who are to be arrested. Some of these have not yet been found. It is considered that to publish the categories at this time would put the individuals concerned on notice and would interfere with their apprehension and punishment, where appropriate. The list of categories is, therefore, withheld from publication for the present.)

If in the light of conditions which you encounter in Germany, you believe that it is not immediately feasible to subject certain persons within these categories to this treatment, you should report your reasons and recommendations to your government through the Joint Chiefs of Staff. If you believe it desirable, you may postpone the arrest of those whose cases you have reported, pending a decision communicated to you by the J.C.S. In no event shall any differentiation be made between or special consideration be accorded to persons arrested, either as to manner of arrest or conditions of detention, upon the basis of wealth or political, industrial, or other rank or position. In your discretion you may make such exceptions as you deem advisable for intelligence or other military reasons.

9. *Political Activities:*

a. No political activities of any kind shall be countenanced unless authorized by you. You will assure that your military government does not become committed to any political group.

b. You will prohibit the propagation in any form of Nazi, militaristic or Pan-German doctrines.

c. No German parades, military or political, civilian or sports shall be permitted by you.

d. To the extent that military interests are not prejudiced and subject to the provisions of the three preceding subparagraphs and of paragraph 10, freedom of speech, press and religious worship will be permitted. Consistent with military necessity, all religious institutions will be respected.

10. *Public Relations and Control of Public Information:*

As a member of the Control Council, you will endeavor to obtain agreement for uniform or coordinated policies with respect to (a) control of public information media in Germany, (b) accrediting of foreign correspondents, (c) press censorship, and (d) issuance of official news communiqués dealing with Control Council matters. United States policies in these matters will be sent to you separately and you will be guided by these in your negotiations on the Control Council.

11. *German Courts:*

a. All extraordinary courts, including the *Volksgerichtshof* (People's Court) and the *Sondergerichte* (Special Courts), and all courts and tribunals of the Nazi Party and of its formations, affiliated associations and supervised organizations will be abolished immediately.

b. All ordinary criminal, civil and administrative courts, except those previously re-established by order of the military government, will be closed. After the elimination of all Nazi features and personnel you will permit those which are to exercise jurisdiction within the boundaries of your zone to resume operations under such regulations, supervision and control as you may consider appropriate. Courts which are to exercise jurisdiction over territory extending beyond the boundaries of your zone will be reopened only with the express authorization of the Control Council and under its regulation, supervision and control. The power to review and veto decisions of German courts shall be included within the power of supervision and control.

12. *Police:*

With the exception of the *Reichskriminalpolizei* (Criminal Police) all elements of the *Sicherheitspolizei* (Security Police) e.g. *Geheimestaatspolizei* (Gestapo), and the *Sicherheitsdienst der S.S.* will be abolished. Criminal and ordinary police will be purged of Nazi personnel and utilized under the control and supervision of the military government.

13. *Political Prisoners:*

Subject to military security and the interests of the individuals concerned, you will release all persons found within your zone who have been detained or placed in custody on grounds of race, nationality, creed or political opinions and treat them as displaced persons. You should make provision for the review of convictions of alleged criminal offenses about which there may be substantial suspicion of racial, religious or political persecution, and in which sentences of imprisonment have not been fully served by persons imprisoned within your zone.

14. *Education:*

a. All educational institutions within your zone except those previously re-established by Allied authority will be closed. The closure of Nazi educational institutions such as Adolf Hitler Schulen, Napolas and

Ordensburgen, and of Nazi organizations within other educational institutions will be permanent.

b. A coordinated system of control over German education and an affirmative program of reorientation will be established designed completely to eliminate Nazi and militaristic doctrines and to encourage the development of democratic ideas.

c. You will permit the reopening of elementary (*Volksschulen*), middle (*Mittelschulen*) and vocational (*Berufsschulen*) schools at the earliest possible date after Nazi personnel has been eliminated. Text books and curricula which are not free of Nazi and militaristic doctrine shall not be used. The Control Council should devise programs looking toward the reopening of secondary schools, universities and other institutions of higher learning. After Nazi features and personnel have been eliminated and pending the formulation of such programs by the Control Council, you may formulate and put into effect an interim program within your zone and in any case may permit the reopening of such institutions and departments which offer training which you consider immediately essential or useful in the administration of military government and the purposes of the occupation.

d. It is not intended that the military government will intervene in questions concerning denominational control of German schools, or in religious instruction in German schools except insofar as may be necessary to insure that religious instruction and administration of such schools conform to such Allied regulations as are or may be established pertaining to purging of personnel and curricula.

15. *Arts and Archives:*

Subject to the provisions of paragraph 6 above, you will make all reasonable efforts to preserve historical archives, museums, libraries and works of art.

PART II

Economic

General Objectives and Methods of Control

16. You will assure that the German economy is administered and controlled in such a way as to accomplish the basic objectives set forth in paragraphs 4 and 5 of this Directive. Economic controls will be imposed only to the extent necessary to accomplish these objectives, provided that

you will impose controls to the full extent necessary to achieve the industrial disarmament of Germany. Except as may be necessary to carry out these objectives, you will take no steps (a) looking toward the economic rehabilitation of Germany, or (b) designed to maintain or strengthen the German economy.

17. To the maximum extent possible without jeopardizing the successful execution of measures required to implement the objectives outlined in paragraphs 4 and 5 of this directive, you will use German authorities and agencies and subject them to such supervision and punishment for non-compliance as is necessary to ensure that they carry out their tasks.

For this purpose you will give appropriate authority to any German agencies and administrative services you consider essential; provided, however, that you will at all times adhere strictly to the provisions of this directive regarding denazification and dissolution or elimination of Nazi organizations, institutions, principles, features, and practices.

To the extent necessary you will establish administrative machinery, not dependent upon German authorities and agencies, to execute or assure the execution of the provisions of paragraphs 19, 20, 30, 31, 32, 39 and 40 and any other measures necessary to an accomplishment of your industrial disarmament objectives.

18. In order to decentralize the structure and administration of the German economy to the maximum possible extent, you will

a. ensure that the action required to maintain or restore essential public utilities and industrial and agricultural activities is taken as far as possible on a local and regional basis;

b. on no account propose or approve in the Control Council the establishment of centralized administration of controls over the German economy except where such centralization of administration is clearly essential to the fulfilment of the objectives listed in paragraphs 4 and 5 of this directive. Decentralization in administration should not be permitted to interfere with attainment of the largest practicable measure of agreement on economic policies in the Control Council.

19. You will institute or assure the maintenance of such statistical records and reports as may be necessary in carrying out the objectives listed in paragraphs 4 and 5 of this directive.

20. You will initiate appropriate surveys which may assist you in achieving the objectives of the occupation. In particular you will promptly undertake surveys of supplies, equipment and resources in your zone. You will endeavor to obtain prompt agreement in the Control Council to the

making of similar surveys in the other zones of occupation, and you will urge appropriate steps to coordinate the methods and results of these and other future surveys conducted in the various zones. You will keep the Control Council, United States Representative on the Reparation Commission and other appropriate authorities, currently apprised of the information obtained by means of intermediate reports or otherwise.

German Standard of Living

21. You will estimate requirements of supplies necessary to prevent starvation or widespread disease or such civil unrest as would endanger the occupying forces. Such estimates will be based upon a program whereby the Germans are made responsible for providing for themselves, out of their own work and resources. You will take all practicable economic and police measures to assure that German resources are fully utilized and consumption held to the minimum in order that imports may be strictly limited and that surpluses may be made available for the occupying forces and displaced persons and United Nations prisoners of war, and for reparation. You will take no action that would tend to support basic living standards in Germany on a higher level than that existing in any one of the neighboring United Nations and you will take appropriate measures to ensure that basic living standards of the German people are not higher than those existing in any one of the neighboring United Nations when such measures will contribute to raising the standards of any such nation.

22. You will urge upon the Control Council that uniform ration scales be applied throughout Germany, that essential items be distributed equitably among the zones, that net surpluses be made available for export to Allied countries, and that imports be limited to the net deficits of Germany as a whole.

Labor, Health, and Social Insurance

23. You will permit the self-organization of employees along democratic lines, subject to such safeguards as may be necessary to prevent the perpetuation of Nazi or militarist influence under any guise or the continuation of any group hostile to the objectives and operations of the occupying forces.

24. You will permit free collective bargaining between employees and employers regarding wage, hour and working conditions and the establishment of machinery for the settlement of industrial disputes. Collective bargaining shall be subject to such wage, hour and other controls, if any, as may be instituted or revived by your direction.

25. Subject to the provisions of paragraph 48 of this directive you are authorized to direct the German authorities to maintain or re-establish nondiscriminatory systems of social insurance and poor relief.

26. You are authorized to direct the German authorities to maintain or re-establish such health services and facilities as may be available to them.

Agriculture, Industry, and Internal Commerce

27. You will require the Germans to use all means at their disposal to maximize agricultural output and to establish as rapidly as possible effective machinery for the collection and distribution of agricultural output.

28. You will direct the German authorities to utilize large-landed estates and public lands in a manner which will facilitate the accommodation and settlement of Germans and others or increase agricultural output.

29. You will protect from destruction by the Germans, and maintain for such disposition as is determined by this and other directives or by the Control Council, all plants, equipment, patents and other property and all books and records of large German industrial companies and trade and research associations that have been essential to the German war effort or the German economy. You will pay particular attention to research and experimental establishments of such concerns.

30. In order to disarm Germany, the Control Council should

a. prevent the production, acquisition by importation or otherwise, and development of all arms, ammunition and implements of war, as well as all types of aircraft, and all parts, components and ingredients specially designed or produced for incorporation therein;

b. prevent the production of merchant ships, synthetic rubber and oil, aluminum and magnesium and any other products and equipment on which you will subsequently receive instructions;

c. seize and safeguard all facilities used in the production of any of the items mentioned in this paragraph and dispose of them as follows:

(1) remove all those required for reparation;

(2) destroy all those not transferred for reparation if they are especially adapted to the production of the items specified in this paragraph and are not of a type generally used in industries permitted to the Germans (cases of doubt to be resolved in favor of destruction);

(3) hold the balance for disposal in accordance with instructions which will be sent to you.

Pending agreement in the Control Council you will take these measures in your own zone. You will not postpone enforcement of the prohibitions contained in subparagraphs *a* and *b* and the instructions in subparagraph *c* without specific approval of your government through the Joint Chiefs of Staff except that, in your discretion, you may permit the production of synthetic rubber and oil, aluminum and magnesium, to the minimum extent necessary to meet the purposes stated in paragraphs 4 and 5 of the directive pending action by the Joint Chiefs of Staff upon such recommendation for postponement as you may make.

31. As an additional measure of disarmament, the Control Council should

a. prohibit initially all research activities and close all laboratories, research institutions and similar technical organizations except those considered necessary to the protection of public health;

b. abolish all those laboratories and related institutions whose work has been connected with the building of the German war machine, safeguard initially such laboratories and detain such personnel as are of interest to your technological investigations, and thereafter remove or destroy their equipment;

c. permit the resumption of scientific research in specific cases, only after careful investigation has established that the contemplated research will in no way contribute to Germany's future war potential and only under appropriate regulations which (1) define the specific types of research permitted, (2) exclude from further research activity any persons who previously held key positions in German war research, (3) provide for frequent inspection, (4) require free disclosure of the results of the research and (5) impose severe penalties, including permanent closing of the offending institution, whenever the regulations are violated.

Pending agreement in the Control Council you will adopt such measures in your own zone.

32. Pending final Allied agreements on reparations and on control or elimination of German industries that can be utilized for war production, the Control Council should:

a. prohibit and prevent production of iron and steel, chemicals, nonferrous metals (excluding aluminum and magnesium), machine tools, radio and electrical equipment, automotive vehicles, heavy machinery and important parts thereof, except for the purposes stated in paragraphs 4 and 5 of this directive;

b. prohibit and prevent rehabilitation of plant and equipment in such industries except for the purposes stated in paragraphs 4 and 5 of this directive; and

c. safeguard plant and equipment in such industries for transfer on reparation account.

Pending agreement in the Control Council, you will put such measures into effect in your own zone as soon as you have had an opportunity to review and determine production necessary for the purposes stated in paragraphs 4 and 5 of this directive.

33. The Control Council should adopt a policy permitting the conversion of facilities other than those mentioned in paragraphs 30 and 32 to the production of light consumer goods, provided that such conversion does not prejudice the subsequent removal of plant and equipment on reparation account and does not require any imports beyond those necessary for the purposes specified in paragraphs 4 and 5 of this directive. Pending agreement in the Control Council, you may permit such conversion in your zone.

34. Subject to the provisions of paragraphs 30 and 32, the Control Council should assure that all feasible measures are taken to facilitate, to the minimum extent necessary for the purposes outlined in paragraphs 4 and 5 of this directive.

a. repairs to and restoration of essential transportation services and public utilities;

b. emergency repair and construction of the minimum shelter required for the civilian population;

c. production of coal and any other goods and services (excluding goods specified in paragraphs 30 and 32 unless measures to facilitate production are specifically approved by this Government through the Joint Chiefs of Staff) required for the purposes outlined in paragraphs 4 and 5 of this directive.

You will assure that such measures are taken in your own zone pending agreement in the Control Council.

35. In your capacity as zone commander and as a member of the Control Council you will take steps to provide for the equitable interzonal distribution and the movement of goods and services essential to the purposes set forth in paragraphs 4 and 5 of this directive.

36. You will prohibit all cartels or other private business arrangements and cartel-like organizations, including those of a public or quasi-public character such as the *Wirtschaftsgruppen* providing for the regulation of marketing conditions, including production, prices, exclusive ex-

change of technical information and processes, and allocation of sales territories. Such necessary public functions as have been discharged by these organizations shall be absorbed as rapidly as possible by approved public agencies.

37. It is the policy of your government to effect a dispersion of the ownership and control of German industry. To assist in carrying out this policy you will make a survey of combines and pools, mergers, holding companies and interlocking directorates and communicate the results, together with recommendations, to your government through the Joint Chiefs of Staff. You will endeavor to obtain agreement in the Control Council to the making of this survey in the other zones of occupation and you will urge the coordination of the methods and results of this survey in the various zones.

38. With due regard to paragraph 4a, the Control Council should adopt such policies as are clearly necessary to prevent or restrain inflation of a character or dimension which would definitely endanger accomplishment of the objectives of the occupation. The Control Council, in particular, should direct and empower German authorities to maintain or establish controls over prices and wages and to take the fiscal and financial measures necessary to this end. Pending agreement in the Control Council you will assure that such measures as you consider necessary are taken in your own zone. Prevention or restraint of inflation should not constitute an additional ground for the importation of supplies, nor shall it constitute an additional ground for limiting removal, destruction or curtailment of productive facilities in fulfillment of the program for reparation, demilitarization and industrial disarmament.

Power, Transportation, and Communications

39. Both as member of the Control Council and zone commander you will take appropriate steps to ensure that

a. power, transportation and communications facilities are directed in such a way as to carry out the objectives outlined in paragraphs 4 and 5 of this directive;

b. Germans are prohibited and prevented from producing, maintaining or operating all types of aircraft.

You will determine the degree to which centralized control and administration of power, transportation and communications is clearly necessary for the objectives stated in paragraphs 4 and 5 and urge the establishment of this degree of centralized control and administration by the Control Council.

Foreign Trade and Reparation

40. The Control Council should establish centralized control over all trade in goods and services with foreign countries. Pending agreement in the Control Council you will impose appropriate controls in your own zone.

41. Both as member of the Control Council and as zone commander you will take appropriate steps to ensure that

a. the foreign trade controls are designed to carry out the objectives stated in paragraphs 4 and 5 of this directive;

b. imports which are permitted and furnished to Germany are confined to those unavoidably necessary to the objectives stated in paragraphs 4 and 5;

c. exports to countries other than the United Nations are prohibited unless specifically authorized by the Allied governments.

42. Both as member of the Control Council and as zone commander you will adopt a policy which would forbid German firms to participate in international cartels or other restrictive contracts and arrangements and order the prompt termination of all existing German participations in such cartels, contracts and arrangements.

43. You will carry out in your zone such programs of reparation and restitution as are embodied in Allied agreements and you will seek agreement in the Control Council on any policies and measures which it may be necessary to apply throughout Germany in order to ensure the execution of such programs.

PART III

Financial

44. You will make full application in the financial field of the principles stated elsewhere in this directive and you will endeavor to have the Control Council adopt uniform financial policies necessary to carry out the purposes stated in paragraphs 4 and 5 of this directive. You will take no steps designed to maintain, strengthen or operate the German financial structure except in so far as may be necessary for the purposes specified in this directive.

45. The Control Council should regulate and control to the extent required for the purposes set forth in paragraphs 4 and 5 the issue and volume of currency and the extension of credit in Germany and in accordance with the following principles:

a. United States forces and other Allied forces will use Allied Military marks and Reichsmark currency or coins in their possession. Allied Military marks and Reichsmark currency and coin now in circulation in Germany will be legal tender without distinction and will be interchangeable at the rate of 1 Allied Military mark for 1 Reichsmark. Reichskreditkassenscheine and other German military currency will not be legal tender in Germany.

b. The Reichsbank, the Rentenbank or any other bank or agency may be permitted or required to issue bank notes and currency which will be legal tender; without such authorization no German governmental or private bank or agency will be permitted to issue bank notes or currency.

c. The German authorities may be required to make available Reichsmark currency or credits free of cost and in amounts sufficient to meet all the expenses of the forces of occupation, including the cost of Allied Military Government and including to the extent that compensation is made therefor, the cost of such private property as may be requisitioned, seized, or otherwise acquired, by Allied authorities for reparations or restitution purposes.

Pending agreement in the Control Council you will follow these policies in your own zone.

You will receive separate instructions relative to the currency which you will use in the event that for any reason adequate supplies of Allied Military marks and Reichsmarks are not available, or if the use of such currency is found undesirable.

You will not announce or establish in your zone, until receipt of further instructions, any general rate of exchange between the Reichsmark on the one hand and the U.S. dollar and other currencies on the other. However, a rate of exchange to be used exclusively for pay of troops and military accounting purposes in your zone will be communicated separately to you.

46. Subject to any agreed policies of the Control Council, you are authorized to take the following steps and to put into effect such further financial measures as you may deem necessary to accomplish the purposes of your occupation:

a. To prohibit, or to prescribe regulations regarding transfer or other dealings in private or public securities or real estate or other property.

b. To close banks, but only for a period long enough for you to introduce satisfactory control, to remove Nazi and other undesirable personnel, and to issue instructions for the determination of accounts to be blocked under subparagraph 48 e below.

c. To close stock exchanges, insurance companies and similar financial institutions for such periods as you deem appropriate.

d. To establish a general or limited moratorium or moratoria only to the extent clearly necessary to carry out the objectives stated in paragraphs 4 and 5 of this directive.

47. Resumption of partial or complete service on the internal public debt at the earliest feasible date is deemed desirable. The Control Council should decide the time and manner of such resumption.

48. Subject to any agreed policies of the Control Council,

a. You will prohibit:

(1) the payment of all military pensions, or emoluments or benefits except compensation for physical disability limiting the recipient's ability to work, at rates which are no higher than the lowest of those for comparable physical disability arising from non-military causes.

(2) the payment of all public or private pensions or other emoluments or benefits granted or conferred:

(a) By reason of membership in or services to the former Nazi party, its formations, affiliated associations or supervised organizations.

(b) to any person who has been removed from an office or position in accordance with paragraph 6, and

(c) to any person arrested and detained in accordance with paragraph 8 during the term of his arrest, or permanently, in case of his subsequent conviction.

b. You will take such action as may be necessary to ensure that all laws and practices relating to taxation or other fields of finance, which discriminate for or against any persons because of race, nationality, creed or political opinion, will be amended, suspended, or abrogated to the extent necessary to eliminate such discrimination.

c. You will hold the German authorities responsible for taking such measures in the field of taxation and other fields of public finance, including restoration of the tax system and maintenance of tax revenues, as will further the accomplishment of the objectives stated in paragraphs 4 and 5.

d. You will exercise general supervision over German public expenditures in order to ensure that they are consistent with the objectives stated in paragraphs 4 and 5.

e. You will impound or block all gold, silver, currencies, securities, accounts in financial institutions, credits, valuable papers, and all other assets falling within the following categories:

(1) Property owned or controlled directly or indirectly, in whole or in part, by any of the following:

(a) The German Reich, or any of the Länder, Gaue or provinces, any Kreis, Municipality or other similar local subdivision; or any agency or instrumentality of any of them including all utilities, undertakings, public corporations or monopolies under the control of any of the above;

(b) Governments, nationals or residents of other nations, including those of territories occupied by them, at war with any of the United Nations at any time since 1 September, 1939;

(c) The Nazi Party, its formations, affiliated associations and supervised organizations, its officials, leading members and supporters;

(d) All organizations, clubs or other associations prohibited or dissolved by military government;

(e) Absentee owners, of non-German nationality including United Nations and neutral governments and Germans outside Germany;

(f) Any institution dedicated to public worship, charity, education or the arts and sciences which has been used by the Nazi Party to further its interests or to cloak its activities;

(g) Persons subject to arrest under provisions of paragraph 8, and all other persons specified by military government by inclusion in lists or otherwise.

(2) Property which has been the subject of transfer under duress or wrongful acts of confiscation, disposition or spoliation, whether pursuant to legislation or by procedure purporting to follow forms of law or otherwise.

(3) Works of art or cultural material of value or importance, regardless of the ownership thereof.

You will take such action as will insure that any impounded or blocked assets will be dealt with only as permitted under licenses or other instructions which you may issue. In the case particularly of property blocked under (1) (a) above, you will proceed to adopt licensing measures which while maintaining such property under surveillance would permit its use in consonance with this directive. In the case of property blocked under (2) above, you will institute measures for prompt restitution, in conformity with the objectives stated in paragraphs 4 and 5 and subject to appropriate safeguards to prevent the cloaking of Nazi and militaristic influence.

49. All foreign exchange transactions, including those arising out of exports and imports, shall be controlled with the aim of preventing Germany from developing a war potential and of achieving the other objectives set forth in this directive. To effectuate these purposes the Control Council should

a. Seek out and reduce to the possession and control of a special agency all German (public and private) foreign exchange and external assets of every kind and description located within or outside Germany.

b. Prohibit, except as authorized by regulation or license, all dealings in gold and silver, foreign exchange, and all foreign exchange transactions of any kind. Make available any foreign exchange proceeds of exports for payment of imports directly necessary to the accomplishment of the objectives stated in paragraphs 4 and 5 of this directive, and authorize no other outlay of foreign exchange assets except for purposes approved by the Control Council or other appropriate authority.

c. Establish effective controls with respect to all foreign exchange transactions, including:

(1) Transactions as to property between persons inside Germany and persons outside Germany;

(2) Transactions involving obligations owed by or to become due from any person in Germany to any person outside Germany; and

(3) Transactions involving the importation into or exportation from Germany of any foreign exchange asset or other form of property. Pending agreement in the Control Council, you will take in your zone the action indicated in subparagraphs a, b and c above. Accordingly, you will in your zone reduce to the possession and control of a special agency established by you, within your Command, all German foreign exchange and external assets as provided in subparagraph a. You will endeavor to have similar agencies for the same purpose established in the other zones of occupation and to have them merged as soon as practicable in one agency for the entire occupied territory. In addition you will provide full reports to your government with respect to all German foreign exchange and external assets.

50. No extension of credit to Germany or Germans by any foreign person or Government shall be permitted except that the Control Council may in special emergencies grant permission for such extension of credit.

51. It is not anticipated that you will make credits available to the Reichsbank or any other bank or to any public or private institution. If, in your opinion, such action becomes essential, you may take such emer-

gency actions as you may deem proper, but in any event, you will report the facts to the Control Council.

52. You will maintain such accounts and records as may be necessary to reflect the financial operations of the military government in your zone and you will provide the Control Council with such information in connection with the use of currency by your forces, any governmental settlements, occupation costs, and other expenditures arising out of operations or activities involving participation of your forces.

Appendix B

Directive to Commander-in-Chief of U.S. Forces of Occupation, Regarding the Military Government of Germany, July 11, 1947

I

1. *Purpose of This Directive*

This directive, issued to you as Commanding General of the United States forces of occupation and as Military Governor in Germany, constitutes a statement of the objectives of your Government in Germany and of the basic policies to which your Government wishes you to give effect from the present time forward. It supersedes JCS 1067/6 and its amendments.

2. *Authority of Military Government*

a. Your authority as Military Governor will be broadly construed and empowers you to take action consistent with relevant international agreements, general foreign policies of this Government and with this directive, appropriate or desirable to attain your Government's objectives in Germany or to meet military exigencies.

b. Pending arrangements for the effective treatment of Germany as an economic and political unit, you will exert every effort to achieve economic unity with other zones.

II

3. *United States Policy toward Germany*

The basic interest of the United States throughout the world is just and lasting peace. Such a peace can be achieved only if conditions of public order and prosperity are created in Europe as a whole. An orderly and prosperous Europe requires the economic contributions of a stable and productive Germany as well as the necessary restraints to insure that Germany is not allowed to revive its destructive militarism.

To accomplish the latter purpose the United States Government has proposed to the other Occupying Powers a treaty for the continuing disarmament and demilitarization of Germany and it has committed itself to maintaining a United States army of occupation as long as foreign occupation of Germany continues.

As a positive program requiring urgent action the United States Government seeks the creation of those political, economic and moral conditions in Germany which will contribute most effectively, to a stable and prosperous Europe.

III

4. *Demilitarization*

There should be no relaxation of effort to complete and effectively to maintain the disarmament and the demilitarization of Germany.

IV

5. *United States Political Objectives in Germany*

It is an objective of the United States Government that there should arise in Germany as rapidly as possible a form of political organization and a manner of political life which, resting on a substantial basis of economic well-being, will lead to tranquillity within Germany and will contribute to the spirit of peace among nations.

Your task, therefore, is fundamentally that of helping to lay the economic and educational bases of a sound German democracy, of encouraging bona fide democratic efforts and of prohibiting those activities which would jeopardize genuinely democratic developments.

6. *German Self-Government*

a. You will continue to promote the development in Germany of institutions of popular self-government and the assumption of direct responsibility by German governmental agencies, assuring them legislative, judicial and executive powers, consistent with military security and the purposes of the occupation.

b. It is the view of your Government that the most constructive development of German political life would be in the establishment throughout Germany of federal German states (Laender) and the formation of a central German government with carefully defined and limited powers and functions. All powers shall be vested in the Laender except such as are expressly delegated to the Central Government.

c. Your Government does not wish to impose its own historically developed forms of democracy and social organization on Germany and believes equally firmly that no other external forms should be imposed. It seeks the establishment in Germany of a political organization which is derived from the people and subject to their control, which operates in accordance with democratic electoral procedures, and which is dedicated to uphold both the basic civil and human rights of the individual. It is opposed to an excessively centralized government which through a concentration of power may threaten both the existence of democracy in Germany and the security of Germany's neighbors and the rest of the world. Your Government believes finally that, within the principles stated above, the ultimate constitutional form of German political life should be left to the decision of the German people made freely in accordance with democratic processes.

7. *Interzonal German Administrative Agencies*

Pending the establishment of central German administrative agencies and of a central German government, you will continue, consistent with the objectives of paragraph 6, to make arrangement with other Zonal Commanders for the creation and operation of interzonal German administrative agencies.

8. *Political Parties*

a. You will adhere to the policy of authorizing and encouraging all political parties whose programs, activities and structure demonstrate their allegiance to democratic principles. Political parties shall be competitive in character, constituted by voluntary associations of citizens in which the leaders are responsible to the members, and with no party enjoying a privileged status.

b. You will likewise give support to the principle that military government and the German authorities should afford non-discriminatory treatment to duly authorized political parties. Every authorized political party should have the right freely to state its views and to present its candidates to the electorate, and you will tolerate no curtailment of nor hindrance to the exercise of that right; if, however, you find that an authorized party is adopting or advocating undemocratic practices or ideas, you may restrict or withdraw its rights and privileges.

c. You will urge in the Control Council the recognition of nation-wide political parties and the uniform treatment of all authorized parties in all zones of occupation. You will advocate quadripartite supervision of political activities and of elections throughout Germany as a whole.

9. *Denazification*

You will implement in your zone the decisions on denazification taken April 23, 1947 by the Council of Foreign Ministers, as may be agreed in ACC.

10. *War Crimes*

You will make every effort to facilitate and bring to early completion the war crimes program subject to the conclusions and recommendations with respect to organizations and members thereof contained in the judgment of the International Military Tribunal.

11. *Courts and Judicial Procedures*

a. You will exercise such supervision over German Courts as is necessary to prevent the revival of National Socialist doctrines, to prohibit discrimination on grounds of race, nationality, creed or political belief, to enforce the application of the principles expressed in Control Council Proclamation No. 3 and compliance with the provisions of Control Council and Military Government legislation. You will foster the independence of the German judiciary by allowing the courts freedom in their interpretation and application of the law and by limiting the control measures instituted by Military Government to the minimum consistent with the accomplishment of the aims of the occupation.

b. You will maintain sufficient Military Government Courts to try persons accused of offenses involving the safety and security of United States and Allied personnel and all cases in which the interest of Military Government requires such procedure.

c. You may extend the jurisdiction of the German courts to all cases which do not involve the interests of Military Government or persons under the protective care of Military Government. Any German Tribunal established for the purpose of determining internal restitution claims may exercise jurisdiction over any person irrespective of his status who institutes a proceeding therein.

d. As a basic objective of the occupation is the reestablishment of the rule of law in Germany, you will require all agencies under your control to refrain from arbitrary and oppressive measures. Except when it clearly appears that detention is necessary for the security of the occupying forces, no person will be detained except when he is charged with a specific

offense and is subject to trial by a duly constituted tribunal. You will
protect the civil rights of persons detained under charges assuring them
a fair trial and ample opportunity to prepare their defense. You will by
regulation limit arrests for security purposes to cases where overriding
considerations of military necessity require such procedure. Persons so
detained will be permitted to communicate with their nearest relative or
friend unless urgent security considerations require an exception, and
you will review their cases periodically to determine whether further
detention is warranted. When in your opinion it will be compatible
with security considerations, you will eliminate such arrests without
prejudice to a revival of the practice in emergencies.

12. *Legislation*

You will exercise your power of disapproval over German legislation
only when such legislation conflicts with the legislation or other policies
of Military Government.

13. *Movement of Persons*

a. You will implement the decisions taken 23 April 1947 by the Council
of Foreign Ministers with regard to United Nations displaced persons and
population transfers.

b. You will, in cooperation with IRO, facilitate the emigration to other
countries of those displaced persons unwilling to be repatriated.

c. Pending the movement of displaced persons you will retain overall
responsibility for their appropriate care, maintenance and protection. You
will utilize the IRO to the maximum possible extent in assisting you to
discharge this responsibility.

d. The term displaced persons as used above refers to displaced persons
and refugees as defined in the IRO Constitution.

e. You will hold the German authorities responsible for the care and
disposition of nationals of former enemy countries not otherwise provided
for herein and you will continue to facilitate their repatriation.

f. You will require that persons of German extraction who have been
transferred to Germany be granted German nationality with full civil and
political rights except in cases of recognized disqualifications under German law. You will take such measures as you may deem appropriate to
assist the German authorities in effecting a program of resettlement.

g. You will continue to permit the exchange of Germans seeking permanent residence between the United States Zone and other zones on a
reciprocal basis. You will permit free movement for temporary purposes

to the greatest possible extent consistent with security considerations and with interzonal or quadripartite agreement.

h. You will continue to receive those Germans whose presence abroad is deemed by your Government to be contrary to the national interest. You will likewise permit the reentry of German and former German nationals who desire to return permanently but in view of restricted facilities you will give priority to those who are willing and able to contribute to the peaceful reconstruction of Germany.

i. You will permit only those Germans to leave Germany who are included in categories approved by Allied agreements or your Government's instructions.

14. *Prisoners of War*

In carrying out the decision of the Council of Foreign Ministers of 23 April 1947, you will press in the Control Council for the earliest possible return of all German prisoners of war still located in the territories of the Allied Powers and in all other territories.

15. *General Economic Objectives*

The economic objectives of the United States Government in Germany are:

    a. to eliminate industry used solely to manufacture and to reduce industry used chiefly to support the production of arms, ammunition and implements of war;

    b. to exact from Germany reparation for the losses suffered by United Nations as a consequence of German aggression; and

    c. to encourage the German people to rebuild a self-supporting State devoted to peaceful purposes, integrated into the economy of Europe.

Although the economic rehabilitation of Germany, within the framework of these objectives, is the task and responsibility of the German people, you should provide them general policy guidance, assist in the development of a balanced foreign trade and ensure that German efforts are consistent with, and contribute to the fulfillment of your Government's objectives.

16. *Economic Disarmament and Reparation*

a. Your Government continues to desire the general fulfillment of the principles of the Potsdam Agreement regarding reparation and industrial disarmament.

b. Your Government believes that the level of industry eventually agreed upon for Germany as a basis for reparation removals, while eliminating excess industrial capacity which has been used by Germany for the purpose of making war, should not permanently limit Germany's industrial capacity. The German people after the period of reparation removals should not be denied the right, consistent with continued disarmament, to develop their resources for the purpose of achieving higher standards of living.

c. Your Government does not agree to reparation from Germany greater than that provided by the Potsdam Agreement. Nor does your Government agree to finance the payment of reparation by Germany to other United Nations by increasing its financial outlay in Germany or by postponing the achievement of a self-sustaining German economy. Your Government reaffirms the principle that the proceeds of authorized exports shall be used in the first place for the payment of authorized imports.

d. You will attempt to obtain Control Council recognition of the principle of compensation for property taken for reparation or where it has been necessary to destroy property under the agreements for economic disarmament, such compensation to constitute a charge against the German economy as a whole. Except in prohibited industries, you will endeavor to ensure, to the greatest extent practicable, that no plant in which there is foreign ownership or control is removed for reparation as long as German-owned plants are available for that purpose.

e. You will continue to assist in the location of cloaked German-owned assets abroad and where possible you will assist in their liquidation.

17. *Restitution*

a. You will proceed, consistent with agreements on restitution reached in the Control Council, to restore such identifiable property other than gold and transport essential to minimum German economy, to the government of the country from which it was taken. You will not consent to any extensive program for the replacement of looted or displaced property which has been destroyed or cannot be located whenever such replacement can be accomplished only at the expense of reparation, a self-sustaining German economy, or the cultural heritage of the German people.

b. You will turn over monetary gold uncovered in Germany to the Tripartite Gold Commission in Brussels for distribution in accordance with the terms of the Paris Act on Reparation.

c. In accordance with JCS 1570/9, you will make available for the rehabilitation and resettlement of non-repatriable victims of German action valuable personal property looted from Nazi victims which is not restitutable.

d. It is the policy of your Government that persons and organizations deprived of their property as a result of National Socialist persecution should either have their property returned or be compensated therefor and that persons who suffered personal damage or injury through National Socialist persecution should receive indemnification in German currency. With respect to heirless and unclaimed property subject to internal restitution you will designate appropriate successor organizations.

18. *Economic Unity and Recovery*

a. Your Government is desirous of securing agreement in the Control Council to the treatment of Germany as an economic unit, the formulation of common policies in all matters affecting Germany as a whole, and the establishment of central German administrative agencies for the purpose of implementing such common policies in the fields of finance, transport, communications, agriculture, economics (including industry and foreign trade) and such other fields as the Control Council may consider necessary and appropriate.

b. Your Government likewise desires to secure the adoption of a production and foreign trade program for Germany as a whole which should be directed toward an increasing standard of living in Germany and the attainment at the earliest practicable date of a self-sustaining German economy. Such a program should give highest priority to increased production of coal, food and export goods; provide for such allocation and distribution of German indigenous output and approved imports throughout Germany as are necessary to carry out the production program and attain the agreed standard of living, ensure full payment for all goods and services exported from Germany (other than reparation or restitution) in approved imports or in foreign exchange which can be utilized for the payment of approved imports, and provide for the pooling of all export proceeds to be made available, first to meet the import needs of Germany as a whole for such time and in such amount as may hereafter be determined, and secondly to compensate the occupying powers for past expenditures pursuant to terms and conditions to be established hereafter, priority in the latter case being given to payment of costs sustained for essential imports in direct proportion to the expenditures made by the occupying powers.

c. In cases where the restoration of normal international commercial relations between Germany and the rest of Europe would involve an increase of US dollar expenditures for the government of Germany, or a delay in the attainment of a self-supporting German economy at an appropriate standard of living, funds for German expenditures shall be increased, or the German economy compensated through provision by the US of sufficient relief monies to the country or countries so benefitted to enable them to pay Germany. You will consult other European countries and international organizations representing such countries in matters of German production and trade mentioned above, and ensure that emphasis is given, in the selection of items for export, to goods needed by European countries for their economic recovery and rehabilitation insofar as these countries may provide in payment needed imports for Germany, or foreign exchange which can pay for such imports. Proposed transactions of a substantial nature which would lead to a restoration of general European trade or normal international commercial relations or restore normal trade exchanges between Germany and other European countries but which would not conform to the principles stated in this paragraph should be referred to the US GOVT for decision.

d. You will support the removal of existing trade barriers and will encourage the return of foreign trade to normal trade channels.

19. *Finance*

a. Your government views the reorganization of German finances on a sound basis and the attainment of financial stability in Germany as among the main factors essential to German economic recovery along democratic and peaceful lines. To that end, you will endeavor to have the Control Council adopt uniform financial policies in conformity with the principles and the objectives set forth in this directive.

b. Pending agreement in the Control Council, or until receipt of further directive from your government, you will continue to be guided by the following policies in your zone:

(1) You will control, within the scope of your authority, all financial transactions of an international character in order to keep Nazi influence out of the field of finance and prevent outward movements of capital from Germany;

(2) You will exercise general supervision over German public expenditures and measures of taxation in order to insure that they are consistent with the objectives of the Military Government;

(3) You will take such action as may be necessary to prevent the establishment of a centralized German banking system and an undue concentration of financial power, but will encourage the establishment

of a central authority for the production, issuance and control of currency and for technical banking supervision. You will also encourage the Germans to reestablish normal banking facilities within the limitation prescribed above and within the present blocking of assets and accounts under Military Government Law No. 52;

(4) You will use the resources of the German economy to the maximum extent possible in order to reduce expenditures from appropriated funds of your government. You are authorized, as provided in the Potsdam Agreement, to use the proceeds of exports to pay for imports which you deem essential, subject to strict accounting and auditing procedures;

(5) You will continue to aid economic recovery by collection of full payment for exports of German goods and services; and

(6) You will continue to prevent non-essential imports.

c. You will press for the adoption by the Control Council of a program for financial reform which provides for a substantial and appropriate reduction in outstanding currency and monetary claims, including public and private debt; for the equitable sharing of the costs of war and defeat; and for ancillary measures including adjustments in the wage-price structure necessary to the restoration of balance between the financial structure and the economic realities.

d. (1) You will maintain such accounts and records as may be necessary to reflect the financial operations of the Military Government (U.S.) in Germany, including also such operations undertaken jointly by you with the Military Government in the British and other zones of occupation in Germany.

(2) You will take measures necessary for calculating occupation costs distinguishing those now incurred within Germany and supported by the Germany economy, and external occupation costs for eventual settlement with Germany. You will endeavor to agree on a definition of occupation costs of both types within the Control Council and to limit and control internal occupation costs on a quadrilateral basis.

20. *Agriculture*

a. In accordance with the decision of 23 April 1947 of the Council of Foreign Ministers, you will ensure the carrying out and completion of land reform in your zone in 1947.

b. You will require the appropriate German authorities to adopt and implement policies and practices which will:

Maximize the production and provide for the effective collection and distribution of agricultural products.

c. You will require the appropriate German authorities to adopt and implement similar policies and practices in respect to forestry and fishing resources.

21. *Economic Institutions*

a. Pending agreement among the occupying powers you will in your zone prohibit all cartels and cartel-like organizations, and effect a dispersion of ownership and control of German industry through the dissolution of such combines, mergers, holding companies and interlocking directorates which represent an actual or potential restraint of trade or may dominate or substantially influence the policies of governmental agencies. You will not, however, prohibit governmental regulation of prices or monopolies subject to government regulation, in fields where competition is impracticable. In so far as possible, you will coordinate your action in this field with the commanders of other zones of occupation.

b. You will permit the formation and functioning of coperatives provided they are voluntary in membership, and are organized along democratic lines and do not engage in activities prohibited under the above paragraph.

c. While it is your duty to give the German people an opportunity to learn of the principles and advantages of free enterprise, you will refrain from interfering in the question of public ownership of enterprises in Germany, except to ensure that any choice for or against public ownership is made freely through the normal processes of democratic government. No measure of public ownership shall apply to foreign-owned property unless arrangements which are satisfactory to your Government have been made for the compensation of foreign owners. Pending ultimate decision as to the form and powers of the central German Government, you will permit no public ownership measure which would reserve that ownership to such central government.

d. Pending agreement among the occupying powers, you will limit new foreign investment in your zone of Germany and will continue to ensure that all property, however owned, and all production and manpower in your zone are subject in all respects to the decisions and directives of the Control Council, and to Military Government and German law.

e. (1) You will permit the organization, operation, and free development of trade unions provided that their leaders are responsible to the membership and their aims and practices accord with democratic principles. Any federation of trade unions shall not impair the financial and organizational autonomy of member unions. You will encourage the trade unions to support programs of adult education and to foster an understanding of democratic processes among their members. You will permit trade unions to act in the interests of their members and to bargain collectively regarding wages, hours and working conditions within the framework of such wage and price controls as it may be necessary to maintain.

(2) Trade unions may represent the occupational, economic and social interests of their members in accordance with the authority contained in their constitutions. Their basic functions may include participation with appropriate authorities in the establishment and development of a peaceful economy.

f. You will permit the organization and functioning of work councils on a democratic basis for the representation of the interests of employees in individual enterprises and will not prohibit the cooperation of trade unions therewith.

g. You will also permit the establishment of machinery for the voluntary settlement of industrial disputes.[1]

VI

22. *Cultural Objectives*
Your Government holds that the reeducation of the German people is an integral part of policies intended to help develop a democratic form of government and to restore a stable and peaceful economy; it believes that there should be no forcible break in the cultural unity of Germany, but recognizes the spiritual value of the regional traditions of Germany and wishes to foster them; it is convinced that the manner and purposes of the reconstruction of the national German culture have a vital significance for the future of Germany.

It is, therefore, of the highest importance that you make every effort to secure maximum coordination between the occupying powers of cultural objectives designed to serve the cause of peace. You will encourage German initiative and responsible participation in this work of cultural reconstruction and you will expedite the establishment of these international cultural relations which will overcome the spiritual isolation im-

---

[1] *Sic.* The official copy reads without a division V. Presumably it should come at the beginning of the economic section. [Ed.]

posed by National Socialism on Germany and further the assimilation of the German people into the world community of nations.

23. *Education*

a. In recognition of the fact that evil consequences to all free men flow from the suppression and corruption of truth and that education is a primary means of creating a democratic and peaceful Germany, you will continue to encourage and assist in the development of educational methods, institutions, programs and materials designed to further the creation of democratic attitudes and practices through education. You will require the German Laender authorities to adopt and execute educational programs designed to develop a healthy, democratic educational system which will offer equal opportunity to all according to their qualifications.

b. You will continue to effect the complete elimination of all National Socialist, militaristic and aggressively nationalistic influences, practices and teachings from the German educational system.

24. *Religious Affairs*

a. You will, in the United States Area of Occupation, continue to assure freedom of religion. You will assure protection of religious activity and support these principles in the deliberations of the Control Council.

b. You will give freedom to the Germans to decide all questions concerning the constitution, the religious activity and the amalgamation of purely ecclesiastical bodies.

c. You will continue to take such action as may be necessary to prevent the revival of National Socialist and militaristic activity under the cloak of a religious program or organization.

25. *Monuments, Fine Arts, and Archives*

a. You will respect, and permit German authorities to protect and preserve, the property of all cultural institutions dedicated to religion, charity, education, the arts and sciences, historic monuments and historic archives, together with their collections and endowments. You will apply the same principle to all other property of cultural value, whether publicly or private owned, except for institutions and monuments specifically devoted to the perpetuation of National Socialism or to the glorification of the German militaristic tradition.

b. You are authorized to make such use of German records and archives as may be appropriate.

26. *Public Information*

a. You will, in the United States Area of Occupation, supervise, encourage and assist in the development by the Germans of media of public information designed to advance the political and cultural objectives stated in this directive.

b. You will arrange through the Allied Control Council for the implementation of the decision of 23 April 1947 of the Council of Foreign Ministers on the free exchange of information and democratic ideas by all media in all of Germany.

c. You will develop and maintain organizations and facilities for the operation of media of information, including those sponsored by Military Government, designed to further the objectives of your Government.

27. *Reestablishment of International Cultural Relations*

In furtherance of the program of the reorientation of the German people and the revival of international cultural relations, you will permit and assist the travel into and out of Germany of persons useful for this program within the availability of your facilities. You will also permit and assist, to the extent of your facilities, the free flow of cultural materials to and from Germany.

Appendix C

Democratization of Germany

A STATEMENT OF POLICY BY GENERAL JOSEPH McNARNEY

July 9, 1946

In general it may be said that the Laender will be given complete power to govern themselves. . . . The only restrictions imposed upon them will be those resulting from:

a) The provisions of the Berlin Protocol and subsequent Four Power agreements which may be forthcoming from further ministerial meetings.

b) Allied Control Council Laws which are binding upon the whole of Germany.

c) Democratization and political decentralization.

d) It is considered the German Government will be "democratized" when the following conditions exist:

1) All political power is recognized as originating with the people and subject to their control.

2) Those who exercise political power are obligated to obtain a man-

date by frequent reference of their programs and leadership to popular elections.

3) Popular elections are conducted under competitive conditions in which not less than two effectively competing political parties submit their programs and candidates for popular review.

4) Political parties must be democratic in character and must be recognized as voluntary associations of citizens, clearly distinguished from rather than identified with the instrumentalities of government.

5) The basic rights of the individual including free speech, freedom of religious preference, and the right of assembly, freedom of political association and other equally basic rights of free men are recognized and guaranteed.

6) Control of the instrumentalities of public opinion such as the radio and press must be diffused and kept free from governmental domination.

7) The rule of law is recognized as the individual's greatest single protection against a capricious and willful exercise of governmental power.

8) Essentially our policy on political decentralization of government is:

A. Power is granted primarily to Laender, and only in specifically enumerated and approved instances to a Federal Government.

B. Powers of basic political implication are reserved to the Laender. Such administrative powers as may be necessary to insure economic unity are allocated to the Reich.

C. All residual powers are reserved to the people except as the people may delegate them to the Laender.

D. A substantial number of functions are delegated by the Laender to the Kreise and the Gemeinden. Those should include all such functions as may be effectively determined and administered by the community.

As these conditions are met the limitations on Laender Government which are imposed by Military Government Regulations will become less stringent. With the definitions of democracy and decentralization and the recognition of the need for economic unity which is contained in the Berlin Protocol, there can never be an effective compromise. These principles must remain as limitations upon Laender activities from this time forward.

Appendix D

MILITARY GOVERNMENT CHANNELS

(Before January, 1946)

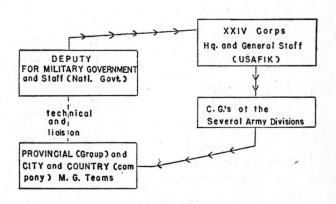

MILITARY GOVERNMENT CHANNELS

(Since January 1946)

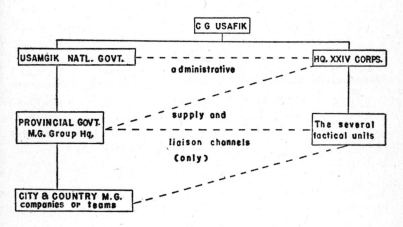

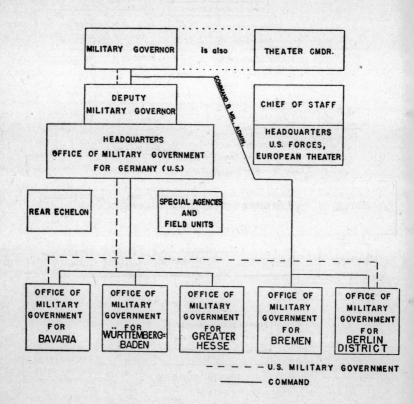

OFFICE OF MILITARY GOVERNMENT FOR GERMANY (U.S.)

COMMAND and MILITARY GOVERNMENT RELATIONSHIPS

INITIAL ORGANIZATION OF MILITARY GOVERNMENT IN KOREA

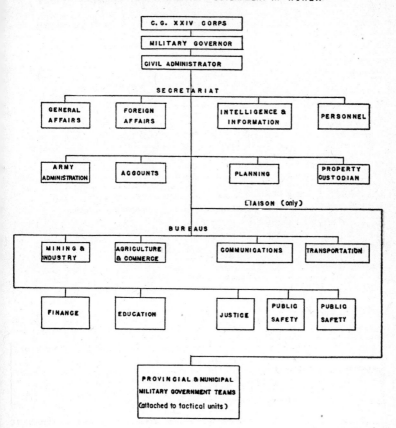

HQ - UNITED STATES ARMY MILITARY GOVERNMENT IN KOREA (USAMGIK)

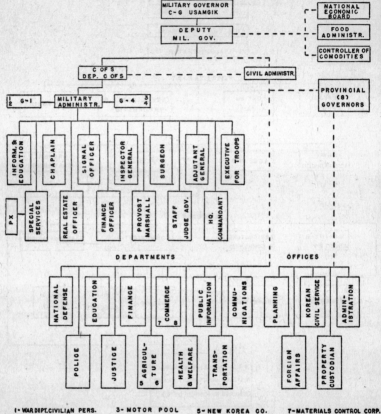

1- WAR DEPT. CIVILIAN PERS.   3- MOTOR POOL   5- NEW KOREA CO.   7- MATERIALS CONTROL CORP.
2- DEPENDENT HOUSING   4- HQ. SUPPLY   6- KOREAN COMMODITY CO.   8- PETROLEUM DISTRIB. AGENCY

G-5 DIV. USFET
(LOCATED AT FRANKFURT)
APRIL, 1946

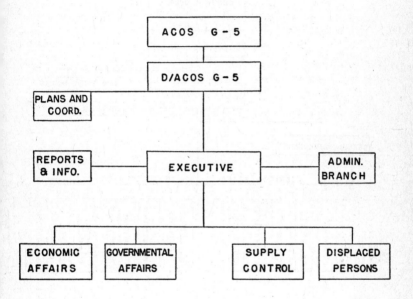

ALLIED CONTROL AUTHORITY

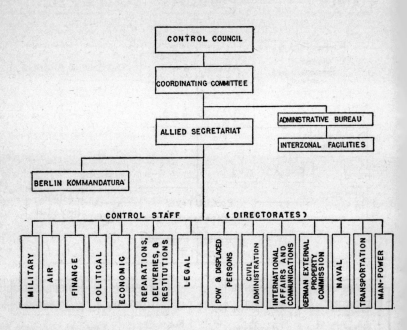

STAFF ORGANIZATION UNDER SCAP

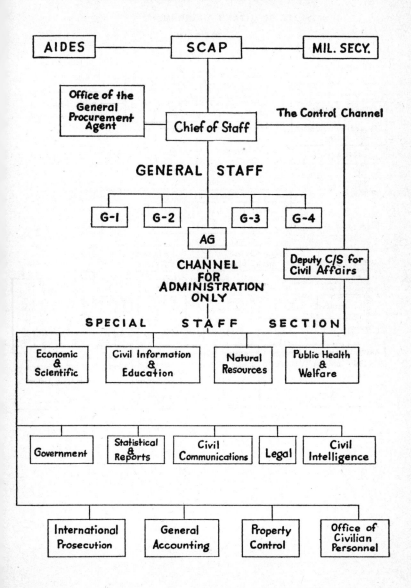

OFFICE OF MILITARY GOVERNMENT FOR GERMANY (U.S.)

BERLIN

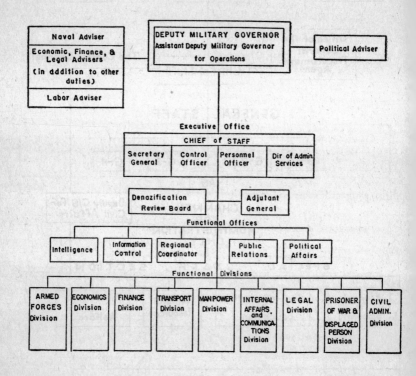

MILITARY GOVERNMENT SECTION AFPAC

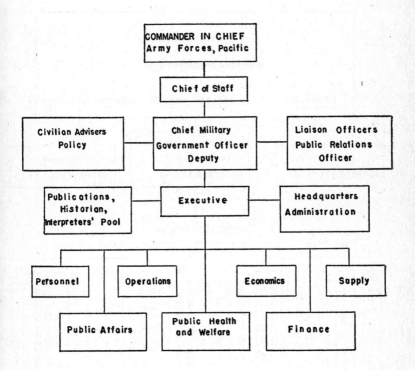

ORGANIZATION OF THE LANDERRAT
(COUNCIL OF LAND MINISTER-PRESIDENTS OF U.S. ZONE)

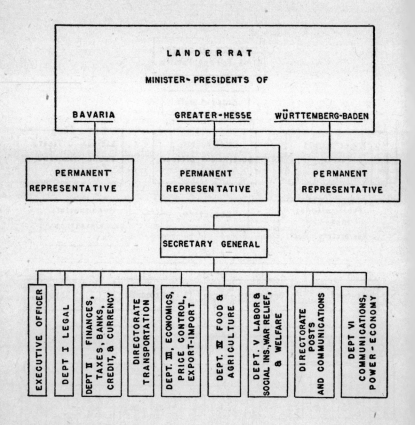

ORGANIZATION
OFFICE OF MILITARY GOVERNMENT FOR BAVARIA

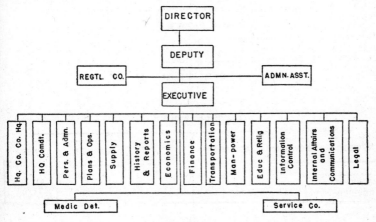

ORGANIZATION
OFFICE OF MILITARY GOVERNMENT FOR WÜRTTEMBERG ⁼ BADEN

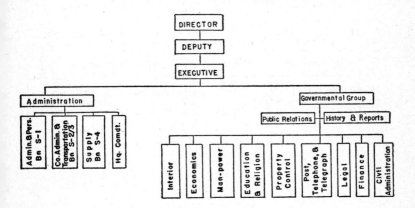

OFFICE OF MILITARY GOVERNMENT FOR GERMANY (U.S.)

REGIONAL GOVERNMENT COORDINATING OFFICE
(Reports to Deputy Military Governor)
(Located at Stuttgart)

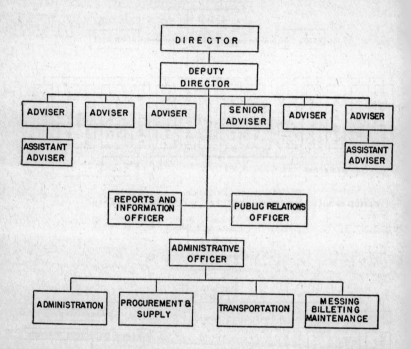

U.S. ORGANIZATION FOR MILITARY GOVERNMENT
BREMEN PORT COMMAND

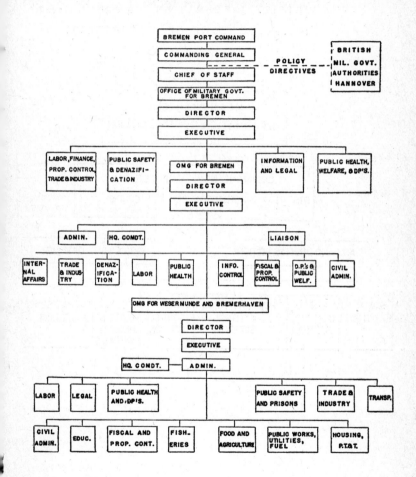

FUNCTIONAL PLAN FOR THE OPERATION
OF A DISTRICT INFORMATION CONTROL UNIT
IN THE U.S. ZONE OF OCCUPATION

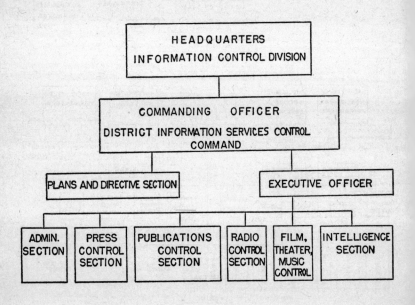

G - 5 DIV. SHAEF
FUNCTIONAL CHART

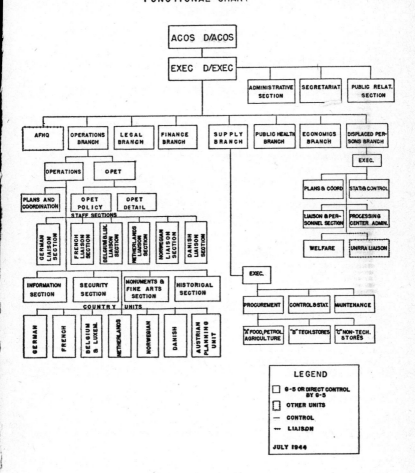

LEGEND

☐ G-5 OR DIRECT CONTROL BY G-5
☐ OTHER UNITS
— CONTROL
--- LIAISON

JULY 1944

Index